PHONETIC READINGS
OF
SONGS AND ARIAS

AUTHENTIC PRONUNCIATION OF 413 ITALIAN, GERMAN, AND FRENCH LYRICS
FROM "THE SINGER'S REPERTOIRE" IN INTERNATIONAL
PHONETIC ALPHABET TRANSCRIPTION

by

BERTON COFFIN

RALPH ERROLLE

WERNER SINGER

PIERRE DELATTRE

PUBLISHED BY PRUETT PRESS, INC. • BOULDER, COLORADO

FOREWORD

"Phonetic Readings of Songs and Arias" is an addition to "The Singer's Repertoire" series of aids for the singer and teacher of singing.

The teacher of singing is faced with many, many challenges — the forming of an individual voice for each of his students, the appropriate use of repertoire for each voice, the teaching of individualized diction of songs in various languages and the stimulation of vocal artistry. Few fields are larger in scope and more challenging than that faced by the serious teacher of singing.

One of the most persistent problems is that of diction in the four principal languages of singing. Molding the pronunciation of lyrics of the basic repertoire of the young singer may be relatively easy but the need for teaching the same pronunciation of the same songs to students over a period of years can easily become an activity of devitalization. To this problem this text has been partially directed.

Another problem is involved with the song needs of the advanced singer. Each individual voice will need its own repertoire. A teacher may not use certain songs for years, but when the time comes, it is urgent that these songs be taught correctly and efficiently as a language. Furthermore, the burden of proof is upon the teacher. He, and he alone, must form the diction, for teachers of languages in the classes of our colleges and universities have little time to serve the individual language needs of students of singing.

Oral assignments can now be made in the text "Phonetic Readings of Songs and Arias" before actual singing is begun. Psychologically it is easier to do one thing at a time — learn the language — read it with the accent of the word — and then place it to music. Many teachers recommend the learning of a lyric prior to the preparation of a song as being an efficient memory device. A fabled teacher was known for her desire to have her students read aloud the poetry of their songs early in the day as an inflective and interpretative device for preparing songs and arias. It was with the above concept in mind that this book of phonetic transcriptions was formed as a reader.

Many students want to hurry the process of learning to sing. Time may be gained in the area of language work faster than in other areas. And, if a language can be learned from the first without the necessity of correction of mistakes, learning can indeed be fast, and the attention of the teacher directed to the use of the language art as it relates to the use of vocal resources and interpretation. Instrumentalists usually observe long practice hours but the singer's work must be accomplished in a shorter length of time because of the nature of the vocal instrument. With the procedure of learning the diction of songs and arias through phonetics more work can be accomplished in a limited time and a larger and more dependable repertoire should evolve.

The singer today is faced with the problem that his art is more international than ever before. Hundreds of American singers are active in
Europe. With the advent of fast transportation a singer is frequently
called upon to sing in several countries and several languages within a
very short time. Furthermore, he is expected to sing each language with
standardized diction. The singer who performs only in our country is still
faced with the singing of several languages, and wherever he appears can be
relatively sure that several persons in his audience will know correct pronunciation of languages due to our traveling, sophisticated culture and to
the enormous influence of recordings by world renowned artists. Now, as
never before, the student must sing well and with correct diction.

As one travels through such countries as Italy, Germany, France, England
and the United States, he is constantly aware of the changing of language
within each nation. Almost any area of a country may be represented by our
language teachers. But as far as singing is concerned, there is a standard
to be used and the standards are subtley changing – witness Webster's Dictionary in this country. Suffice it to say that the transcriptions found in
this text have been made according to the most recent techniques of phonetic
transcriptions and accepted standards of language. The phonetics used are
those of the International Phonetic Association of which at least half of the
symbols are already known to the singer. With the memorization of the re-
maining symbols the pronunciation of the basic lyric repertoire will be easily
available to every singer. A clear statement concerning the symbols of each
of the languages is found in the foreword of each of the divisions.

The Italian standard, used by Italian radio announcers and actors, is
Zingarelli – "Vocabulario della Lingua Italiana." Although this reference does
not use the International Phonetic Alphabet, pronunciation is clearly marked
and is in this text transferred to I. P. A. symbols with few changes. Certain
exceptions of the unaccented e and o vowels have been transcribed open (ɛ and
ɔ) for singing, p. 1. The authors hope that these exceptions do not serve as
license to open all other unaccented e and o vowels.

The German standard used has been Siebs – "Deutsche Hochsprache," the use
of which has been further strengthened by the reference "Deutsche Phonetik" by
Martens. These sources differ from earlier use of I. P. A. transcriptions primarily in the treatment of diphthongs.

Eis	is now	ae	rather than	aɪ
Leute	is now	ɔø	rather than	ɔɪ
Haus	is now	ao	rather than	au

French, the most standardized of the languages, is written in open syllabli-
fication for better flow of the language in this text, designed as a phonetic
reader. French is essentially a language of open syllables. In this reference
the closing consonant has been transposed to the right, becoming a part of the
consonant cluster at the beginning of the next syllable. Americans have the
tendency of closing the syllables, thus anglicizing the French. The standard for
the French transcription has been Fouché – "Traite de Prononciation Française."

For the experienced singer who kinesthetically knows the following modifications or for the teacher of singing or coach with a sensitive ear, the phenomenon herein described is probably already observed but not categorized. For the untrained singer, the teacher of singing, and coach with limited experience, a <u>definition of vowel modification</u> is probably necessary in a book of phonetic transcription to avoid a forced, uniform phonetic forming of vowels in voices. Such inflexible treatment might impare the musicality, expressiveness and survival of some voices.

Italian teachers have long preferred the vowel <u>a</u> for the vocalization and training of the singing voice. There is a fundamental reason why this is true which is also related to the modification of other vowels. In short, the phenomenon is as follows:

1. Vowels are caused by two cavities, the cavity of the pharynx and the cavity of the mouth.

2. <u>The frequencies of these cavities for the various vowels are the same for men and women.</u>

3. The frequency of the boccal cavity may be heard by <u>whispering</u> the vowels.

4. The frequency of the pharyngeal cavity may be heard by forming the vowel then <u>thumping</u> on the base of the tongue, below the jaw bone. The frequencies are better heard when the glottis is closed as before the explosion of a cough. The vowels i – e – a – o – u in order will give a rising and falling pattern of frequencies.

5. Frequencies of the pharyngeal cavity for the various vowels in <u>male and female</u> throats are

æ	a	ɑ (750 cps)	roughly g^2
ɛ	œ	ɔ (600 cps)	roughly d^2
e	ø	o (456 cps)	roughly a^1
i	y	u (350 cps)	roughly f^1

   I   II   III   Series (Modified from Howie and Delattre.)

6. There are three series of vowel modifications, I – front vowels, II – middle vowels, and III – back vowels.

7. There is loss of understandability of a given vowel when it is sung on a pitch above the frequency of the larynx cavity of that vowel, and it will tend to sound like the vowel in its series on that particular note, i.e. the vowel i (see Series I in No. 5) will tend to sound like æ on g^2, ɛ on d^2, and e on a^1. The same is true of any vowel in its particular series.

8. Vowels sung higher than the above pitches tend to be harsh when an unmodified form is forced upon the voice.

9. The law of cavity frequency and vowel modification is primarily concerned with <u>female voices</u> because this phenomenon occurs between f^1 and g^2.

10. The observation can be made in the above chart that in the female voice 12 vowels are possible on f^1, 9 vowels possible on a^1, 6 vowels possible on d^2 and three vowels possible on g^2. An adroit use of modified vowels in context with consonants should create the illusion of good diction. At the same time the fundamental of the pitch being sung will be heard. If it is not, the tone will be a fraction of what it should be.

11. If the law is disregarded (without intuitive change) there may be difficulty with timbre, pitch, agility and flexibility of dynamics.

12. The above definition is a substantiation of the preferable <u>a</u> vowel of the Italians — it is the only vowel that can be sung freely on all pitches! Albert Bach in "Musical Education and Vocal Culture" quotes Anna Maria Celoni as saying, "Le vocali l'i ed l'u si devono evitare a lasciarle a coloro che avessero la mania d'imitare i cavalli ed i lupi." (The vowels <u>i</u> and <u>u</u> should be left for those who desire to imitate horses and wolves.) Apparently <u>i</u> and <u>u</u> were considered to be unfavorable vowels for training most voices. BUT we must sing on these vowels in all languages. The above law indicates how these and related vowels can be sung.

13. The stated law should indicate approximately how the vowels will be used by the various voice classifications. In female voices there must be a great deal of modification. Male voices are hardly touched by this law.

14. The law of modification of <u>male voices</u> is that in ascending, open vowels close and close vowels open. (Witherspoon)

15. Vowels vary their modification with emotional coloring. With joy the vowels become brighter and vary towards the front vowels, with sadness the vowels become more sombre and vary toward the back series of vowels.

Thus, there is a high art with which the wedding of language and musical line (vocal line) must be accomplished. Traditionally this has occurred quite late in study and is the mark of an artist. Why can it not occur earlier if the above phenomena are understood and observed in the study of languages through phonetics?

I believe that this volume of "The Singer's Repertoire" series has been most fortunate in the selection of its co-authors.

<u>Ralph Errolle</u>, former leading tenor of the Metropolitan, Chicago and San Francisco opera companies is the author of "Italian Diction for Singers," Pruett Press, 1963. He was formerly Professor of Music and Director of Opera at Louisiana State University, and Director of the Opera Arts Association of

Atlanta, Georgia. He has taught American Institute of Vocal Pedagogy seminars in Italian and French Diction at several National Association of Teachers of Singing Workshops. He is presently teaching in Chicago.

Werner Singer, Coach-Accompanist of New York City, is German-born and was trained at the Staatliche Hochschule für Musik, Berlin. He has conducted operas at the Hamburg Volksoper and the Theatro Municipal, Rio de Janeiro, Brazil. In this country he is widely known, having been a coach and/or accompanist to Mmes. Barbieri, Berger, Leider, Loevberg, Tebaldi and Yeend, and Messrs. Bernac, de Luca, Gedda, London, Svanholm, Tagliavini and Vinay. In the academic field, Mr. Singer has established and has been successfully holding summer classes in "Repertoire for Singers" at the University of Colorado.

Pierre Delattre, Professor of French, University of Colorado, is a French-born specialist in phonetics. He was trained at the University of Paris and the University of Michigan. He was Head of the Department of Phonetics at Middlebury summer schools for 20 years and has been phonetics editor of the French Review since 1939. He has probably built the best experimental phonetics laboratory, for the analysis of accents in foreign languages and the acoustic analysis of vowels and consonants, in the United States. Contributor to Bulletin, National Association of Teachers of Singing — Vol. XV No. 1, October 1958, "Vowel Color and Voice Quality" (most important for comparison of speech and singing vowel qualities and vocal positions); Vol. XVIII No. 4, May 1962, "Effect of Pitch on the Intelligibility of Vowels." Lecturer at NATS Workshops. French editor for Webster Dictionaries since 1941.

Acknowledgements for counsel and valued assistance should be made to Clara Regnoni-Macera, Assistant Professor of Italian at the University of Colorado, formerly of St. Cecilia, Rome; Lola Martini, Tuscan Italian, and Dr. Anton Burzle, phonetician and Professor of German at the University of Kansas and Director of the German Summer Institute, Holzkirchen O.B.B. Germany.

Without the assistance and the permission of the following publishers to use copyrighted lyrics, the extent of the repertoire included would have been seriously limited: Associated Music Publishers, Inc.; Boston Music Company; Durand et Cie; Elkan-Vogel Co., Inc.; Chas. W. Homeyer and Co., Inc.; Theodore Presser Company; G. Ricordi and Co.; and G. Schirmer, Inc. Vera Tügel, copyright owner of "Wiegenlied" has granted permission for the use of that lyric.

A grant from the Council on Research and Creative Work at the University of Colorado has made this study possible.

Berton Coffin, Professor and
Head, Division of Voice
University of Colorado
Boulder, Colorado

July 18, 1963

RELATED BIBLIOGRAPHY

Bach, Albert.   Musical Education and Vocal Culture.
Kegan, Paul and Trench. London, 1898.

Cartier, Frances A.   The Phonetic Alphabet. Wm. C. Brown.
Dubuque, Iowa, 1954. (English vowels.)

Coffin, Berton.   The Singer's Repertoire. Vol. I.
Coloratura, Lyric and Dramatic Soprano.
Vol. II. Mezzo Soprano and Contralto.
Vol. III. Lyric and Dramatic Tenor.
Vol. IV. Baritone and Bass. The Scarecrow
Press, New York, 1960.

Coffin, Berton and
Werner Singer.   Program Notes for The Singer's Repertoire.
The Scarecrow Press, New York, 1962.

Gray, Giles Wilkerson
and Claude M. Wise.   The Bases of Speech. Harper, New York,
1946.

Howie, John and
Pierre Delattre.   "An Experimental Study of the Effect of
Pitch on the Intelligibility of Vowels,"
Bulletin, National Association of Teachers
of Singing, Vol. XVIII, No. 4, May 15, 1962.

Kantner, Claude and
Robert West.   Phonetics. Harper, New York, 1941.

Wise, Claude M.   Introduction to Phonetics. Prentice Hall,
New York, 1958.

Witherspoon, Herbert.   Singing. G. Schirmer, New York, 1925.

(See bibliography for each language at the end
of each preliminary statement.)

PHONETIC TRANSCRIPTION OF ITALIAN SONGS AND ARIAS

Ralph Errolle and Berton Coffin

Vocal coaches in Italy are striving to limit the concessions in pronunciation asked for by singers and to keep the pronunciation in singing as nearly as possible to recognized academic rules. This text is the transcription of classic Italian with permissible concessions to singing.

PROBLEMS OF ITALIAN DICTION

The basic problems of Italian diction are concerned with the pronunciation of orthographic e, o, s, z, and zz. The mispronouncing of accented e and o may affect meaning:

venti. . . vẹnti -- winds, but venti -- twenty

dei. . . . . dẹi --- gods, but dẹi ---- of the

mezzo. . . mẹd:zo- medium, but mẹt:so -- over-ripe

Stressed e and o

1. The principle problems in Italian diction are concerned with the open and close e, ɛ and e, and open and close o, ɔ and o. Dictionaries do not always agree on the close and open e and o in accented syllables. In such cases the vowel most conducive to vocal emission has been indicated. Please see Bibliography page 4.

2. Accented finale e – è has been transcribed close and accented final o – ò has been transcribed open according to present usage.

perchè. . . . . .pɛrkẹ   salpò. . . .salpọ

fè. . . . . . . .fe   farò. . . .farọ

Unaccented e and o

According to accepted academic rules the orthographic e and o are always close when not the vowel of the tonic syllable. The following concessions to singing are included in this transcription.

1. e in apocopation (the dropping of the final vowel) tends to open to ɛ and is so transcribed – della. . .del:la, del. . . . .dɛl. But, since there is a more marked difference between e and ɛ than o and ɔ, the o in apocopation remains close. ancora. . .aŋkọra, ankor. . .aŋkọr.

2. In singing, unstressed e tends to open before m, l, n, r when followed by another consonant and is transcribed ɛ.

M	L	N	R
ɛmblɛma	bɛltà	ɛntità	vɛrbɛna
tɛmperare	dɛlfịn	sɛntịre	cɛrvɛllo

3. The unstressed o tends to open before r when followed by another consonant and is transcribed as follows:

mortal.....mǫrtal   sortire.....sǫrtire

Note that the following is <u>not</u> an exception: unaccented final e may sound to some persons as a change in value to an intermediate vowel or even the open vowel. This is incorrect. Final e should be considered as <u>the close sound in unstressed form</u>, and should never be pronounced ε. Hence unstressed final e is always transcribed e.

Intervocalic s

Intervocalic s is pronounced soft z –even when pronounced s in speech, because the American singer will tend to emphasize the s so much that it will be heard as ss. If s follows a prefix, it is pronounced s.

Intervocalic   rosa...rǫza   pisa...pi̱za

With prefix   disegno...dise̱ɲo   risuonò...riswonǫ

Pronunciation of z and zz

The two pronunciations of z and zz, which are almost without rules, are indicated in this text by ts, dz, and when doubled t:s and d:z.

danza....da̱ntsa   bonzo....bǫndzo

pazzo....pa̱t:so   mezzo....me̱d:zo

Tonic accent

In this transcription the tonic accent or elevation of the tone is indicated by the vowel being underlined (bεl:la) rather than accented (ˋbεl:la) for easier reading and for a clearer indication of the lengthening of the syllable.

Textual Diphthongs

When the final vowel of a word is tied to the initial vowel of the succeeding word and is sung on a single note, the combination is referred to as a textual diphthong. The textual diphthong is indicated by a tie and the stressed vowel is underlined.

che un   che ai   cento e

Each such cluster must be uttered with one impulse of the breath and should never be broken into separate sounds – the composer would have written separate notes had he so desired. (Errolle)

Double Consonants

Double consonants are stressed in articulation and the sound is <u>prolonged</u>. Since the double consonant is of such importance in Italian and is so frequently neglected by American singers, all double consonants have been separated in this text by a colon to remind the singer that the utterance of the consonant should be prolonged.

letto – lε̱t:to   bocca – bǫk:ka   giammai – dʒam:ma̱i
legge – lε̱d:ʒe   mezzo – me̱d:zo   prezzo – prε̱t:so

Value of the phonetic symbols used in the transcription of Italian

Phonetic Symbol	Sound as derived from English sounds	As found in Italian words
VOWELS		
a*	father (in middle west)	casa.....k<u>a</u>za
ɛ	pet	ecco.....<u>ɛ</u>k:ko
e	pate, without the diphthong vanish ei	che.....ke
i	me	mi.....mi
o	loan, roll, without diphthong glide ou to u	voce.....v<u>o</u>tʃe
ɔ	orphan	oggi.....<u>ɔ</u>dʒi
u	rule	muto.....m<u>u</u>to
CONSONANTS		
b	bond	banco.....b<u>a</u>ŋko
d	<u>d</u>ental, with tongue touching the upper front teeth	dente.....d<u>ɛ</u>nte
dʒ	Affricate of d and ʒ as in ju<u>dg</u>e	gioja.....dʒ<u>ɔ</u>ja
f	fat	fatto.....f<u>a</u>t:to
g	gamble	gamba.....g<u>a</u>mba
j	yes	ieri.....j<u>ɛ</u>ri
k	keel	caro.....k<u>a</u>ro
l	love dentalized, with tongue touching upper front teeth	lunga.....l<u>u</u>ŋga
ʎ	mil<u>li</u>on li or lj becomes ʎ when tongue touches lower front teeth	gli.....ʎi
m	mine	mio.....m<u>i</u>o
n	dent dentalized, with tongue touching upper front teeth	notte.....n<u>ɔ</u>t:te
ŋ	ring	anche.....<u>a</u>ŋke

*Do not confuse this **IPA** symbol with the a used in French where it represents a sound acoustically between æ and ɑ.

CONSONANTS continued

ɲ	pinion, ni becomes ɲ when tongue touches lower front teeth	ogni.....oɲi
p	pull	pace.....patʃe
r	rock – but always rolled in Italian	riso.....rizo
s	sell	sapete.....sapete
t	try – dentalized with the tongue touching upper front teeth	testa.....tͼsta
tʃ	Affricate of t and ʃ as in chess	voce.....votʃe
v	vine	vino.....vino
w	went	guerra....gwͼr:ra
z	zoo	rosa.....roza

BIBLIOGRAPHY

Bianchi, Enrico. *Come si dice, Come si scrive*. Casa Editrice. Adriano, Salani Firenze, 1947.

Edgren, Hjalmor. *An Italian and English Dictionary*. Henry Holt & Co., New York 1929. (Contains many words used in songs not found in other works.)

Errolle, Ralph. *Italian Diction for Singers*. Third Edition. Pruett Press, Boulder, Colorado, 1963. (Adjustments from speech to singing explained.) Recommended by Dr. Riccardo Picozzi, Teatro alla Scala, Milano and Teatro dell'Opera di Roma.

Grandgent & Wilkens. *Italian Grammar*. D. C. Heath Co., New York, 1915.

Hoare, Alfred. *A Short Italian Dictionary*. Cambridge University Press, 1950.

Russo, Joseph Louis. *Present Day Italian*. D. C. Heath Co., Boston, 1947.

Zingarelli, Nicola. *Vocabolario Della Lingua Italiana*. Eighth Edition. Nicola Zanichelli Editore, Bologna, 1959.

Beethoven   In questa tomba oscura
               in kwesta tomba oskura

In questa tomba oscura lasciami riposar;
in kwesta tomba oskura laʃami ripozar;

quando vivevo, ingrata, dovevi a me pensar.
kwando vivevo, iŋgrata, dovevi a me pɛnsar.*

Lascia che l'ombre ignude godansi pace almen,
laʃa ke lombre iɲude godansi patʃe almɛn,

e non bagnar mie ceneri d'inutile velen.
e non baɲar mie tʃeneri dinutile velɛn.*

Bellini   Casta Diva, from "Norma"
bel:lini   kasta diva norma

Casta Diva, che inargenti
kasta diva, ke inardʒɛnti

queste sacre, antiche piante,
kweste sakre, antike pjante,

a noi volgi il bel sembiante,
a noi voldʒi il bɛl sembjante,

senza nube e senza vel, si.
sɛntsa nube e sɛntsa vel, si.

Tempra, o Diva, tempra tu de' cori ardenti,
tɛmpra, o diva, tɛmpra tu de kori ardɛnti,

tempra ancora, tempra ancor lo zelo audace,
tɛmpra aŋkora, tɛmpraŋkor lo dzɛlo audatʃe,

spargi in terra, ah, quella pace,
spardʒin tɛr:ra, a, kwel:la patʃe,

che regnar tu fai nel ciel.
ke reɲar tu fai nɛl tʃɛl.

Bencini   Tanto sospirerò
bentʃini   tanto sospirerɔ

Tanto sospirerò, tanto mi lagnerò,
tanto sospirerɔ, tanto mi laɲerɔ,

*See page 1 for unusual openings of unaccented vowels.

che intender le farò, che per lei moro!
ke intɛndɛr le faro, ke per lɛi moro!

Pur l'alma le dirà: "Cara, t'adoro"!
pur lalma le dira: "kara tadoro"!

Boïto L'altra notte in fondo al mare, from "Mefistofele"
boito laltra not:te in fondo al mare mefistofele

L'altra notte in fondo al mare
laltra not:te in fondo al mare

il mio bimbo hanno gittato,
il mio bimbo an:no dʒit:tato,

or per farmi delirare diconch'io
or per farmi delirare dikoŋkio

l'abbia affogato.
lab:bjaf:fogato.

L'aura è fredda, il carcer fosco,
laura ɛ frɛd:da, il kartʃɛr fosko,

e la mesta anima mia
e la mɛsta anima mia

come il passero del bosco
kome il pas:sero dɛl bosko

vola via. Ah! di me pietà!
vola via. a di me pjeta!

In funereo sopore è mia madre addormentata
in funɛreo sopore ɛ mia madre ad:dormɛntata*

e per colmo dell'orrore diconch'io
e per kolmo del:lor:rore dikoŋkio

l'abbia attoscata.
lab:bjat:toskata.

Bononcini L'esperto nocchiero
bonontʃini lespɛrto nok:kjero

L'esperto nocchiero perchè torna al lido, appena partì?
lespɛrto nok:kjero pɛrke tornal lido, ap:pena parti

*See pages 1 and 2 for unusual openings of unaccented vowels.

Del vento cangiato, del flutto turbato s'accorse e fuggi!
dɛl vɛnto kandʒato, dɛl flut:to turbato sak:korse fud:ʒi!

Se il mar lusinghiero sapea ch'era infido,
se il mar luziŋgjero sapɛa kɛra infido,

perchè mai salpò? Salpò ma ingannato,
pɛrkɛ mai salpo?   salpo ma ingan:nato,

al lido lasciato in breve tornò!
al lido laʃato in brɛve torno!

Bononcini   Per la gloria
bonontʃini   per la glɔrja

Per la gloria d'adorarvi
per la glɔrja dadorarvi

voglio amarvi, o luci care.
vɔʎo amarvi, o lutʃi kare.

Amando penerò, ma sempre v'amerò,
amando penero, ma sɛmpre vamero,

sì, sì, nel mio penare.
si, si, nɛl mio penare.

Penerò, v'amerò luci care.
penero, vamero lutʃi kare.

Senza speme di diletto vano affetto
sɛntsa spɛme di dilɛt:to vano af:fɛt:to

è sospirare, ma i vostri dolci rai
ɛ sospirare, ma i vɔstri dɔltʃi rai

chi vagheggiar può mai, e non v'amare?
ki vaged:ʒar pwɔ mai, e non vamare?

Penerò, v'amerò, luci care!
penero, vamero, lutʃi kare!

Caccini	Amarilli, mia bella
katːʃini	amarilːli, mia bɛlːla

Amarilli, mia bella,
amarilːli, mia bɛlːla,

non credi, o del mio cor
non krɛdi, o dɛl mio kɔr

dolce desío, d' esser tu l' amor mio?
doltʃe dezio, dɛsːser tu lamor mio?

Credilo pur: e se timor t' assale,
krɛdilo pur: e se timor tasːsale,

dubitar non ti vale.
dubitar non ti vale.

Aprimi il petto
apri mil pɛtːto

E vedrai scritto in core:
e vedrai skritːto in kɔre

Amarilli è il mio amore.
amarilːli ɛ il mio amore.

Caldara	Alma del core
kaldara	alma dɛl kɔre

Alma del core, spirto dell' alma,
alma dɛl kɔre, spirto delːlalma,

sempre costante t' adorerò.
sɛmpre kostante tadorerɔ.

Sarò contento nel mio tormento
sarɔ kontɛnto nɛl mio tormɛnto

se quel bel labbro baciar potrò.
se kwel bɛl labːbro batʃar potrɔ.

Caldara	Come raggio di sol
kaldara	kome radːʒo di sol

Come raggio di sol mite e sereno,
kome radːʒo di sol mite serɛno,

8

sovra placidi flutti si riposa,
sovra platʃidi flut:ti si ripoza,

mentre del mare nel profondo seno
mentre dɛl mare nɛl profondo seno

sta la tempesta ascosa:
sta la tempɛsta askoza:

così riso talor gaio e pacato di contento,
kozi rizo talor gajo e pakato di kontɛnto,

di gioia un labbro infiora,
di dʒoja un lab:bro infjora,

mentre nel suo segreto il cor piagato
mentre nɛl suo segreto il kor pjagato

s'angoscia e si martora.
saŋgoʃa   e si martora.

Caldara   Sebben, crudele
kaldara   seb:ben krudɛle

Sebben, crudele, mi fai languir,
seb:ben, krudɛle, mi fai laŋgwir,

sempre fedele ti voglio amar.
sɛmpre fedɛle ti voʎo amar.

Con la lunghezza del mio servir
kon la luŋget:sa dɛl mio sɛrvir

la tua fierezza saprò stancar.
la tua fjeret:sa sapro staŋkar.

Caldara   Selve amiche
kaldara   sɛlve amike

Selve amiche, ombrose piante
sɛlve amike, ombroze pjante,

fido albergo del mio core,
fido albɛrgo dɛl mio kore,

chiede a voi quest' alma amante
kjede a voi kwestalma amante

qualche pace al suo dolore.
kwalke patʃe al suo dolore.

Carissimi   Vittoria, mio core!
karis:simi vit:tɔrja, mio kɔre!

Vittoria, mio core!   non lagrimar più,
vit:tɔrja, mio kɔre!   non lagrimar pju,

è sciolta d' Amore la vil servitù.
ɛ ʃɔlta damɔre la vil servitu.

Già l' empia a' tuoi danni
dʒa lempja twoi dan:ni

fra stuolo di sguardi,
fra stwɔlo di zgwardi,

con vezzi bugiardi dispose gl' inganni;
kon vet:si budʒardi dispoze ʎiŋgan:ni;

le frode, gli affanni non hanno più loco,
le frɔde, ʎaf:fan:ni non an:no pju lɔko,

del crudo suo foco è spento l' ardore!
dɛl krudo suo fɔko ɛ spento lardɔre!

Da luci ridenti non esce più strale,
da lutʃi ridɛnti non ɛʃe pju strale,

che piaga mortale nel petto m' avventi:
ke pjaga mortale nɛl pɛt:to mav:venti,

nel duol, ne' tormenti io più non mi sfaccio
nɛl dwɔl, ne tormenti io pju non mi sfat:ʃo

è rotto ogni laccio, sparito il timore!
ɛ rɔt:toni lat:ʃo, sparito il timɔre!

10

Catalani   Ebben, ne andrò lontana, from "La Wally"
katalani   eb:bɛn, ne andrɔ lontana   la val:li

Ebben, ne andrò lontana,
eb:bɛn, ne andrɔ lontana,

come va l'eco della pia campana,
kome va lɛko del:la pia kampana,

là, fra la neve bianca, là, fra le nubi d'ôr,
la, fra la neve bjaŋka, la, fra le nubi dɔr,

laddove la speranza è rimpianto, è dolor!
lad:dove la sperantsa ɛ rimpjanto, ɛ dolor!

O della madre mia casa gioconda,
o del:la madre mia kaza dʒokonda,

la Wally ne andrà da te,
la val:li ne andra da te,

da te lontana assai,
da te lontanas:sai,

e forse a te non farà mai più ritorno,
e forse a te non fara mai pju ritorno,

nè più la rivedrai! mai più.
ne pju la rivedrai! mai pju.

Ne andrò sola e lontana
ne andrɔ sola e lontana

come l'eco della pia campana,
kome lɛko del:la pia kampana,

là fra la neve bianca, n'andrò,
la, fra la neve bjaŋka, nandrɔ,

n'andrò sola e lontana
nandrɔ sola e lontana

e fra le nubi d'ôr!
e fra le nubi dɔr!

Ma fermo è il pie'! n'andiam,
ma fermo ɛ il pje! nandjam,

chè lunga è la via, n'andiam.
ke lunga ɛ la via, nandjam.

11

```
Cavalli      Donzelle, fuggite
kaval:li     dondzɛl:le, fud:ʒite
```

```
Donzelle, fuggite procace beltà!  Fuggite!
dondzɛl:le, fud:ʒite prokatʃe bɛltà!  fud:ʒite!
```

```
Se lucido sguardo vi penetra il core,
se lutʃido zgwardo vi pɛnetra il kɔre,
```

```
Lasciate quel' dardo del perfido amore,
laʃate kwɛl dardo dɛl pɛrfido amore,
```

```
Che insidie scaltrite tramando vi sta!
ke insidje skaltrite tramando vi sta!
```

```
Cesti      Intorno all'idol mio, from "Il Pomo d'Oro"
tʃɛsti     intorno al:lidol mio      "il pomo dɔro"
```

```
Intorno all' idol mio spirate pur,
intorno al:lidol mio spirate pur,
```

```
aure soavi e grate, e nelle guancie elette
aure soavi e grate, e nɛl:le gwan tʃe lɛt:te
```

```
baciatelo per me, cortesi aurette!
batʃatelo per me, kɔrtezi auret:te!
```

```
Al mio ben, che riposa su l'ali della
al mio bɛn, ke ripoza su lali dɛl:la
```

```
quiete, grati sogni assistete
kwiɛte, grati soɲi as:sistete
```

```
E il mio racchiuso ardore
e il mio rak:juzo ardore
```

```
svelategli per me, o larve d'amore!
zvelateʎi per me, o larve damore!
```

```
Cesti      Tu mancavi a tormentarmi
tʃɛsti     tu maŋkavi a tormentarmi
```

```
Tu mancavi a tormentarmi
tu maŋkavi a tormentarmi,
```

```
crudelissima speranza,
krudelis:sima sperantsa,
```

e con dolce rimembranza vuoi
e kon doltʃe rimɛmbrantsa vwɔi

di nuovo avvelenarmi.
di nwɔvo av:velenarmi.

Ancor dura la sventura
aŋkor dura la zvɛntura

d'una fiamma incenerita,
duna fjam:ma intʃenerita,

la ferita ancora aperta par
la ferita aŋkora apɛrta par

m'avverta nuove pene.
mav:vɛrta nwɔve pene.

Dal rumor delle catene
dal rumor dɛl:le katene

mai non vedo allontanarmi.
mai non vedo al:lontanarmi.

Cilea   Il Lamento di Federico, from "L'Arlesiana"
tʃilɛa   il lamento di federiko larlezjana

È la solita storia del pastore
ɛ la solita stɔrja dɛl pastore

Il povero ragazzo voleva raccontarla e s'addormì
il povero ragat:so voleva rak:kontarla e sad:dormi

C'è nel sonno l'oblio come l'invidio!
tʃe nɛl son:no loblio kome linvidjo!

Anch'io vorrei dormir così
aŋkio   vor:rɛi dormir kozi

Nel sonno almen l'oblio trovar!
nɛl son:no almɛn loblio trovar!

La pace sol cercando io vo.
la patʃe sol tʃɛrkando io vɔ.

Vorrei poter tutto scordar!
vor:rɛi poter tut:to skordar!

Ma ogni sforzo è vano ;
ma oɲi sfɔrtso ɛ vano ;

Davanti ho sempre di lei
davanti ɔ sempre di lɛi

il dolce sembiante.
il doltʃe sembjante.

La pace tolta è solo a me!
la patʃe tɔlta ɛ solo a me!

Perchè degg' io tanto penar?
perke ded:ʒio tanto penar?

Lei sempre lei mi parla al cor...
lɛi sempre lɛi mi par lal kɔr...

Mi fai tanto male! ahimè! Fatale vision, mi lascia!
mi fai tanto male! aimɛ! fatale vizjɔn, mi laʃa!

Cimara   Fiocca la neve
tʃimara   fjɔk:ka la neve

Lenta la neve fiocca, fiocca, fiocca.
lɛnta la neve fjɔk:ka, fjɔk:ka, fjɔk:ka.

Senti, una zana dondola pian piano.
sɛnti, una dzana dɔndola pjan pjano.

Un bimbo piange, il piccol dito in bocca.
un bimbo pjandʒe, il pik:kol dito in bɔk:ka.

Canta una vecchia, il mento sulla mano.
kanta una vɛk:kja, il mɛnto sul:la mano.

La vecchia canta: "Intorno al tuo lettino
la vɛk:kja kanta: "intɔrno al tuo let:tino

c'è rose e gigli come un bel giardino."
tʃɛ rɔze dʒiʎi kome un bɛl dʒardino."

Nel bel giardino il bimbo s'addormenta,
nɛl bɛl dʒardino il bimbo sad:dormɛnta,

fiocca la neve lenta, fiocca la neve.
fjɔk:ka la neve lɛnta, fjɔk:ka la neve.

Donaudy   O del mio amato ben
donaudi   o dɛl mio amato bɛn

O del mio amato ben perduto incanto!
o dɛl mio amato bɛn pɛrduto iŋkanto!

Lungi è dagli occhi miei chi m'era gloria e vanto!
lundʒi ɛ da ʎok:ki mjɛi ki mɛra glɔrja e vanto!

Or per le mute stanze sempre la cerco e chiamo
or per le mute stantse sɛmpre la tʃɛrko e kjamo

con pieno il cor di speranze ma cerco invan,
kon pjɛno il kor di sperantse ma tʃɛrko invan,

chiamo invan! E il pianger m'è sì caro,
kjamo invan!   e il pjandʒɛr mɛ si karo,

che di pianto sol nutro il cor.
ke di pjanto sol nutro il kor.

Mi sembra, senza lei, triste ogni loco.
mi sɛmbra, sɛntsa lɛi, triste ɔni lɔko.

Notte mi sembra il giorno, mi sembra gelo il foco.
nɔt:te mi sɛmbra il dʒorno, mi sɛmbra dʒɛlo il fɔko.

Se pur tal volta spero di darmi ad altra cura,
se pur tal vɔlta spɛro di darmi ad altra kura,

sol mi tormenta un pensiero: ma, senza lei, che farò?
sol mi tormɛnta un pensjɛro, ma, sɛntsa lɛi, ke farɔ?

Mi par così la vita vana cosa senza il mio ben.
mi par kozi la vita vana kɔza sɛntsa il mio bɛn.

Donizetti   O mio Fernando, from "La Favorita"
donidzɛt:ti o mio fɛrnando la favorita

Fia dunque vero.. oh Ciel!   desso Fernando
fia duŋkwe vɛro   o tʃɛl!   dɛs:so fɛrnando

lo sposo di Leonora! Ah!
lo spɔzo di leonɔra! a!

Tutto mel dice.. e dubbia l'alma ancora
tut:to mel ditʃe e dub:bja lalma aŋkɔra

all' inattesa gioja.
al:linat:tɛza dʒɔja.

Oh Dio!   sposarlo... Oh mia vergogna estrema...
o dio   spozarlo   o mia vergoɲa estrema...

in doteal prode recar il disonor!
in doteal prode rekar il dizonor!

no... mai dovessi esecrarmi...fuggir!
nɔ mai doves:si ezekrarmi, fud:ʒir!

saprà in brev' ora chi sia la donna che cotanto adora.
sapra in brevɔra ki sia la don:na ke kotanto adora.

O mio Fernando!   della terra il trono
o mio fernando!   del:la ter:ra il trono

A possederti avrai donato il cor;
a pos:sederti avrai donato il kɔr;

Ma puro l' amor mio come il perdono,
ma puro lamor mio kome il perdono,

Dannato ahì lassa! e a disperato orror...
dan:nato ai las:sa! e a disperator:rɔr...

Il ver fia noto, e in tuo dispregio estremo
il ver fia nɔto, e in tuo dispredʒo estremo

La pena avrommi che maggior si de'! ah!
la pena avrɔm:mi ke mad:ʒor si de! a!

Se il giusto tuo disdegno allor,   allor fia scemo.
se il dʒusto tuo dizdeɲo al:lor, al:lor fia ʃemo.

Piombi, gran Dio, ... la folgor tua su me.
pjombi, gran dio,   la folgor tua su me.

Ah, se fia scemo il tuo disdegno, piombi, o Dio,
a, se fia ʃemo il tuo dizdeɲo, pjombi, o dio,

la folgor tua su me!
la folgor tua su me!

Su, crudeli... e chi v' arresta?
su krudeli.... e ki var:resta?

Scritto è in cielo il mio dolor!
skrit:to ɛ in tʃelo il mio dolɔr!

Su, venite, ell' è una festa, Sparsa l' ara sia di fior,
su, venite, el:lɛ una fɛsta,   sparsa lara sia di fjor,

Già la tomba a me s'appresta,   E coperta in negro vel.
dʒa la tomba a me sap:presta,   e kopɛrta in negro vel.

16

Sia la trista fidanzata,
sịa la trịsta fidantsạta,

Che rejetta, disperata, Non avrà perdono in ciel
ke rejẹt:ta disperạta, non avrạ pɛrdọno in tʃɛl

maledetta, disperata, non avrà perdono in ciel!
maledẹt:ta, disperạta, non avrạ pɛrdọno in tʃɛl!

Donizetti   Regnava nel silenzio, from "Lucia di Lammermoor"
donidzẹt:ti   reɲạva nɛl silɛntsjo   lutʃịa di lạm:mermur

Regnava nel silenzio alta la notte bruna,
reɲạva nɛl silɛntsjo ạlta la nọt:te brụna,

colpía la fonte un pallido raggio di tetra Luna,
kolpịa la fọnte un pạl:lido rạd:ʒo di tẹtra lụna,

quando un sommesso gemito fra l'aure udir si fe',
kwạndo un som:mẹs:so dʒẹmito fra lạure ụdịr si fe,

ed ecco su quel margine l'ombra mostrarsi a me, ah!
ed ɛk:ko su kwɛl mạrdʒine lọmbra mostrạrsi ạ me, a!

qual di chi parla muoversi il labbro suo vedea,
kwal di ki pạrla mwọvɛrsi il lạb:bro sụo vedẹa,

e con la mano esanime chiamarmi a sé parea;
e kon la mạno ẹzạnime kjamạrmi ạ se parẹa;

stette un momento immobile, poi ratta dileguò
stẹt:te un momẹnto im:mọbile, pọi rạt:ta dilegwọ

e l'onda pria si limpida di sangue rosseggiò.
e lọnda prịa si lịmpida di sạngwe ros:sẹd:ʒọ.

Quando rapita in estasi del più cocente ardore
kwạndo rapịtạ in ɛstazi dɛl pju kotʃɛnte ạrdọre

col favellar del core mi giura eterna fé
kol favel:lạr dɛl kọre mi dʒụra ẹtɛrna fe

gli affanni miei dimentico gioja diviene il pianto,
ʎaf:fạn:ni mjɛi dimẹntiko dʒọja divjẹnẹ il pjạnto,

parmi, che a lui d'accanto si schiuda il ciel per me, ah!
pạrmi, ke ạ lụi dak:kạnto si skjụda il tʃɛl per me, a!

17

Donizetti   Spirto gentil, from " La Favorita"
donidzet:ti   spirto dzɛntil   la favorita

Spirto gentil, ne' sogni miei
spirto dzɛntil, ne soɲi mjɛi

brillasti un dì, ma ti perdei,
bril:lasti un di, ma ti pɛrdei,

fuggi dal cor mentita speme,
fud:ʒi dal kɔr mɛntita spɛme,

larve d' amor, fuggite insieme, larve d' amor!
larve damɔr, fud:ʒite insjɛme, larve damɔr!

A te d' accanto del genitore
a te dak:kanto dɛl dzenitore

scordava il pianto, la patria, il Ciel!
skɔrdava il pjanto, la patria, il tʃɛl!

donna sleal, in tanto amore,
dɔn:na zleal, in tanto amore,

segnasti il core d' onta mortal, ahimè!
seɲastil   kɔre dɔnta mortal, aimɛ!

Donizetti   Una furtiva lagrima, from " L' Elisir d' Amore"
donidzet:ti   una furtiva lagrima   lelizir damore

Una furtiva lagrima negl' occhi suoi spuntò:
Una furtiva lagrima neʎok:ki   swɔi spunto,

quelle festose giovani, invidiar sembrò;
kwɛl:le festoze dʒovani, invidiar sembrɔ;

che più cercando io vo? m' ama, si m' ama, lo vedo!
ke pju tʃɛrkando io vɔ? mama, si mama, lo vedo!

un solo istante i palpiti del suo bel cor sentir;
un solo istante i palpiti dɛl suo bɛl kɔr sentir;

i miei sospir confondere, per poco a' suoi sospir,
i mjɛi sospir konfondere, per pɔko a swɔi sospir,

i palpiti sentir, confondere i miei, coi suoi sospir.
i palpiti sentir, konfondere i mjɛi, kɔi swɔi sospir.

Cielo si può morir; di più non chiedo!
tʃɛlo si pwɔ morir; di pju non kjɛdo!

18

Durante   Danza, danza, fanciulla
durante   da̠ntsa, da̠ntsa, fantʃul:la

Danza, fanciulla, al mio cantar;
da̠ntsa, fantʃul:la, al mi̠o kanta̠r;

danza, fanciulla gentile, al mio cantar.
da̠ntsa, fantʃul:la dʒenti̠le, al mi̠o kanta̠r.

Gira leggera, sottile al suono,
dʒi̠ra led:ʒɛra, sot:ti̠le al swo̠no,

al suono dell' onde del mar.
al swo̠no del:lo̠nde dɛl mar.

Senti il vago rumore dell' aura scherzosa
sɛn til vago rumo̠re del:laura skɛrtso̠za

che parla al core con languido suon,
ke pa̠r lal ko̠re kon la̠ŋgwido swon,

e che invita a danzar, senza posa,
e ke̠ invi̠ta dantsa̠r, sɛntsa po̠za,

che invita a danzar.
ke invi̠ta dantsa̠r.

Durante   Vergin, tutta amor
durante   ve̠rdʒin, tu̠t:tamo̠r

Vergin, tutta amor, O Madre di bontade,
ve̠rdʒin, tu̠t:tamo̠r, o ma̠dre di bonta̠de,

o Madre pia, ascolta, dolce Maria,
o ma̠dre pi̠a, asko̠lta, do̠ltʃe mari̠a,

la voce del peccator.
la vo̠tʃe dɛl pek:kato̠r.

Il pianto suo ti muova,
il pja̠nto su̠o ti mwo̠va,

giungano a te i suoi lamenti,
dʒu̠ŋgano a̠ te i swo̠i lame̠nti,

suo duol, suoi tristi accenti
su̠o dwo̠l, swo̠i tri̠sti a̠t:ʃɛnti

oda pietoso quel tuo cor.
o̠da pje to̠zo kwɛl tu̠o kor.

Flotow   M' apparì tutt' amor, from "Martha"
floto   map:pari tut:tamor   marta

M' apparì tutt' amor, il mio sguardo l' incontrò;
map:pari tut:tamor, il mio zgwardo linkontro;

bella si che il mio cor ansioso a lei volò;
bel:la si ke il mio kor anzjozo a lei volo;

mi ferì, m'invaghì quell' angelica beltà,
mi feri, minvagi kwel:landzelika belta,

sculta in cor dall' amor, cancellarsi non potrà:
skulta in kor dal:lamor, kantʃel:larsi non potra:

il pensier di poter palpitar con lei d' amor,
il pensjer di poter palpitar kon lei damor,

può sopir il martir che m' affanna e strazia il cor,
pwɔ sopir il martir ke maf:fan:na e stratsja il kor,

Marta, Marta, tu sparisti, e il mio cor col tuo n' andò!
marta, marta, tu sparisti, e il mio kor kol tuo nando!

tu la pace mi rapisti, di dolor io morirò,
tu la patʃe mi rapisti, di dolor io moriro,

ah, di dolor morrò, si, morrò!
a, di dolor mor:rɔ, si, mɔr:rɔ!

Flotow   Qui sola vergin rosa, from "Martha"
floto   kwi sola verdʒin roza   marta

Qui sola vergin rosa, come puoi tu fiorir?
kwi sola verdʒin roza, kome pwɔi tu fjorir?

Ancora mezzo ascosa e presso già morir!
ankora med:ʒo askoza e pres:so dʒa morir!

Non ha per te rugiade, già colta sei dal gel!
non a per te rudʒade, dʒa kolta sei dal dʒel!

Il capo tuo già cade, chino sul verde stel.
il kapo tuo dʒa kade, kino sul verde stɛl.

Perchè sola ignorata languir nel tuo giardin,
perke sola inorata langwir nɛl tuo dʒardin,

dal vento tormentata in preda a un rio destin.
dal vɛnto tormentata in prɛda un rio destin.

20

Sul cespite tremante ti colgo, giovin fior!
sul tʃɛspite tremante ti kɔlgo, dʒovin fjor!

Su questo core amante così morrai d'amor.
su kwesto kɔre amante kozi mor:rai damɔr.

Giordani   Caro mio ben
dʒordani   karo mio bɛn

Caro mio ben, credimi almen,
karo mio bɛn, kredimi almɛn,

senza di te languisce il cor.
sɛntsa di te laŋgwiʃe il kɔr.

Il tuo fedel sospira ognor.
il tuo fedɛl sospira ɔnor.

Cessa, crudel, tanto rigor!
tʃɛs:sa, krudɛl, tanto rigor!

Giordano   Nemico della patria? from "Andrea Chenier"
dʒordano   nemiko del:la patria   andrɛa ʃeɲe

Nemico della patria?! È vecchia fiaba che beatamente
nemiko del:la patria! ɛ vɛk:kja fjaba ke beatamente

ancor la beve il popolo. Nato a Castantinopoli?
aŋkɔr la beve il pɔpolo. nato a kostantinɔpoli?

Straniero! Studiò a Saint Cyr?
stranjero! studjɔ a sɛn sir?

Soldato! Traditore! Di Dumouriez un complice!
soldato! traditɔre! di dumurje un komplitʃe!

È poeta? Sovvertitor di cuori e di costumi!
ɛ pɔeta? sov:vertitɔr di kwori e di kostumi!

Un dì m'era di gioia passar fra gli odì e le vendette,
un di mɛra di dʒɔja pas:sar fra ʎodi e le vɛndet:te,

puro, innocente e forte! Gigante, mi credea!
puro, in:notʃɛnte forte! dʒigante, mi kredea!

Son sempre un servo!   Ho mutato padrone!
son sempre un sɛrvo!   ɔ mutato padrone!

Un servo obbediente di violenta passione!   Ah, peggio!
un sɛrvob:bedjɛnte di vjolɛnta pas:sjone!   a, pɛd:ʒo!

Uccido e tremo, e mentre uccido, io piango!
ut:ʃido e trɛmo, e mɛntre ut:ʃido, io pjaŋgo!

Io della Redentrice figlio pel primo ho udito il grido
io del:la redɛntritʃe fiʎo pel pri mo udito il grido

suo pel mondo ed ho al suo il mio grido unito....
suo pel mondo ed ɔ al suo il mio grido unito ...

Or smarrita ho la fede nel sognato destino?
or zmar:rita ɔ la fede nɛl soɲato destino?

Com' era irradiato di gloria il mio cammino!
komɛra ir:radjato di glɔrja il mio kam:mino!

La coscienza nei cuor ridestar de le genti!
la koʃɛntsa nei kwor ridestar de le dʒɛnti!

Raccogliere le lagrime dei vinti e sofferenti!
rak:kɔʎere le lagrime dei vinti e sof:ferɛnti!

Fare del mondo un Pantheon!   Gli uomini in dii mutare
fare dɛl mondo un panteon!   ʎi wɔmini in dii mutare

e in un sol bacio e abbraccio tutte le genti amar!
e in un sol batʃo e ab:bratʃo tut:te le dʒɛnti amar!

Gluck   Che farò senza Eudidice, from '' Orfeo''
gluk   ke farɔ sɛntsa euriditʃe   orfeo

Ahimè!   dove trascorsi, ove mi spinse un delirio d' amor?
aimɛ!   dove traskorsi, ɔve mi spinse un delirjo damor?

Sposa Euridice Consorte
spɔza euriditʃe konsɔrte

Ah! più non vive la chiamo invan!
a!   pju non vive la kjamo invan!

Misero me! la perdo e di nuovo e per sempre! oh legge!
mizero me! la pɛrdo e di nwɔvo e per sɛmpre! o lɛd:ʒe!

oh morte! oh ricordo crudel!
o mɔrte! o rikɔrdo krudɛl!

Non ho soccorso non m' avanza consiglio io veggo solo
non ɔ sok:kɔrso non mavantsa konsiʎo io veg:go sɔlo

(Oh fiera vista!)
o fjɛra vista!

il luttoso aspetto dell' orrido mio stato!
il lut:tozo aspɛt:to del:lɔr:rido mio stato!

Saziati, sorte rea son disperato!
satsjati, sɔrte rɛa son disperato!

Che farò senza Euridice? Dove andrò senza il mio ben?
ke farɔ sɛntsa euriditʃe? dove andrɔ sɛntsa il mio bɛn?

Euridice! oh Dio! rispondi.
euriditʃe! o dio rispɔndi.

Io son pur il tuo fedele,
io son pur il tuo fedele,

Ah! non m' avanza più soccorso,
a! non mavantsa pju sok:kɔrso,

più speranza nè dal mondo, nè dal ciel!
pju sperantsa ne dal mɔndo, ne dal tʃɛl!

Gluck   O del mio dolce ardor, from "Paride ed Elena"
gluk   o dɛl mio dɔltʃe ardɔr   paride ed ɛlena

O del mio dolce ardor bramato oggetto,
o dɛl mio dɔltʃe ardɔr bramato od:ʒɛt:to,

L' aura che tu respiri, alfin respiro,
laura ke tu respiri, alfin respiro,

Ovunque il guardo io giro,
ovunkwe il gwardo io dʒiro,

Le tue vaghe sembianze Amore in me dipinge:
le tue vage sɛmbjantse amore in me dipindʒe,

Il mio pensier si finge
il mio pɛnsjɛr si findʒe

Le più liete speranze;
le pju ljɛte sperantse;

23

E nel desio che così m'empie il petto
e nɛl dezi̯o ke kozi mɛmpi̯e il pɛt:to

Cerco te, chiamo te, spero e sospiro. Ah!
tʃɛrko te, ki̯amo te, spɛro e sospiro. a!

Gluck   Spiagge amate, from "Paride ed Elena"
gluk   spi̯ad:ʒe amate   paride ed ɛlena

Spiagge amate ove talora
spi̯ad:ʒe amate ove talora

l'idol mio lieto s'aggira,
lidol mi̯o li̯eto sad:ʒira,

ruscelletti, ove si mira
ruʃel:let:ti, ove si mira

quando infiora il crine o il sen,
kwando infi̯ora il krine o il sen,

chiari fonti, ove si bagna,
ki̯ari fonti, ove si baɲa,

erbe in cui posa le piante,
ɛrbe in kui poza le pi̯ante,

voi pietose a un core amante,
voi pi̯etoze a un kore amante,

dite voi che fa il mio ben,
dite voi ke fa il mi̯o bɛn,

chiari fonti, ruscelletti.
ki̯ari fonti, ruʃel:let:ti.

Handel   Ah! mio cor!, from "Alcina"
a mi̯o kɔr   altʃina

Ah! mio cor, schernito sei.
a mi̯o kɔr, skɛrnito sɛi.

Stelle, Dei, Nume d'amore!   traditore,
stel:le, dɛi, nume damore!   traditore,

24

t'amo tanto, puoi lasciarmi sola in pianto?
tamo tanto, pwɔi laʃarmi sola in pjanto?

Oh!Dei! puoi lasciarmi, perchè?
o dɛi! pwɔi laʃarmi, pɛrke?

Handel   Alma mia (Aria di Floridante from Floridante)
           alma mia   floridante

Alma mia, sì, sol tu sei la mia gloria, il mio diletto.
alma mia, si sol tu sɛi la mia glɔrja, il mio dilɛt:to.

Dal poter de' sommi Dei più bel dono io non aspetto.
dal potɛr de sɔm:mi dɛi pju bɛl dono io non aspɛt:to.

Handel   Care selve, from "Atalanta"
           kare selve   atalanta

Care selve, ombre beate,
kare selve, ombre beate,

vengo in traccia del mio cor.
vɛngo in trat:ʃa dɛl mio kor.

Handel   Lascia ch'io pianga, from "Rinaldo"
           laʃa kio pjaŋga   rinaldo

Armida, dispietata colla forza d'abisso rapimmi
armida, dispjetata kɔl:la fɔrtsa dabis:so rapim:mi

al caro ciel de'miei contenti,
al karo tʃɛl de mjɛi kontɛnti,

e qui, con duolo eterno,
e kwi, kon dwɔlo etɛrno,

vivo mi tiene in tormentoso inferno!
vivo mi tjɛne in tormentozo infɛrno!

Signor, deh! per pietà, lasciami piangere!
siɲor, dɛ! per pjeta, laʃami pjandʒere!

Lascia ch' io pianga la cruda sorte,
laʃa   kio pjaŋga la kruda sorte,

e che sospiri la libertà,
e ke sospiri la libɛrta,

Il duolo infranga queste ritorte,
il dwolo infraŋga kwɛste ritorte,

de' miei martiri sol per pietà
de mjɛi martiri sol per pjeta!

Handel   Lusinghe più care, from "Alessandro"
              luziŋge pju kare   ales:sandro

Ne trionfa d'Alessandro, trionfa ancor quest' alma,
ne trionfa dales:sandro, trionfaŋkor kwestalma,

ma funesta Zisaura ogni mia palma ma sentirò
ma funɛsta tsizaura oɲi mia palma ma sentiro

tutte d'amor le vie, perchè allettato il vincitore
tut:te damor le vie, pɛrke al:let:tato il vintʃitore

amante, infido altrui, sia solo a me costante.
amante, infido altrui, sia solo a me kostante.

Lusinghe più care, d'amor veri dardi, vezzose volate
luziŋge pju kare, damor vɛri dardi, vet:soze volate

sul labbro, nei guardi, e tutta involate l'altrui libertà,
sul lab:bro, nɛi gwardi, e tut:ta involate laltrui libɛrta,

Gelosi sospetti, diletti con pene, fra gioie e tormenti,
dʒelozi sospɛt:ti, dilɛt:ti kon pene, fra dʒoje tormenti,

momenti di spene voi l'armi sarete di vaga beltà.
momenti di spɛne voi larmi sarete di vaga bɛlta.

Handel   Ombra mai fu, from "Serse"
              ombra mai fu   sɛrse

Frondi tenere e belle
frondi tɛnere e bɛl:le

del mio platano amato, per voi risplende il fato
dɛl mio platano amato, per voi risplɛnde il fato

26

tuoni, lampi e procelle non v'oltraggino mai
tw<u>o</u>ni, l<u>a</u>mpi e prot∫<u>ɛ</u>l:le non voltr<u>a</u>d:ʒino m<u>ai</u>

la cara pace, nè giunga a profanarvi,
la k<u>a</u>ra p<u>a</u>t∫e, ne dʒ<u>u</u>ŋga profan<u>a</u>rvi,

austro rapace!
<u>a</u>ustro rap<u>a</u>t∫e!

Ombra mai fu di vegetabile,
<u>o</u>mbra m<u>ai</u> fu di vedʒet<u>a</u>bile,

cara ed amabile, soave più.
k<u>a</u>ra ed am<u>a</u>bile, so<u>a</u>ve pju.

Handel   Sì, tra i ceppi, from "Berenice"
             si, tr<u>ai</u> t∫<u>ɛ</u>p:pi   berenit∫e

Sì tra i ceppi e le ritorte
si, tr<u>ai</u> t∫<u>ɛ</u>p:pi e le rit<u>o</u>rte

La mia fè tra le ritorte,
la m<u>i</u>a fe tra le rit<u>o</u>rte,

La mia fè risplenderà.
la m<u>i</u>a fe rispl<u>ɛ</u>ndera.

Nò, nè pur la stessa morte
nɔ, ne pur la st<u>ɛ</u>s:sa m<u>o</u>rte

Il mio foco estinguerà.
il m<u>i</u>o f<u>o</u>ko estiŋgwera.

Legrenzi   Che fiero costume
legr<u>ɛ</u>ntsi   ke fj<u>ɛ</u>ro kost<u>u</u>me

Che fiero costume d'aligero nume,
ke fj<u>ɛ</u>ro kost<u>u</u>me dal<u>i</u>dʒero n<u>u</u>me,

che a forza di pene si faccia adorar!
ke <u>a</u> f<u>o</u>rtsa di p<u>ɛ</u>ne si f<u>a</u>t:∫adorar!

E pur nell'ardore il dio traditore
e pur nel:lard<u>o</u>re il d<u>i</u>o tradit<u>o</u>re

un vago sembiante mi fe' idolatrar.
un vago sɛmbjante mi fe idolatrar.

Che crudo destino che un cieco bambino
ke krudo destino ke un tʃeko bambino

con bocca di latte si faccia stimar!
kon bok:ka di lat:te si fat:ʃa stimar!

Ma questo tiranno con barbaro inganno,
ma kwesto tir:rano kon barbaro iŋgan:no,

entrando per gli occhi, mi fe' sospirar.
ɛntrando per ʎok:ki mi fe sospirar.

Leoncavallo Prologue, from "Pagliacci"
leonkaval:lo   paʎat:ʃi

Si può? Si può? Signore! Signori!
si pwɔ si pwɔ siɲore siɲori

Scusatemi se da sol mi presento.
skuzatemi se da sol mi prezɛnto.

Io sono il Prologo:
io sonɔ il prɔlogo,

Poichè in iscena ancor
poike in iʃʃnaŋkor

le antiche maschere mette l'autore;
le antike maskere mɛt:te lautore;

in parte ei vuol riprendere le vecchie usanze,
in partei vwɔl riprɛndere le vɛk:kje uzantse,

e a voi di nuovo inviami.
e a voi di nwɔvo inviami.

Ma non per dirvi come pria:
ma non per dirvi kome pria:

"Le lacrime che noi versiam son false!
le lakrime ke noi vɛrsjam son false!

Degli spasimi e de' nostri martir non allarmatevi."
deʎi spazimi e de nɔstri martir non al:larmatevi."

No! No! L'autore ha cercato
nɔ! nɔ! lautore a tʃɛrkato

28

invece pingervi uno squarcio di vita.
invetʃe pindʒɛrvi uno skwartʃo di vita.

Egli ha per massima sol che l'artista è un uom
eʎa   per mas:sima sol ke lartista ɛ un wɔm

e che per gli uomini scrivere ei deve.
e ke per ʎwomini skriverei deve.

Ed al vero ispiravasi.
ed al vero ispiravasi.

Un nido di memorie in fondo a l'anima cantava un giorno,
un nido di memorje in fondo a lanima kantava un dʒorno,

ed ei con vere lacrime scrisse,
ed ei kon vere lakrime skris:se,

e i singhiozzi il tempo gli battevano!
e i siŋgjot:si il tɛmpo ʎi bat:tevano!

Dunque, vedrete amar sì come s'amano gli esseri umani;
duŋkwe, vedrete amar si kome samano ʎɛs:seri umani;

vedrete de l'odio i tristi frutti, Del dolor gli spasimi,
vedrete de lodjo i tristi frut:ti, dɛl dolor ʎi spazimi,

urli di rabbia, udrete e risa ciniche!
urli di rab:bja udrete e riza tʃinike!

E voi, piuttosto, che le vostre povere gabbane d'istrioni,
e voi, pjut:tosto, ke le vostre povere gab:bane distrjoni,

le nostr'anime considerate,
le nostranime konsiderate,

poichè siam uomini di carne e d'ossa,
poike sjam womini di karne e dɔs:sa,

e che di quest'orfano mondo
e ke di kwestorfano mondo

al pari di voi spiriamo l'aere!
al pari di voi spirjamo laere!

Il concetto vi dissi...Or ascoltate com'egli è svolto.
il kontʃɛt:to vi dis:si, or askoltate komeʎɛ zvɔlto.

Andiam, Incominciate!
andjam, iŋkomintʃate!

Leoncavallo   Vesti la giubba, from "Pagliacci"
leoŋkaval:lo   vɛsti la dʒub:ba   paʎat:ʃi

Vesti la giubba e la faccia infarina.
vɛsti la dʒub:ba e la fat:ʃa infarina.

La gente paga e rider vuole qua.
la dʒɛnte paga e ridɛr vwɔle kwa.

E se Arlecchin t' invola Colombina,
e se arlek:kin tinvɔla kolombina,

ridi, Pagliaccio e ognun applaudirà!
ridi, paʎat:ʃo e oɲun ap:plaudira!

Tramuta in lazzi lo spasmo ed il pianto;
tramuta in lad:zi lo spazmo ed il pjanto;

in una smorfia il singhiozzo e'l dolor Ah!
in una zmɔrfja il siŋgjɔt:so el dolɔr a!

Ridi, Pagliaccio, sul tuo amore infranto!
ridi, paʎat:ʃo,   sul tuo amɔre infranto!

Ridi del duol che t' avvelena il cor!
ridi dɛl dwɔl ke tav:velɛna il kor!

Lotti   Pur dicesti, o bocca bella
lɔt:ti   pur ditʃesti, o bok:ka bɛl:la

Pur dicesti, o bocca, bocca bella,
pur ditʃesti, o bok:ka, bok:ka bɛl:la,

quel soave e caro sì,
kwɛl soave karo si.

sì, che fa tutto il mio piacer.
si, ke fa tut:to il mio pjatʃɛr.

Per onor di sua facella
per onɔr di sua fatʃɛl:la

con un bacio Amor t' aprì,
kon un batʃo amɔr tapri,

dolce fonte del goder, ah!
dɔltʃe fɔnte dɛl godɛr, a!

Marcello   Il mio bel foco
martʃɛl:lo il mio bɛl fɔko

Il mio bel foco, o lontano o vicino
il mio bɛl fɔko, o lontano vitʃino

ch' esser poss' io, senza cangiar mai tempre
kɛs:ser pos:sio, sɛntsa kandʒar mai tɛmpre

per voi, care pupille, arderà sempre.
per voi, kare pupil:le, ardera sɛmpre.

Quella fiamma che m' accende,
kwɛl:la fjam:ma ke matːʃɛnde,

piace tanto all' alma mia,
pjatʃe tanto al:lalma mia,

che giammai s' estinguerà.
ke dʒam:mai sestiŋgwera.

E se il fato a voi mi rende,
e se il fato a voi mi rɛnde,

vaghi rai del mio bel sole,
vagi rai dɛl mio bɛl sɔle,

altra luce ella non vuole
altra lutʃel:la non vwɔle

nè voler giammai potrà.
ne volɛr dʒam:mai potra.

Mascagni   Voi lo sapete, from "Cavalleria Rusticana"
maskaɲi   voi lo sapete   kaval:leria rustikana

Voi lo sapete, o mamma, prima d' andar soldato
voi lo sapete, o mam:ma, prima dandar soldato

Turiddu aveva a Lola eterna fè giurato.
turid:du aveva lola etɛrna fe dʒurato.

Tornò, la seppe sposa;
tornɔ, la sep:pe spɔza;

e con un nuovo amore volle spegner la fiamma
e kon un nwɔvo amore vol:le speɲer la fjam:ma

che gli bruciava il core m' amò, l' amai, ah!
ke ʎi brutʃava il kɔre mamɔ, lamai, a!

31

Quell' invida d'ogni delizia mia,
kwel:linvida doɲi delitsja mia,

del suo sposo dimentica,
dɛl suo spozo dimentika,

arse di gelosia, Me l' ha rapito.
arse di dʒelozia, me la rapito.

Priva dell' onor mio rimango:
priva del:lonor mio rimaŋgo,

Lola e Turiddu s'amano, io piango!
lola e turid:du samano, io pjaŋgo!

Monteverdi   Lasciatemi morire
monteverdi   laʃatemi morire

Lasciatemi morire!
laʃatemi morire!

e che volete che mi conforte
e ke volete ke mi konforte

in così dura sorte,
in kozi dura sorte,

in così gran martire?
in kozi gran martire?

Mozart   Aprite un po' quegl'occhi, from ''Le Nozze di Figaro''
          aprite un po kweʎɔk:ki   le nɔt:se di figaro

Aprite un po' quegl'occhi, Uomini incauti e schiocchi,
aprite un po kweʎɔk:ki, wominiŋkauti e ʃɔk:ki,

Guardate queste femmine, guardate cosa son!
gwardate kweste fem:mine, gwardate koza son!

Queste chiamate dee, Dagli ingannati sensi,
kweste kjamate dɛɛ, daʎingan:nati sɛnsi,

A cui tributa incensi La debole ragion.
a kui tributa intʃɛnsi la debole radʒon.

32

Son streghe che incantano per farci penar,
son strege ke iŋkantano per fartʃi penar,

Sirene che cantano per farci affogar,
sirɛne ke kantano per fartʃi af:fogar,

Civette che allettano per trarci le piume,
tʃivɛt:te ke al:let:tano per trartʃi le pjume,

Comete che brillano per toglierci il lume,
komɛte ke bril:lano per toʎertʃil lume,

Son rose spinose, Son volpi vezzose,
son roze spinoze, son volpi vet:soze,

Son orse benigne, Colombe, maligne, Maestre d'inganni,
son ɔrse benine, kolombe, maline, maɛstre diŋgan:ni,

Amiche d'affanni, Che fingono, mentono, amore
amike daf:fani, ke fiŋgono, mentono, amore

Non senton pietà, non senton pietà, no.
non sɛnton pjeta, non sɛnton pjeta, nɔ.

Il resto nol dico, già ognuno lo sa.
il rɛsto nol diko, dʒa onuno lo sa.

Mozart   Batti, batti, o bel Masetto, from "Don Giovanni"
              bat:ti, bat:ti, o bɛl mazet:to   dɔn dʒovan:ni

Batti, batti, o bel Masetto, la tua povera Zerlina:
bat:ti, bat:ti, o bɛl mazet:to, la tua povera dzɛrlina,

starò qui come agnellina le tue botte ad aspettar.
starɔ kwi kome anel:lina le tue bɔt:te ad aspet:tar.

Lascierò straziarmi il crine,
laʃerɔ stratsjarmil krine,

lascierò cavarmi gli occhi,
laʃerɔ kavarmi ʎɔk:ki,

le care tue manine lieta poi saprò baciar.
le kare tue manine ljeta pɔi saprɔ batʃar.

Ah, lo vedo non hai core.
a, lo vedo non ai kɔre.

33

Pace, pace, o vita mia!
patʃe, patʃe, o vita mia!

In contento ed allegria notte e dì vogliam passar.
in kontento ed al:legria not:te di voʎam pas:sar.

Mozart Dalla sua pace, from ''Don Giovanni''
     dal:la sua patʃe   don dʒovan:ni

Dalla sua pace la mia dipende,
dal:la sua patʃe la mia dipende,

quel che a lei piace vita mi rende,
kwɛl ke a lɛi pjatʃe vita mi rende,

quel che le incresce, morte mi dà,
kwɛl ke le iŋkreʃe, morte mi da,

S'ella sospira, sospiro anch'io,
sel:la sospira, sospiro aŋkio,

è mia quell'ira, quel pianto è mio;
ɛ mia kwel:lira, kwɛl pjanto ɛ mio;

e non ho bene, s'ella non l'ha!
e non ɔ bɛne, sel:la non la!

Mozart Deh vieni alla finestra, from ''Don Giovanni''
     dɛ vjɛni al:la finɛstra don dʒovan:ni

Deh vieni alla finestra, o mio tesoro,
dɛ, vjɛni al:la finɛstra, o mio tezoro,

Deh vieni a consolar il pianto mio!
de vjɛni a konsolar il pjanto mio!

Se neghi a me di dar qualche ristoro,
se negi a me di dar kwalke ristoro,

Davanti agli occhi tuoi morir vogl'io!
davanti a ʎok:ki twoi morir voʎio!

Tu ch'hai la bocca dolce più del miele,
tu kai la bok:ka doltʃe pju dɛl mjɛle,

34

Tu che il zucchero porti in mezzo al core!
tu ke il dzuk:kero pɔrti in mɛd:zo al kɔre!

Non esser, gioja mia, con me crudele!
non ɛs:ser, dʒɔja mia, kon me krudɛle!

Lasciati almen veder, mio bell'amore!
laʃati almɛn vedɛr, mio bɛl:lamore!

Mozart   Deh, vieni, non tardar, from "Le Nozze di Figaro"
          dɛ, vjɛni non tardar   le nɔt:se di figaro

Giunse alfin il momento che godrò senza affanno
dʒunse alfin il momɛnto ke godrɔ sɛntsaf:fan:no

in braccio all'idol mio!   Timide cure!
in brat:ʃo al:lidol mio!   timide kure!

uscite dal mio petto:
uʃite dal mio pɛt:to,

a turbar non venite il mio diletto!
a turbar non venite il mio dilɛt:to!

Oh! come par, che all'amoroso foco
o, kɔme par, ke al:lamorozo fɔko

l'amenità del loco, la terra e il ciel risponda!
lamenita dɛl lɔko, la tɛr:ra e il tʃɛl rispɔnda!

Come la notte i furti miei seconda!
kɔme la nɔt:te i furti mjɛi sekɔnda!

Deh, vieni, non tardar, o gioja bella!
dɛ, vjɛni, non tardar, o dʒɔja bɛl:la!

vieni ove amore per goder t'appella
vjɛni ove amore per godɛr tap:pɛl:la

finchè non splende in ciel notturna face,
fiŋke non splɛnde in tʃɛl not:turna fatʃe,

finchè l'aria è ancor bruna, e il mondo tace.
fiŋke larja ɛ aŋkor bruna, e il mondo tatʃe.

Qui mormora il ruscel quì scherza l'aura,
kwi mɔrmora il ruʃɛl kwi skɛrtsa laura,

che col dolce sussurro il cor ristaura;
ke kol dɔltʃe sus:sur:ro il kɔr ristaura,

35

Qui ridono i fioretti, e l'erba è fresca!
kwi ridono i fjoret:ti, e lɛrba ɛ freska!

ai piaceri d'amor qui tutto adesca.
ai pjatʃeri damor kwi tut:to adeska.

Vieni, ben mio! tra queste piante ascose.
vjɛni, bɛn mio! tra kwɛste pjante askoze.

ti vo' la fronte incoronar di rose.
ti vɔ la fronte iŋkoronar di rɔze!

Mozart   Dove sono, from "Le Nozze di Figaro"
              dove sono   le nɔt:se di figaro

Dove sono i bei momenti Di dolcezza, e di piacer!
dove sono i bɛi momenti di doltʃet:sa, e di pjatʃɛr!

Dove andaro i giuramenti Di quel labbro menzogner!
dove andaro i dʒuramenti di kwɛl:lab:bro mɛntsoŋɛr!

Perchè mai se in pianti, e in pene
pɛrke mai se in pjanti, e in pene

Per me tutto si cangiò. La memoria di quel bene
per me tut:to si kandʒɔ. la memɔrja di kwɛl bɛne

Dal mio sen non trapassò!
dal mio sen non trapas:sɔ!

Ah! se almen la mia costanza Nel languire amando ognor
a   se almɛn la mia kostantsa nɛl laŋgwire amando oŋor

Mi portasse una speranza Di cangiar l'ingrato cor!
mi portas:se una sperantsa di kandʒar liŋgrato kɔr!

Mozart   Finch' han dal vino, from "Don Giovanni"
              fiŋkan dal vino   dɔn dʒovan:ni

Finch' han dal vino calda la testa,
fiŋkan   dal vino kalda la tɛsta,

una gran festa fa preparar!
una gran fɛsta fa preparar!

Se trovi in piazza qualche ragazza,
se tro vin pjat:sa kwalke ragat:sa,

teco ancor quella cerca menar.
teko aŋkor kwel:la tʃerka menar.

Senza alcun ordine la danza sia,
sentsa alkun ordine la dantsa sia,

chi'l menuetto, chi la follia,
kil menuet:to, ki la fol:lia,

chi l'alemana farai ballar!
ki lalemana farai bal:lar!

Ed io frattanto dall' altro canto
ed io frat:tanto dal:laltro kanto

con questa e quella vo' amoreggiar;
kon kwesta e kwel:la vo amored:ʒar;

Ah, la mia lista doman mattina
a, la mia lista doman mat:tina

d'una decina devi aumentar.
duna detʃina devi aumentar.

Mozart   Il mio tesoro, from "Don Giovanni"
             il mio tezoro   don dʒovan:ni

Il mio tesoro intanto, andate, a consolar!
il mio tezoro intanto, andate, a konsolar!

e del bel ciglio il pianto cercate di asciugar, cercate,
e del bel tʃiʎo il pjanto tʃerkate di aʃugar, tʃerkate,

Ditele che i suoi torti a vendicar io vado,
ditele ke i swoi torti a vendikar io vado,

che sol di stragi e morti Nunzio vogl' io tornar.
ke sol di stradʒi e morti nuntsjo voʎio tornar.

Mozart   Madamina, from "Don Giovanni"
             madamina   don dʒovan:ni

Madamina!   Il catalogo è questo,
madamina!   il katalogo ɛ kwesto,

37

delle belle, che amò il padron mio
del:le bɛl:le, ke amo il padron mio

un catalogo è gli è, che ho fatto io,
un katalogo ɛ ʎɛ,   ke ɔ fat:to io,

osservate, leggete con me!
os:servate, led:ʒete kon me!

In Italia sei cento e quaranta;
in italja sɛi tʃɛnto e kwaranta;

in Almagna due cento e trent' una,
in almaɲa due tʃɛnto e trentuna,

cento in Francia, in Turchia novant' una;
tʃɛnto in frantʃa, in turkia novant una;

ma in Ispagna son già mille e tre!
ma in ispaɲa son dʒa mil:le tre!

V'han fra queste contadine, cameriere, cittadine.
van   fra kweste kontadine, kamerjere, tʃit:tadine,

V'han contesse, baronesse, marchesane,
van kontes:se, barones:se, markezane,

principesse, e v'han donne d'ogni grado,
printʃipes:se, e van don:ne doɲi grado

d'ogni forma, d'ogni età.
doɲi forma, doɲi eta.

Nella bionda egli ha l'usanza
nel:la bjonda eʎa   luzantsa

di lodar la gentilezza, nella bruna
di lodar la dʒentilɛt:sa, nel:la bruna

la costanza nella bianca la dolcezza.
la kostantsa, nel:la bjaŋka la doltʃet:sa.

Vuol d'inverno la grassotta,
vwol dinvɛrno la gras:sot:ta,

vuol d'estate la magrotta, e la grande maestosa
vwol destate la magrot:ta, e la grande maestoza

La piccina è ognor vezzosa,
la pit:ʃina, ɛ oɲor vet:soza,

delle vecchie fa conquista pel piacer di porle in lista
del:le vɛk:kje fa koŋkwista pel pjatʃɛr di porle in lista

sua passion predominante è la giovin principiante;
sua pas:sjon predominante ɛ la dʒovin printʃipjante;

38

non si picca se sia ricca, se sia brutta,
non si pik:ka se sia rik:ka, se sia brut:ta,

se sia bella, se sia ricca, brutta, se sia bella,
se sia bɛl:la, se sia rik:ka, brut:ta, se sia bɛl:la,

purchè porti la gonella,   voi sapete quel che fa,
purke pɔrti la gonɛl:la,   vɔi sapete kwɛl ke fa.

Mozart   Non più andrai, from "Le Nozze di Figaro"
              non pju andrai   le nɔt:se di figaro

Non più andrai farfallone amoroso,
non pju andrai farfal:lone amorozo,

notte e giorno d'intorno girando,
nɔt:te dʒorno dintorno dʒirando,

delle belle turbando il riposo,
dɛl:le bɛl:le turbando il ripozo,

Narcisetto, Adoncino d'amor!
nartʃizet:to, adontʃino d'amor!

Non più avrai questi bei pennacchini,
non pju avrai kwesti bɛi pen:nak:kini,

quel cappello leggiero e galante,
kwɛl kap:pɛl:lo led:ʒero e galante,

quella chioma, quell'aria brillante,
kwel:la kjoma, kwel:larja bril:lante,

quel vermiglio donnesco color!
kwɛl vermiʎo dɔn:nesko kolor!

Fra guerrieri, poffar Bacco!
fra gwer:rjeri, pɔf:far bak:ko!

gran mustacchi, stretto sacco,
gran mustak:ki, stret:to sak:ko,

schioppo in spalla, sciabla al fianco,
skjɔp:po in spal:la, ʃa blal fjaŋko,

collo dritto, muso franco;
kɔl:lo drit:to, muzo fraŋko;

un gran casco, o un gran turbante,
un gran kasko, o un gran turbante,

39

molto onor, poco contante!
mɔlto onor, pɔko kontante!

Ed in vece del fandango
ed in vetʃe dɛl fandaŋgo

una marcia per il fango,
una martʃa per il faŋgo,

per montagne, per valloni,
per montaɲe, per val:lɔni,

colle nevi, e i sollioni,
kɔl:le nevi, e i sol:ljɔni,

al concerto di tromboni,
al kontʃɛrto di trombɔni,

di bombarde, di cannoni,
di bombarde, di kan:nɔni,

che le palle in tutti i tuoni
ke le pal:le in tut:ti twɔni

all' orecchio fan fischiar!
al:lorɛk:kjo fan fiskjar!

Cherubino, alla vittoria!   alla gloria militar!
kerubino, al:la vit:tɔrja! al:la glɔrja militar!

Mozart   Non so più cosa son, from "Le Nozze di Figaro"
            non sɔ pju kɔza son   le nɔt:se di figaro

Non so più cosa son, cosa faccio
non sɔ pju kɔza son, kɔza fat:ʃo

or di foco, ora sono di ghiaccio,
or di fɔkɔra   sɔno di gjat:ʃo,

ogni donna cangiar di colore,
oɲi dɔn:na kandʒar di kolɔre,

ogni donna mi fa palpitar.
oɲi dɔn:na mi fa palpitar.

Solo ai nomi d' amor di diletto
sɔlo ai nɔmi damor di dilɛt:to

mi si turbami s' altera il petto;
mi si turbami saltera il pɛt:to;

40

e a parlare mi sforza d' amore
e a parl<u>a</u>re mi sf<u>o</u>rtsa dam<u>o</u>re

un des<u>í</u>o ch' io non posso spiegar.
un dez<u>i</u>o k<u>i</u>o non p<u>o</u>s:so spjegar.

Parlo d' amor vegliando, parlo d' amor sognando,
p<u>a</u>rlo dam<u>o</u>r veʎando,   p<u>a</u>rlo dam<u>o</u>r soɲando,

all' acqua, all' ombra, ai monti,
al:l<u>a</u>k:kwa, al:l<u>o</u>m br<u>ai</u> m<u>o</u>nti,

ai fiori, all' erbe, ai fonti,
<u>ai</u> fj<u>o</u>rjal:l<u>ɛ</u>rb<u>e</u>, <u>ai</u> f<u>o</u>nti,

all' eco, all' aria, ai venti,
al:l<u>ɛ</u>ko, <u>a</u>l:l<u>a</u>rj<u>ai</u>   v<u>ɛ</u>nti,

che il suon de' vani accenti
ke il swon dev<u>a</u>ni <u>a</u>t:ʃ<u>ɛ</u>nti

portano via con sé
p<u>o</u>rtano v<u>i</u>a kon se

E se non ho chi m' oda,
e se non ɔ ki m<u>o</u>da,

parlo, d' amor con me.
p<u>a</u>rlo, dam<u>o</u>r kon me.

Mozart   Porgi amor, from ''Le Nozze di Figaro''
            p<u>o</u>rdʒi am<u>o</u>r   le n<u>o</u>t:se di f<u>i</u>garo

Porgi amor qualche ristoro al mio duolo,
p<u>o</u>rdʒi <u>a</u>m<u>o</u>r kw<u>a</u>lke rist<u>o</u>ro al m<u>i</u>o dw<u>o</u>lo,

a miei sospir! O mi rendi il mio tesoro,
a mj<u>ɛ</u>i sosp<u>i</u>r! o mi r<u>ɛ</u>ndil m<u>i</u>o tez<u>o</u>ro,

o mi lascia almen morir!
o mi l<u>a</u>ʃalm<u>ɛ</u>n   mor<u>i</u>r!

Mozart   Se vuol ballare, from ''Le Nozze di Figaro''
            se vwɔl b<u>a</u>l:lare   le n<u>o</u>t:se di f<u>i</u>garo

Se vuol ballare, Signor contino,
se vwɔl bal:l<u>a</u>re siɲor kont<u>i</u>no,

il chitarrino le suonerò, sì, le suonerò.
il kitar:rino le swonerǫ, si, le swonerǫ.

Se vuol venire nella mia scuola,
se vwɔl venire nɛl:la mia skwǫla,

la capriola le insegnerò.
la kapriǫla lɛ inseɲerǫ.

Saprò, ma piano, meglio ogni arcano
saprǫ, ma pjano, mɛʎoɲi arkano

dissimulando scoprir potrò.
dis:simulando skoprir potrǫ.

L' arte schermendo, l' arte adoprando,
larte skɛrmɛndo, larte adoprando,

di qua pungendo, di là scherzando,
di kwa pundzɛndo, di la skɛrtsando,

tutte le macchine rovescierò!
tut:te le mak:kine roveʃerǫ!

Mozart   Vedrai, carino, from "Don Giovanni"
           vedrai, karino   don dʒovan:ni

Vedrai, carino, se sei buonino,
vedrai, karino, se sɛi bwonino,

che bel rimedio ti voglio dar.
ke bɛl rimɛdjo ti vǫʎo dar.

È naturale, non dà disgusto
ɛ naturale, non da dizgusto

e lo speziale non lo sa far.
e lo spetsjale non lo sa far.

È un certo balsamo che porto addosso,
ɛ un tʃɛrto balsamo ke pɔrto ad:sɔs:so,

dare t' el posso, se il vuoi provar.
dare tɛl pɔs:so, se il vwǫi provar.

Saper vorresti dove mi sta?
saper vor:rɛsti dǫve mi sta?

Sentilo battere, toccami qua.
sentilo bat:tere, tǫk:kami kwa.

Mozart   Voi, che sapete, from "Le Nozze di Figaro"
         vɔi, ke sapete   le nɔt:se di figaro

Voi, che sapete che cosa è amor,
vɔi, ke sapete ke kɔza ɛ amɔr,

donne, vedete, s'io l'ho nel cor,
dɔn:ne vedete, sio lo nɛl kɔr,

Quello ch'io provo, vi ridirò,
kwɛl:lo kio prɔvo, vi ridirɔ,

è per me nuovo capir nol so.
ɛ per me nwɔvo kapir nol sɔ.

Sento un affetto pien di desir,
sɛnto un af:fɛt:to pjɛn di dezir,

ch'ora è diletto, ch'ora è martir.
kɔra ɛ dilɛt:to   kɔra ɛ martir.

Gelo, e poi sento l'alma avvampar,
dzɛlo, e pɔi sɛnto lal mav:vampar,

e in un momento torno a gelar!
e in un momɛnto tɔrno a dzelar!

Ricerco un bene fuori di me,
ritʃerko un bɛne fwɔri di me,

non so chi il tiene, non so cos' è,
non sɔ kil tjɛne, non sɔ kɔzɛ,

sospiro e gemo senza voler,
sospiro e dzɛmo sɛntsa volɛr,

palpito e tremo senza saper,
palpito e trɛmo sɛntsa sapɛr,

non trovo pace notte, nè dì,
non trɔvo patʃe nɔt:te, ne di,

ma pur mi piace languir così.
ma pur mi pjatʃe laŋgwir kozi.

Paisiello   Chi vuol la zingarella
paizjɛl:lo   ki vwɔl la tsiŋgarɛl:la

Chi vuol la zingarella graziosa, accorta e bella?
ki vwɔl la tsiŋgarɛl:la gratsjɔ zak:kɔrta e bɛl:la?

Signori, eccola qua, signori, eccola qua.
siɲori, ɛk:kola kwa, siɲori, ɛk:kola kwa

Le donne sul balcone so bene indovinar.
le don:ne sul balkone so bɛne indovinar.

I giovani al cantone so meglio stuzzicar.
i dʒovan:ni al kantone so mɛʎo stut:tsikar.

A vecchi innamorati scaldar fo le cervella.
a vɛk:kin:namorati skaldar fo le tʃɛrvɛl:la.

Paisiello   Nel cor più non mi sento
paizjɛl:lo   nɛl kor pju non mi sɛnto

Nel cor più non mi sento brillar la gioventù;
nɛl kor pju non mi sɛnto bril:lar la dʒoventu,

cagion del mio tormento, amor, sei colpa tu.
kadʒon dɛl mio tormento, amor, sɛi kolpa tu.

Mi pizzichi, mi stuzzichi, mi pungichi, mi mastichi;
mi pit:siki, mi stut:siki, mi pundʒiki, mi mastiki;

che cosa è questo, ahimè? Pietà, pietà, pietà!
ke koza ɛ kwesto, aimɛ?   pjeta, pjeta, pjeta!

Amore è un certo che disperar mi fa.
amore ɛ un tʃɛrto che disperar mi fa.

Pergolesi   Se tu m' ami
pergolezi   se tu mami

Se tu m' ami, se tu sospiri Sol per me, gentil pastor,
se tu mami, se tu sospiri sol per me dʒɛntil pastor,

Ho dolor de' tuoi martiri, Ho diletto del tuo amor,
ɔ dolor de twoi martiri, ɔ dilɛt:to dɛl tuo amor,

Ma se pensi che soletto Io ti debba riamar,
ma se pɛnsi ke solet:to io ti dɛb:ba riamar,

Pastorello, sei soggetto Facilmente a t' ingannar.
pastorɛl:lo, sɛi sod:ʒɛt:to fatʃilmente a tiŋgan:nar.

Bella rosa porporina Oggi Silvia sceglierà,
bɛl:la rɔza porporina ɔd:ʒi silvja ʃeʎera,

Con la scusa della spina Doman poi la sprezzerà.
kon la skuza del:la spina doman pɔi la spret:sera.

Ma degli uomini il consiglio Io per me non seguirò.
ma deʎi wɔmini il konsiʎo io per me non segwirɔ.

Non perchè mi piace il giglio
non pɛrke mi pjatʃe il dʒiʎo

Gli altri fiori sprezzerò.
ʎaltri fjɔri spret:serɔ.

Pergolesi   Stizzoso, mio stizzoso, from "La Serva Padrona"
pergolezi   stit:sɔzo, miɔ stit:sɔzo   la sɛrva padrɔna

Stizzoso, mio stizzoso, voi fate il borioso, ma no,
stit:sɔzo miɔ stit:sɔzo, vɔi fate il boriɔzo, ma nɔ,

ma non vi può giovare;
ma non vi pwɔ dʒovare;

bisogna al mio divieto star cheto;
bizɔɲal   miɔ divjeto star keto;

e non parlare, zit Serpina vuol così.
e non parlare, tsit sɛrpina vwɔl kozi.

Cred' io che m' intendete, sì.
krediɔ   ke   mintɛndete, si,

da che mi conoscete son molti e molti dì.
da ke   mi konoʃete son mɔlti e mɔlti di.

Pergolesi   Tre giorni son che Nina
pergolezi   tre dʒɔrni son ke nina

Tre giorni son che Nina
tre dʒɔrni son ke nina

a letto se ne sta.
a lɛt:to se ne sta.

45

Pifferi, cembali, timpani,
pif:feri, tʃembali, timpani,

svegliatemi Ninetta, acciò non dorma più.
zveʎatemi ninet:ta, at:ʃɔ non dɔrma pju.

Peri   Invocazione di Orfeo, from "Euridice"
peri   invokatsjone di orfɛo   euriditʃe

Gioite al canto mio, selve frondose,
dʒoite al kanto mio, sɛlve frondoze,

Gioite amati colli, e d'ogn' intorno.
dʒoite amati kɔl:li, e dɔnintorno.

Eco rimbombi dalle valli ascose.
ɛko rimbombi dal:le val:li askoze,

Risorto è il mio bel sol di raggi adorno
rizɔrto ɛ il mio bɛl sol di rad:ʒi adorno

E coi begli occhi, onde fa scorno a Delo,
e koi beʎok:ki,   onde fa skorno a dɛlo,

Raddoppia fuoco all'alme e luce al giorno,
rad:dop:pja fwɔko al:lalme e lutʃe al dʒorno,

E fa servi d'amor la terra e il cielo.
e fa sɛrvi damor   la tɛr:ra e il tʃɛlo.

Ponchielli   Cielo e mar, from "La Gioconda"
poŋkjɛl:li   tʃɛlo e mar   la dʒokɔnda

Cielo e mar! l'etereo velo splende come un santo altar.
tʃɛlo e mar!   letɛreo velo splɛnde kɔme un santo altar.

L'angiol mio verrà dal cielo? l'angiol mio verrà dal mare?
landʒol mio ver:ra dal tʃɛlo? landʒol mio ver:ra dal mare?

Qui l'attendo; ardente spira oggi il vento dell'amor
kwi lat:tɛndo; ardɛnte spira ɔd:ʒil vɛnto del:lamor

Ah! quell'uom che vi sospira vi conquide, o sogni d'ôr,
a! kwɛl:lwɔm ke vi sospira vi koŋkwide, soɲi dor,

Per l'aura fonda non appar nè suol, nè monte,
per laura fonda non ap:par ne swɔl, ne monte,

L'orizzonte bacia l'onda! l'onda bacia l'orizzonte!
lorid:zɔnte batʃa lɔnda! lɔnda batʃa lorid:zɔnte!

Qui nell'onda ov'io mi giaccio coll'anelito del cor,
kwi nel:lɔnda, ovio mi dʒat:ʃo kol:laŋelito dɛl kɔr,

vieni, o donna, vieni al bacio della vita e dell'amor,
vjɛni, o dɔn:na, vjɛni al batʃo dɛl:la vita e dɛl:lamɔr,

vieni, o donna, qui t'attendo coll'anelito del cor
vjɛni, o dɔn:na, kwi tat:tɛndo kol:laŋelito dɛl kɔr

vieni al bacio della vita e dell'amor ah! vien!
vjɛni al batʃo dɛl:la vita e dɛl:lamɔr, a vjɛn!

Ponchielli   Suicidio! from "La Gioconda"
poŋkjɛl:li   suitʃidjo   la dʒokɔnda

Suicidio! In questi fieri momenti tu sol mi resti,
suitʃidjo! in kwesti fjeri momenti tu sol mi rɛsti,

e il cor mi tenti. Ultima voce del mio destino,
e il kɔr mi tɛnti. ultima vɔtʃe dɛl mio destino,

ultima croce del mio cammin!
ultima krɔtʃe dɛl mio kam:min!

E un dì leggiadre volavan l'ore, perdei la madre,
e un di led:ʒadre volavan lore, pɛrdei la madre,

perdei l'amore, vinsi l'infausta gelosa febbre!
pɛrdei lamore, vinsi linfausta dʒeloza fɛb:bre!

or piombo esausta, fra le tenebre!
or pjɔmbo ezausta, fra le tɛnebre!

Tocco alla meta,
tɔk:ko al:la mɛta,

domando al cielo di dormir queta dentro l'avel.
domando al tʃɛlo di dormir kwɛta dɛntro lavɛl.

Ponchielli   Voce di donna, from "La Gioconda"
poŋkjɛl:li   vot∫e di dɔn:na   la dʒokonda

Voce di donna o d' angelo
vot∫e di dɔn:na o dandʒelo

le mie catene ha sciolto;
le mie katene a ∫ɔlto;

Mi vietan le mie tenebre
mi vjetan le mie tenebre

di quella santa il volto.
di kwɛl:la santa il vɔlto.

Pure da me non partasi,
pure da me non partasi,

senza un pietoso don, no! no!
sɛntsa un pjetozo dɔn, nɔ! nɔ!

A te questo rosario che le preghiere aduna,
a te kwɛsto rozarjo ke le pregjere aduna,

Io te lo porgo, accettalo, ti porterà fortuna.
io te lo pɔrgo, at:∫ɛt:talo, ti portera fortuna.

Sulla tua testa vigili la mia benedizion.
sul:la tua tɛsta vidʒili la mia beneditsjɔn.

Puccini   Che gelida manina, from "La Bohême"
put:∫ini   ke dʒɛlida manina   la bɔɛm

Che gelida manina, se la lasci riscaldar.
ke dʒɛlida manina, se la la∫i riskaldar.

Cercar che giova? - Al buio non si trova.
t∫ɛrkar ke dʒɔva? - al bujo non si trɔva.

Ma per fortuna è una notte di luna,
ma per fortuna ɛ una nɔt:te di luna,

e qui la luna l'abbiamo vicina.
e kwi la luna lab:bjamo vit∫ina.

Aspetti, signorina, le dirò con due parole
aspɛt:ti, siɲorina, le dirɔ kon due parɔle

chi son, e che faccio, come vivo. Vuole?
ki son, e ke fat:∫o, kome vivo.   vwɔle?

Chi son? - Sono un poeta.
ki son? - sono un poɛta.

Che cosa faccio? – Scrivo.
ke kɔza fat:ʃo? – skrivo.

E come vivo? – Vivo.
e kome vivo? – vivo.

In povertà mia lieta scialo da gran signore
in povɛrta mia ljeta ʃalo da gran siɲore

rime ed inni d'amore.
rime din:ni damore.

Per sogni e per chimere e per castelli in aria
per soɲi e per kimɛre e per kastɛl:lin arja

l'anima ho milionaria.
lanima ɔ miʎonaria.

Talor dal mio forziere ruban tutti i gioielli
talor dal mio fɔrtsjere ruban tut:ti dʒojɛl:li

due ladri: gli occhi belli.
due ladri,   ʎɔk:ki bɛl:li.

V'entrar con voi pur ora, ed i miei sogni usati
vɛntrar kon voi pur ɔra, ed i mjɛi soɲi uzati

e i bei sogni miei tosto si dileguar!
e i bɛi soɲi mjɛi tɔsto si dilegwar!

Ma il furto non m'accora poichè vi ha preso stanza
ma il furto non mak:kɔra poike vi a prezo stantsa

la dolce speranza!
la dɔltʃe sperantsa!

Or che mi conoscete parlate voi. Chi siete?
or ke mi konoʃete parlate voi.   ki sjete?

Vi piaccia dir?
vi pjat:ʃa dir?

Puccini   E lucevan le stelle, from "La Tosca"
put:ʃini   e lutʃevan le stɛl:le   la toska

E lucevan le stelle ed olezzava la terra
e lutʃevan le stɛl:le ed oled:zava la tɛr:ra

e stridea l'uscio dell'orto
e stridɛa luʃo   del:lɔrto

49

e un passo sfiorava la rena.
e un pas:so sfjorava la rena.

Entrava ella, fragrante,
ɛntrava el:la, fragrante,

mi cadea fra le braccia.
mi kadea fra le brat:ʃa.

Oh! dolci baci, o languide carezze,
o!   doltʃi batʃi, o laŋgwide karet:se,

mentr' io fremente
mɛntrio fremɛnte

le belle forme disciogliea dai veli!
le bɛl:le forme diʃoʎea dai veli!

Svanì per sempre il sogno mio d' amore...
zvani per sɛmpre il soɲo mio damore...

l' ora è fuggita e muoio disperato!...
lora ɛ fud:ʒita e mwojo disperato!...

E non ho amato mai tanto la vita!
e non o amato mai tanto la vita!

Puccini   In quelle trine morbide, from ''Manon Lescaut''
put:ʃini   in kwel:le trine morbide   manon lesko

In quelle trine morbide nell' alcova dorata
in kwel:le trine morbide nel:lalkova dorata

v' è un silenzio, un gelido mortal,
vɛ un silɛntsjo, un dʒelido mortal,

v' è un silenzio, un freddo che m' agghiaccia!
vɛ un silɛntsjo, un fred:do ke mag:gjat:ʃa!

Ed io che m' ero avvezza
ed io ke mero av:vetsa

a una carezza voluttuosa
a una karet:sa volut:twoza

di labbra ardenti e d' infuocate braccia
di lab:brardɛnti e dinfwokate   brat:ʃa

or ho tutt' altra cosa!
or o tut:taltra koza!

O mia dimora umile, tu mi ritorni innanzi
o mia dimora umile, tu mi ritornin:nantsi

gaia, isolata, bianca come un sogno gentile
gaja, izolata, bjanka kome un soɲo dzentile

e di pace e d' amor!
e di patʃe damor!

Puccini   O mio babbino caro, from "Gianni Schicchi"
put:ʃini   o mio bab:bino karo   dzan:ni skik:ki

O mio babbino caro, mi piace, è bello;
o mio bab:bino karo, mi pjatʃe ɛ bɛl:lo;

vo' andare in Porta Rossa
vo andare in porta ros:sa

a comperar l' anello! Sì, ci voglio andare!
a komperar lanɛl:lo! si, tʃi voʎo andare!

e se l' amassi indarno, andrei sul Ponte Vecchio,
e se lamas:si indarno, andrɛi sul ponte vɛk:kjo,

ma per buttarmi in Arno!
ma per but:tar min arno!

Mi struggo e mi tormento!   O Dio, vorrei morir
mi strug:go e mi tormento! o dio vor:rɛi morir

Babbo, pietà, pietà!
bab:bo, pjeta, pjeta!

Puccini   Quando me' n vo', from "La Bohême"
put:ʃini   kwando men vo   la boɛm

Quando me' n vo' soletta per la via la gente sosta e mira
kwando men vo solet:ta per la via la dzente sosta e mira

e la bellezza mia tutta ricerca in me da capo a piè;
e la bel:let:sa mia tut:ta ritʃerka in me da kapo a pje;

ed assaporo allor la bramosìa sottil,
ed as:saporo al:lor la bramozia sot:til,

che da gl'occhi traspira e dai palesi vezzi intender sa
ke da ʎok:ki   traspira e dai palezi vet:sintɛnder sa

alle occulte beltà.
al:le ok:kulte bɛlta.

Così l'effluvio del desìo tutta m'aggira
kozi lef:fluvjo dɛl dezio tut:ta mad:ʒira

felice mi fa, felice mi fa.
felitʃe mi fa, felitʃe mi fa.

E tu che sai che memori e ti struggi,
e tu ke sai ke memori e ti strud:ʒi,

da me tanto rifuggi?
da me tanto rifud:ʒi?

So ben: le angoscie tue non le vuoi dir,
so bɛn, le aŋgoʃe tue non le vwoi dir,

so ben ma ti senti morir!
so bɛn ma ti sɛnti morir!

Puccini   Recondita armonia, from "La Tosca"
put:ʃini   rekonditarmonia   la toska

Recondita armonia di bellezze diverse!...
rekonditarmonia di bel:let:se divɛrse!...

È bruna Floria, l'ardente amante mia,
ɛ bruna floria, lardɛnte amante mia,

e te, beltade ignota
e te, bɛltade inota

cinta di chiome bionde!
tʃinta di kjome bjonde!

Tu azzurro hai l'occhio Tosca ha l'occhio nero!
tu ad:zur:ro ai lok:kjo toska a lok:kjo nero!

L'arte nel suo mistero
larte nɛl suo mistɛro

le diverse bellezze insiem confonde:
le divɛrse bel:let:se insjɛm konfonde,

ma nel ritrar costei
ma nel ritrar kostεi

il mio solo pensiero,
il m$\underline{i}$o s$\underline{o}$lo pεnsj$\underline{e}$ro,

ah! il mio sol pensier sei tu!
a! il m$\underline{i}$o sol pεnsjεr sεi tu!

Tosca sei tu!
t$\underline{o}$ska sεi tu!

Puccini   Si, mi chiamano Mimì, from ''La Bohême''
put:$\int$ini   si, mi kj$\underline{a}$mano mim$\underline{i}$ la boεm

Si, mi chiamano Mimì ma il mio nome è Lucia.
si, mi kj$\underline{a}$mano mim$\underline{i}$ m$\underline{a}$ il m$\underline{i}$o n$\underline{o}$mε lut$\int$$\underline{i}$a.

La storia mia è breve: A tela o a seta
la st$\underline{o}$rja m$\underline{i}$a ε br$\underline{e}$ve, a t$\underline{e}$la o a s$\underline{e}$ta

ricamo in casa e fuori......
rik$\underline{a}$mo $\underline{i}$n k$\underline{a}$za e fw$\underline{o}$ri......

Son tranquilla e lieta ed è mio svago far gigli e rose.
son traηkw$\underline{i}$l:l$\underline{a}$ e lj$\underline{e}$ta ed ε m$\underline{i}$o zv$\underline{a}$go far d$\du{z}$i$\int$e r$\underline{o}$ze.

Mi piaccion quelle cose che han sì dolce malìa,
mi pj$\underline{a}$t$\int$on kw$\underline{e}$l:le k$\underline{o}$ze ke $\underline{a}$n si d$\underline{o}$lt$\int$e mal$\underline{i}$a,

che parlano d'amor, di primavere,
ke p$\underline{a}$rlano dam$\underline{o}$r, di primav$\underline{e}$re,

che parlano di sogni e di chimere,
ki p$\underline{a}$rlano di s$\underline{o}$$\eta$e di kim$\underline{e}$re,

quelle cose che han nome poesia, Lei m'intende?
kw$\underline{e}$l:le k$\underline{o}$ze ke $\underline{a}$n n$\underline{o}$me poez$\underline{i}$a, lεi mint$\underline{e}$nde?

Mi chiamano Mimì, il perchè non so.
mi kj$\underline{a}$mano mim$\underline{i}$, il pεrk$\underline{e}$ non sυ.

Sola, mi fo il pranzo da me stessa.
s$\underline{o}$la, mi fo il pr$\underline{a}$ntso da me st$\underline{e}$s:sa.

Non vado sempre a messa ma prego assai il Signor.
non v$\underline{a}$do s$\underline{e}$mpre $\underline{a}$ m$\underline{e}$s:sa ma pr$\underline{e}$go as:sail si$\eta$$\underline{o}$r.

Vivo sola, soletta, Là in una bianca cameretta:
v$\underline{i}$vo s$\underline{o}$la, sol$\underline{e}$t:ta, la in $\underline{u}$na bj$\underline{a}$$\eta$ka kamer$\underline{e}$t:ta,

53

guardo sui tetti e in cielo,
gwardo sui tet:ti e in tʃɛlo,

ma quando vien lo sgelo il primo sole è mio,
ma kwando vjɛn lo zdʒɛlo il primo solɛ mio,

il primo bacio dell' aprile è mio!
il primo batʃo del:laprile ɛ mio!

Il primo sole è mio!
il primo solɛ ɛ mio!

Germoglia in un vaso una rosa.
dʒɛrmoʎa in un vazo una roza.

Foglia a foglia la spio! Così gentil
foʎa foʎa la spio!   kozi dʒɛntil

il profumo d' un fior! Ma i fior ch' io faccio,
il profumo dun fjor! ma i fjor kio fat:ʃo,

ahimè! non hanno odore!
aimɛ!   non an:nodore!

Altro di me non le saprei narrare:
altro di me non le saprɛi nar:rare.

sono la sua vicina che la vien fuori d'ora a importunare.
sono la sua vitʃina ke la vjɛn fwori dora importunare.

Puccini   Un bel dì, from " Madama Butterfly"
put:ʃini   un bɛl di   madama botɛrflai

Un bel dì, vedremo levarsi un fil di fumo
un bɛl di, vedremo levarsi un fil di fumo

sull' estremo confin del mare.
sul:lestrɛmo konfin dɛl mare.

E poi la nave appare
e poi la nave ap:pare

Poi la nave bianca entra nel porto,
poi la nave bjaŋka ɛntra nɛl porto,

romba il suo saluto. Vedi?
romba il suo saluto. vedi?

È venuto! Io non gli scendo incontro.
ɛ venuto! io non ʎi ʃendo iŋkontro.

Io no. Mi metto là sul ciglio del colle
i̯o nɔ. mi mɛt:to la sul tʃiʎo dɛl kɔl:le

e aspetto gran tempo e non mi pesa, la lunga attesa.
e aspɛt:to gran tɛmpo e˙non mi peza, la luŋgat:teza.

È uscito dalla folla cittadina
ɛ uʃito dal:la fɔl:la tʃit:tadina

un uomo, un picciol punto s'avvia per la collina.
un u̯ɔmo, un pitʃɔl punto sav:vi̯a per la kɔl:lina.

Chi sarà? E come sarà giunto che dirà?
ki sara? e kɔme sara dʒunto ke dira?

Chiamerà Butterfly dalla lontana.
kjamera botɛrflai̯ dal:la lontana.

Io senza dar risposta me ne starò nascosta
i̯o sɛntsa dar rispɔsta me ne starɔ naskɔsta

un po' per celia
un pɔ per tʃɛlja

e un po' per non morire al primo incontro,
e un pɔ per non morire al primo iŋkontro,

ed egli alquanto in pena chiamerà,
ed e ʎalkwanto in pena kjamera,

Piccina mogliettina olezzo di verbena,
pitʃina moʎetina   oled:zo di vɛrbena,

i nomi che mi dava al suo venire
i nomi ke mi dava l suo venire

Tutto questo avverrà, te lo prometto.
tut:to kwesto av:ver:ra, te lo promɛt:to.

Tienti la tua paura,
tjɛnti la tu̯a pau̯ra,

io con sicura fede l'aspetto.
i̯o kon sikura fede laspɛt:to.

Puccini   Vissi d'arte from "La Tosca"
put:ʃini   vis:si darte   la tɔska

Vissi d'arte, vissi d'amore,
vis:si darte, vis:si damore,

non feci mai male ad anima viva!
non fetʃi mai male ad anima viva!

Con man furtiva quante miserie conobbi, aiutai.
kon man furtiva kwante mizɛrje konɔb:bi, ajutai.

Sempre con fè sincera
sempre kon fe sintʃɛra

la mia preghiera ai santi tabernacoli salì.
la mia pregjera ai santi tabɛrnakoli sali.

Sempre con fè sincera diedi fiori agli altar.
sempre kon fe sintʃɛra djedi fjɔri aʎaltar.

Nell'ora del dolore perchè, perchè,
nel:lora dɛl dolɔre pɛrke, pɛrke,

Signore, perchè me ne rimuneri così?
siɲore, pɛrke me ne rimuneri kozi?

Diedi gioielli della Madonna al manto, e diedi il canto
djedi dʒojɛl:li dɛl:la madɔn:nal manto, e djedil kanto

agli astri, al ciel, che ne ridean più belli.
aʎastri, al tʃɛl, ke ne ridɛan pju bɛl:li.

Nell'ora del dolor perchè, perchè,
nel:lora dɛl dolor pɛrke, pɛrke,

Signor, ah, perchè me ne rimuneri cosi?
siɲor, a, pɛrke me ne rimuneri kozi?

Respighi   Nebbie
respigi   nɛb:bje

Soffro Lontan lontano Le nebbie sonnolente
sof:fro lontan lontano le nɛb:bje son:nolɛnte

Salgono dal tacente Piano.
salgono dal tatʃɛnte pjano.

Alto gracchiando, i corvi, Fidati all'ali nere,
alto grak:kjando, i kɔrvi, fidati al:lali nere,

Traversan le brughiere torvi.
travɛrsan le brugjere tɔrvi.

Dell'aere ai morsi crudi Gli addolorati tronchi
del:laɛre ai mɔrsi krudi ʎad:dolorati troŋki

Offron, pregando, i bronchi nudi.
of:fron, pregando, i bronki nudi.

Come ho freddo! Son sola;
kome o fred:do! son sola;

Pel grigio ciel sospinto Un gemito d'estinto vola;
pel gridʒo tʃɛl sospinto un dʒemito destinto vola;

E mi ripete: Vieni; È buia la vallata.
e mi ripɛte: vjɛni; ɛ buja la val:lata.

O triste, o disamata vieni! Vieni!
O triste, o dizamata vjɛni! vjɛni!

Rosa   Star vicino
roza   star vitʃino

Star vicino al bel idol che s'ama,
star vitʃino al bɛl idol ke sama,

è il più vago diletto d'amor!
ɛ il pju vago dilɛt:to damor!

Star lontan da colei che si brama,
star lontan da kolɛi ke si brama,

è d'amor il più mesto dolor!
ɛ damor il pju mɛsto dolor!

Rossini   Ecco ridente in cielo, from "Il Barbiere di Siviglia"
ros:sini   ɛk:ko ridɛnte in tʃɛlo   il barbjɛre di siviʎa

Ecco ridente in cielo, Spunta la bella aurora,
ɛk:ko ridɛnte in tʃɛlo, spunta la bɛl:la aurora,

E tu non sorgi ancora E puoi dormir così? Ah!
e tu non sordʒi aŋkora e pwoi dormir kozi? a!

Sòrgi mia dolce speme, Vieni bell'Idol mio,
sordʒi mia doltʃe spɛme, vjɛni bel:lidol mio,

57

Rendi men crudo, oh Dio!   Lo stral che mi ferì;
rɛndi men krudo dio!   lo stral ke mi feri;

Oh, sorte! già veggo?   Quel caro sembiante;
o, sɔrte! dʒa veg:go? kwɛl karo sembjante;

Quest' anima amante ottenne pietà?
kwestanima amante ot:tɛn:ne pjeta?

Rossini   La calunnia è un venticello, from "Il Barbiere di Sivigli
ros:sini   la kalun:nja ɛ un vɛntitʃɛl:lo   il barbjɛre di siviʎa

La calunnia è un venticello, un' auretta assai gentile,
la kalun:nja ɛ un vɛntitʃɛl:lo, un aurɛt:ta as:sai dʒentile,

che insensibile e sottile, leggermente, dolcemente,
ke insɛnsibile sot:tile, led:ʒɛrmente, doltʃemente,

incomincia a sussurrar. Piano piano, terra terra,
iŋkomintʃa sus:sur:rar. pjano pjano, tɛr:ra tɛr:ra,

sotto voce, sibilando, va scorrendo, va ronzando,
sot:to votʃe, sibilando, va skor:rɛndo, va rondzando,

nelle orecchie della gente s' introduce destramente,
nɛl:le orɛk:kje dɛl:la dʒɛnte sintrodutʃe destramente,

alle teste ed i cervelli, fa stordire e fa gonfiar.
al:le tɛste di tʃɛrvɛl:li, fa stordire fa gonfjar.

Dalla bocca fuori uscendo, lo schiamazzo va crescendo;
dal:la bok:ka fwori uʃɛndo, lo skjamat:so va kreʃɛndo;

prende forza a poco a poco, vola già di loco in loco
prɛnde fortsa poko a poko, vola dʒa di lɔko in lɔko

sembra il tuono, la tempesta, che nel sen della foresta
sɛmbra il twɔno, la tempɛsta, ke nɛl sen dɛl:la forɛsta

va fischiando, brontolando, e ti fa d' orror gelar.
va fiskjando, brontolando, e ti fa dor:ror dʒelar.

Alla fin trabocca e scoppia, si propaga, si raddoppia
al:la fin trabok:ka e skɔp:pja, si propaga, si rad:dɔp:pja

e produce un' esplosione come un colpo di cannone
e produtʃe un esplozjone kome un kolpo di kan:none

un tremuoto, un temporale che fa l' aria rimbombar;
un tremwɔto, un tɛmporale ke fa larja rimbombar;

58

E il meschino calunniato, avvilito, calpestato,
e il meskino kalun:njato, av:vilito, kalpestato,

sotto il pubblico flagello per gran sorte va a crepar!
·sot:to il pub:bliko fladʒel:lo per gran sorte va krepar!

Rossini   La Danza
ros:sini   la dantsa

Già la luna è in mezzo al mare, mamma mia, si salterà!
dʒa la luna ɛ in mɛd:ʒo al mare, mam:ma mia, si saltera!

L'ora è bella per danzare, chi è in amor non mancherà.
lora ɛ bɛl:la per dantsare, kjɛ in amor non maŋkera.

Già la luna è in mezzo al mare, mamma mia, si salterà!
dʒa la luna ɛ in mɛd:ʒo al mare, mam:ma mia, si saltera!

Presto in danza a tondo, a tondo, donne mie venite qua,
prɛsto in dantsa tondo, a tondo, don:ne mie venite kwa,

un garzon bello e giocondo a ciascuna toccherà,
un gardzon bɛl:lo e dʒokondo a tʃaskuna tok:kera,

finchè in ciel brilla una stella e la luna splenderà.
fiŋke in tʃɛl bril:la una stɛl:la e la luna splɛndera.

Il più bel con la più bella tutta notte danzerà.
il pju bɛl kon la pju bɛl:la tut:ta not:te dantsera.

Mamma mia, già la luna è in mezzo al mare,
mam:ma mia, dʒa la luna ɛ in mɛd:ʒo al mare,

mamma mia, si salterà. Frinche, mamma mià, si salterà
mam:ma mia, si saltera. friŋke, mam:ma mia, si saltera!

Salta, salta, gira, gira, ogni coppia a cerchio va,
salta, salta, dʒira, dʒira, oni kop:pja tʃɛrkjo va,

già s'avanza, si ritira e all' assalto tornerà.
dʒa savantsa, si ritira e al:las:salto tornera.

Serra, serra, colla bionda, colla bruna va qua e là
sɛr:ra, sɛr:ra, kol:la bjonda, kol:la bruna va kwa e la

colla rosa va a seconda, colla smorta fermo sta.
kol:la roza va a sekonda, kol:la smorta fɛrmo sta.

Viva il ballo a tondo a tondo, sono un Re, sono un Pascià,
viva il bal:lo a tondo a tondo, sono un re, sono un paʃa,

59

e il più bel piacer del mondo la più cara voluttà.
e il pju bɛl pjatʃɛr dɛl mondo la pju kara volut:ta...

Rossini   Largo al factotum della città, from "Il Barbiere di Sivi‹
ros:sini   largo al faktotum del:la tʃit:ta   il barbjɛre di sivi‹

Largo al factotum della città, largo! la!
largo al faktotum del:la tʃit:ta, largo! la.

Presto a bottega, che l'alba è già, presto! la!
prɛsto a bot:tega, ke lalba ɛ dʒa, prɛsto! la.

Ah, che bel vivere, che bel piacere,
a, ke bɛl vivere, ke bɛl pjatʃere,

per un barbiere di qualità,
per un barbjɛre di kwalita,

Ah bravo, Figaro, bravo bravissimo, bravo
a bravo, figaro, bravo bravis:simo, bravo.

Fortunatissimo per verità; bravo! la!
fortunatis:simo per verita; bravo! la!

Pronto a far tutto la notte e il giorno,
pronto a far tut:to la not:te il dʒorno,

sempre d'intorno in giro sta.
sempre dintorno in dʒiro sta.

Miglior cuccagna per un barbiere,
miʎor kuk:kaɲa per un barbjɛre,

vita più nobile, nò, non si dà!
vita pju nɔbile, nɔ, non si da!

Rasori, pettini, lancette e forbici
razori, pɛt:tini, lantʃet:te forbitʃi

al mio comando tutto qui sta.
al mio komando tut:to kwi sta.

V'è la risorsa poi del mestiere
vɛ la rizɔrsa poi dɛl mestjere

colla donnetta, col cavaliere, la ran larala.
kol:la don:net:ta, kol kavaljere, la ran larala.

Tutti mi chiedono, tutti mi vogliono,
tut:ti mi kjɛdono, tut:ti mi voʎono,

donne, ragazzi, vecchie, fanciulle.
don:ne, ragat:si, vɛk:kje, fantʃul:le.

Qua la parrucca! presto la barba!
kwa la par:ruk:ka! prɛsto la barba!

qua la sanguigna! presto il biglietto!
kwa la saŋgwiɲa! prɛsto il biʎet:to!

Figaro! ohimè! che furia, ohimè!
figaro! ɔimɛ! ke furja, ɔimɛ!

che folla! un' alla volta per carità,
ke fɔl:la! un al:la vɔlta per karita,

Figaro! Son qua. Figaro qua, Figaro là,
figaro! son kwa. figaro kwa, figaro la,

Figaro sù, Figaro giù!
figaro su, figaro dʒu!

Pronto prontissimo son come un fulmine,
prɔnto prontis:simo son kome un fulmine,

sono il factotum della città!
sono il faktotum del:la tʃit:ta!

Ah, bravo Figaro, bravo bravissimo!
a, bravo, figaro, bravo bravis:simo!

Rossini   Una voce poco fa, from "Il Barbiere di Siviglia"
ros:sini   una votʃe poko fa   il barbjɛre di siviʎa

Una voce poco fa: Qui nel cor mi risuonò!
una votʃe poko fa, kwi nɛl kɔr mi riswonɔ!

Il mio cor ferito è già; E Lindor fu che il piagò.
il mio kɔr ferito ɛ dʒa; e lindɔr fu ke il pjagɔ.

Sì, Lindoro mio sarà! Lo giurai, la vincerò.
si, lindɔro mio sara! lo dʒurai, la vintʃerɔ.

Il tutor ricuserà; Io l'ingegno aguzzerò:
il tutor rikuzera; io lindʒeɲo agut:serɔ,

Alla fin s' acchetterà, E contenta io resterò,
al:la fin sak:ket:tera, e kontɛnta io resterɔ,

Si, Lindoro mia sarà!   Lo giurai – la vincerò.
si, lindoro mi̯o sara! lo dʒurai – la vintʃero.

Io sono docile, Son rispettosa, Sono obbediente
i̯o sono dotʃile, son rispet:toza, sono ob:bedjɛnte

Dolce amorosa; Mi lascio reggere, Mi fo guidar,
doltʃe amoroza; mi laʃo rɛd:ʒere, mi fo gwidar,

Ma se mi toccano dov'è il mio debole, Sarò una
ma se mi tok:kano dove il mi̯o debole, saro una

vipera, sarò, E cento trappole prima di cedere,
vipera, saro, e tʃɛnto trap:pole prima di tʃedere,

farò giocar.
faro dʒokar.

Sarti|sarti| Lungi dal caro bene
Secchi|sek:ki| lundʒi dal karo bɛne

Lungi dal caro bene vivere non poss'io!
lundʒi dal karo bɛne vivere non pos:sio!

Sono in un mar di pene, Lungi dal caro bene,
sono in un mar di pene, lundʒi dal karo bɛne,

sento mancarmi il cor! Un dolce estremo sonno
sɛnto maŋkarmil kor!   un doltʃestrɛmo son:no

se lei mirar non ponno, mi chiuda i lumi ancor.
se lɛi mirar non pon:no, mi kjuda i lumi aŋkor.

Scarlatti   Chi vuole innamorarsi
skarlat:ti   ki vwole in:namorarsi

Chi vuole innamorarsi, Ci deve ben pensar!
ki vwole in:namorarsi, tʃi deve bɛn pensar!

Amore è un certo foco, Che, se s'accende un poco,
amorɛ un tʃerto foko, ke, se sat:ʃende un poko,

Eterno suol durar, eterno suol durare, suol durar.
etɛrno swɔl durar, etɛrno swɔl durare, swɔl durar.

Non è lieve tormento, Aver piagato il cor!
non ɛ ljeve tormɛnto, avɛr pjagato il kɔr!

Soggetta ogni volere A due pupille arciere,
sodʒɛt:ta oni volere a due pupil:le artʃere,

Chi serve al Dio d'amor.
ki sɛrve al dio damɔr.

Scarlatti   Già il sole dal Gange
skarlat:ti   dʒa il sole dal gandʒe

Già il sole dal Gange più chiaro sfavilla
dʒa il sole dal gandʒe pju kjaro sfavil:la

e terge ogni stilla dell'alba che piange.
e tɛrdʒe oni stil:la del:lalba ke pjandʒe.

Col raggio dorato ingemma ogni stelo,
kol rad:ʒo dorato indʒɛm:ma oni stɛlo,

e gli astri del cielo dipinge nel prato.
e   ʎastri dɛl tʃɛlo dipindʒe nɛl prato.

Scarlatti   O cessate di piagarmi
skarlat:ti   o tʃes:sate di pjagarmi

O cessate di piagarmi, o lasciatemi morir!
o tʃes:sate di pjagarmi, o laʃatemi morir!

Luc'ingrate dispietate più del gelo e più dei marmi
lutʃingrate dispjetate pju dɛl dʒelo e pju dei marmi

fredde e sorde ai miei martir!
frɛd:de sorde ai mjɛi martir!

Più d'un angue, più d'un aspe
pju dun aŋgwe, pju dun aspe

crude e sorde ai miei sospir!
krude sorde ai mjɛi sospir!

Occhi alteri, voi petete,
ɔk:ki altɛri vɔi potɛte,

Voi potete risanarmi,
vɔi potɛte risanarmi,

e godete al mio languir!
e godɛte al mio laŋgwir!

Scarlatti   Rugiadose, odorose
skarlat:ti   ruʤadoze, odoroze

Rugiadose, odorose, Violette graziose,
ruʤadoze, odoroze, violɛt:te gratsioze,

Voi vi state vergognose, mezzo ascose
vɔi vi state vɛrgoɲoze, mɛd:zo askoze

tra le foglie, e sgridate le mie voglie
tra le foʎe,   e zgridate le mie voʎe

che son troppo ambiziose.
ke son trɔp:po ambitsioze.

Scarlatti   Se Florindo è fedele
skarlat:ti   se florindo ɛ fedɛle

Se Florindo è fedele io m'innamorerò,
se florindo ɛ fedɛle io min:namorerɔ,

s'è fedele Florindo m'innamorerò.
sɛ fedɛle florindo min:namorerɔ.

Potrà ben l'arco tendere il faretrato arcier,
potra bɛn larko tɛndere il faretrato artʃɛr.

ch'io mi saprò difendere d'un guardo lusinghier.
kio mi saprɔ difɛndere dun gwardo luziŋgjɛr.

Preghi, pianti e querele, io non ascolterò,
prɛgi, pjanti e kwerɛle, io non askolterɔ,

ma se sarà fedele io m'innamorerò
ma se sara fedɛle io min:namorerɔ.

Scarlatti   Sento nel core
skarla̱t:ti   se̱nto nɛl ko̱re

Sento nel core certo dolore,
se̱nto nɛl ko̱re tʃɛ̱rto dolo̱re,

che la mia pace turbando va: nel core.
ke la mi̱a pa̱tʃe turba̱ndo va, nɛl ko̱re.

Splende una face che l' alma accende,
splɛ̱nde u̱na fa̱tʃe ke la̱l   mat:ʃɛ̱nde,

se non è amore, amor sarà.
se non ɛ amo̱re, amo̱r ꞌsara̱.

Stradella   Per Pietà
stradɛ̱l:la   per pjeta̱

Per pietà, deh, torna a me!   Amor mio e dove sei?
per pjeta̱, dɛ, to̱rna a me!   amo̱r mi̱o e do̱ve sɛ̱i?

Son dolenti i lumi miei Non san viver senza te.
son dolɛ̱nti   lu̱mi mjɛ̱i non   san vi̱vɛr sɛ̱ntsa te.

Torelli   Tu lo sai
torɛ̱l:li   tu lo sa̱i

Tu lo sai quanto t' amai
tu lo sa̱i kwa̱nto tama̱i

tu lo sai, lo sai crudel!
tu lo sa̱i, lo sa̱i krudɛ̱l!

Io non bramo altra mercé,
i̱o non bra̱mo a̱ltra mɛrtʃe̱,

Ma ricordati di me
ma riko̱rdati di me,

E poi sprezza un infedel!
e po̱i sprɛt:sa un infedɛ̱l!

Verdi   Addio del passato, from "La Traviata"
verdi   ad:di̯o dɛl pas:sa̱to   la travja̱ta

Attendo, attendo, nè a me giungon mai!
at:te̱ndo, at:te̱ndo, ne a̱ me dʒuŋgo̱n ma̱i!

Oh come son mutata!   Ma il Dottore
o ko̱me son muta̱ta!   ma̱ il dot:to̱re

a sperar pure m' esorta!   Ah, con tal morbo
a spera̱r pu̱re mezo̱rta!   a,   kon tal mo̱rbo

ogni speranza è morta!
o̱ni spera̱ntsa ɛ mo̱rta!

Addio del passato, bei sogni ridenti,
ad:di̯o dɛl pas:sa̱to, bɛi so̱ni ride̱nti,

le rose del volto già sono pallenti;
le ro̱ze dɛl vo̱lto dʒa so̱no pal:lɛ̱nti;

l' amore d' Alfredo perfino mi manca,
lamo̱re dalfre̱do pɛrfi̱no mi ma̱ŋka,

conforto, sostegno dell' anima stanca,
konfo̱rto, soste̱no del:la̱nima sta̱ŋka,

conforto, sostegno. Ah! della Traviata
konfo̱rto, soste̱no. a!   de̱l:la travja̱ta

sorridi al desío, a lei deh perdona,
sor:ri̱di al dezi̱o, a lɛi dɛ pɛrdo̱na,

tu accoglila, o Dio!   Ah! tutto finì, or tutto finì!
tu ak:ko̱ʎila, o di̱o!   a!   tut:to fini̱, or tut:to fini̱!

Le gioje, i dolori tra poco avran fine;
le dʒo̱je, i dolo̱ri tra po̱ko avra̱n fi̱ne;

la tomba ai mortali di tutto è confine!
la to̱mba a̱i morta̱li di tut:to ɛ konfi̱ne!

Non lagrima o fiore avrà la mia fossa!
non la̱grima o̱ fjo̱re avra̱ la mi̱a fo̱s:sa!

non croce col nome che copra quest' ossa!
non kro̱tʃe kol no̱me ke ko̱pra kwesto̱s:sa!

Non croce, non fior!   Ah!   della Traviata . . . . .
non kro̱tʃe, non fjor!   a!   de̱l:la travja̱ta . . . . .

Verdi   Ah, fors' è lui, from "La Traviata"
verdi   a, fɔrsɛ lui   la travjata

È strano! è strano!
ɛ strano! ɛ strano!

in core scolpiti ho quegli accenti!
in kɔre skolpiti o kweʎatːʃɛnti!

Saría per me sventura un serio amore?
saria per me zvɛntura un sɛrjo amɔre?

Che risolvi, o turbata anima mia?
ke rizɔlvi, o turbatanima mia?

Null' uomo ancora l' accendeva.
nulːlwɔmo aŋkɔra latːʃɛndeva.

Oh gioja ch' io non conobbi, esser amato amando!
o dʒɔja kio non konɔbːbi, ɛsːser amato amando!

E sdegnarla poss' io per l' aride follie del viver mio?
e zdeɲarla pɔsːsio per laride folːlie dɛl vivɛr mio?

Ah, fors' è lui che l' anima solinga ne' tumulti,
a, fɔrsɛ lui ke lanima soliŋga ne tumulti,

godea sovente pingere de suoi colori occulti!
godɛa sovɛnte pindʒere de swɔi kolorjokːkulti!

Lui, che modesto e vigile all' egre soglie ascese,
lui, ke modɛsto e vidʒile alːlegre soʎe aʃeze,

e nuova febbre accese, destandomi all' amor!
e nwɔva fɛbːbre atːʃeze, destandomi alːlamɔr!

A quell' amor, ch' e palpito
a kwɛlːlamɔr, ke palpito

dell' universo intero, misterioso, altero,
delːlunivɛrso intɛro, misteriozo, altɛro,

croce e delizia, delizia al cor.
krɔtʃe delitsja, delitsjal kɔr.

Follie! follie! delirio vano è questo!
folːlie! folːlie! delirjo vano ɛ kwɛsto!

Povera donna, sola, abbandonata
pɔvera dɔnːna, sɔla, abːbandonata

in questo popoloso deserto che appellano Parigi,
in kwɛsto popoloso dezɛrto ke apːpelːlano paridʒi,

che spero or più' che far degg' io? gioire!
ke spɛror pju? ke far dedːʒio? dʒɔire!

67

di voluttà ne' vortici, di voluttà perir!   Gioir!
di volut:t̪a̠ ne vo̠rtit̠ʃi, di volut:t̪a̠ perir! d̠ʒo̠ir!

Sempre libera degg'io folleggiare di gioja in gioja,
sɛmpre li̠bera ded:ʒio fol:led:ʒare di d̠ʒo̠ja in d̠ʒo̠ja,

vo' che scorra il viver mio pei sentieri del piacer.
vo ke sko̠r:ra̠ il vi̠ver mi̠o pe̠i sentjeri dɛl pjat̠ʃɛr.

Nasca il giorno, o il giorno muoja,
na̠ska̠ il d̠ʒo̠rno, o̠ il d̠ʒo̠rno mwo̠ja,

sempre lieta ne' ritrovi,
sɛmpre lje̠ta ne ritro̠vi,

a diletti sempre nuovi dee volare il mio pensier.
a dilɛt:ti sɛmpre nwo̠vi de volare il mi̠o pɛnsjɛr.

Ave Maria, piena di grazia,
a̠ve mari̠a, pje̠na di gra̠tsja,

eletta Fra le spose e le vergini sei tu,
elɛt:ta fra le spo̠ze le vɛrd̠ʒini se̠i tu,

Sia benedetto il frutto,
si̠a benede̠t:to̠ il fru̠t:to,

Di tue materne viscere: Gesù!
di tu̠e matɛrne vi̠ʃere, d̠ʒezu̠!

 Prega per chi adorando a te si prostra,
prɛga per kjadora̠ndo a te si pro̠stra,

Prega pel peccator, per l'innocente,
prɛga pel pek:ʃato̠r, per lin:not̠ʃɛnte,

E pel debole oppresso e pel possente,
e pel de̠bole op:prɛs:so̠ e pel pos:sɛnte,

Misero anch'esso, tua pietà dimostra.
mi̠zero a̠ŋke̠s:so, tu̠a pje̠ta̠ dimo̠stra.

Prega per chi sotto l'oltraggio piega la fronte
prɛga per ki so̠t:to lo̠ltra̠d:ʒo pje̠ga la fro̠nte

e sotto la malvagia sorte;
so̠t:to la malva̠d̠ʒa so̠rte;

Per noi, per noi, tu prega, prega sempre
per noi, per noi, tu prega, prega sempre

e nell'ora della morte nostra, Prega per noi,
e nel:lora del:la morte nostra, prega per noi,

Ave Maria Ave! Amen!
ave maria ave amɛn!

Verdi   Caro nome, from "Rigoletto"
verdi   karo nome   rigolet:to

Gualtier Maldè! nome di lui si amato,
gwaltjɛr malde! nome di lui si amato,

ti scolpisci nel core innamorato!
ti skolpiʃi nɛl kore in:namorato!

Caro nome che il mio cor festi primo palpitar,
karo nome ke il mio kor fɛsti primo palpitar,

le delizie dell'amor mi déi sempre rammentar!
le delitsje del:lamor mi dei sɛmpre ram:mentar!

Col pensier il mio desir a te sempre volerà,
kol pɛnsjɛr il mio dezir a te sɛmpre volera,

e fin l'ultimo sospir, caro nome, tuo sarà.
e fin lultimo sospir, karo nome, tuo sara.

...tuo sarà, il mio desir a te ognora volerà,
   tuo sara, il mio dezir a te oɲora volera,

fin l'ultimo sospiro tuo sarà!
fin lultimo sospiro tuo sara!

Verdi   Celeste Aïda, from "Aïda"
verdi   tʃelɛste aida

Se quel guerrier io fossi!
se kwɛl gwer:rjɛr io fos:si!

se il mio sogno si avverasse!
se il mio soɲo si av:veras:se!

Un esercito di prodi da me guidato,
un ezɛrtʃito di prɔdi da me gwidato,

e la vittoria e il plauso di Menfi tutta!
e la vit:tɔrja e il plauzo di mɛnfi tut:ta!

E a te, mia dolce Aïda,
e a te, mia doltʃe aida,

tornar di lauri cinto dirti:
tornar di lauri tʃinto dirti,

per te ho pugnato, per te ho vinto!
per te ɔ puɲato, per te ɔ vinto!

Celeste Aïda, forma divina,
tʃelɛste aida, forma divina,

mistico serto di luce e fior,
mistiko sɛrto di lutʃe fjor,

del mio pensiero tu sei regina,
del mio pensjɛro tu sɛi redʒina,

tu di mia vita sei lo splendor.
tu di mia vita sɛi lo splɛndor.

Il tuo bel cielo vorrei ridarti,
il tuo bɛl tʃɛlo vor:rɛi ridarti,

le dolci brezze del patrio suol;
le doltʃe brɛd:ze dɛl patrjo swɔl;

un regal serto sul crin posarti,
un regal sɛrto sul krin pozarti,

ergerti un trono vicino al sol, ah!
ɛrdʒɛrti un trɔno vitʃino al sol, a!

Celeste Aïda, forma divina,
tʃelɛste aida, forma divina,

mistico raggio di luce e fior.....
mistiko rad:ʒo di lutʃe fjor.....

Verdi   Credo, from "Otello"
verdi   krɛdo   otɛl:lo

Vanne; la tua meta già vedo.
van:ne; la tua mɛta dʒa vedo.

Ti spinge il tuo dimone e il tuo dimon son io,
ti spindʒe il tuo dimone e il tuo dimon son io,

e me trascina il mio,
e me traʃina il mio,

nel quale io credo inesorato Iddio:
nɛl kwale io kredo inezorato id:dio

Credo in un Dio crudel che m'ha creato simile a sè,
kredo in un dio krudɛl ke ma kreato simile a se,

e che nell'ira io nomo.
e ke nel:lira io nomo.

Dalla viltà d'un germe o d'un atòmo vile son nato.
dal:la vilta dun dʒɛrme o dun atomo vile son nato.

Son scellerato perchè son uomo, e sento il fango
son ʃel:lerato pɛrke son womo, e sɛnto il faŋgo

originario in me. Sì! quest'è la mia fè!
oridʒinarjo in me. si, kwɛst ɛ la mia fe!

Credo con fermo cuor,
kredo kon fermo kwɔr,

siccome crede la vedovella al tempio,
sik:kome krede la vedovɛl:lal tɛmpjo,

che il mal ch'io penso e che da me procede
ke il mal kio pɛnso e ke da me protʃɛde

per mio destino adempio.
per mio destino adɛmpjo.

Credo che il giusto è un istrion beffardo
kredo ke il dʒusto ɛ un istrjon bef:fardo

e nel viso e nel cuor,
e nɛl vizo e nɛl kwɔr,

che tutto è in lui bugiardo, lagrima, bacio,
ke tut:to ɛ in lui budʒardo, lagrima, batʃo,

sguardo, sacrificio ed onor.
zgwardo, sakrifitʃo ed onɔr.

E credo l'uom gioco d'iniqua sorte
e kredo lwɔm dʒoko dinikwa sɔrte

dal germe della culla al verme dell'avel.
dal dʒɛrme dɛl:la kul:la al vɛrme del:lavɛl.

71

Vien dopo tanta irrision la Morte. E poi?
vjɛn dopo tanta ir:rizjon la morte. e poi?

La Morte è il Nulla è vecchia fola il Ciel.
la morte ɛ il nul:la ɛ vɛk:kja fola il tʃɛl.

Verdi   Di Provenza il mar, from "La Traviata"
verdi   di provɛntsa il mar   la travjata

Di Provenza il mar, il suol chi dal cor ti cancellò?
di provɛntsa il mar, il swol ke dal kor ti kantʃel:lo

Al natio fulgente sol qual destino ti furò?
al natio fuldʒɛnte sol kwal destino ti furo?

Oh rammenta pur nel duol ch'ivi gioia a te brillò,
o ram:mɛnta pur nɛl dwol kivi dʒoja te bril:lo,

e che pace colà sol su te splendere ancor può,
e ke patʃe kola sol su te splɛndere aŋkor pwo,

Dio mi guidò!
dio mi gwido!

Ah il tuo vecchio genitor tu non sai quanto soffrì!
a il tuo vɛk:kjo dʒenitor tu non sai kwanto sof:fri

Te lontano di squallor il suo tetto si coprì.
te lontano di skwal:lor il suo tɛt:to si kopri.

Ma se alfin ti trovo ancor, se in me speme non fallì,
ma se alfin ti trovo aŋkor, se in me spɛme non fal:li,

se la voce dell'onor in te appien non ammutì
se la votʃe del:lonor in te ap:pjɛn non am:muti

ma se il fin ti trovo ancor,
ma se il fin ti trovo aŋkor,

se in me speme non fallì, Dio m'esaudì!
se in me spɛme non fal:li, dio mezaudi!

Verdi   Ella giammai m'amò, from "Don Carlo"
verdi   el:la dʒam:mai mamo   don karlo

Ella giammai m'amò! no! quel cor chiuso è a me,
el:la dʒam:mai mamo! no! kwɛl kor kjuzo ɛ a me,

72

amor per me non ha!   Io la rivedo ancor
amor per me non a!   io la rivedo aŋkor

contemplar trista in volto
kontɛmplar trista in vɔlto

il mio crin bianco il dì che qui di Francia venne.
il mio krin bjaŋko il di ke kwi di frantʃa vɛn:ne.

No, amor per me non ha!
nɔ, amor per me non a!

Ove son?   Quei doppier presso a finir!
ɔve son?   kwei dop:pjɛr prɛs:so a finir,

L'aurora imbianca il mio veron già spunta il dì!
laurɔra imbjaŋka il mio veron dʒa spunta il di!

Passar veggo i miei giorni lenti!
pas:sar veg:go i mjɛi dʒorni lɛnti!

il sonno o Dio, sparì da' miei occhi languenti.
il son:no dio, spari da mjɛi ɔk:ki laŋgwɛnti.

Dormirò sol nel manto mio regal,
dormirɔ sol nɛl manto mio regal,

quando la mia giornata è giunta a sera,
kwando la mia dʒornata ɛ dʒunta sera,

dormirò sol sotto la volta nera, avel dell'Escurial.
dormirɔ sol sɔt:to la vɔlta nɛra, avɛl del:leskurial.

Se il serto regal a me desse il poter
se il sɛrto regal a me dɛs:se il potɛr

di leggere nei cor, che Dio può sol può sol veder!
di lɛd:ʒere nei kɔr, ke dio pwɔ sol pwɔ sol vedɛr!

Se dorme il prence, veglia il traditore;
se dɔrme il prɛntʃe, veʎa il traditore;

il serto perde il re, il consorte l'onore!
il sɛrto pɛrde il re, il konsɔrte lonore!

Verdi   Eri tu, from "Un Ballo in Maschera"
verdi   ɛri tu   un bal:lo in maskera

Alzati! là tuo figlio a te concedo riveder.
altsati! la tuo fiʎo a te kontʃedo vedɛr.

73

Nell'ombra e nel silenzio,
nel:lombra e nɛl silɛntzjo,

là il tuo rossore e l'onta mia nascondi!
la il tuo ros:sore lonta mia naskondi!

Non è su lei, nel suo fragile petto
non ɛ su lɛi, nɛl suo fradʒile pɛt:to

che colpir degg'io.   Altro,
ke kolpir dedːʒio. altro,

ben altro sangue a terger dessi l'offesa.
bɛn altro saŋgwe a tɛrdʒɛr dɛs:si lof:feza.

Il sangue tuo!
il saŋgwe tuo!

E lo trarrà il pugnale dallo sleal tuo core:
e lo trar:ra il puɲale dal:lo zlɛal tuo kore,

delle lacrime mie vendicator!
del:le lakrime mie vɛndikator!

Eri tu che macchiavi quell'anima,
ɛri tu ke mak:kjavi kwel:lanima,

la delizia dell'anima mia...
la delitsja del:lanima mia...

che m'affidi e d'un tratto esecrabile
ke maf:fidi e dun trat:to ezekrabile

l'universo avveleni per me!
lunivɛrso av:velɛni per me!

Traditor!   che compensi in tal guisa
traditor!   ke kompɛnsin tal gwiza

dell'amico tuo primo,...la fè!
del:lamiko tuo primo ...la fe!

O dolcezze perdute! o memorie
o doltʃet:se pɛrdute! o memorje

d'un amplesso che l'essere india!
dun amplɛs:so ke lɛs:sere india!

quando Amelia, sì bella, si candida
kwando amelja, si bɛl:la, si kandida

sul mio seno brillava d'amor!
sul mio seno bril:lava damor!

È finita: non siede che l'odio,
ɛ finita, non sjede ke lɔdjo,

e la morte nel vedovo cor!
e la mɔrte nɛl vedovo kɔr!

O dolcezze perdute!
o doltʃet:se pɛrdute!

o speranze d'amor!
o sperantse damɔr!

Verdi   Il lacerato spirito, from "Simon Boccanegra"
verdi   il latʃerato spirito   simon bok:kanegra

A te l'estremo addio palagio altero,
a te lestrɛmo ad:dio paladzo altɛro,

freddo sepolcro dell'angiolo mio!
frɛd:do sepɔlkro del:landzolo mio!

Nè a proteggerti valsi!...
ne a protɛd:ʒerti valsi!

Oh maledetto!... oh vile seduttore!...
o maledɛt:to!   o vile sedut:tore!

E tu, Vergin, soffristi
e tu, vɛrdʒin, sof:fristi

rapita lei la verginal corona?
rapita lɛi la vɛrdʒinal korɔna?

Ah! che dissi?...deliro!...ah, mi perdona!
a! ke dis:si?   deliro!   a, mi pɛrdɔna!

Il lacerato spirito del mesto genitore
il latʃerato spirito dɛl mɛsto dʒenitore

era serbato a strazio d'infamia e di dolore.
ɛra sɛrbato a stratsjo dinfamja e di dolore.

Il serto a lei de'martiri pietoso il cielo diè
il sɛrto a lɛi de martiri pjetozo il tʃɛlo dje

Resa al fulgor degli angeli, prega, Maria per me.
rezal fulgor de ʎandʒeli, prɛga, maria per me.

75

Verdi   Infelice, from "Ernani"
verdi   infelitʃe   ernani

Che mai vegg' io
ke mai ved:ʒio

nel penetral più sacro di mia magione,
nɛl penetral pju sakro di mia madʒone,

presso a lei che sposa, esser dovrà d'un Silva,
prɛs:so a lɛi ke spoza, ɛs:ser dovra dun silva,

due seduttori io scorgo!
due sedut:tori io skorgo!

Entrate, olà miei fidi cavalieri!
ɛntrate, ola, mjɛi fidi kavaljeri!

Sia ognun testimon del disonore
sia oɲun testimon dɛl dizonore

Dell' onta che si reca al suo signore.
del:lonta ke si rɛkal suo siɲore.

Infelice! e tu credevi Si bel giglio immaculato!
infelitʃe e tu kredevi si bɛl giʎo im:makulato

Del tuo crine fra le nevi
dɛl tuo krine fra le nevi

piomba invece il disonor.
pjomba invetʃe il dizonor.

Ah perchè perchè l'etade in seno
a pɛrke pɛrke letade in seno

Giovin core m'ha serbato!
dʒovin kore ma sɛrbato!

Mi dovevan gli anni almeno
mi dovevan ʎi an:ni almeno

Far di gelo, far di gelo ancora il cor!
far di dʒɛlo, far di dʒɛlo aŋkora il kor!

Verdi   La donna è mobile, from "Rigoletto"
verdi   la don:na ɛ mobile   rigolet:to

La donna è mobile qual piuma al vento,
la don:na ɛ mobile kwal pjumal vɛnto,

muta d'accento e di pensiero.
muta dat:ʃɛnto e di pɛnsjero.

Sempre un amabile leggiadro viso,
sɛmpre un amabile led:ʒadro vizo,

in pianto o in riso, è menzognero.
in pjanto in   riso, ɛ mɛntsoɲero.

La donna è mobil qual piuma al vento
la don:na ɛ mobil kwal pjumal vɛnto

muta d'accento e di pensier.
muta dat:ʃɛnto e di pɛnsjɛr.

È sempre misero chi a lei s'affida,
ɛ sɛmpre mizero ki a lɛi saf:fida,

chi le confida mal cauto il core!
ki le konfida mal kauto il kɔre!

Pur mai non sentesi felice appieno
pur mai non sɛntesi felitʃe ap:pjeno

chi su quel seno non liba amore!
ki su kwɛl seno non libamore!

Verdi   O don fatale, from "Don Carlo"
vɛrdi   o don fatale   don karlo

O don fatale, o don crudel,
o don fatale, o don krudɛl,

che in suo furor mi fece il cielo!
ke in suo furor mi fetʃe il tʃɛlo!

Tu che ci fai Si vane altere,
tu ke tʃi fai si vane altɛre,

ti maledico, o mia beltà!
ti malediko, o mia bɛlta!

Versar, sol posso il pianto,
vɛrsar, sol pɔs:so il pjanto,

Speme non ho, soffrir dovrò,
spɛme non ɔ,   sof:frir dovrɔ,

Il mio delitto è orribil tanto,
il mio delit:to ɛ or:ribil tanto,

Che cancellar mai nol potrò.
ki kantʃelːar mai nol potrọ.

O mia regina, io t'immolai
o mịa redʒịna, ịo timːolại

Al folle error di questo cor!
al fọlːe erːrọr di kwẹsto kọr!

Solo in un chiostro al mondo omai
sọlọ in un kjọstro al mọndomại

Potrò celar il mio dolor.
potrọ tʃelar il mịo dolọr.

Ohimè! O mia regina, solo in un chiostro
ɔimẹ! o mịa redʒịna, sọlọ in un kjọstro

al mondo omai Potrò celar il mio dolore.
al mọndomại potrọ tʃelar il mịo dolọre.

Oh ciel! e Carlo a morte domani gran Dio,
o tʃɛl! e kạrlo a mọrte domạni gran dịo,

forse andrà! Ah!
fọrse ạndrạ! a!

un dì mi resta, la speme m'arride!
un di mi rẹsta, la spẹme marːrịde!

Sia benedetto il ciel, lo salverò!
sịa benedẹtọ il tʃɛl, lo salverọ!

Verdi   O tu, Palermo, from " I Vespri Siciliani"
verdi   o tu, palẹrmo   i vẹspri sitʃiljạni

O patria, o cara patria, alfin ti veggo,
o pạtria, o kạra pạtria, alfịn ti vẹgːgo,

l'esule ti saluta dopo sì lunga assenza.
lẹzule ti salụta dopo si lụŋga asːsẹntsa.

Il fiorente tuo suolo repien d'amore io bacio,
il fjorẹnte tụo swọlo ripjẹn damọre ịo batʃo,

reco il mio voto a te col braccio e il core!
rẹko il mịo vọto a te kol bratːʃo e il kọre!

O tu, Palermo, terra adorata,
o tu palẹrmo, tɛrːra adorạta,

a me sì caro riso d'amor, ah,
a me si k̠aro ri̠so dam̠or, a,

alza la fronte tanto oltraggiata,
a̠ltsa la fron̠te ta̠nto oltrad:z̠ata,

il tuo ripiglia primier splendor!
il tu̠o ripi̠ʎa primj̠er splen̠dor!

Chiesi aïta a straniere nazioni,
kj̠ezi ai̠ta stranj̠ere natsj̠oni,

ramingai per castella città;
ramiŋga̠i per kastel̠:la e tʃit:ta̠;

ma insensibil al fervido sprone dicea ciascun:
ma insen̠sibil al f̠ervido spron̠e di̠tʃea tʃasku̠n,

Siciliani, ov' è il prisco valor?
sitʃiljani, ov e̠ il pri̠sko valor̠?

Su, sorgete a vittoria all' onor!
su, sordʒ̠ete a vit:to̠rja a̠l:lonor̠!

....il tuo ripiglia almo splendor,
il tu̠o ripi̠ʎalmo splendor̠,

ah, torna al primiero, almo splendor!
a, to̠rnal primj̠ero, a̠lmo splendor!

Verdi   Pace, pace, mio Dio, from "La Forza del Destino"
ve̠rdi   pa̠tʃe, pa̠tʃe mi̠o di̠o   la fo̠rtsa del destino̠

Pace, mio Dio!
pa̠tʃe, mi̠o di̠o!

Cruda sventura M' astringe, ahimè a languir;
kru̠da zventu̠ra mastrindʒe, ai̠me a laŋgwi̠r;

Come il dì primo da tant' anni dura
ko̠me il di pri̠mo da tanta̠n:ni du̠ra

Profonde il mio soffrir. Pace, mio Dio!
profon̠de il mi̠o sof:fri̠r. pa̠tʃe, mi̠o di̠o!

L' amai, gli è ver! ma di beltà e valore
lama̠i, ʎe ver! ma di belta̠ e valo̠re

Cotanto Iddio l'ornò, Che l'amo ancor,
kotan̠to id:di̠o lorno̠, ke la̠mo aŋkor,

nè togliermi dal core L' immagin sua saprò.
ne toʎermi   dal kɔre lim:madʒin sua saprɔ.

Fatalità! un delitto Disgiunti n'ha quaggiù!
fatalita! un delit:to dizdʒunti na kwad:ʒu!

Alvaro, io t'amo, e su nel cielo è scritto:
alvaro, io tamo, e su nɛl tʃɛlo ɛ skrit:to,

Non ti vedrò mai più! Oh Dio, Dio, fa ch'io muoja;
non ti vedrɔ mai pju! o dio, dio, fa kio mwɔja;

chè la calma può darmi morte sol.
ke la kalma pwɔ darmi mɔrte sol.

Invan la pace qui sperò quest' alma
invan la patʃe kwi spero kwest alma

In preda a tanto, a tanto duol,
in prɛda tanto, a tanto dwɔl,

in mezzo a tanto, a tanto duol.
in mɛd:ʒo a tanto, a tanto dwɔl.

Invan la pace quest' alma,
invan la patʃe kwestalma,

invan la pace quest' alma invan sperò.
invan la patʃe kwestalma invan sperɔ.

Misero pane a prolungar mi vieni la sconsolata vita.
mizɛro pane a proluŋgar mi vjɛni la skonsolata vita.

Ma chi giunge? Chi profanare ardisce il sacro loco?
ma ki dʃundʒe? ki profanare ardiʃe il sakro lɔko?

Maledizione!
maleditsjone!

Verdi   Questa o quella, from ''Rigoletto''
verdi   kwesta o kwɛl:la   rigolet:to

Questa o quella per me pari sono
kwesta o kwɛl:la per me pari sono

a quant'altre d'intorno,
a kwantaltre dintɔrno,

d'intorno mi vedo, del mio core l'impero non cedo
dintɔrno mi vedo, dɛl mio kɔre limpɛro non tʃɛdo

meglio ad una, che ad altra beltà.
meʎo ad una, ke ad altra bɛlta.

La costoro avvenenza è qual dono
la kostoro av:venɛntsa ɛ kwal dono

di che il fato ne infiora la vita; s'oggi questa
di ke il fato ne infjora la vita; sɔd:ʒi kwesta

mi torna gradita, forse un' altra doman lo sarà,
mi torna gradita, forse un altra doman lo sara,

La costanza, tiranna del core, detestiamo qual morbo,
la kostantsa, tiran:na dɛl kore, detestjamo kwal morbo,

qual morbo crudele, sol chi vuole si serbi fedele;
kwal morbo krudele, sol ki vwole si sɛrbi fedele;

Non v'ha amor se non v'è libertà.
non va amor se non vɛ liberta.

De' mariti il geloso furore,
de maritil dʒelozo furore,

degli amanti le smanie derido,
deʎamanti le zmanje derido,

anco d'Argo i cent'occhi disfido se mi punge,
aŋko dargo i tʃɛntok:ki disfido se mi pundʒe,

se mi punge una qualche beltà.
se mi pundʒe una kwalke bɛlta.

Verdi   Ritorna vincitor, from "Aida"
verdi   ritorna vintʃitor   aida

Ritorna vincitor! E dal mio labbro uscì l'empia parola!
ritorna vintʃitor! e dal mio lab:bro uʃi lempja parola!

Vincitor del padre mio, di lui che impugna l'armi per me
vintʃitor dɛl padre mio, di lui ke impuɲa larmi per me

per ridonarmi una patria, una reggia e il nome illustre
per ridonarmi una patria, una rɛd:ʒa e il nome il:lustre

che qui celar m'è forza! Vincitor de' miei fratelli
ke kwi tʃelar mɛ fortsa! vintʃitor de mjɛi fratɛl:li

ond'io lo vegga, tinto del sangue amato,
ondio lo vɛg:ga, tinto dɛl saŋgwe amato,

trionfar nel plauso dell' Egizie coorti!
trionfar nɛl plauzo del:ledʑitsje koorti!

E dietro il carro, un Re mio padre di catene avvinto!
e djɛtro il kar:ro, un re mio padre di katene av:vinto!

L' insana parola, o Numi, sperdete! —
linsana parola, o numi, spɛrdete!

Al seno d'un padre la figlia rendete;
al seno dun padre la fiʎa rɛndete;

Struggete le squadre dei nostri oppressor! Ah!
strud:ʑete le skwadre dei nostri op:pres:sor! a!

sventurata! che dissi? e l'amor mio?
zvɛnturata! ke dis:si? e lamor mio?

Dunque scordar poss'io
duŋkwe skordar pos:sio

Questo fervido amore che, oppressa e schiava,
kwɛsto fɛrvido amore ke, op:pres:sa e skjava,

Come raggio di sol qui mi beava?
kome rad:ʒo di sol kwi mi beava?

Imprecherò la morte a Radamès, a lui ch'amo pur tanto?
imprekero la mɔrte a radamɛs, a lui kamo pur tanto?

Ah! non fu in terra mai da più crudeli
a, non fu in tɛr:ra mai da pju krudɛli

angoscie un core affranto!
aŋgoʃe un kore af:franto!

I sacri nomi di padre, d'amante,
i sakri nomi di padre, damante,

Nè profferir poss'io, nè ricordar,
ne prof:ferir pos:sio, ne rikordar,

Per l'un per l'altro confusa,
per lun per laltro konfuza,

tremante Io piangere vorrei pregar.
tremante io pjandʒere vor:rɛi pregar.

Ma la mia prece in bestemmia si muta.
ma la mia prɛtʃe in bestem:mja si muta.

Delitto è il pianto a me, colpa il sospir,
delit:to ɛ il pjanto a me kolpa il sospir,

In notte cupa la mente è perduta,
in nɔt:te kupa la mente ɛ pɛrduta,

82

E nell'ansia crudel vorrei morir!
e nel:lạnsja krudɛl vor:rɛi morịr!

Numi, pietà del mio soffrir!
nụmi, pjeta dɛl mịo sof:frịr!

Speme non v'ha pel mio dolor;
spɛme non va pel mịo dolọr;

Amor fatal, tremendo amor spezzami il cor, fammi morir!
amọr fatạl, tremɛndo amọr spɛt:samil kọr, fạm:mi morịr!

Numi, pietà del mio soffrir.
nụmi, pjeta dɛl mịo sof:frịr.

Verdi   Stride la vampa, from "Il Trovatore"
vɛrdi   strịde la vạmpa   il trovatọre

Stride la vampa, la folla indomita corre a quel foco,
strịde la vạmpa, la fọl:la indomita kọr:re a kwɛl fọko,

lieta in sembianza, urli di gioja intorno echeggiano,
ljẹta in sembjạntsa, ụrli di dʒọja intọrno ekẹd:ʒano,

cinta di sgherri donna s'avanza;
tʃịnta di zgɛr:ri dọn:na savạntsa;

sinistra splende sui volti orribile
sinịstra splɛnde sụi vọlti or:rịbile

La tetra fiamma che s'alza,
la tɛtra fjạm:ma ke sạltsa,

che s'alza al ciel, che s'alza al ciel.
ke sạltsa al tʃɛl, ke sạl tsal tʃɛl.

Stride la vampa, giunge la vittima nero vestita,
strịde la vạmpa, dʒundʒe la vịt:tima nɛro vestịta,

discinta e scalza; grido feroce di morte levasi,
diʃịnta e skạltsa; grido ferọtʃe di mọrte lɛvasi,

l'eco il ripete di balza in balza;
lɛkọ il ripɛte di bạltsa in bạltsa;

sinistra splende sui volti orribili
sinịstra splɛnde sụi vọlti or:rịbili

la tetra fiamma che s'alza al ciel.
la tɛtra fjạm:ma ke sạltsal tʃɛl.

Verdi   Volta la terrea, from "Un Ballo in Maschera"
verdi   vǫlta la tɛr:rɛa   un bal:lo in maskera

Volta la terrea fronte alle stelle!
vǫlta la tɛr:rɛa frǫnte al:le stɛl:le!

come sfavilla la sua pupilla,
kǫme sfavil:la la sụa pupil:la,

quando alle belle il fin predice
kwạndo al:le bɛl:le il fin preditʃe

mesto o felice dei loro amor!
mẹsto o felitʃe dei lǫro amǫr!

Ah, e con Lucifero d'accordo ognor!
a, e kon lutʃifero dak:kǫr doɲọr!

Chi la profetica sua gemma afferra,
ki la profɛtika sụa dʒem:ma af:fɛr:ra,

o passi'l mare voli alla guerra,
o pas:sil mạre vǫli al:la gwɛr:ra,

le sue vicende soavi, amare,
le sụe vitʃɛnde soạvi, amare,

da questa apprende nel dubbio cor.
da kwẹsta ap:prɛnde nɛl dụb:bjo kǫr.

Vivaldi   Un certo non so che
vivạldi   un tʃɛrto non sɔ ke

Un certo non so che Mi giunge e passa il cor,
un tʃɛrto non sɔ ke mi dʒụndʒe pas:sa il kɔr,

Eppur dolor non è, Se questo fosse amor?
ep:pur dolǫr non ɛ, se kwẹsto fǫs:se amǫr?

Nel suo vorace ardor, Già posi incauta, posi il piè?
nel sụo voratʃe ardǫr, dʒa posiŋkạuta, pǫsil pje?

PHONETIC TRANSCRIPTION OF GERMAN SONGS AND ARIAS

Werner Singer and Berton Coffin

The German songs have been transcribed phonetically according to the principles used in Siebs, "Deutsche Hochsprache," Gruyter, Berlin, 1958, with the following indicated exceptions. These exceptions are due to the fact that this book is written primarily for singers, that this is a transcription of phonetic principles used in the singing of the German language, as used by German singers, and that the transcription is written for a fluent reading of the phonetic sounds and accents.

Punctuation

Punctuation is placed in the phonetic transcription to enable the singer to read the phonetics with the phrasing of the text. (Note: the punctuation of the colon : has been replaced by the comma in the transcription to avoid conflict with the : symbol of lengthened vowel.)

Indication of Accent

It is felt that the underlined accent (fɛrge:blɪçəs ʃtɛntçən) will read more fluently than (fɛr'ge:blɪçəs'ʃtɛntçən) the usual accent indication.

Double Liquid Consonants

In this text the double liquid consonants mm, nn, ll and rr will be written as two consonants as in the following words: Himmel, Wellen, Sonne and Herren. While it may be correct to call such combinations long consonants, it is not necessary that they be long but that they be split in the middle. The split being accompanied by a variation of breath pressure or a wave in which a slight decrease of pressure is followed by an increase of pressure. This applies only to singing (according to Wilcke), not to the speech of the stage German (according to Siebs). It is necessary because singing is usually more prolonged than speech.

Wilcke in "German Diction in Singing" (translated from the German) states, "in singing, the student should accustom himself to lightly strike the first consonant at the utmost end of the syllable, as for instance in the Himmel, alle, Nonne . . . ., then to clearly articulate the following consonant."

Do not sing:	a-lle	Wo-nnen
nor	all-e	Wonn-en
but sing:	al le	Won nen

ig Endings

All ig endings have been transcribed as ɪç with the following exception. When the ig ending is followed in a word by ich suffix the ig is transcribed as ɪk, ie königlich would sound better to the ear pronounced kø:nɪklɪç rather than kø:nɪçlɪç according to authorities, see Bithell. Apparently the double fricative is of questionable taste.

85

The combination of d and t between two words

In words ending in d̲ or t̲ followed by words beginning with d̲ or t̲, a strong t̲ is used to give the articulation. However, in this transcription it is indicated by a tie in the four possible combinations, ie, und‿Treu, bist‿du, nicht‿treu, and und‿das. The tie is also used when the same sounds occur phonetically, ie bist zu . . . . . bɪst‿tsu:

Long and Short Vowels

The singer should at all times note the difference between the long and short vowels which are characteristic of the German language. The vowels e:, i:, etc., should be held as long as possible in the time value allotted by the music and in contrast the short vowels ɛ, ɪ, ʏ, etc., should be shortened by the slight anticipation of the closing consonant of the syllable. The symbol : indicates a vowel is long. Absence ·) of the symbol indicates a short vowel.

Symbol for glottal attack, | rather than ?

The | symbol for glottal attack has been used instead of the ? symbol frequently used. Siebs 1958. The glottal attack, long feared by singers and teachers of singing, has been transcribed only during the flow of a phrase, not at the beginning. Artistic use of this interruption of vocal line is necessary for intelligibility of the German language.

Value of the phonetic symbols used in the transcription of German

Phonetic Symbol		Sounds as derived from English sounds	As found in German words
VOWELS			
long	a:	a little brighter than a in Father (pronounced long)	Kahn . . . . . ka:n
short	a	father (pronounced short)	Mann . . . . . man
long	ɛ:	men, set, (pronounced long)	währen . . . . vɛ̲:rən
short	ɛ	men, set, (pronounced short)	weg . . . . . vɛk
long	e:	as in grey (without the diphthong vanish to i.)	Teer . . . . . te:r
short	e	as above but short duration	der . . . . . der
	ə	like e in quicken	baden . . . . . ba̲:dən
long	i:	believe	Sieb . . . . . zi:p
short	ɪ	in, is	in . . . . . ɪn
long	o:	Rose, loan (without diphthong vanish to ʊ.)	Rose . . . . . ro̲:zə

86

short	ɔ	got, with lips more rounded	Gott . . . . . gɔt
long	u:	food, loom	Kuh . . . . . ku:
short	ʊ	put, book	unter . . . . . u̠ntər
long	ø:	gate pronounced with kiss formation (tongue position of e, lip position of u)	Löhne . . . . . lø̠:nə
short	œ	met pronounced with rounded lips	Götter . . . . . gœtər
long	y:	meat with rounded lips	Lüge . . . . . ly̠:gə
short	ʏ	it with rounded lips	Müller . . . . . my̠llər

DIPHTHONGS

	a̠e	mine, thy	Mein . . . . . ma̠en
	a̠o	house, mount	Haus . . . . . ha̠os
	ɔ̠ø	boy	treu . . . . . trɔ̠ø

CONSONANTS

b	bad, both		Bote . . . . . bo̠:tə
ç	human |çuman|, frictional and whispered		Licht . . . . . lɪçt
d	dine, tongue almost touching upper teeth		dein . . . . . da̠en
f	fine		fein . . . . . fa̠en
g	give, God		geben . . . . . ge̠:bən
h	His, house		Herr . . . . . hɛr
x	very slowly whisper the word ho<u>ck</u> so that the back of the tongue rises slowly towards the |k| without the tongue contacting the velum		Bach . . . . . bax
j	yes		ja . . . . . ja:
k	key		Kopf . . . . . kɔpf
l	clear l, even after vowels more fronted and dental than in English. May be obtained by taking position and tongue tension of th in English and pronouncing it l		Welle . . . . . vɛ̠llə
m	mine		Mein . . . . . ma̠en
n	nine		Nein . . . . . na̠en

CONSONANTS continued

ŋ	Ring	Ring . . . . . rɪŋ
p	past	Post . . . . . pɔst
r	roll, but with rolled r	reden . . . . . reːdən (little heard on endings)
s	less, best	es . . . . . ɛs
ʃ	shine	Schein . . . . . ʃaen
t	tall, tongue touching upper teeth	Tahl . . . . . taːl
v	voice, vine	Wein . . . . . vaen
z	zoo	so . . . . . zoː
|	glottal stop produced by sudden release of breath after it has been banked up behind the vocal chords. The variation of intensity in the glottal stop is of a high artistic importance	nur |alleine |ist's

BIBLIOGRAPHY

Siebs. — Deutsche Hochsprache Bühnenaussprache. Stage pronunciation in phonetics, Berlin, 1958, Gryter and Co. Called by some, "the bible."

Wilcke, Eva. — German Diction in Singing. tr and ed by Bainbridge Crist, N. Y. 1930, Dutton.

Wardale, W. L. — German Pronunciation. Edinburgh, Edinburgh University Press, 1955.

Bithell, Jethro. — German Pronunciation and Phonology. Methuen and Co., London, 1952.

Martens, Carl & Peter — Phonetik der Deutschen Sprache. Hueber Verlag, München, 1961. (Excellent photographs of pronunciation of German vowels and consonants).

Bach   Bist du bei mir
                bɪst duː bae miːr

Bist du bei mir, geh ich mit Freuden
bɪst duː bae miːr, geː |ɪç mɪt frøødən

zum Sterben und zu meiner Ruh!
tsum ʃtɛrbən |ʊnt tsuː maenər ruː!

Ach, wie vergnügt wär so mein Ende,
ax, viː fɛrgnyːkt vɛːr zoː maen |ɛndə,

es drückten deine lieben Hände
ɛs drʏktən daenə liːbən hɛndə

mir die getreuen Augen zu!
miːr di gətrøøn |aogən tsuː!

Bach   Es ist vollbracht
                ɛs |ɪst fɔlbraxt

Es ist vollbracht!
ɛs |ɪst fɔlbraxt!

Vergiss ja nicht dies Wort,
fɛrgɪs jaː nɪçt diːs vɔrt,

mein Herz, das Jesus spricht,
maen hɛrts, das jeːzus ʃprɪçt,

da er am Kreuze für dich stirbet
daː |eːr |am krøøtsə fyːr dɪç ʃtɪrbət

und dir die Seligkeit erwirbet,
|ʊnt diːr di zeːlɪçkaet |ɛrvɪrbət,

da er, der Alles, Alles wohl gemacht
daː |eːr der |aləs, aləs voːl gəmaxt

nunmehro spricht: es ist vollbracht!
nuːnmero ʃprɪçt, ɛs |ɪst fɔlbraxt!

Bach   Komm, süsser Tod
                kɔm, zyːsər toːt

Komm, süsser Tod, komm, sel'ge Ruh'!
kɔm, zyːsər toːt, kɔm, zeːlgə ruː,

Komm und führe mich in Friede,
kɔm |ʊnt fy:rə mɪç |ɪn fri̯:də,

weil ich der Welt bin müde.
va̯el |ɪç der vɛlt bɪn my̤:də.

Ach komm, ich wart' auf dich,
ax kɔm, ɪç vart |a̤of dɪç,

komm bald und führe mich,
kɔm balt |ʊnt fy̤:rə mɪç,

drück' mir die Augen zu.
drʏk mi̯:r di |a̤ogən tsu:.

Komm, sel'ge Ruh'!
kɔm, ze̤:lgə ru:!

Beethoven   Abscheulicher! wo eilst du hin? from "Fidelio"
             apʃo̤ølɪçər!   vo: |a̤elst du: hɪn?   fidḛljo

Abscheulicher! wo eilst du hin? was hast du vor,
apʃo̤ølɪçər! vo: |a̤elst du: hɪn? vas hast du: for,

was hast du vor in wildem Grimme? Des Mitleids Ruf,
vas hast du: for |ɪn vi̤ldəm grɪmmə? dɛs mi̤tla̯ets ru:f,

der Menschheit Stimme rührt nicht mehr deinen Tigersinn.
der mḛnʃha̯et ʃtɪmmə ry̤:rt nɪçt me:r da̤enən ti̤:gərzɪn.

Doch toben auch wie Meereswogen
dɔx to̤:bən |a̤ox vi: mḛ:rəsvo:gən

dir in der Seele Zorn und Wuth,
di:r |ɪn der ze̤:lə tsɔrn |ʊnt vu:t,

so leuchte mir ein Farbenbogen,
zo: lo̤øçtə mi:r |a̤en farbənbo:gən,

der hell auf dunklen Wolken ruht.
der hɛl |a̤of dṳŋklən vo̤lkən ru:t.

Der blickt so still', so friedlich nieder,
der blɪkt zo: ʃtɪl, zo: fri̤:tlɪç ni̤:dər,

der spiegelt alte Zeiten wieder,
der ʃpi̤:gəlt |altə tsa̤etən vi:dər,

und neu besänftigt wallt mein Blut.
|ʊnt no̤ø bəzḛnftɪçt valt ma̤en blu:t.

Komm Hoffnung, lass den letzten Stern
kɔm hɔfnʊŋ, las den lɛtstən ʃtɛrn

der Müden nicht erbleichen,
der myːdən nɪçt |ɛrblaeçən,

o komm erhell', erhell' mein Ziel, sei's noch so fern,
oː kɔm |ɛrhɛl, ɛrhɛl maen tsiːl, zaes nɔx zoː fɛrn,

die Liebe, sie wird's erreichen,
di liːbə, ziː vɪrts |ɛrraeçən,

ja, ja, sie wird's erreichen.
jaː, jaː, ziː vɪrts |ɛrraeçən.

Komm, o komm, komm, o Hoffnung!
kɔm, oː kɔm, kɔm, oː hɔfnʊŋ!

Lass den letzten Stern, der Müden nicht erbleichen!
las den lɛtstən ʃtɛrn, der myːdən nɪçt |ɛrblaeçən!

Erhell' ihr Ziel, sei's noch so fern,
ɛrhɛl |iːr tsiːl, zaes nɔx zoː fɛrn,

die Liebe wird's erreichen. Ich folg' dem innern Triebe,
di liːbə vɪrts |ɛrraeçən.   ɪç fɔlk dem |ɪnnərn triːbə,

ich wanke nicht,
ɪç vaŋkə nɪçt,

mich stärkt die Pflicht der treuen Gattenliebe.
mɪç ʃtɛrkt di pflɪçt der trɔøən gatənliːbə.

O du, für den ich alles trug,
oː duː, fyːr den |ɪç |aləs truːk,

könnt' ich zur Stelle dringen,
kœnt |ɪç tsuːr ʃtɛllə drɪŋən,

wo Bosheit dich in Fesseln schlug,
voː boːzhaet dɪç |ɪn fɛsəln ʃluːk,

und süssen Trost dir bringen!
ʊnt syːsən troːst diːr brɪŋən!

Beethoven   Adelaide
            adəlaiːdə

Einsam wandelt dein Freund im Frühlingsgarten,
aenzam vandəlt daen frɔønt |ɪm fryːlɪŋsgartən,

mild vom lieblichen Zauberlicht umflossen,
mɪlt vɔm liːplɪçən tsaobərlɪçt |umflɔsən,

das durch wankende Blüthenzweige zittert,
das dʊrç vaŋkəndə blyːtəntsvaegə tsɪtərt,

Adelaide!   Adelaide!
adəlai̯ːde! adəlai̯ːde!

In der spiegelnden Fluth, im Schnee der Alpen,
ɪn der ʃpiːgəlndən fluːt, ɪm ʃneː der |alpən,

in des sinkenden Tages Goldgewölken,
ɪn dəs zɪŋkəndən taːgəs gɔltgevœlkən,

im Gefilde der Sterne strahlt dein Bildnis, Adelaide!
ɪm gəfɪldə der ʃtɛrnə ʃtraːlt daen bɪltnɪs, adəlai̯ːdə!

Abendlüftchen im zarten Laube flüstern,
aːbəntlʏftçən |ɪm tsaːrtən laobə flʏstərn,

Silberglöckchen des Mai's im Grase säuseln,
zɪlbərglœkçən dəs maes|ɪm graːzə zɔøzəln,

Wellen rauschen und Nachtigallen flöten: Adelaide!
vɛllən raoʃən |ʊnt naxtigallən fløːtən, adəlai̯ːdə!

Einst, o Wunder! entblüht auf meinem Grabe
aenst, oː vʊndər! ɛntblyːt |aof maenəm graːbə

eine Blume der Asche meines Herzens,
|aenə bluːmə der |aʃə maenəs hɛrtsəns,

deutlich schimmert, auf jedem Purpurblättchen: Adelaide!
dɔøtlɪç ʃɪmmərt, aof jeːdəm pʊrpurblɛtçən, adəlai̯ːdə!

Beethoven   Die Ehre Gottes aus der Natur
              di |eːrə gɔtəs |aos der natuːr

Die Himmel rühmen des Ewigen Ehre,
di hɪmməl ryːmən dəs |eːvɪgən |eːrə,

ihr Schall pflanzt seinen Namen fort.
iːr ʃal pflantst zaenən naːmən fɔrt.

Ihn rühmt der Erdkreis,
iːn ryːmt der |eːrtkraes,

ihn preisen die Meere, vernimm, o Mensch,
iːn praezən di meːrə, fɛrnɪm, o mɛnʃ,

92

ihr göttlich Wort!
iːr gœtliç vɔrt!

Wer trägt der Himmel unzählbare Sterne?
veːr trɛːkt der hɪmməl |ʊntsɛːlbarə ʃtɛrne?

Wer führt die Sonn' aus ihrem Zelt?
veːr fyːrt di zɔn |aʊs |iːrəm tsɛlt?

Sie kommt und leuchtet und lacht uns von ferne
ziː kɔmt |ʊnt lɔøçtət |ʊnt laxt |ʊns fɔn fɛrnə

und läuft den Weg gleich als ein Held.
|ʊnt lɔøft den veːk glaeç |als |aen hɛlt.

Beethoven   Die Trommel gerühret
              di   trɔmməl gəryːrət

Die Trommel gerühret, das Pfeifchen gespielt!
di   trɔmməl gəryːrət, das pfaefçən gəʃpiːlt!

Mein Liebster gewaffnet dem Haufen befiehlt,
maen liːpstər gəvafnət dem haʊfən bəfiːlt,

die Lanze hoch führet, die Leute regieret.
di   lantsə hoːx fyːrət, di lɔøtə rəgiːrət.

Wie klopft mir das Herz! Wie wallt mir das Blut!
viː klɔpft miːr das hɛrts! viː valt miːr das bluːt!

O hätt ich ein Wämslein und Hosen und Hut!
oː hɛt |ɪç |aen vɛmslaen |ʊnt hoːzən |ʊnt huːt!

Ich folgt' ihm zum Thor 'naus mit muthigem Schritt,
ɪç fɔlkt |iːm tsum toːr naʊs mɪt muːtɪgəm ʃrɪt,

ging' durch die Provinzen, ging' überall mit.
gɪŋ dʊrç di   provɪntsən, gɪŋ |yːbər|al mit.

Die Feinde schon weichen, wir schiessen da drein;
di faendə ʃoːn vaeçən, viːr ʃiːsən daː draen;

Welch' Glück sondergleichen, ein Mannsbild zu sein!
velç glʏk zɔndərglaeçən, aen mansbɪlt tsuː zaen!

Beethoven   Freudvoll und leidvoll
             frɔøtfɔl |ʊnt laetfɔl

Freudvoll und leidvoll, gedankenvoll sein;
frɔøtfɔl |ʊnt laetfɔl, gədaŋkənfɔl zaen;

Hangen und bangen in schwebender Pein;
haŋən |ʊnt baŋən |ɪn ʃveːbəndər paen;

himmelhoch jauchzend; zum Tode betrübt;
hɪmməloːx jaoxtsənt; tsʊm toːdə bətryːpt;

glücklich allein ist die Seele, die liebt!
glʏklɪç |allaen |ɪst di zeːlə, di liːpt!

Beethoven   Ich liebe dich
             ɪç liːbə dɪç

Ich liebe dich, so wie du mich,
ɪç liːbə dɪç, zoː viː duː mɪç,

am Abend und am Morgen,
am |aːbənt |ʊnt |am mɔrgən,

noch war kein Tag, wo du und ich
nɔx vaːr kaen taːk, voː duː |ʊnt mɪç

nicht theilten uns're Sorgen.
nɪçt taeltən |ʊnzrə zɔrgən.

Auch waren sie für dich und mich
aox vaːrən ziː fyːr dɪç |ʊnt mɪç

getheilt leicht zu ertragen;
gətaelt laeçt tsuː |ɛrtraːgən,

du tröstetest im Kummer mich,
duː trøːstətəst |ɪm kʊmmər mɪç,

ich weint' in deine Klagen,
ɪç vaent |ɪn daenə klaːgən,

D'rum Gottes Segen über dir,
drʊm gɔtəs zeːgən |yːbər diːr,

du meines Lebens Freude,
duː maenəs leːbəns frɔødə,

Gott schütze dich, erhalt' dich mir,
gɔt ʃʏtsə dɪç, ɛrhalt dɪç miːr,

schütz' und erhalt' uns beide!
ʃʏts |ʊnt |ɛrhalt |ʊns baedə!

Beethoven   Mailied
             maeliːt

Wie herrlich leuchtet mir die Natur,
viː hɛrlɪç loøçtət miːr di natuːr,

wie glänzt die Sonne, wie lacht die Flur!
viː glɛntst di zɔnnə, viː laxt di fluːr!

Es dringen Blüthen aus jedem Zweig und tausend Stimmen
ɛs drɪŋən blyːtən |aos jeːdəm tsvaek |unt taozənt ʃtɪmmən

aus dem Gesträuch
|aos dem gəʃtrɔøç

und Freud' und Wonne aus jeder Brust:
|unt frɔøt |unt vɔnnə |aos jeːdər brust,

O Erd' o Sonne, o Glück, o Lust!
oː |eːrt, oː zɔnnə, oː glʏk, oː lust!

O Lieb', o Liebe, so golden schön,
oː liːp, oː liːbə, zoː gɔldən ʃøːn,

wie Morgenwolken auf jenen Höh'n!
viː mɔrgənvolkən |aof jeːnən høːn!

Du segnest herrlich das frische Feld,
duː zeːgnəst hɛrlɪç das frɪʃə fɛlt,

im Blüthendampfe die volle Welt.
ɪm blyːtəndampfə di fɔllə vɛlt.

O Mädchen, Mädchen, wie lieb' ich dich!
oː mɛːtçən, mɛːtçən, viː liːp |ɪç dɪç!

wie blickt dein Auge, wie liebst du mich!
viː blɪkt daen |aogə, viː liːpst duː mɪç!

So liebt die Lerche Gesang und Luft,
zoː liːpt di lɛrçə gəzaŋ |unt luft,

und Morgenblumen den Himmelsduft,
unt mɔrgənbluːmən den hɪmməlsduft,

wie ich dich liebe mit warmem Blut,
viː |ɪç dɪç liːbə mɪt varməm bluːt,

die du mir Jugend und Freud' und Muth
di duː miːr juːgənt |unt frɔøt |unt muːt

zu neuen Liedern und Tänzen gibst.
tsuː nɔøən liːdərn |unt tɛntsən giːpst.

Sei ewig glücklich, wie du mich liebst!
zae |eːvɪç glʏklɪç, viː duː mɪç liːpst!

Beethoven   Mit einem gemalten Band
             mɪt |aenəm gəmaltən bant

Kleine Blumen, kleine Blätter
klaenə blu:mən, klaenə blɛtər

streuen mir mit leichter Hand
ʃtrøøən mi:r mɪt laeçtər hant

gute junge Frühlingsgötter tändelnd auf ein luftig Band
gu:tə juŋə fry:lɪŋsgœttər tɛndəlnt |aof |aen lʊftɪç bant.

Zephyr, nimm's auf deine Flügel,
tse:fɪr, nɪms |aof daenə fly:gəl,

schling's um meiner Liebsten Kleid;
ʃlɪŋs |um maenər li:pstən klaet;

und so tritt sie vor den Spiegel
ʊnt zo: trɪt zi: for den ʃpi:gəl

all' in ihrer Munterkeit.
|al |ɪn |i:rər mʊntərkaet.

Sieht mit Rosen sich umgeben,
zi:t mɪt ro:zən zɪç |umge:bən,

selbst wie eine Rose jung.
zelpst vi: |aenə ro:zə juŋ.

Einen Blick, geliebtes Leben!
aenən blɪk, gəli:ptəs le:bən!

und ich bin belohnt genung.
ʊnt |ɪç bɪn bəlo:nt genuŋ.

Fühle, fühle, was dies Herz empfindet,
fy:lə, fy:lə, vas di:s herts |empfɪndət,

reiche frei mir deine Hand,
raeçə frae mi:r daenə hant,

und das Band, das uns verbindet,
ʊnt das bant, das |uns ferbɪndət,

sei kein schwaches Rosenband,
zae kaen ʃvaxəs ro:zənbant,

Fühle, was dies Herz empfindet,
fy:lə, vas di:s herts |empfɪndət,

reiche frei mir deine Hand,
raeçə frae mi:r daenə hant,

und das Band, das uns verbindet,
ʊnt das bant, das |uns ferbɪndət,

sei kein schwaches Rosenband!
zae kaen ʃvaxəs ro:zənbant!

96

Beethoven   Wonne der Wehmuth
             v̯ɔnnə der veːmuːt

Trocknet nicht, Thränen der ewigen Liebe!
trɔknət nɪçt, trɛːnən der |evɪgən liːbə!

Ach, nur dem halb getrockneten Auge wie öde,
ax, nuːr dem halp gətrɔknətən |a̯ogə viː |øːdə,

wie todt die Welt ihm erscheint!
viː toːt d̯i vɛlt |iːm |ɛrʃa̯ent!

Trocknet nicht, Thränen unglücklicher Liebe.
trɔknət nɪçt, trɛːnən |ʊnglʏlɪçər liːbə,

Bohm   Still wie die Nacht
            ʃtɪl viː di naxt

Still wie die Nacht, tief wie das Meer,
ʃtɪl viː di naxt, tiːf viː das meːr,

soll deine Liebe sein!
zɔl d̯a̯enə liːbə za̯en!

Wenn du mich liebst so wie ich dich,
vɛn duː mɪç liːpst so viː |ɪç dɪç,

will ich dein eigen sein.
vɪl |ɪç d̯a̯en |a̯egən za̯en.

Heiss wie der Stahl und fest wie der Stein
ha̯es viː der ʃtaːl |ʊnt fɛst viː der ʃta̯en

soll deine Liebe sein!
zɔl d̯a̯enə liːbə za̯en!

Brahms   An die Nachtigall
           an di naxtigal

Geuss' nicht so laut der liebentflamten Lieder
gɔøs nɪçt zoː la̯ot der liːp|ɛntflamtən liːdər

tonreichen Schall
toːnra̯eçən ʃal

vom Blütenast des Apfelbaums hernieder,
fom blyːtən|ast dɛs |apfəlba̯oms hɛrniːdər,

97

O Nachtigall!
oː n<u>a</u>xtigal!

Du tönest mir mit deiner süssen Kehle die Liebe wach;
duː tø̯ːnəst miːr mɪt d<u>ae</u>nər zy̆ːsən ke̯ːlə di l<u>i</u>ːbə vax;

denn schon durchbebt die Tiefen meiner Seele
dɛn ʃoːn durçb<u>e</u>ːpt di tiːfən m<u>ae</u>nər z<u>e</u>ːlə

dein schmelzend '' Ach.''
d<u>ae</u>n ʃm<u>ɛ</u>ltsənt |''ax''.

Dann flieht der Schlaf von neuem dieses Lager,
dan fliːt der ʃlaːf fon n<u>øø</u>m d<u>iː</u>zəs laːgər,

ich starre dann
ɪç ʃt<u>a</u>rrə dan

mit nassem Blick und todtenbleich und hager
mɪt n<u>a</u>səm blɪk |ʊnt t<u>o</u>ːtənblae̯ç |ʊnt haːgər

den Himmel an
den hɪmməl |an.

Fleuch, Nachtigall, in grüne Finsternisse,
flɔ̯øç, n<u>a</u>xtigal, ɪn gry̆ːnə fɪnstərnisə,

ins Haingesträuch,
ɪns h<u>ae</u>ngəʃtrɔ̯øç,

und spend' im Nest der treuen Gattin Küsse, entfleuch!
ʊnt ʃpɛnt |ɪm nɛst der tr<u>øø</u>ən g<u>a</u>tɪn ky̆sə, ɛntflɔ̯øç!

Brahms   An eine Aeolsharfe
Wolf   an |<u>ae</u>nə |<u>ɛ</u>ːɔlsharfə

Angelehnt an die Efeuwand dieser alten Terrasse,
angəl<u>e</u>ːnt |an di |<u>e</u>ːfø̯øvant d<u>iː</u>zər |<u>a</u>ltən tɛrr<u>a</u>sə,

du, einer luftgebornen Muse geheimnisvolles Saitenspiel,
duː, <u>ae</u>nər l<u>ʊ</u>ftgəbornən m<u>u</u>ːzə gəh<u>ae</u>mnɪsfɔlləs z<u>ae</u>tənʃpiːl,

fang' an, fange wieder an deine melodische Klage.
faŋ |an, f<u>a</u>ŋə v<u>iː</u>dər |an d<u>ae</u>nə melo̯ːdɪʃə kl<u>a</u>ːgə.

Ihr kommet, Winde, fern herüber,
iːr k<u>o</u>mmət, vɪndə, fɛrn hɛry̆ːbər,

ach! von des Knaben, der mir so lieb war,
ax! fɔn dɛs kn<u>a</u>ːbən der miːr zoː liːp vaːr,

frisch grünendem Hügel.
friʃ   gry:nəndəm hy:gəl.

Und Frühlingsblüten unterweges streifend,
ʊnt fry:lɪŋsbly:tən |ʊntərve:gəs ʃtraefənt,

übersättigt mit Wohlgerüchen,
y:bərzɛtɪçt mɪt vo:lgəryçən,

wie süss bedrängt ihr dies Herz!
vi: zy:s bədrɛŋt |i:r di:s hɛrts!

Und säuselt her in die Saiten,
ʊnt zɔøzəlt he:r |ɪn di zaetən,

angezogen von wohllautender Wehmut,
angətso:gən fɔn vo:llaotəndər ve:mu:t,

wachsend im Zug meiner Sehnsucht und hinsterbend wieder.
vaksənt |ɪm tsu:k maenər ze:nzuxt |ʊnt hɪnʃtɛrbənt vi:dər.

Aber auf einmal, wie der Wind heftiger herstösst,
a:bər |aof |aenma:l, vi: der vɪnt hɛftɪgər hɛrʃtø:st,

ein holder Schrei der Harfe
aen hɔldər ʃrae der harfə

wiederholt mir zu süssem Erschrecken
vi:dərho:lt mi:r tsu: zy:səm |ɛrʃrɛkən

meiner Seele plötzliche Regung,
maenər ze:lə plœtslɪçə re:gʊŋ,

und hier, die volle Rose streut geschüttelt
ʊnt hi:r, di fɔllə ro:zə ʃtrɔøt gəʃytəlt

all' ihre Blätter vor meine Füsse!
|al |i:rə blɛtər fɔr maenə fy:sə!

Brahms   Auf dem Kirchhofe
             aof dem kɪrçho:fə

Der Tag ging regenschwer und sturmbewegt,
der ta:k gɪŋ re:gənʃve:r |ʊnt ʃtʊrmbəve:kt,

ich war an manch' vergess'nem Grab' gewesen,
ɪç va:r |an manç fɛrgɛsnəm gra:p gəve:zən,

verwittert Stein und Kreuz, die Kränze alt,
fɛrvɪtərt ʃtaen |ʊnt krɔøts, di krɛntsə |alt,

die Namen überwachsen, kaum zu lesen.
ði na:mən |y:bərvaxsən, kaom tsu: le:zən.

Der Tag ging sturmbewegt und regenschwer,
der ta:k gɪŋ ʃturmbəve:kt |unt re:gənʃve:r,

auf allen Gräbern fror das Wort: Gewesen.
|aof |allən grɛ:bərn fror das vort, gəve:zən.

Wie sturmestot die Särge schlummerten,
vi: ʃturməsto:t di zɛrgə ʃlummərtən,

auf allen Gräbern taute still: Genesen.
aof |allən grɛ:bərn taotə ʃtɪl, gəne:zən.

Brahms   Botschaft
              bo:tʃaft

Wehe, Lüftchen, lind und lieblich
ve:ə, lyftçən, lɪnt |unt li:plɪç

um die Wange der Geliebten,
|um di vaŋə der gəli:ptən,

spiele zart in ihrer Locke,
ʃpi:lə tsart |ɪn |i:rər lɔke,

eile nicht, hinweg zu flieh'n.
aelə nɪçt, hɪnvɛk tsu: fli:n.

Tut sie dann vielleicht die Frage,
tu:t zi: dan filaeçt di fra:gə,

wie es um mich Armen stehe,
vi: |ɛs |um mɪç |a:rmən ʃte:ə,

sprich, "Unendlich war sein Wehe,
ʃprɪç, "|un|ɛntlɪç va:r zaen ve:ə,

höchst bedenklich seine Lage;
hœçst bədɛŋklɪç zaenə la:gə;

aber jetzo kann er hoffen,
a:bər jɛtso kan |e:r hɔfən,

wieder herrlich aufzuleben,
vi:dər hɛrlɪç |aoftsule:bən,

denn du, Holde, denkst an ihn."
dɛn du:, hɔldə, dɛŋkst |an |i:n."

Brahms   Das Mädchen spricht
                das mɛ:tçən ʃprɪçt

Schwalbe, sag' mir an, ist's dein alter Mann
ʃvalbə, za:k mi:r |an, ɪsts daen |altər man,

mit dem du's Nest gebaut, mit dem du's Nest gebaut?
mɪt dem du:s nɛst gəbaot, mɪt dem du:s nɛst gəbaot?

oder hast du jüngst erst dich ihm vertraut?
o:dər hast du: jʏŋst |ɛrst dɪç |i:m fɛrtraot?

Sag', was zwitschert ihr, sag', was flüstert ihr
za:k, vas tsvɪtʃərt |i:r, za:k vas flʏstərt |i:r

des Morgens so vertraut, des Morgens so vertraut?
dɛs mɔrgəns zo: fɛrtraot, dɛs mɔrgəns zo: fɛrtraot?

Gelt, du bist wohl auch noch nicht lange Braut?
gɛlt, du: bɪst vo:l |aox nox nɪçt laŋə braot?

Brahms   Dein blaues Auge
                daen blaoəs |aogə

Dein blaues Auge hält so still,
daen blaoəs |aogə hɛlt zo: ʃtɪl,

ich blicke bis zum Grund.
ɪç blɪkə bɪs tsum grʊnt.

Du fragst mich, was ich sehen will?
du: fra:kst mɪç, vas |ɪç ze:ən vɪl?

Ich sehe mich gesund.
ɪç ze:ə mɪç gəzʊnt.

Es brannte mich ein glühend Paar,
ɛs brantə mɪç |aen gly:ənt pa:r,

noch schmerzt das Nachgefül:
nox ʃmɛrtst das naxgəfy:l,

das deine ist wie See so klar
das daenə |ɪst vi: ze: zo: kla:r

und wie ein See so kühl.
|ʊnt vi: |aen ze: zo: ky:l.

101

Brahms   Der Schmied
              der ʃmiːt

Ich hör' meinen Schatz, den Hammer er schwinget,
ıç høːr maenən ʃats,   den hammər |eːr ʃvıŋət,

das rauschet, das klinget, das dringt in die Weite
das raoʃət,   das klıŋət,   das drıŋt |ın di vaetə

wie Glockengeläute, durch Gassen und Platz.
viː glɔkəngəloøtə, durç gasən |unt plats.

Am schwarzen Kamin, da sitzet mein Lieber,
am ʃvartsən kamiːn, daː zıtsət maen liːbər,

doch, geh' ich vorüber, die Bälge dann sausen,
dɔx, geː |ıç fɔryːbər, di bɛlgə dan zaosən,

die Flammen aufbrausen, und lodern um ihn.
di flammən |aofbraozən, unt loːdərn |um |iːn.

Brahms   Der Tod, das ist die kühle Nacht
              der toːt, das |ıst di kyːlə naxt

Der Tod, das ist die kühle Nacht,
der toːt, das |ıst di kyːlə naxt,

das Leben ist der schwüle Tag.
das leːbən |ıst der ʃvyːlə taːk.

Es dunkelt schon, mich schläfert,
ɛs duŋkəlt ʃoːn, mıç ʃlɛːfərt,

der Tag hat mich müd' gemacht.
der taːk hat mıç myːt gəmaxt.

Über mein Bett erhebt sich ein Baum,
yːbər maen bɛt |ɛrheːpt zıç |aen baom,

d'rin singt die junge Nachtigall;
drın zıŋt di juŋə naxtigal;

sie singt von lauter Liebe,
ziː zıŋt fɔn laotər liːbə,

ich hör' es sogar im Traum.
ıç høːr |ɛs zogaːr |ım traom.

102

Brahms   Die Mainacht
               di ma͟enaxt

Wann der silberne Mond durch die Gesträuche blinkt,
van   der zɪlbərnə moːnt‿durç di   gəʃtro͟øçə blɪŋkt,

und sein schlummerndes Licht über den Rasen streut,
ʊnt za͟en ʃlu͟mmərndəs lɪçt |y͟ːbər den ra͟ːzən ʃtro͟øt,

und die Nachtigall flötet, wandl' ich
ʊnt‿di na͟xtigal fløːtət, vandl |ɪç

traurig von Busch zu Busch.
tra͟orɪç fon bʊʃ tsuː bʊʃ.

Überhüllet vom Laub girret ein Taubenpaar
y͟ːbərhy͟llət fom la͟op gɪrrət |a͟en ta͟obənpa͟ːr

sein Entzücken mir vor; aber ich wende mich,
za͟en |ɛnttsy͟kən miːr for, a͟ːbər |ɪç vɛndə mɪç,

suche dunklere Schatten, und die einsame Träne rinnt.
zu͟ːxə du͟ŋklərə ʃa͟tən,   ʊnt‿di |a͟enza͟ːmə trɛ͟ːnə rɪnt.

Wann, o lächelndes Bild, welches wie Morgenrot
van, o: lɛ͟çəlndəs bɪlt, vɛ͟lçəs vi: mo͟rgənroːt

durch die Seele mir strahlt, find ich auf Erden dich?
dʊrç di   ze͟ːlə miːr ʃtra͟ːlt, fɪnt |ɪç |a͟of |e͟ːrdən dɪç?

Und die einsame Träne bebt
ʊnt‿di |a͟enzamə trɛ͟ːnə beːpt

mir heisser, heisser die Wang herab.
miːr ha͟esər, ha͟esər di vaŋ hɛra͟p.

Brahms   Feldeinsamkeit
               fɛ͟lt| a͟enza͟ːmka͟et

Ich ruhe still im hohen grünen Gras
ɪç ru͟ːə ʃtɪl |ɪm ho͟ːən gry͟ːnən gra͟ːs

und sende lange meinen Blick nach oben,
|ʊnt zɛ͟ndə la͟ŋə ma͟enən blɪk na͟ːx |o͟ːbən,

von Grillen rings umschwirrt ohn' Unterlass,
fon grɪ͟llən rɪŋs |ʊmʃvɪrt |o͟ːn |u͟ntərlas,

von Himmelsbläue wundersam umwoben.
fon hɪ͟mməlsbloøə vu͟ndərzaːm |ʊmvo͟ːbən.

Die schönen weissen Wolken zieh'n dahin
di ʃø͟ːnən va͟esən vo͟lkən tsiːn dahɪ͟n

durch's tiefe Blau, wie schöne stille Träume,
durçs   ti:fə blao, vi: ʃø:nə stɪllə trɔømə,

mir ist, als ob ich längst gestorben bin
mi:r |ɪst, als |ɔp |ɪç lɛŋst gəʃtɔrbən bɪn

und ziehe selig mit durch ew'ge Räume.
ʊnt tsi:ə ze:lɪç mɪt durç |e:vgə rɔømə.

Brahms   Immer leiser wird mein Schlummer
              ɪmmər laezər vɪrt maen ʃlʊmmər

Immer leiser wird mein Schlummer,
ɪmmər laezər vɪrt maen ʃlʊmmər,

nur wie Schleier liegt mein Kummer
nu:r vi: ʃlaeər li:kt maen kʊmmər

zitternd über mir, über mir.
tsɪtərnt |y:bər mi:r, y:bər mi:r.

Oft im Traume hör' ich dich
ɔft |ɪm traomə hø:r |ɪç dɪç

rufen draus vor meiner Tür,
ru:fən draos fɔr maenər ty:r,

niemand wacht und öffnet dir,
ni:mant vaxt |ʊnt |œfnət di:r,

ich erwach' und weine bitterlich.
ɪç |ɛrvax |ʊnt vaenə bɪtərlɪç.

Ja, ich werde sterben müssen,
ja:, ɪç ve:rdə ʃtɛrbən mysən,

eine Andre wirst du küssen,
aenə |andrə vɪrst du: kysən,

wenn ich bleich und kalt;
vɛn |ɪç blaeç |ʊnt kalt;

eh' die Maienlüfte weh'n,
e: di maeənlyftə ve:n,

eh' die Drossel singt im Wald:
e: di drɔsəl zɪŋkt |ɪm valt,

Willst du mich noch einmal seh'n,
vɪlst du: mɪç nɔx |aenma:l ze:n,

komm', o komme bald, komm' o komme bald!
kɔm, oː kɔmmə balt, kɔm oː kɔmmə balt!

Brahms   In der Fremde
Schumann   ɪn der frɛmde

Aus der Heimat hinter den Blitzen rot,
aos der haemat hɪntər den blɪtsən roːt,

da kommen die Wolken her.
daː kɔmmən di vɔlkən hɛr.

Aber Vater und Mutter sind lange tot,
aːbər faːtər ǀunt mutər zɪnt laŋə toːt,

es kennt mich dort keiner mehr.
ɛs kɛnt mɪç dort kaenər meːr.

Wie bald, ach, wie bald kommt die stille Zeit,
viː balt, ax, viː balt kɔmt di stɪllə tsaet,

da ruhe ich auch, und über mir rauscht
daː ruːə ǀɪç ǀaox, unt ǀyːbər miːr raoʃt

die schöne Waldeinsamkeit,
di ʃøːnə valtǀaenzaːmkaet,

und keiner kennt mich mehr hier.
unt kaenər kɛnt mɪç meːr hiːr.

Brahms   In Waldeseinsamkeit
           ɪn valdəsǀaenzaːmkaet

Ich sass zu deinen Füssen in Waldeseinsamkeit;
ɪç zaːs tsuː daenən fyːsən ǀɪn valdəsǀaenzaːmkaet,

Windesatmen, Sehnen ging durch die Wipfel breit.
vɪndəsǀaːtmən, zeːnən gɪŋ durç di vɪpfəl braet.

In stummen Ringen senkt' ich das Haupt in deinen Schoss,
ɪn stummən rɪŋən zɛŋkt ǀɪç das haopt ǀɪn daenən ʃoːs,

und meine bebenden Hände um deine Knie ich schloss.
unt maenə beːbəndən hɛndə ǀum daenə kniː ǀɪç ʃlɔs.

105

Die Sonne ging hinunter, der Tag verglühte all,
di zɔnnə gɪŋ hɪnʊntər,   der taːk fɛrglyːtə |al,

ferne, sang eine Nachtigall, sang eine Nachtigall.
fɛrnə, zaŋ |aenə naxtigal, zaŋ |aenə naxtigal.

Brahms   Liebestreu
              liːbəstrøø

"O versenk', o versenk' dein Leid, mein Kind,
"oː fɛrzɛŋk, oː fɛrzɛŋk daen laet, maen kɪnt,

in die See, in die tiefe See!"
ɪn di zeː, ɪn di tiːfə zeː."

Ein Stein wohl bleibt auf des Meeres Grund,
aen ʃtaen voːl blaept |aof des meːrəs grʊnt,

mein Leid kommt stets in die Höh'.
maen laet komt ʃteːts |ɪn di høː.

"Und die Lieb', die du im Herzen trägst,
"ʊnt di liːp, di duː |ɪm hɛrtsən trɛːkst,

brich sie ab, brich sie ab, mein Kind!"
brɪç ziː |ap, brɪç ziː |ap, maen kɪnt!"

Ob die Blum' auch stirbt, wenn man sie bricht,
op di bluːm |aox ʃtɪrpt, vɛn man ziː brɪçt,

treue Lieb' nicht so geschwind.
trɔøə liːp nɪçt zoː gəʃvɪnt.

"Und die Treu', 's war nur ein Wort,
"ʊnt di trɔø, svaːr nuːr |aen vort,

in den Wind damit hinaus!"
|ɪn den vɪnt damɪt hɪnaos!"

O Mutter, und splittert der Fels auch im Wind,
oː mʊtər, ʊnt ʃplɪtərt der fɛls |aox |ɪm vɪnt,

Meine Treue, die hält ihn aus.
maenə trɔø, di hɛlt |iːn |aos.

Brahms   Meine Liebe ist grün
             mae̯nə li̱ːbə |ɪst gryːn

Meine Liebe ist grün wie der Fliederbusch,
mae̯nə li̱ːbə |ɪst gryːn viː der fli̱ːdərbuʃ,

und mein Lieb ist schön wie die Sonne,
|ʊnt mae̯n liːp |ɪst ʃøːn viː di zo̱nnə,

die glänzt wohl herab auf den Fliederbusch
di glɛntst voːl hɐrap |ao̯f den fli̱ːdərbuʃ

und füllt ihn mit Duft und mit Wonne.
|ʊnt fʏlt |iːn mɪt duft |ʊnt mɪt vo̱nnə.

Meine Seele hat Schwingen der Nachtigall
mae̯nə ze̱ːlə hat ʃvɪŋən   der na̱xtigal

und wiegt sich in blühendem Flieder,
|ʊnt viːkt zɪç |ɪn bly̱ːəndəm fliːdər,

und jauchzet und singet von Duft berauscht
ʊnt jao̯xtsət |ʊnt zɪŋət fon duft bərao̯ʃt

viel liebestrunkene Lieder.
fiːl li̱ːbəstrʊŋkənə li̱ːdər.

Brahms   Minnelied
             mɪnnəliːt

Holder klingt der Vogelsang, wenn die Engelreine,
ho̱ldər klɪŋt der fo̱ːgəlzaŋ, vɛn di |ɛŋəlrae̯nə,

die mein Jünglingsherz bezwang, wandelt durch die Haine.
di mae̯n jʏŋlɪŋshɛrts bətsvaŋ, va̱ndəlt dʊrç di hae̯nə.

Röter blühen Tal und Au, grüner wird der Wasen,
røːtər bly̱ːən taːl |ʊnt |ao̯, gryːnər vɪrt der va̱ːzən,

wo die Finger meiner Frau Maienblumen lasen.
voː di fɪŋər mae̯nər frao̯ mae̯ənbluːmən la̱ːzən.

Ohne sie ist alles tot, welk sind Blüt' und Kräuter:
o̱ːnə ziː |ɪst |alləs toːt, vɛlk zɪnt bly̱ːt |ʊnt krɔøtər,

und kein Frühlingsabendrot dünkt mir schön und heiter.
ʊnt kae̯n fry̱ːlɪŋs|aːbəntroːt dʏŋkt miːr ʃøːn |ʊnt hae̯tər.

Traute, minnigliche Frau wollest nimmer fliehen,
trao̯tə, mɪnnɪklɪçə frao̯ vo̱lləst nɪmmər fliːən,

dass mein Herz, gleich dieser Au,
das maen hɛrts, glaeç diːzər |ao,

mög' in Wonne blühen, mög' in Wonne blühen.
møːk |ɪn vɔnnə blyːən, møːk |ɪn vɔnnə blyːən.

Brahms   Nachtigall
              naxtigal

O Nachtigall, dein süsser Schall,
oː naxtigal, daen zyːsər ʃal,

er dringet mir durch Mark und Bein.
eːr drɪŋət miːr durç mark |unt baen.

Nein, trauter Vogel, nein!
naen, traotər foːgəl, naen!

Was in mir schafft so süsse Pein,
vas |ɪn miːr ʃaft zoː zyːsə paen,

das ist nicht dein,
das |ɪst nɪçt daen,

das ist von andern, himmelschönen,
das |ɪst fon |andərn, hɪmməlʃøːnən,

nun längst für mich verklungenen Tönen
nuːn lɛŋst fyːr mɪç fɛrkluŋənən tøːnən

in deinem Lied ein leiser Wiederhall!
|ɪn daenəm liːt |aen laezər viːdərhal!

Brahms   Nicht mehr zu dir zu gehen
              nɪçt meːr tsuː diːr tsuː geːən

Nicht mehr zu dir zu gehen,
nɪçt meːr tsuː diːr tsuː geːən,

beschloss ich und beschwor ich,
bəʃlɔs |ɪç |unt bəʃvoːr |ɪç,

und gehe jeden Abend,
unt geːə jeːdən |aːbənt,

108

denn jede Kraft, denn jede Kraft
dɛn jeːdə kraft, dɛn jeːdə kraft

und jeden Halt verlor ich.
|ʊnt jeːdən halt fɛrloːr |ɪç.

Ich möchte nicht mehr leben,
ɪç mœçtə nɪçt meːr leːbən,

möcht augenblicks, augenblicks verderben,
mœçt |aogənblɪks, aogənblɪks fɛrdɛrbən,

und möchte doch auch leben für dich, mit dir,
ʊnt mœçtə dɔx |aox leːbən fyːr dɪç, mɪt diːr,

und nimmer, nimmer sterben.
ʊnt nɪmmər, nɪmmər ʃtɛrbən.

Ach, rede, sprich ein Wort nur,
ax, reːdə, ʃprɪç |aen vɔrt nuːr,

ein einziges, ein klares;
aen |aentsɪgəs, aen klaːrəs;

gib Leben oder Tod mir, nur dein Gefühl,
giːp leːbən |oːdər toːt miːr, nuːr daen gəfyːl,

nur dein Gefühl enthülle mir, dein wahres!
nuːr daen gəfyːl |ɛnthʏllə miːr, daen vaːrəs!

Brahms   O kühler Wald
            oː kyːlər valt

O kühler Wald, wo rauschest du,
oː kyːlər valt, voː raoʃəst duː,

in dem mein Liebchen geht?
ɪn dem maen liːpçən geːt?

O Wiederhall, wo lauschest du,
oː viːdərhal, voː laoʃəst duː,

der gern mein Lied versteht?
der gɛrn maen liːt fɛrʃteːt?

Im Herzen tief da rauscht der Wald,
ɪm hɛrtsən tiːf daː raoʃt der valt,

in dem mein Liebchen geht,
ɪn dem maen liːpçən geːt,

in Schmerzen schlief der Wiederhall,
ɪn ʃmɛrtsən ʃliːf der viːdərhal,

die Lieder sind verweht.
di liːdər zɪnt fɐveːt.

Brahms   O liebliche Wangen
             oː liːplɪçə vaŋən

O liebliche Wangen, ihr macht mir Verlangen,
oː liːplɪçə vaŋən, |iːr maxt miːr fɐlaŋən,

dies rote, dies weisse zu schauen mit Fleisse.
diːs roːtə, diːs vaesə tsuː ʃaoən mɪt flaesə.

Und dies nur alleine ist's nicht, was ich meine;
ʊnt diːs nuːr |allaenə |ɪsts nɪçt, vas |ɪç maenə;

zu schauen, zu grüssen, zu rühren, zu küssen!
tsuː ʃaoən, tsuː gryːsən, tsuː ryːrən, tsuː kʏsən!

ihr macht mir Verlangen, o liebliche Wangen!
iːr maxt miːr fɐlaŋən, oː liːplɪçə vaŋən!

O Sonne der Wonne!   O Wonne der Sonne!
oː zɔnnə der vɔnnə! oː vɔnnə der zɔnnə!

O Augen, so saugen das Licht meiner Augen.
oː |aogən, zoː zaogən das lɪçt maenər |aogən.

O englische Sinnen!   O himmlisch Beginnen!
oː |ɛŋlɪʃə zɪnnən!   oː hɪmlɪʃ bəgɪnnən!

O Himmel auf Erden! magst du mir nicht werden,
oː hɪmməl |aof |eːrdən! makst duː miːr nɪçt veːrdən,

O Wonne der Sonne, O Sonne der Wonne!
oː vɔnnə der zɔnnə, oː zɔnnə der vɔnnə!

O Schönste der Schönen!   benimm mir dies Sehnen,
oː ʃøːnstə der ʃøːnən!   bənɪm miːr diːs zeːnən,

komm eile, komm, komme, du Süsse du Fromme!
kom |aelə, kom, kɔmmə, duː zyːsə duː frɔmmə!

Ach Schwester, ich sterbe, ich sterb', ich verderbe,
ax ʃvɛstər, ɪç ʃtɛrbə, ɪç stɛrp, ɪç fɐdɛrbə,

komm, komme, komm eile, komm, komme, komm eile,
kom, kɔmmə, kom |aelə, kom, kɔmmə, kom |aelə,

benimm mir dies Sehnen, O Schönste der Schönen.
bənɪm miːr diːs zeːnən, oː ʃøːnstə der ʃøːnən.

Brahms   O wüsst ich doch den Weg zurück
         oː vyːst |ɪç dɔx den veːk tsurʏk

O wüsst' ich doch den Weg zurück,
oː vyːst |ɪç dɔx den veːk tsurʏk,

den lieben Weg zum Kinderland!
den liːbən veːk tsum kɪndərlant!

O warum sucht' ich nach dem Glück
oː vaːrʊm zuːxt |ɪç naːx dem glʏk

und liess der Mutter Hand?
ʊnt liːs der mʊtər hant?

O wie mich sehnet auszuruh'n,
oː viː mɪç zeːnət |aostsuruːn,

von keinem Streben aufgeweckt,
fɔn kaenəm ʃtreːbən |aofgəvɛkt,

die müden Augen zuzutun,
di myːdən |aogən tsuːtsutuːn,

von Liebe sanft bedeckt!
fɔn liːbə zanft bədɛkt!

Und nichts zu forschen, nichts zu späh'n,
ʊnt nɪçts su: fɔrʃən, nɪçts su: ʃpɛːn,

und nur zu träumen leicht und lind,
ʊnt nuːr tsu: trɔømən laeçt |ʊnt lɪnt,

der Zeiten Wandel nicht zu seh'n,
der tsaetən vandəl nɪçt tsu: zeːn,

zum zweiten Mal ein Kind!
tsum tsvaetən mːal |aen kɪnt!

O zeigt mir doch den Weg zurück,
oː tsaekt miːr dɔx den veːk tsurʏk,

den lieben Weg zum Kinderland!
den liːbən veːk tsum kɪndərlant!

Vergebens such' ich nach dem Glück,
fɛrgeːbəns zuːx|ɪç naːx dem glʏk,

111

ringsum ist öder Strand, öder Strand!

rɪŋs|ʊm |ɪst |ø:dər ʃtrant, ø:dər ʃtrant!

Brahms   Sapphische Ode

zafɪʃə |o:də

Rosen brach ich nachts mir am dunklen Hage;

ro:zən bra:x |ɪç naxts mi:r |am dʊŋklən ha:gə,

süsser hauchten Duft sie als je am Tage;

zy:sər haoxtən dʊft zi: als je: |am ta:gə,

doch verstreuten reich die bewegten Äste

dɔx fɛrʃtrɔøtən raeç di bəve:ktən |ɛstə

Tau, der mich nässte.

tao, der mɪç nɛstə.

Auch der Küsse Duft mich wie nie berückte,

aox der kysə dʊft mɪç vi: ni: bərʏktə,

die ich nachts vom Strauch deiner Lippen pflückte:

di |ɪç naxts fɔm ʃtraox daenər lɪpən pflʏktə,

doch auch dir, bewegt im Gemüt gleich jenen,

dɔx |aox di:r, bəve:kt |ɪm gəmy:t glaeç je:nən,

tauten die Tränen.

taotən di trɛ:nən.

Brahms   Sonntag

zɔnta:k

So hab' ich doch die ganze Woche

zo: ha:p |ɪç dɔx di gantsə vɔxə

mein feines Liebchen nicht geseh'n,

maen faenəs li:pçən nɪçt gəze:n,

ich sah es an einem Sonntag

ɪç za: |ɛs |an |aenəm zɔnta:k

wohl vor der Türe steh'n:

vo:l fɔr der ty:rə ʃte:n,

das tausendschöne Jungfräulein,
das taozəntʃøːnə jʊŋfroølaen,

das tausendschöne Herzelein,
das taozəntʃøːnə hɛrtsəlaen,

wollte Gott, wollte Gott,
vɔltə gɔt, vɔltə gɔt,

ich wär' heute bei ihr!
|ɪç vɛːr hɔøtə bae |iːr!

So will mir doch die ganze Woche
zo| vɪl miːr dɔx di gantsə vɔxə

das Lachen nicht vergeh'n,
das laxən nɪçt fɛrgeːn,

ich sah es an einem Sonntag
ɪç za |ɛs |an |aenəm zɔntaːk

wohl in die Kirche geh'n:
voːl |ɪn di kɪrçə geːn,

das tausendschöne Jungfräulein,
das taozəntʃøːnə jʊŋfroølaen,

das tausendschöne Herzelein,
das taozəntʃøːnə hɛrtsəlaen,

wollte Gott, wollte Gott,
vɔltə gɔt, vɔltə gɔt,

ich wär' heute bei ihr!
|ɪç vɛːr hɔøtə bae |iːr!

Brahms   Ständchen
          ʃtɛntçən

Der Mond steht über dem Berge,
der moːnt ʃteːt |yːbər dem bɛrgə,

so recht für verliebte Leut;
zoː rɛçt fyːr fɛrliːptə lɔøt;

im Garten rieselt ein Brunnen,
ɪm gartən riːzəlt |aen brʊnnən,

sonst Stille weit und breit.
zɔnst ʃtɪllə vaet |ʊnt braet.

Neben der Mauer im Schatten,
neːbən der maoər |ɪm ʃatən,

da steh'n der Studenten drei
daː ʃteːn der ʃtudɛntən draɛ

mit Flöt' und Geig' und Zither,
mɪt fløːt |ʊnt gaɛk |ʊnt‿tsɪtər,

und singen und spielen dabei.
ʊnt zɪŋən |ʊnt ʃpiːlən dabaɛ.

Die Klänge schleichen der Schönsten
di klɛŋə   ʃlaɛçən der   ʃøːnstən

sacht in den Traum hinein,
zaxt |ɪn den traom hɪnaɛn,

sie schaut den blonden Geliebten
ziː ʃaot‿den blɔndən gəliːptən

und lispelt: "vergiss nicht mein!"
|ʊnt lɪspəlt, "fɛrgɪs nɪçt maɛn."

Brahms   Therese
                tereːzə

Du milchjunger Knabe, wie schaust du mich an?
duː mɪlçjuŋər knaːbə, vi ʃaost‿duː mɪç |an?

Was haben deine Augen für eine Frage getan!
vas haːbən daɛnə |aogən fyːr |aɛnə fraːgə gətaːn!

Alle Ratsherrn in der Stadt und alle Weisen der Welt
allə raːtshɛrn |ɪn der ʃtat |ʊnt |allə vaɛzən der vɛlt

bleiben stumm auf die Frage, die deine Augen gestellt!
blaɛbən ʃtʊm |aof di fraːgə, di daɛnə |aogən gəʃtɛlt!

Eine Meermuschel liegt auf dem Schrank
aɛnə meːrmuʃəl   liːkt |aof dem ʃraŋk

meiner Bas': da halte dein Ohr d'ran,
maɛnər baːz, daː haltə daɛn |oːr dran,

dann hörst du etwas!
dan høːrst duː |ɛtvas!

114

Brahms   Vergebliches Ständchen
                fɛrge:blɪçəs ʃtɛntçən

Guten Abend, mein Schatz, guten Abend, mein Kind!
gu:tən |a:bənt maen ʃats, gu:tən |a:bənt, maen kɪnt!

Ich komm' aus Lieb' zu dir, ach, mach' mir auf die Tür.
ɪç kɔm |aos li:p tsu: di:r, ax max mi:r |aof di ty:r.

Mein' Tür ist verschlossen, ich lass' dich nicht ein;
maen ty:r |ɪst fɛrʃlɔsən, ɪç las dɪç nɪçt |aen;

Mutter, die rät mir klug, wärst du herein mit Fug
mutər, di rɛ:t mi:r klu:k, vɛrst du: hɛraen mɪt fu:k

wär's mit mir vorbei!
vɛ:rs mɪt mi:r fɔrbae!

So kalt ist die Nacht, so eisig der Wind,
zo: kalt |ɪst di naxt, zo: |aezɪç der vɪnt,

dass mir das Herz erfriert, mein Lieb' erlöschen wird,
das mi:r das hɛrts |ɛrfri:rt, maen li:p |ɛrlœʃən vɪrt,

öffne mir, mein Kind, öffne mir, mein Kind!
œfnə mi:r, maen kɪnt, œfnə mi:r, maen kɪnt!

Löschet dein' Lieb', lass' sie löschen nur!
lœʃət daen li:p, las zi: lœʃən nu:r!

Löschet sie, immerzu, geh' heim zu Bett, zur Ruh',
lœʃət zi:, ɪmmərtsu:, ge: haem tsu: bɛt, tsu:r ru:,

gute Nacht, mein Knab', gute Nacht, mein Knab'!
gu:tə naxt, maen kna:p, gu:tə naxt, maen kna:p!

Brahms   Verrat
          fɛrra:t

Ich stand in einer lauen Nacht an einer grünen Linde,
ɪç ʃtant |ɪn |aenər laoən naxt |an |aenər gry:nən lɪndə,

der Mond schien hell, der Wind ging sacht,
der mo:nt ʃi:n hɛl, der vɪnt gɪŋ zaxt,

der Giessbach floss geschwinde, geschwinde.
der gi:sbax flɔs gəʃvɪndə, gəʃvɪndə.

Die Linde stand vor Liebchens Haus,
di lɪndə ʃtant fɔr li:pçəns haos,

die Türe hört ich knarren.
di ty:rə hø:rt |ɪç knarrən.

115

Mein Schatz liess sacht ein Mannsbild 'raus:
maen ʃats li:s zaxt |aen mansbɪlt raos,

"Lass morgen mich nicht harren;
las mɔrgən mɪç nɪçt harrən,

lass mich nicht harren, süsser Mann,
las mɪç nɪçt harrən, zy:sər man,

wie hab ich dich so gerne!
vi: ha:p |ɪç dɪç zo: gɛrnə.

Ans Fenster klopfe leise an,
ans fɛnstər klɔpfə laezə |an,

mein Schatz ist in der Ferne, ja Ferne!"
maen ʃats |ɪst |ɪn der fɛrnə, ja: fɛrnə."

Lass ab vom Druck und Kuss, Feinslieb,
las |ap fɔn druk |ʊnt kʊs, faensli:p,

du Schöner im Sammetkleide,
du: ʃø:nər |ɪm zammətklaedə,

nun spute dich, du feiner Dieb,
nu:n ʃpu:tə dɪç, du: faenər di:p,

ein Mann harrt auf der Heide, ja Heide.
aen man hart |aof der haedə, ja: haedə.

Der Mond scheint hell, der Rasen grün
der mo:nt ʃaent hɛl, der ra:zən gry:n

ist gut zu unsrem Begegnen,
|ɪst gu:t tsu: |ʊnzrəm bəge:gnən,

du trägst ein Schwert und nickst so kühn,
du: trɛ:kst |aen ʃve:rt |ʊnt nɪkst zo: ky:n,

Dein Liebschaft will ich segnen, ja segnen!
daen li:pʃaft vɪl |ɪç ze:gnən, ja: ze:gnən!

Und als erschien der lichte Tag,
ʊnt |als |ɛrʃi:n der lɪçtə ta:k,

dein Liebschaft will ich segnen, ja segnen!
daen li:pʃaft vɪl |ɪç ze:gnən, ja: ze:gnən!

was fand er auf der Heide?
vas fant |e:r |aof der haedə?

Ein Toter in den Blumen lag
aen to:tər |ɪn den blu:mən la:k

zu einer Falschen Leide, ja Leide.
tsu: |aenər falʃən laedə, ja: laedə.

116

Brahms   Vier Ernste Gesänge
              1. Denn es gehet dem Menschen
                  dɛn |ɛs ge͜ːət dem mɛnʃən

Denn es gehet dem Menschen, wie dem Vieh,
dɛn |ɛs ge͜ːət dem mɛnʃən, viː dem fiː,

wie dies stirbt, so stirbt er auch;
viː diːs ʃtɪrpt, zoː ʃtɪrpt |eːr |a͜ox;

und haben alle einerlei Odem;
ʊnt ha͜ːbən |allə |a͜enərla͜e |o͜ːdəm;

und der Mensch hat nichts mehr, denn das Vieh:
ʊnt͜ der mɛnʃ hat nɪçts meːr, dɛn das fiː,

denn es ist alles eitel.
dɛn |ɛs |ɪst |allǝs |a͜etəl.

Es fährt alles an einen Ort;
ɛs fɛːrt |allǝs |an |a͜enən |ort;

es ist alles von Staub gemacht,
ɛs |ɪst |allǝs von ʃta͜op gəma͜xt,

und wird wieder zu Staub.
ʊnt vɪrt viːdər tsuː ʃta͜op.

Wer weiss ob der Geist des Menschen aufwärts fahre,
veːr va͜es |ɔp der ga͜est dɛs mɛnʃən |a͜ofvɛrts fa͜ːrə,

und der Odem des Viehes unterwärts
ʊnt͜ der |o͜ːdəm dɛs fi͜ːəs |ʊntərvɛrts

unter die Erde, unterwärts unter die Erde fahre?
|ʊntər di e͜ːrdə, ʊntərvɛrts ʊntər di |e͜ːrdə fa͜ːrə?

Darum sahe ich, dass nichts bessers ist,
da͜rʊm za͜ːə |ɪç, das nɪçts bɛsərs ɪst,

denn dass der Mensch fröhlich sei in seiner Arbeit,
dɛn das der mɛnʃ frøːlɪç za͜e |ɪn za͜enər |arba͜et,

denn das ist sein Teil.
dɛn das |ɪst za͜en ta͜el.

Denn wer will ihn dahin bringen,
dɛn veːr vɪl |i͜ːn da͜hɪn brɪ͜ŋən,

dass er sehe, was nach ihm geschehen wird?
das |eːr ze͜ːə, vas na͜x |i͜ːm gəʃe͜ːən vɪrt?

117

Brahms   Vier Ernste Gesänge
            2.   Ich wandte mich
               ɪç vantə mɪç

Ich wandte mich und sahe an alle,
ɪç vantə mɪç |unt zaːə |an |allə,

die Unrecht leiden unter der Sonne;
di |u̯nrɛçt laedən |untər der zɔnnə;

und siehe, da waren Tränen,
unt ziːə, daː vaːrən trɛːnən,

Tränen derer die Unrecht litten,
trɛːnən deːrər di |u̯nrɛçt lɪtən,

und hatten keinen Tröster;
unt hatən kaenən trøːstər;

und die ihnen Unrecht täten waren zu mächtig,
unt di |iːnən |u̯nrɛçt tɛːtən vaːrən tsuː mɛktɪç,

dass sie keinen Tröster haben konnten.
das ziː kaenən trøːstər haːbən kɔntən.

Da lobte ich die Toten,
daː loːptə |ɪç di toːtən,

die schon gestorben waren,
di ʃoːn gəʃtɔrbən vaːrən,

mehr als die Lebendigen,
meːr |als di lebɛndɪgən,

die noch das Leben hatten.
di nɔx das leːbən hatən.

Und der noch nicht ist,
unt der nɔx nɪçt |ɪst,

ist besser, als alle beide,
ɪst bɛsər, als |allə baedə,

und des Bösen nicht inne wird,
unt dəs bøːzən nɪçt |ɪnnə vɪrt,

das unter der Sonne geschieht.
das |untər der zɔnnə gəʃiːt.

118

Brahms   Vier Ernste Gesänge
          3.   O Tod, wie bitter bist du
              o: to:t, vi: bɪtər bɪst du:

O Tod, o Tod, wie bitter bist du,
o: to:t, o: to:t, vi: bɪtər bɪst du:,

wenn an dich gedenket ein Mensch,
vɛn |an dɪç gədɛŋkət |aen mɛnʃ,

der gute Tage und genug hat
der gu:tə ta:gə |unt gənu:k hat

und ohne Sorge lebet;
|unt |o:nə zɔrgə le:bət;

und dem es wohlgeht in allen Dingen
unt dem |ɛs vo:lge:t |ɪn |allən dɪŋən

und noch wohl essen mag!
|unt nɔx vo:l |ɛsən ma:k!

O Tod, wie wohl tust du dem Dürftigen,
o: to:t, vi: vo:l tu:st du: dem dyrftɪgən,

der da schwach und alt ist,
der da: ʃvax |unt |alt |ɪst,

der in allen Sorgen steckt,
der |ɪn |allən zɔrgən ʃtɛkt,

und nichts Bessers zu hoffen,
unt nɪçts bɛsərs tsu: hɔfən,

noch zu erwarten hat!
nɔx tsu: |ɛrvartən hat!

O Tod, o Tod, wie wohl tust du.
o: to:t, o: to:t, vi: vo:l tu:st du.

Brahms   Vier Ernste Gesänge
          4.   Wenn ich mit Menschen und mit Engelszungen redete
              vɛn |ɪç mɪt mɛnʃən |unt mɪt |ɛŋəlstsuŋən re:dətə

Wenn ich mit Menschen und mit Engelszungen redete,
vɛn |ɪç mɪt mɛnʃən |unt mɪt |ɛŋəlstsuŋən re:dətə,

und hätte der Liebe nicht,
unt hɛtə   der li:bə nɪçt,

so wär ich ein tönend Erz, oder eine klingende Schelle.
zo: vɛ:r |ɪç |aen tø:nənt |ɛrts, o:dər |aenə klɪŋəndə ʃɛllə.

119

Und wenn ich weissagen könnte, und wüsste
ʊnt vɛn |ɪç vaesaːgən kœntə, ʊnt vʏstə

alle Geheimnisse und alle Erkenntniss,
|alə gəhaemnɪsə |ʊnt |alə |ɛrkɛntnis,

und hätte allen Glauben, also,
ʊnt hɛtə |alən glaobən, |alzo,

dass ich Berge versetzte;
das |ɪç bɛrgə fɛrzɛtstə;

und hätte der Liebe nicht, so wäre ich nichts.
ʊnt hɛtə der liːbə nɪçt, zoː vɛːrə |ɪç nɪçts.

Und wenn ich alle meine Habe den Armen gäbe,
ʊnt vɛn |ɪç |alə maenə haːbə den |armən gɛːbə,

und liesse meinen Leib brennen;
ʊnt liːsə maenən laep brɛnən;

und hätte der Liebe nicht,
ʊnt hɛtə der liːbə nɪçt,

so wäre mir's nichts nütze.
zoː vɛːrə miːrs nɪçts nʏtsə.

Wir sehen jetzt durch einen Spiegel
viːr zeːən jɛtst durç |aenən ʃpiːgəl

in einem dunkeln Worte;
|ɪn |aenəm dʊŋkəln vɔrtə;

dann aber von Angesicht zu Angesichte.
dan |aːbər fɔn |angəzɪçt tsuː |angəzɪçt.

Jetzt erkenne ich's stückweise,
jɛtst |ɛrkɛnə |ɪçs ʃtʏkvaezə,

dann aber werd' ich's erkennen,
dan |aːbər veːrt |ɪçs |ɛrkɛnən,

gleich wie ich erkennet bin.
glaeç viː |ɪç |ɛrkɛnət bɪn.

Nun aber bleibet Glaube, Hoffnung,
nuːn |aːbər blaebət glaobə, hɔfnʊŋ,

Liebe, diese drei;
liːbə, diːzə drae;

aber die Liebe ist die grösseste unter ihnen.
aːbər di liːbə |ɪst di grøːsəstə |ʊntər |iːnən.

Brahms   Von ewiger Liebe
fɔn |eːvɪgər liːbə

Dunkel, wie dunkel im Wald und in Feld.
dʊŋkəl, viː dʊŋkəl |ɪm valt |ʊnt |ɪn fɛlt!

Abend schon ist es, nun schweiget die Welt.
aːbənt ʃoːn |ɪst |ɛs, nuːn ʃvaegət di vɛlt.

Nirgend noch Licht, und nirgend noch Rauch, ja,
nɪrgənt nɔx lɪçt, ʊnt nɪrgənt nɔx raox, jaː,

und die Lerche sie schweiget nun auch.
ʊnt di lɛrçə zi: ʃvaegət nuːn |aox.

Kommt aus dem Dorfe der Bursche heraus,
kɔmt |aos dem dɔrfə der bʊrʃə hɛraos,

gibt das Geleit der Geliebten nach Haus,
giːpt das gəlaet der gəliːptən nax haos,

führt sie an Weidengebüsche vorbei,
fyːrt zi: |an vaedəngəbyʃə fɔrbae,

redet so viel und so mancherlei:
reːdət zo: fiːl |ʊnt zo: mançərlae,

"Leidest du Schmach und betrübest du dich,
laedəst du: ʃmax |ʊnt bətryːbəst du: dɪç,

leidest du Schmach von andern um mich,
laedəst du: ʃmax fɔn |andərn |ʊm mɪç,

werde die Liebe getrennt so geschwind,
veːrdə di liːbə gətrɛnt zo: gəʃvɪnt,

schnell wie wir früher vereiniget sind.
ʃnɛl viː viːr fryːər fɛr|aenɪgət zɪnt.

Scheide mit Regen und scheide mit Wind,
ʃaedə mɪt reːgən |ʊnt ʃaedə mɪt vɪnt,

schnell wie wir früher vereiniget sind."
ʃnɛl viː viːr fryːər fɛr|aenɪgət zɪnt."

Spricht das Mägdelein, Mägdelein spricht:
ʃprɪçt das mɛːkdəlaen, mɛːkdəlaen ʃprɪçt,

"Unsere Liebe, sie trennet sich nicht!
ʊnzərə liːbə, zi: trɛnnət zɪç nɪçt!

Fest ist der Stahl und das Eisen gar sehr,
fɛst |ɪst der ʃtaːl |ʊnt das |aezən gaːr zeːr,

unsere Liebe ist fester noch mehr.
ʊnzərə liːbə |ɪst fɛstər nɔx meːr.

121

Eisen und Stahl, man schmiedet sie um,
aezən |ʊnt ʃtaːl, man ʃmiːdət ziː |ʊm,

unsere Liebe, wer wandelt sie um?
ʊnzərə liːbə, veːr vandəlt ziː |ʊm?

Eisen und Stahl, sie können zergehn,
aezən |ʊnt ʃtaːl, ziː kœnnən tsɛrgeːn,

unsere Liebe muss ewig, ewig bestehn.''
ʊnʃərə liːbə mʊs |eːvɪç, eːvɪç bəʃteːn.''

Brahms   Wie bist du meine Königin
                viː bɪst duː maenə køːnɪgɪn

Wie bist du meine Königin, durch sanfte Güte wonnevoll!
viː bɪst duː maenə køːnɪgɪn, dʊrç zanftə gyːtə vɔnnəfɔl!

Du lächle nur, Lenzdüfte wehn durch mein Gemüte,
duː lɛçlə nuːr, lɛntsdyftə veːn dʊrç maen gəmyːtə,

wonnevoll, wonnevoll!
vɔnnəfɔl, vɔnnəfɔl!

Frisch aufgeblühter Rosen Glanz,
frɪʃ |aofgəblyːtər roːzən glants,

vergleich ich ihn den deinigen?
fɛrglaeç |ɪç |iːn den daenigən?

Ach, über alles, was da blüht,
ax, yːbər |alləs, vas daː blyːt,

ist deine Blüte, wonnevoll!
ɪst daenə blyːtə, vɔnnəfɔl!

Durch tote Wüsten wandle hin,
dʊrç toːtə vyːstən vandlə hɪn,

und grüne Schatten breiten sich,
ʊnt gryːnə ʃatən braetən zɪç,

ob fürchterliche Schwüle dort
ɔp fʏrçtərlɪçə ʃvyːlə dɔrt

ohn' Ende brüte, wonnevoll.
|oːn |ɛndə bryːtə, vɔnnəfɔl.

Lass mich vergehn in deinem Arm!
las mɪç fɛrgeːn |ɪn daenəm |arm!

Es ist in ihm ja selbst der Tod,
ɛs |ɪst |ɪn |iːm jaː zɛlpst der toːt,

ob auch die herbste Todesqual
ɔp |aoҫ diː hɛrpstə toːdəskvaːl

die Brust durchwüte, wonnevoll, wonnevoll!
di brʊst dʊrҫvyːtə, vɔnnəfɔl, vɔnnəfɔl!

Brahms   Wiegenlied
              viːgənliːt

Guten Abend, gut' Nacht,
guːtən |aːbənt, guːt naxt,

mit Rosen bedacht, mit Näg'lein besteckt,
mɪt roːzən bədaxt, mɪt nɛːklaen bəʃtɛkt,

schlupf' unter die Deck'.
ʃlʊpf |ʊntər di dɛk.

Morgen früh, wenn Gott will,
mɔrgən fryː, vɛn gɔt vɪl,

wirst du wieder geweckt.
vɪrst duː viːdər gəvɛkt.

Guten Abend, gut' Nacht,
guːtən |aːbent, guːt naxt,

von Eng'lein bewacht
fɔn |ɛŋlaen bəvaxt,

die zeigen im Traum
di tsaegən |ɪm traom

dir Christkindleins Baum:
diːr krɪstkɪntlaens baom,

Schlaf' nun selig und süss,
ʃlaːf nuːn zeːlɪҫ |ʊnt zyːs,

schau' im Traum's Paradies.
ʃao |ɪm traoms paradiːs.

Brahms   Wie Melodien zieht es mir
              viː melodiːən tsiːt |ɛs miːr

Wie Melodien zieht es mir leise durch den Sinn,
viː melodiːən tsiːt |ɛs miːr laezə durç den zɪn,

wie Frühlingsblumen blüht es, und schwebt wie Duft dahin.
viː fryːlɪŋsbluːmən blyːt |ɛs, ʊnt ʃveːpt viː duft dahɪn.

Doch kommt das Wort und fasst es und führt es vor das Aug',
dɔx kɔmt das vɔrt |ʊnt fast |ɛs |ʊnt fyːrt |ɛs fɔr das aok,

wie Nebelgrau erblasst es und schwindet wie ein Hauch.
viː neːbəlgrao |ɛrblast |ɛs |ʊnt ʃvɪndət viː |aen haox.

Und dennoch ruht im Reime verborgen wohl ein Duft,
ʊnt dɛnnɔx ruːt |ɪm raemə fɛrbɔrgən voːl |aen duft,

den mild aus stillem Keime ein feuchtes Auge ruft.
den mɪlt |aos ʃtɪlləm kaemə |aen fɔøçtəs |aogə ruːft.

Brahms   Wir wandelten, wir zwei zusammen
              viːr vandəltən, viːr tsvae tsuzammən

Wir wandelten, wir zwei zusammen,
viːr vandəltən, viːr tsvae tsuzammən,

ich war so still und du so stille;
ɪç vaːr zoː ʃtɪl |ʊnt du: zoː ʃtɪllə;

ich gäbe viel, um zu erfahren,
ɪç gɛːbə fiːl, ʊm tsu: |ɛrfaːrən,

was du gedacht in jenem Fall.
vas du: gədaxt |ɪn jeːnəm fal.

Was ich gedacht, unausgesprochen verbleibe das!
vas |ɪç gədaxt, ʊn|aosgəʃproxən fɛrblaebə das!

Nur Eines sag' ich, Eines sag' ich:
nuːr |aenəs zaːk |ɪç, aenəs zaːk |ɪç,

So schön war alles, was ich dachte,
zoː ʃøːn vaːr |alləs, vas |ɪç daxtə,

so himmlisch heiter war es all'.
zoː hɪmlɪʃ haetər vaːr |ɛs |al.

In meinem Haupte die Gedanken,
ɪn maenəm haoptə di gədaŋkən,

sie läuteten wie gold'ne Glöckchen;
ziː lɔøtətən viː gɔldnə glœkçən;

so wundersüss, so wunderlieblich
zoː vʊndərzyːs, zoː vʊndərliːplɪç

ist in der Welt kein and'rer Hall.
|ɪst |ɪn der vɛlt kaen |andrər hal.

Handel   Dank sei Dir, Herr
          daŋk zae diːr, hɛr

Dank sei Dir, Herr,
daŋk zae diːr, hɛr,

Du hast Dein Volk mit Dir geführt,
duː hast daen fɔlk mɪt diːr gəfyːrt,

Israel hin durch das Meer.
iːzrael hɪn dʊrç das meːr.

Wie eine Heerde zog es hindurch,
viː |aenə heːrdə tsoːk |ɛs hɪndʊrç,

Herr, Deine Hand schützte es
hɛr, daenə hant ʃʏtstə |ɛs

in Deiner Güte gabst Du ihm Heil.
ɪn daenər gyːtə gaːpst duː |iːm hael.

Dank sei Dir Herr.
daŋk zae diːr hɛr.

Liszt   Es muss ein Wunderbares sein
         ɛs mʊs |aen vʊndərbaːrəs zaen

Es muss ein Wunderbares sein
ɛs mʊs |aen vʊndərbaːrəs zaen

ums Lieben zweier Seelen,
|ums liːbən tsvaeər zeːlən,

sich schliessen ganz einander ein,
zɪç ʃliːsən gants |aen|andər |aen,

125

sich nie ein Wort verhehlen,
zɪç niː |a͜en vɔrt fɛrheːlən,

und Freud und Leid und Glück und Noth
ʊnt frɔøt |ʊnt la͜et |ʊnt glʏk |ʊnt noːt

so mit einander tragen;
zoː mɪt |a͜en|andər traːgən,

vom ersten Kuss bis in den Tod
fɔm |eːrstən kʊs bɪs |ɪn den toːt

sich nur von Liebe sagen.
zɪç nuːr fɔn liːbə zaːgən.

Mahler   Blicke mir nicht in die Lieder
            blɪkə miːr nɪçt |ɪn di liːdər

Blicke mir nicht in die Lieder!
blɪkə miːr nɪçt |ɪn di liːdər!

Meine Augen schlag' ich nieder,
ma͜enə |a͜ogən ʃlaːk |ɪç niːdər,

wie ertappt auf böser Tat.
viː |ɛrtapt |a͜of bøːzər taːt.

Selber darf ich nicht getrauen,
zɛlbər darf |ɪç nɪçt gətra͜oən,

ihrem Wachsen zuzuschauen.
iːrəm vaksən tsuːtsuʃa͜oən.

Blicke mir nicht in die Lieder!
blɪkə miːr nɪçt |ɪn di liːdər!

Deine Neugier ist Verrat, ist Verrat!
da͜enə nɔøgiːr |ɪst fɛrraːt, ɪst fɛrraːt!

Bienen, wenn sie Zellen bauen,
biːnən, vɛn ziː tsɛllən ba͜oən,

lassen auch nicht zu sich schauen,
lasən |a͜ox nɪçt‿tsuː zɪç ʃa͜oən,

schauen selbst auch nicht zu.
ʃa͜oən zɛlpst |a͜ox nɪçt‿tsuː.

Wenn die reichen Honigwaben
vɛn di ra͜eçən hoːnɪçvaːbən

sie zu Tag gefördert haben,
zi: tsu: ta:k gəfœrdərt ha:bən,

dann vor allen nasche du.
dan fɔr |allən naʃə du:.

Mahler   Der Tamboursg'sell
              der tambu:rsgzɛl

Ich armer Tamboursg'sell!
ıç |armər tambu:rsgzɛl!

Man führt mich aus dem G'wölb,
man fy:rt mıç |aos dem gvœlp,

Wär' ich ein Tambour blieben,
vɛ:r |ıç |aen tambu:r bli:bən,

dürft' ich nicht gefangen liegen!
dyrft |ıç nıçt gəfaŋən li:gən!

O Galgen, du hohes Haus, du siehst so furchtbar aus!
o: galgən, du: ho:əs haos, du: zi:st zo: furçtba:r |aos!

Ich schau' dich nicht mehr an!
ıç ʃao dıç nıçt me:r |an!

weil i weiss, dass i g'hör d'ran!
vael |i: vaes, das |i: ghø:r dran!

Wenn Soldaten vorbeimarschier'n,
vɛn zɔldatən fɔrbaemarʃi:rn,

bei mir nit einquartier'n,
bae mi:r nıt |aenkvarti:rn,

wenn sie fragen, wer i g'wesen bin:
vɛn zi: fra:gən, ve:r |i: gve:zən bın,

Tambour von der Leibkompanie!
tambu:r fɔn der laepkɔmpani:.

Gute Nacht, ihr Marmelstein',
gu:tə naxt, i:r marməlʃtaen,

ihr Berg' und Hügelein!
i:r bɛrk |unt hy:gəlaen!

Gute Nacht, ihr Offizier, Korporal und Musketier!
gu:tə naxt, i:r |ɔfitsi:r, kɔrpora:l |unt muskəti:r!

Ich schrei' mit heller Stimm':
ɪç ʃrae mɪt hɛllər ʃtɪm,

von Euch ich Urlaub nimm! Gute Nacht!
fon |ɔøç |ɪç |uːrlaop nɪm! guːtə naxt!

Mahler   Ich atmet' einen linden Duft
              ɪç |atmət |aenən lɪndən duft

Ich atmet' einen linden Duft.
ɪç |atmət |aenən lɪndən duft.

Im Zimmer stand ein Zweig der Linde,
ɪm tsɪmmər ʃtant |aen tsvaek der lɪndə,

ein Angebinde von lieber Hand.
aen |angəbɪndə fon liːbər hant.

Wie lieblich war der Lindenduft.
viː liːplɪç vaːr der lɪndənduft.

Wie lieblich ist der Lindenduft.
viː liːplɪç |ɪst der lɪndənduft.

das Lindenreis brachst du gelinde!
das lɪndənraes braːxst duː gəlɪndə!

Ich atme leis im Duft der Linde,
ɪç |atmə laes |ɪm duft der lɪndə,

der Liebe linden Duft.
der liːbə lɪndən duft.

Mahler   Ich bin der Welt abhanden gekommen
              ɪç bɪn der vɛlt |aphandən gəkɔmmən

Ich bin der Welt abhanden gekommen,
ɪç bɪn der vɛlt |aphandən gəkɔmmən,

mit der ich sonst viele Zeit verdorben;
mɪt der |ɪç zɔnst fiːlə tsaet fɛrdɔrbən;

sie hat so lange nichts von mir vernommen
ziː hat zoː laŋə nɪçts fon miːr fɛrnɔmmən

128

sie mag wohl glauben, ich sei gestorben!
zi: ma:k vo:l glaobən, ıç zae gəʃtɔrbən!

Es ist mir auch gar nichts daran gelegen,
ɛs |ɪst mi:r |aox ga:r nıçts daran gəle:gən,

ob sie mich für gestorben hält.
ɔp zi: mıç fy:r gəʃtɔrbən hɛ:lt.

Ich kann auch gar nichts sagen dagegen,
ıç kan |aox ga:r nıçts za:gən dage:gən,

denn wirklich bin ich gestorben der Welt.
dɛn vırklıç bın |ıç gəʃtɔrbən der vɛlt.

Ich bin gestorben dem Weltgetümmel
ıç bın gəʃtɔrbən dem vɛltgətʏmməl.

und ruh' in einem stillen Gebiet.
|ʊnt ru: |ın |aenəm ʃtıllən gəbi:t.

Ich leb' allein in meinem Himmel,
ıç le:p |allaen |ın maenem hımməl,

in meinem Lieben, in meinem Lied.
ın maenəm li:bən, ın maenəm li:t.

Mahler   Liebst du um Schönheit
              li:pst du: |ʊm ʃø:nhaet

Liebst du um Schönheit, o nicht mich liebe!
li:pst du: |ʊm ʃø:nhaet, o: nıçt mıç li:bə!

Liebe die Sonne, sie trägt ein goldnes Haar!
li:bə di zɔnnə, zi: trɛ:kt |aen gɔldnəs ha:r!

Liebst du um Jugend, o nicht mich liebe!
li:pst du ʊm ju:gənt, o: nıçt mıç li:bə!

Liebe den Frühling, der jung ist jedes Jahr!
li:bə den fry:lıŋ, der jʊŋ |ıst je:dəs ja:r!

Liebst du um Schätze, o nicht mich liebe!
li:pst du |ʊm ʃɛtsə, o: nıçt mıç li:bə!

Liebe die Meerfrau, sie hat viel Perlen klar!
li:bə di me:rfrao, zi: hat fi:l pɛrlən kla:r!

Liebst du um Liebe, o ja, mich liebe!
li:pst du: |ʊm li:bə, o: ja:, mıç li:bə!

Liebe mich immer, dich lieb' ich immer, immerdar!
liːbə mɪç |ɪmmər, dɪç liːp |ɪç |ɪmmər, ɪmmərdaːr!

Mahler   Um Mitternacht
             um mɪtərnaxt

Um Mitternacht hab' ich gewacht
um mɪtərnaxt haːp |ɪç gəvaxt

und aufgeblickt zum Himmel;
|unt |aofgəblɪkt tsum hɪmməl;

kein Stern vom Sterngewimmel
kaen ʃtɛrn fom ʃtɛrngəvɪmməl

hat mir gelacht um Mitternacht.
hat miːr gəlaxt |um mɪtərnaxt.

Um Mitternacht hab' ich gedacht
um mɪtərnaxt haːp |ɪç gədaxt

hinaus in dunkle Schranken.
hinaos |ɪn duŋklə ʃraŋkən.

Es hat kein Lichtgedanken
ɛs hat kaen lɪçtgədaŋkən

mir Trost gebracht um Mitternacht.
miːr troːst gəbraxt |um mɪtərnaxt.

Um Mitternacht nahm ich in acht
um mɪtərnaxt naːm |ɪç |ɪn |axt

die Schläge meines Herzens;
di ʃlɛːgə maenəs hɛrtsəns;

ein einz'ger Puls des Schmerzens
aen |aentsgər puls dɛs ʃmɛrtsəns

war angefacht um Mitternacht.
vaːr |angəfaxt |um mɪtərnaxt.

Um Mitternacht kämpft' ich die Schlacht,
um mɪtərnaxt kɛmpft |ɪç di ʃlaxt,

O Menschheit, deiner Leiden;
oː mɛnʃhaet, daenər laedən;

nicht konnt' ich sie entscheiden
nɪçt kont |ɪç ziː |əntʃaedən

mit meiner Macht um Mitternacht.
mɪt maenər maxt |ʊm mɪtərnaxt.

Um Mitternacht hab' ich die Macht
ʊm mɪtərnaxt haːp |ɪç di maxt

in Deine Hand gegeben; Herr! Herr über Tod und Leben,
|ɪn daenə hant gəgeːbən; hɛr! hɛr |yːbər toːt |ʊnt leːbən,

Du hälst die Wacht, um Mitternacht!
duː hɛlst‿di vaxt, ʊm mɪtərnaxt!

Mozart   Abendempfindung
             aːbənt|ɛmpfɪndʊŋ

Abend ist's, die Sonne ist verschwunden,
aːbənt |ɪsts, di zɔnnə |ɪst fɛrʃvʊndən,

und der Mond strahlt Silberglanz;
ʊnt‿der moːnt ʃtraːlt zɪlbərglants;

so entflieh'n des Lebens schönste Stunden,
zoː |ɛntfliːn dɛs leːbəns ʃøːnstə stʊndən,

flieh'n vorüber wie im Tanz.
fliːn foryːbər viː |ɪm tants.

Bald entflieht des Lebens bunte Szene,
balt |ɛntfliːt dɛs leːbəns bʊntə stseːnə,

und der Vorhang rollt herab; aus ist unser Spiel,
ʊnt‿der foːrhaŋ rɔlt hɛrap; aos |ɪst |ʊnzər ʃpiːl,

des Freundes Träne fliesset schon auf unser Grab.
dɛs frɔendəs trɛːnə fliːsət ʃoːn |aof |ʊnzər graːp.

Bald vielleicht mir weht,
balt fɪllaeçt miːr veːt,

wie Westwind leise, eine stille Ahnung zu,
viː vɛstvɪnt laezə, aenə stɪllə |aːnʊŋ tsuː,

schliess ich dieses Lebens Pilgerreise, fliege in das Land der Ruh!
ʃliːs |ɪç diːzəs leːbəns pɪlgərraezə, fliːgə |ɪn das lant der ruː.

Werd't ihr dann an meinem Grabe weinen,
veːrt |iːr dan |an maenəm graːbə vaenən,

trauernd meine Asche sehn,
traoərnt maenə |aʃə zeːn,

dann, O Freunde, will ich euch erscheinen
dan, o: frøendə, vɪl |ɪç |ɔøç |ɛrʃaenən

und will Himmel auf euch wehn.
|ʊnt vɪl hɪmməl aof |ɔøç ve:n.

Schenk' auch du ein Tränchen mir
ʃɛŋk |aox du |aen trɛ:nçən mi:r

und pfücke mir ein Veilchen auf mein Grab,
ʊnt pflykə mi:r |aen faelçən |aof maen gra|p,

und mit deinem seelenvollen Blicke
ʊnt mɪt daenəm ze:lənfɔllən blɪkə

sieh' dann sanft auf mich herab.
zi: dan zanft |aof mɪç herap.

Weih' mir eine Träne, und ach!
vae mi:r |aenə trɛ:nə, ʊnt ax!

schäme dich nur nicht, sie mir zu weih'n,
ʃɛ:mə dɪç nu:r nɪçt, zi: mi:r tsu vaen,

O sie wird in meinem Diademe
o: zi: vɪrt |ɪn maenəm diade:mə

dann die schönste Perle sein.
dan di ʃø:nstə pɛrlə zaen.

Mozart   Ach, ich fühl's, from "Die Zauberflöte"
              ax, ɪç fy:ls   di tsaobərflø:tə

Ach, ich fühl's, es ist verschwunden,
ax, ɪç fy:ls, ɛs |ɪst fɛrʃvʊndən,

ewig hin der Liebe Glück!
e:vɪç hɪn der li:bə glʏk!

Nimmer kommt ihr, Wonnestunden,
nɪmmər kɔmt |i:r, vɔnnəʃtʊndən,

meinem Herzen mehr zurück.
maenəm hɛrtsən me:r tsurʏk.

Sieh', Tamino, diese Tränen fliessen,
zi:, tamino, di:zə trɛ:nən fli:sən,

Trauter, dir allein.
traotər, di:r |allaen.

132

Fühlst du nicht der Liebe Sehnen,
fyːlst du nɪçt der liːbə zeːnən,

so wird Ruh' im Tode sein.
zoː vɪrt ruː |ɪm toːdə zaen.

Mozart   Als Luise die Briefe
             als luiːzə di briːfə

Erzeugt von heisser Phantasie,
ɛrtsɔøkt fon haesər fantaziː,

in einer schwärmerischen Stunde zur Welt gebrachte,
ɪn |aenər ʃvɛrmərɪʃən   ʃtʊndə tsuːr vɛlt gəbraxtə,

geht zu Grunde, ihr Kinder der Melancholie!
geːt tsuː grʊndə, iːr kɪndər der melaŋkoliː!

Ihr danket Flammen euer Sein,
iːr daŋkət flammən |ɔøer zaen,

ich geb euch nun den Flammen wieder,
ɪç geːp |ɔøç nuːn den flammən viːdər,

und all' die schwärmerischen Lieder, denn ach!
ʊnt |al di ʃvɛrmərɪʃən   liːdər, dɛn |ax!

er sang nicht mir allein.
eːr zaŋ nɪçt miːr |allaen.

Ihr brennet nun, und bald, ihr Lieben,
iːr brɛnnət nuːn, ʊnt balt, iːr liːbən,

ist keine Spur von euch mehr hier.
ɪst kaenə ʃpuːr fon |ɔøç meːr hiːr.

Doch ach! der Mann, der euch geschrieben,
dɔx |ax! der man, der |ɔøç gəʃriːbən,

brennt lange noch vielleicht in mir.
brɛnt laŋə nɔx fillaeçt |ɪn miːr.

Mozart   An Chloe
             an kloːe

Wenn die Lieb' aus deinen blauen,
vɛn di liːp |a͜os da͜enən bla͜oən,

hellen, offnen Augen sieht,
hɛllən, ofnən |a͜ogən ziːt,

und vor Lust hinein zu schauen
unt fɔr lʊst hɪna͜en tsu ʃa͜oən

mir's im Herzen klopft und glüht;
miːrs |ɪm hɛrtsən klɔpft |unt glyːt;

und ich halte dich und küsse deine Rosenwangen warm,
unt |ɪç haltə dɪç |unt kysə da͜enə roːzənvaŋən varm,

liebes Mädchen,
liːbəs mɛːtçən,

und ich schliesse zitternd dich in meinen Arm!
unt |ɪç ʃliːsə tsɪtərnt dɪç |ɪn ma͜enən |aːrm!

Mädchen, und ich drücke dich an meinen Busen fest,
mɛːtçən, unt |ɪç drykə dɪç |an ma͜enən buːzən fɛst,

der im letzten Augenblicke sterbend,
der |ɪm lɛtstən |a͜ogənblɪkə ʃtɛrbənt,

sterbend nur dich von sich lässt;
ʃtɛrbənt nuːr dɪç fɔn zɪç lɛst;

den berauschten Blick umschattet eine düstre Wolke mir,
den bəra͜oʃtən blɪk |umʃatət |a͜enə dyːstrə vɔlkə miːr,

und ich sitze dann ermattet, ermattet,
unt |ɪç zɪtsə dan |ermatət, ermatət,

aber selig neben dir.
aːbər zeːlɪç neːbən diːr.

Mozart   Das Veilchen
             das fa͜elçən

Ein Veilchen auf der Wiese stand,
a͜en fa͜elçən |a͜of der viːzə ʃtant,

gebückt in sich und unbekannt:
gəbykt |ɪn zɪç |unt |unbəkant,

es war ein herzig's Veilchen.
ɛs vaːr |a͜en hɛrtsɪçs fa͜elçən.

Da kam ein' junge Schäferin mit leichtem Schritt
daː kaːm |ae̯n jʊ̯ŋə ʃɛːfərɪn mɪt lae̯çtəm ʃrɪt

und munterm Sinn daher,
|ʊnt mʊ̯ntərm zɪn dahe̯ːr,

daher, die Wiese her und sang.
dahe̯ːr, di vi̯ːzə heːr |ʊnt zaŋ.

Ach! denkt das Veilchen,
ax! dɛŋkt das fa̯e̯lçən,

wär' ich nur die schönste Blume der Natur,
vɛːr |ɪç nuːr di ʃøːnstə blu̯ːmə der natu̯ːr,

ach, nur ein kleines Weilchen,
ax, nuːr |ae̯n kla̯e̯nəs va̯e̯lçən,

bis mich das Liebchen abgepflückt
bɪs mɪç das li̯ːpçən |a̯pgəpflʏkt

und an dem Busen matt gedrückt,
|ʊnt |an dem bu̯ːzən mat gədrʏkt,

ach nur ein Viertelstündchen lang.
ax nuːr |ae̯n fi̯ːrtəlʃtʏntçən laŋ.

Ach, aber ach! das Mädchen kam
ax, a̯ːbər |ax! das mɛ̯ːtçən kaːm

und nicht in Acht das Veilchen nahm,
|ʊnt nɪçt |ɪn |axt das fa̯e̯lçən naːm,

ertrat das arme Veilchen.
ɛrtra̯ːt das |a̯rmə fa̯e̯lçən.

Es sank und starb und freut' sich noch:
ɛs zaŋk |ʊnt ʃtarp |ʊnt fro̯ø̯t zɪç nɔx,

und sterb' ich denn, so sterb' ich doch durch sie,
ʊnt ʃtɛrp |ɪç dɛn, zoː ʃtɛrp |ɪç dɔx dʊrç ziː,

zu ihren Füssen doch.
tsuː |i̯ːrən fy̯ːsən dɔx.

Das arme Veilchen! es war ein herzig's Veilchen.
das |a̯rmə fa̯e̯lçən! ɛs vaːr |ae̯n hɛrtsɪçs fa̯e̯lçən.

Mozart   Der Hölle Rache kocht in meinem Herzen, from "Die Zauberflöt
           der hœllə raxə kɔxt |ɪn maenem hɛrtsən   di tsaobərflø:t

Der Hölle Rache kocht in meinem Herzen,
der hœllə raxə kɔxt |ɪn maenəm hɛrtsən,

Tod und Verzweiflung flammet um mich her!
to:t |ʊnt fɛrtsvaefluŋ flammət |ʊm mɪç he:r!

Fühlt nicht durch dich Sarastro Todesschmerzen,
fy:lt nɪçt durç dɪç sarastro to:dəsʃmɛrtsən,

so bist du meine Tochter nimmermehr.
zo: bɪst du: maenə tɔxtər nɪmmərme:r.

Verstossen sei auf ewig, verlassen sei auf ewig,
fɛrʃto:sən zae |aof |e:vɪç, vɛrlasən zae |aof |e:vɪç,

zertrümmert sein auf ewig alle Bande der Natur,
tsɛrtrʊmmərt zaen |aof |e:vɪç |allə bandə der natu:r,

wenn nicht durch dich Sarastro wird erblassen!
vɛn nɪçt durç dɪç sarastro vɪrt |ɛrblasən!

Hört Rachegötter!   hört der Mutter Schwur!
hø:rt raxəgœtər!   hø:rt der mutər ʃvu:r!

Mozart   Dies Bildnis ist bezaubernd schön, from "Die Zauberflöte"
           di:s bɪltnɪs |ɪst bətsaobərnt ʃø:n   di tsaobərflø:te

Dies Bildnis ist bezaubernd schön,
di:s bɪltnɪs |ɪst bətsaobərnt ʃø:n,

wie noch kein Auge je geseh'n!
vi: nɔx kaen |aogə je: gəze:n!

Ich fühl' es, wie dies Götterbild
ɪç fy:l |ɛs, vi: di:s gœtərbɪlt

mein Herz mit neuer Regung füllt.
maen hɛrts mit nøər re:guŋ fy:lt.

Dies Etwas kann ich zwar nicht nennen,
di:s |ɛtvas kan |ɪç tsva:r nɪçt nɛnnən,

doch fühl' ich's hier wie Feuer brennen.
dɔx fy:l |ɪçs hi:r vi: føər brɛnnən.

Soll die Empfindung Liebe sein?
zɔl di |ɛmpfɪnduŋ li:bə zaen?

Ja, ja, die Liebe ist's allein.
ja:, ja:, di li:bə |ɪsts |allaen.

O, wenn ich sie nur finden könnte!
oː, vɛn |ɪç ziː nuːr fɪndən kœnte!

O, wenn sie doch schon vor mir stände!
oː, vɛn ziː dox ʃoːn for miːr ʃtɛndə!

Ich würde, warm und rein, was würde ich? Ich würde sie voll Entzücken
ɪç vʏrdə, varm |unt raen, vas vʏrdə |ɪç? ɪç vʏrdə ziː fol ɛnttsʏkən

an diesen heissen Busen drücken, und ewig wäre sie dann mein!
|an diːzən haesən buːzən drʏkən, unt |eːvɪç vɛːrə ziː dan maen!

Mozart   In diesen heil'gen Hallen, from "Die Zauberflöte"
             ɪn diːzən haelgən hallən   di tsaobərfløːte

In diesen heil'gen Hallen kennt man die Rache nicht,
ɪn diːzən haelgən hallən kɛnt man di raxə nɪçt,

und ist der Mensch gefallen, führt Liebe ihn zur Pflicht.
unt |ɪst der mɛnʃ gəfallən, fyːrt liːbə |iːn tsur pflɪçt.

Dann wandelt er an Freundes Hand
dan vandəlt |eːr |an frɔøndəs hant

vergnügt und froh in's bess're Land!
fɛrgnyːkt |unt froː |ɪns bɛsrə lant.

In diesen heil'gen Mauern, wo Mensch den Menschen liebt,
ɪn diːzən haelgən maoərn, voː mɛnʃ den mɛnʃən liːpt.

kann kein Verräther lauern, weil man dem Feind vergiebt.
kan kaen fɛrrɛːtər laoərn, vael man dem faent fɛrgiːpt.

Wen solche Lehren nicht erfreu'n,
veːn zolçə leːrən nɪçt |ɛrfrɔøn,

verdienet nicht ein Mensch zu sein.
fɛrdiːnət nɪçt |aen mɛnʃ tsuː zaen.

Mozart   O Isis und Osiris, from "Die Zauberflöte"
             oː |iːzɪs |unt |oziːrɪs di tsaobərfløːte

O Isis und Osiris, schenket der
oː |iːzɪs |unt |oziːrɪs, ʃɛŋkət

Weisheit Geist dem neuen Paar!
der vaeshaet gaest dem nɔøən paːr!

137

Die ihr der Wandrer Schritte lenket,
di |i:r der vandrər ʃrɪtə lɛŋkət,

stärkt mit Geduld sie in Gefahr.
ʃtɛrkt mɪt gədu̯lt zi: |ɪn gəfa:r.

Lasst sie der Prüfung Früchte sehen;
last zi: der pry:fuŋ fryçtə ze:ən;

doch sollten sie zu Grabe gehen,
dɔx zɔltən zi: tsu: gra:bə ge:ən,

so lohnt der Tugend kühnen Lauf,
zo: lo:nt der tu̯:gənt ky:nən la̯of,

nehmt sie in euren Wohnsitz auf.
ne:mt zi: |ɪn |ɔørən vo:nzɪts |a̯of.

Mozart   Warnung
          varnuŋ

Männer suchen stets zu naschen,
mɛnnər zu̯xən ʃte:ts tsu̯: na̯ʃən,

lässt man sie allein,
lɛst man zi: |alla̯en,

leicht sind Mädchen zu erhaschen,
la̯eçt zɪnt mɛ:tçən tsu: ɛrha̯ʃən,

weiss man sie zu überraschen.
va̯es man zi: tsu: |y:bərra̯ʃən.

Soll das zu verwundern sein?
zɔl das tsu: fɛrvu̯ndərn za̯en?

Mädchen haben frisches Blut,
mɛ:tçən ha:bən frɪ̯ʃəs blu:t,

und das Naschen schmeckt so gut.
u̯nt das na̯ʃən ʃmɛkt zo: gu̯:t.

Doch das Naschen vor dem Essen
dɔx das na̯ʃən fɔr dem |ɛsən

nimmt den Appetit.
nɪmt den̯ |appəti̯:t.

Manche kam, die das vergessen,
ma̯nçə ka:m, di das fɛrgɛsən,

um den Schatz, den sie besessen,
um den ʃats,   den ziː bəzɛ̯sən,

und um ihren Liebsten mit.
ʊnt |ʊm |iːrən liːpstən mɪt.

Väter, lasst euch's Warnung sein,
fɛːtər, last |ɔøçs varnʊŋ zaen,

sperrt die Zuckerplätzchen ein!
ʃpɛrt di̯ tsu̯kərplɛtsçən |aen!

sperrt die jungen Mädchen ein!
ʃpɛrt di̯ ju̯ŋən mɛːtçən |aen!

Reger   Maria Wiegenlied
             mari̯a viːgənliːt

Maria sitzt am Rosenhag und wiegt ihr Jesuskind,
mari̯a zɪtst |am roːzənhaːk |ʊnt viːkt |iːr jeːsuskɪnt,

durch die Blätter leise weht der warme Sommerwind.
dʊrç di blɛtər lae̯zə veːt der varmə zɔmmərvɪnt.

Zu ihren Füssen singt ein buntes Vögelein:
tsuː |iːrən fyːsən zɪŋt |aen bu̯ntəs føːgəlaen,

Schlaf', Kindlein, süsses, schlaf' nun ein!
ʃlaːf, kɪntlaen, zyːsəs, ʃlaːf nuːn |aen!

Hold ist dein Lächeln, holder deines Schlummers Lust,
hɔlt |ɪst dae̯n lɛçəln, hɔldər daenəs ʃlu̯mmərs lʊst,

leg dein müdes Köpfchen fest an deiner Mutter Brust!
leːk daen myːdəs kœpfçən fɛst |an daenər mu̯tər brʊst!

Schlaf', Kindlein, süsses, schlaf' nun ein.
ʃlaːf, kɪntlaen, zyːsəs, ʃlaːf nuːn |aen.

Schubert   Am Grabe Anselmo's
             am graːbə |anzɛlmos

Dass ich dich verloren habe, dass du nicht mehr bist,
das |ɪç dɪç fɛrloːrən ha̯ːbə, das duː nɪçt meːr bɪst,

139

ach, dass hier in diesem Grabe
ax, das hiːr |ɪn diːzəm graːbə

mein Anselmo ist, das ist mein Schmerz!
maen |anzɛlmo |ɪst, das |ɪst maen ʃmɛrts!

Seht, wie liebten wir uns beide,
zeːt, viː liːptən viːr |uns baedə,

und, so lang' ich bin,
unt, zoː laŋ |ɪç bɪn,

kommt Freude niemals wieder in mein Herz.
komt frɔødə niːmals viːdər |ɪn maen hɛrts.

Schubert   Am Meer
              am meːr

Das Meer erglänzte weit hinaus
das meːr |ɛrglɛntstə vaet hɪnaos

im letzten Abendscheine;
|ɪm lɛtstən |aːbəntʃaenə;

wir sassen am einsamen Fischerhaus,
viːr zasən |am |aenzaːmən fɪʃərhaos,

wir sassen stumm und alleine.
viːr zasən ʃtʊm |unt |allaenə.

Der Nebel stieg, das Wasser schwoll,
der neːbəl ʃtiːk, das vasər ʃvɔl,

die Möve flog hin und wieder;
di møːvə floːk hɪn |unt viːdər;

aus deinen Augen liebevoll
aos daenən |aogən liːbəfɔl

fielen die Thränen nieder.
fiːlən di trɛːnən niːdər.

Ich sah sie fallen auf deine Hand
ɪç zaː ziː falən |aof daenə hant

und bin aufs Knie gesunken;
unt bɪn |aofs kniː gəzʊŋkən;

ich hab von deiner weissen Hand
ɪç haːp fon daenər vaesən hant

140

die Thränen fortgetrunken.
di trɛːnən fɔrtgətruŋkən.

Seit jener Stunde
zaet jeːnər ʃtʊndə

verzehrt sich mein Leib,
fɛrtseːrt zɪç maen laep,

die Seele stirbt vor Sehnen;
di zeːlə ʃtɪrpt fɔr zeːnən;

mich hat das unglücksel'ge Weib
mɪç hat das |ʊnglʏkzeːlgə vaep

vergiftet mit ihren Thränen.
fɛrgɪftət mɪt |iːrən trɛːnən.

Schubert   An die Leier
             an di laeər

Ich will von Atreus' Söhnen,
ɪç vɪl fɔn |aːtrøøs zøːnən,

von Kadmus will ich singen!
fɔn katmʊs vɪl |ɪç zɪŋən!

Doch meine Saiten tönen nur Liebe im Erklingen.
dɔx maenə zaetən tøːnən nuːr liːbə |ɪm |ɛrklɪŋən.

Ich tauschte um die Saiten,
ɪç taoʃtə |ʊm di zaetən,

die Leier möcht ich tauschen!
di laeər mœçt |ɪç taoʃən!

Alcidens Siegesschreiten
altʃiːdəns ziːgəsʃraetən

sollt' ihrer Macht entrauschen!
zɔlt |iːrər maxt |ɛntraoʃən!

Doch auch die Saiten tönen nur Liebe im Erklingen.
dɔx |aox di zaetən tøːnən nuːr liːbə |ɪm |ɛrklɪŋən.

So lebt denn wohl,
zoː leːpt dɛn voːl,

Heroen!   denn meine Saiten tönen,
heroːən! dɛn maenə zaetən tøːnən,

141

statt Heldensang zu drohen, nur Liebe im Erklingen.
ʃtat hɛldənzaŋ tsuː droːən, nuːr liːbə |ɪm |ɛrkliŋən.

Schubert   An die Musik
               an di muziːk

Du holde Kunst, in wie viel grauen Stunden,
duː hɔldə kʊnst, ɪn viː fiːl graʊən ʃtʊndən,

wo mich des Lebens wilder Kreis umstrickt,
voː mɪç dɛs leːbəns vɪldər kraes |umʃtrɪkt,

hast du mein Herz zu warmer Lieb entzunden,
hast duː maen hɛrts tsuː varmər liːp |ɛntsʊndən,

hast mich in eine bessre Welt entrückt!
hast mɪç |ɪn |aenə bɛsrə vɛlt |ɛntrʏkt!

Oft hat ein Seufzer, deiner Harf entflossen,
ɔft hat |aen zɔøftsər, daenər harf |ɛntflɔsən,

ein süsser, heiliger Akkord von dir
aen zyːsər, haelɪgər |akɔrt fɔn diːr

den Himmel bessrer Zeiten mir erschlossen,
den hɪmməl bɛsrər tsaetən miːr |ɛrʃlɔsən,

du holde Kunst, ich danke dir dafür.
duː hɔldə kʊnst, ɪç daŋkə diːr dafyːr.

Schubert   An Silvia
               an sɪːlvja

Was ist Silvia, saget an,
vas |ɪst sɪːlvja zaːgət |an,

dass sie die weite Flur preist?
das ziː di vaetə fluːr praest?

Schön und zart seh ich sie nahn,
ʃøːn |unt tsaːrt zeː |ɪç ziː naːn,

auf Himmels Gunst und Spur weist,
aof hɪmməls gunst |unt ʃpuːr vaest,

142

dass ihr alles untertan.
das |iːr |a̰lləs |ṵntərtaːn.

Ist sie schön und gut dazu?
ɪst ziː ʃøːn |ʊnt guːt datsṵː?

Reiz labt wie milde Kindheit;
ra̰ets la̰ːpt viː mɪldə kɪnthaet;

ihrem Aug eilt Amor zu,
ḭːrəm |a̰ok |aelt |a̰ːmɔr tsuː,

dort heilt er seine Blindheit,
dɔrt ha̰elt |eːr zaenə blɪnthaet,

und verweilt in süsser Ruh.
ʊnt fɛrva̰elt |ɪn zṵːsər ruː.

Darum Silvia tön, o Sang,
darṵm sɪːlvja tøːn, oː zaŋ,

der holden Silvia Ehren;
der ho̰ldən sɪːlvja |ḛːrən;

jeden Reiz besiegt sie lang,
jḛːdən ra̰ets bəzḭːkt ziː laŋ,

den Erde kann gewähren:
den |ḛːrdə kan gəvɛ̰ːrən,

Kränze ihr und Saitenklang!
krɛ̰ntsə |iːr |ʊnt za̰etənklaŋ!

Schubert   Auf dem Wasser zu singen
              a̰of dem va̰sər tsuː zɪ̰ŋən

Mitten im Schimmer der spiegelnden Wellen
mɪtən |ɪm ʃɪ̰mmər der ʃpḭːgəlndən vɛllən

gleitet, wie Schwäne, der wankende Kahn;
gla̰etət, viː ʃvɛ̰ːnə, der va̰ŋkəndə kaːn,

ach, auf der Freude sanft schimmernden Wellen
ax, a̰of der frøːdə zanft ʃɪmmərndən vɛllən

gleitet die Seele dahin wie der Kahn;
gla̰etət‿di zeːlə dahɪ̰n viː der kaːn,

denn von dem Himmel herab auf die Wellen
dɛn fɔn dem hɪ̰mməl hɛra̰p |a̰of di vɛllən

143

tanzet das Abendroth rund um den Kahn.
tantsət das |aːbəntroːt rʊnt |ʊm den kaːn.

Über den Wipfeln des westlichen Haines
yːbər den vɪpfəln dɛs vɛstlɪçən haenəs

winket uns freundlich der rötliche Schein,
vɪŋkət |ʊns frɔøntlɪç der røːtlɪçə ʃaen,

unter den Zweigen des östlichen Haines
ʊntər den tsvaegən dɛs |œstlɪçən haenəs

säuselt der Kalmus im rötlichen Schein;
zɔøzəlt der kalmʊs |ɪm røːtlɪçən ʃaen;

Freude des Himmels und Ruhe des Haines
frɔødə dɛs hɪmməls |ʊnt ruːə dɛs haenəs

atmet die Seel im errötenden Schein.
aːtmət di zeːl |ɪm |ɛrrøːtəndən ʃaen.

Ach, es entschwindet mit tauigem Flügel
ax, ɛs |ɛntʃvɪndət mɪt taoɪgəm flyːgəl

mir auf den wiegenden Wellen die Zeit.
miːr |aof den viːgəndən vɛllən di tsaɪt.

Morgen entschwinde mit schimmerndem Flügel
mɔrgən |ɛntʃvɪndə mɪt ʃɪmmərndəm flyːgəl

wieder wie gestern und heute die Zeit,
viːdər viː gɛstərn |ʊnt hɔøtə di tsaet,

bis ich auf höherem strahlenden Flügel
bɪs |ɪç |aof høːərəm ʃtraːləndən flyːgəl

selber entschwinde der wechselnden Zeit.
zɛlbər |ɛntʃvɪndə der vɛksəlndən tsaet.

Schubert   Aufenthalt
            aofəntalt

Rauschender Strom, brausender Wald,
raoʃəndər ʃtroːm, braozəndər valt,

starrender Fels mein Aufenthalt.
starrəndər fɛls maen aofəntalt.

Wie sich die Welle an Welle reiht,
viː zɪç di vɛllə |an vɛllə raet,

fliessen die Tränen mir ewig erneut.
fliːsən di trɛːnən miːr |eːvɪç |ɛrnɔøt.

Hoch in den Kronen wogend sich's regt,
hoːx |ɪn den kroːnən voːgənt zɪçs reːkt,

so unaufhörlich mein Herze schlägt.
zoː |unaofhøːrlɪç maen hɛrtsə ʃlɛːkt.

Und wie des Felsen uraltes Erz,
unt viː dɛs fɛlzən |uːr|altəs |ɛrts,

ewig derselbe bleibet mein Schmerz.
eːvɪç deːrzɛlbə blaebət maen ʃmɛrts.

Schubert   Ave Maria
              aːvɛ mariːa

Ave Maria!   Jungfrau mild,
aːvɛ mariːa! juŋfrao mɪlt,

erhöre einer Jungfrau Flehen,
ɛrhøːrə |aenər juŋfrao fleːən,

aus diesem Felsen starr und wild
aos diːzəm fɛlzən ʃtar |unt vɪlt

soll mein Gebet zu dir hin wehen.
zɔl maen gəbeːt t͡su: diːr hɪn veːən.

Wir schlafen sicher bis zum Morgen,
viːr ʃlaːfən zɪçər bɪs t͡sum mɔrgən,

ob Menschen noch so grausam sind.
ɔp mɛnʃən   nɔx   zoː graozam zɪnt.

O Jungfrau, sieh der Jungfrau Sorgen,
oː juŋfrao, ziː der juŋfrao zɔrgən,

o Mutter, hör ein bittend Kind!
oː mutər, høːr |aen bɪtənt kɪnt!

Ave Maria!
aːvɛ mariːa!

Ave Maria!   Unbefleckt!
aːvɛ mariːa! unbəflɛkt!

Wenn wir auf diesen Fels hinsinken zum Schlaf,
vɛn viːr |aof diːzən fɛls hɪnzɪŋkən t͡sum ʃlaːf,

und uns dein Schutz bedeckt,
unt |uns daen ʃuts bedɛkt,

wird weich der harte Fels uns dünken.
vɪrt vaeç der hartə fɛls |uns dʏŋkən.

Du lächelst, Rosendüfte wehen
du: lɛçəlst, ro:zəndʏftə ve:ən

in dieser dumpfen Felsenkluft.
|ɪn di:zər dʊmpfən fɛlzənkluft.

O Mutter, höre Kindes Flehen,
o: mʊtər, hø:rə kɪndəs fle:ən,

o Jungfrau, eine Jungfrau ruft!
o: jʊŋfrao, aenə jʊŋfrao ru:ft!

Ave Maria! Reine Magd!
a:vɛ mari:a! raenə ma:kt!

Der Erde und der Luft Dämonen,
der |e:rdə |unt der luft dɛmo:nən,

von deines Auges Huld verjagt,
fon daenəs |aogəs hʊlt fərja:kt,

sie können hier nicht bei uns wohnen.
zi: kœnnən hi:r nɪçt bae |uns vo:nən.

Wir wolln uns still dem Schicksal beugen,
vi:r voln |uns ʃtɪl dem ʃɪkza:l bøøgən,

da uns dein heilger Trost anweht;
da: |uns daen haelgər tro:st |anve:t;

der Jungfrau wolle hold dich neigen,
der jʊŋfrao vollə holt dɪç naegən,

dem Kind, das für den Vater fleht! Ave Maria!
dem kɪnt, das fy:r den fa:tər fle:t! a:vɛ mari:a!

Schubert   Das Wandern
             das vandərn

Das Wandern ist des Müllers Lust, das Wandern!
das vandərn |ɪst des mʏllərs lʊst, das vandərn!

Das muss ein schlechter Müller sein,
das mʊs |aen ʃlɛçtər mʏllər zaen,

dem niemals fiel das Wandern ein,
dem niːmaːls fiːl das vandərn |aen,

das Wandern, das Wandern.
das vandərn, das vandərn.

Vom Wasser haben wir's gelernt, vom Wasser!
fɔm vasər haːbən viːrs gəlɛrnt, fɔm vasər!

Das hat nicht Rast bei Tag und Nacht,
das hat nɪçt rast bae taːk |unt naxt,

ist stets auf Wanderschaft bedacht,
ɪst ʃteːts |aof vandərʃaft bədaxt,

das Wasser, das Wasser.
das vasər, das vasər.

Das sehn wir auch den Rädern ab, den Rädern!
das zeːn viːr |aox den rɛːdərn |ap, den rɛːdərn!

Die gar nicht gerne stille stehn,
di gaːr nɪçt gɛrnə ʃtɪllə ʃteːn,

die sich mein Tag nicht müde drehn, die Räder.
di zɪç maen taːk nɪçt myːdə dreːn, di rɛːdər.

Die Steine selbst, so schwer sie sind, die Steine!
di ʃtaenə zɛlpst, zoː ʃveːr ziː zɪnt, di ʃtaenə!

Sie tanzen mit den muntern Reih'n
ziː tantsən mɪt den muntərn raen

und wollen gar noch schneller sein,
|unt vɔllən gaːr nɔx ʃnɛllər zaen,

die Steine, die Steine.
di ʃtaenə, di ʃtaenə.

O Wandern, Wandern, meine Lust, o Wandern!
oː vandərn, vandərn, maenə lust, oː vandərn!

Herr Meister und Frau Meisterin,
hɛr maestər |unt frao maestərɪn,

lasst mich in Frieden weiterzieh'n
last mɪç |ɪn friːdən vaetərtsiːn

und wandern, und wandern.
|unt vandərn, unt vandərn.

Schubert   Das Wirtshaus
            das vɪrtshaos

Auf einen Totenacker hat mich mein Weg gebracht.
aof |aenən to̯:tən|akər hat mɪç maen ve:k gəbraxt.

Allhier will ich einkehren, hab ich bei mir gedacht.
alhi̯:r vɪl |ɪç |aenke:rən, ha:p |ɪç bae mi:r gədaxt.

Ihr grünen Totenkränze könnt wohl die Zeichen sein,
i:r gry:nən to̯:tənkrɛntsə kœnt vo:l di tsaeçən zaen,

die müde Wandrer laden ins kühle Wirtshaus ein.
di my:də vandrər la:dən |ɪns ky:lə vɪrtshaos |aen.

Sind denn in diesem Hause die Kammern all besetzt?
zɪnt dɛn |ɪn di̯:zəm haozə di kammərn |al bəzɛtst?

bin matt zum Niedersinken, bin tödlich schwer verletzt.
bɪn mat tsum ni̯:dərzɪŋkən, bɪn tø̯:tlɪç ʃve:r fɛrlɛtst.

O unbarmherzge Schenke, doch weisest du mich ab?
o: |unbarmhɛrtsgə ʃɛŋkə, dox vaezəst du: mɪç |ap?

Nun weiter denn, nur weiter, mein treuer Wanderstab!
nu:n vaetər dɛn, nu:r vaetər, maen tro̯ʏər vandərʃta:p!

Schubert   Dem Unendlichen
            dem |un|ɛntlɪçən

Wie erhebt sich das Herz,
vi: |ɛrhe̯:pt zɪç das hɛrts,

wenn es dich, Unendlicher, denkt!
vɛn |ɛs dɪç, un|ɛntlɪçər, dɛnkt!

Wie sinkt es, wenn es auf sich herunterschaut!
vi: zɪŋkt |ɛs, vɛn |ɛs |aof zɪç həruntərʃaot!

Elend schauts wehklagend dann und Nacht und Tod!
e̯:lənt ʃaots ve:kla:gənt dan unt naxt |unt to̯:t!

Allein du rufst mich aus meiner Nacht,
allaen du: ru:fst mɪç |aos maenər naxt,

der im Elend, der im Tode hilft!
der |ɪm |e̯:lənt, der |ɪm to̯:də hɪlft!

Dann denk' ich es ganz, dass du ewig mich schufst,
dan dɛŋk |ɪç |ɛs gants, das du: |e̯:vɪç mɪç ʃu:fst,

Herrlicher, den kein Preis, unten am Grab,
hɛrlɪçər, den kaen praes, untən |am gra:p,

oben am Thron, Herr, Gott, den, dankend entflammt,
oːbən |am troːn, hɛr, gɔt, den, daŋkənt |ɛntflamt,

kein Jubel genug besingt!
kaen juːbəl gənuːk bəzɪŋkt!

Weht, Bäume des Lebens, in's Harfengetön!
veːt, bøømə dɛs leːbəns, ɪns harfəngətøːn!

Rausche mit ihnen in's Harfengetön,
raoʃə mɪt |iːnən |ɪns harfəngətøːn,

krystallner Strom!
krɪstalnər ʃtroːm!

Ihr lispelt und rauscht,
iːr lɪspəlt |unt raoʃt,

und, Harfen, ihr tönt nie es ganz!
unt, harfən, iːr tøːnt niː |ɛs gants!

Gott ist es, Gott ist es,   den ihr preist.
gɔt |ɪst |ɛs, gɔt |ɪst |ɛs, den |iːr praest.

Welten donnert im feierlichen Gang!
vɛltən dɔnnərt |ɪm faeərlɪçən gaŋ!

Welten, donnert in der Posaunen Chor!
vɛltən, dɔnnərt |ɪn der pozaonən koːr!

Tönt, all' ihr Sonnen auf der Strasse voll Glanz,
tøːnt, al |iːr zɔnnən aof der ʃtrasə fɔl glants,

in der Posaunen Chor!
ɪn der pozaonən koːr!

Ihr Welten, ihr donnert, du, der Posaunen Chor,
iːr vɛltən, iːr dɔnnərt, duː, der pozaonən koːr,

hallest nie es ganz! Gott, nie es ganz!
halləst niː |ɛs gants! gɔt, niː |ɛs gants!

Gott ist es, den ihr preist!
gɔt |ɪst |ɛs, den |iːr praest!

Schubert   Der Atlas
             der |atlas

Ich unglückselger Atlas!
ɪç |unglʏkzeːlgər |atlas!

Eine Welt, die ganze Welt der Schmerzen,
aenə vɛlt, di gantsə vɛlt der ʃmɛrtsən,

muss ich tragen,
mʊs |ɪç trɑːgən,

ich trage Unerträgliches,
ɪç trɑːgə |ʊnɛrtrɛːklɪçəs,

und brechen will mir das Herz im Leibe.
ʊnt brɛçən vɪl miːr das hɛrts |ɪm laebə.

Du stolzes Herz, du hast es ja gewollt!
duː ʃtɔltsəs hɛrts, duː hast |ɛs jɑː gəvɔlt!

Du wolltest glücklich sein,
duː vɔltəst glʏklɪç zaen,

unendlich glücklich, oder unendlich elend,
ʊn|ɛntlɪç glʏklɪç, oːdər |ʊn|ɛntlɪç |eːlənt,

stolzes Herz, und jetzo bist du elend.
ʃtɔltsəs hɛrts, ʊnt jɛtso bɪst duː |eːlənt.

Ich unglücksel'ger Atlas!
ɪç |ʊnglʏkzeːlgər |atlas!

Die ganze Welt der Schmerzen muss ich tragen!
di gantsə vɛlt der ʃmɛrtsən mʊs |ɪç trɑːgən!

Schubert   Der Doppelgänger
                der dɔpəlgɛŋər

Still ist die Nacht, es ruhen die Gassen,
ʃtɪl |ɪst di naxt, ɛs ruːən di gasən,

in diesem Hause wohnte mein Schatz;
ɪn diːzəm haozə voːntə maen ʃats;

sie hat schon längst die Stadt verlassen,
ziː hat ʃoːn lɛŋst di ʃtat fɛrlasən,

doch steht noch das Haus auf demselben Platz.
dɔx ʃteːt nɔx das haos |aof demzɛlbən plats.

Da steht auch ein Mensch und starrt in die Höhe,
daː ʃteːt |aoç |aen mɛnʃ ʊnt ʃtart |ɪn di høːə,

und ringt die Hände vor Schmerzensgewalt;
ʊnt rɪŋt di hɛndə for ʃmɛrtsənsgəvalt;

mir graust es, wenn ich sein Antlitz sehe,
miːr graost |ɛs, vɛn |ɪç zaen |antlɪts zeːə,

der Mond zeigt mir meine eigne Gestalt.
der moːnt tsaekt miːr maenə |aegnə gəʃtalt.

Du Doppelgänger, du bleicher Geselle!
duː dɔpəlgɛŋər, duː blaeçər gəzɛllə!

Was äffst du nach mein Liebesleid
vas |ɛfst duː nax maen liːbəslaet

das mich gequält auf dieser Stelle
das mɪç gəkvɛːlt |aof diːzər ʃtɛllə

so manche Nacht, in alter Zeit?
zoː mançə naxt, ɪn |altər tsaet?

Schubert   Der Erlkönig
             der |ɛrlkøːnɪç

Wer reitet so spät durch Nacht und Wind?
veːr raetət zoː spɛːt dʊrç naxt |ʊnt vɪnt?

Es ist der Vater mit seinem Kind;
ɛs |ɪst der faːtər mɪt zaenəm kɪnt;

er hat den Knaben wohl in dem Arm,
eːr hat den knaːbən voːl |ɪn dem |arm,

er fasst ihn sicher, er hält ihn warm.
ɛːr fast |iːn zɪçər, eːr hɛːlt |iːn varm.

Mein Sohn, was birgst du so bang dein Gesicht?
maen zoːn, vas bɪrkst duː zoː baŋ daen gəzɪçt?

Siehst, Vater, du den Erlkönig nicht?
ziːst, faːtər, duː den |ɛrlkøːnɪç nɪçt?

Den Erlenkönig mit Kron und Schweif?
den |ɛrlənkøːnɪç mɪt kroːn |ʊnt ʃvaef?

Mein Sohn, es ist ein Nebelstreif.
maen zoːn, ɛs ɪst |aen neːbəlʃtraef.

"Du liebes Kind, komm, geh mit mir!
"duː liːbəs kɪnt, kɔm, geː mɪt miːr!

gar schöne Spiele spiel ich mit dir;
gaːr ʃøːnə ʃpiːlə ʃpiːl |ɪç mɪt diːr;

manch bunte Blumen sind an dem Strand,
manç bʊntə bluːmən zɪnt |an dem ʃtrant,

meine Mutter hat manch gülden Gewand."
maenə mʊtər hat manç gʏldən gəvant."

Mein Vater, mein Vater,   und hörest du nicht,
maen faːtər, maen faːtər, ʊnt høːrəst duː nɪçt,

was Erlenkönig mir leise verspricht?
vas |ɛrlənkøːnɪç miːr laezə fɛrʃprɪçt?

Sei ruhig, bleibe ruhig, mein Kind:
zae ruːɪç, blaebə ruːɪç, maen kɪnt,

in dürren Blättern säuselt der Wind.
ɪn dʏrrən blɛtərn zɔøzəlt der vɪnt.

"Willst, feiner Knabe, du mit mir gehn?
vɪlst, faenər knaːbə, duː mɪt miːr geːn?

meine Töchter sollen dich warten schön;
maenə tœçtər zɔllən dɪç varten ʃøːn;

meine Töchter führen den nächtlichen Reihn
maenə tœçtər fyːrən den nɛçtlɪçən raen

und wiegen und tanzen und singen dich ein,
|ʊnt viːgən |ʊnt tantsən |ʊnt zɪŋən dɪç |aen,

sie wiegen und tanzen und singen dich ein."
ziː viːgən |ʊnt tantsən |ʊnt zɪŋən dɪç |aen."

Mein Vater, mein Vater, und siehst du nicht dort
maen faːtər, maen faːtər, ʊnt ziːst duː nɪçt dɔrt

Erlkönigs Töchter am düstern Ort?
ɛrlkøːnɪçs tœçtər |am dyːstərn |ɔrt?

Mein Sohn, mein Sohn, ich seh es genau,
maen zoːn, maen zoːn, ɪç zeː |ɛs gənao,

es scheinen die alten Weiden so grau.
ɛs ʃaenən di |altən vaedən zoː grao.

"Ich liebe dich, mich reizt deine schöne Gestalt,
"ɪç liːbə dɪç, mɪç raetst daenə ʃøːnə gəʃtalt."

und bist du nicht willig, so brauch ich Gewalt."
ʊnt bɪst duː nɪçt vɪllɪç, zoː braox |ɪç gəvalt."

"Mein Vater, mein Vater, jetzt fasst er mich an!
"maen faːtər, maen faːtər, jɛtst fast |eːr mɪç |an!

Erlkonig hat mir ein Leids getan!''
ɛrlkøːnɪç hat miːr |aen laets gətaːn!''

Dem Vater grauset's, er reitet geschwind,
dem faːtər graozəts, eːr raetət gəʃvɪnt,

er hält in Armen das ächzende Kind,
eːr hɛːlt |ɪn |armən das |ɛçtsəndə kɪnt,

erreicht den Hof mit Müh und Not;
ɛrraeçt den hoːf mɪt myː |ʊnt noːt;

in seinen Armen das Kind war tot.
ɪn zaenən |armən das kɪnt vaːr toːt.

Schubert   Der Leiermann
              der laeərman

Drüben hinterm Dorfe steht ein Leiermann,
dryːbən hɪntərm dorfə ʃteːt |aen laeərman,

und mit starren Fingern dreht er, was er kann.
ʊnt mɪt ʃtarrən fɪŋərn dreːt |eːr, vas |eːr kan.

Barfuss auf dem Eise wankt er hin und her,
barfuːs aof dem |aezə vaŋkt |eːr hɪn |ʊnt heːr,

und sein kleiner Teller bleibt ihm immer leer.
ʊnt zaen klaenər tɛllər blaept |iːm |ɪmmər leːr.

Keiner mag ihn hören, keiner sieht ihn an,
kaenər maːk |iːn høːrən, kaenər ziːt |iːn |an,

und die Hunde knurren um den alten Mann.
ʊnt di hʊndə knʊrrən |ʊm den |altən man.

Und er lässt es gehen alles, wie es will,
ʊnt |eːr lɛst |ɛs geːən |alləs, viː |ɛs vɪl,

dreht, und seine Leier steht ihm nimmer still.
dreːt, ʊnt zaenə laeər ʃteːt |iːm nɪmmər ʃtɪl.

Wunderlicher Alter, soll ich mit dir gehn?
vʊndərlɪçər |altər, zɔl |ɪç mɪt diːr geːn?

Willst zu meinen Liedern deine Leier drehn?
vɪlst tsuː maenən liːdərn daenə laeər dreːn?

153

Schubert　　Der Lindenbaum
　　　　　　der lɪndənbaom

Am Brunnen vor dem Tore da steht ein Lindenbaum;
am brʊnən for dem toːrə daː ʃteːt |aen lɪndənbaom;

ich träumt' in seinem Schatten so manchen süssen Traum.
ɪç trɔømt |ɪn zaenəm ʃatən　zoː mançən　zyːsən　traom.

Ich schnitt in seine Rinde so manches liebe Wort;
ɪç ʃnɪt　|ɪn zaenə rɪndə zoː mançəs liːbə vɔrt;

es zog in Freud und Leide zu ihm mich immerfort.
ɛs tsoːk |ɪn frɔøt |ʊnt laedə zuː |iːm mɪç |ɪmmərfort.

Ich musst auch heute wandern vorbei in tiefer Nacht,
ɪç　mʊst |aoç hɔøtə　vandərn forbae |ɪn tiːfər naxt,

da hab ich noch im Dunkel die Augen zugemacht.
daː haːp |ɪç nɔx |ɪm dʊŋkəl di |aogən tsuɡəmaxt.

Und seine Zweige rauschten, als riefen sie mir zu:
ʊnt zaenə tsvaegə raoʃtən,　als riːfən ziː miːr tsuː,

komm her zu mir, Geselle, hier findst du deine Ruh!
kɔm heːr tsuː miːr, ɡəzɛllə, hiːr fɪndst duː daenə ruː!

Die kalten Winde bliesen mir grad ins Angesicht,
di kaltən　vɪndə　bliːzən miːr graːt |ɪns |aŋɡəzɪçt,

der Hut flog mir vom Kopfe, ich wendete mich nicht.
der huːt floːk miːr fɔm kɔpfə, ɪç vɛndətə mɪç nɪçt.

Nun bin ich manche Stunde entfernt von jenem Ort,
nuːn bɪn |ɪç mançə ʃtʊndə |ɛntfɛrnt fɔn jeːnəm |ort,

und immer hör ich's rauschen:　du fändest Ruhe dort!
ʊnt |ɪmmər høːr |ɪçs raoʃən,　duː fɛndəst ruːə dort!

Schubert　　　Der Musensohn
　　　　　　　der muːzənzoːn

Durch Feld und Wald zu schweifen,
dʊrç fɛlt |ʊnt valt tsuː ʃvaefən,

mein Liedchen weg zu pfeifen,
maen liːtçən vɛk tsuː pfaefən,

so geht's von Ort zu Ort!　　Und nach dem Takte reget
zoː ɡeːts fɔn |ort tsuː |ort! ʊnt nax dem taktə reːɡət

und nach dem Mass beweget sich alles an mir fort.
unt nax dem maːs bəveːgət zɪç |alləs |an miːr fort.

Ich kann sie kaum erwarten, die erste Blum im Garten,
ɪç kan ziː kaom |ɛrvartən, di |ɛrstə bluːm |ɪm gartən,

die erste Blüt am Baum. Sie grüssen meine Lieder,
di |ɛrstə blyːt |am baom. ziː gryːsən maenə liːdər,

und kommt der Winter wieder, sing ich noch jenen Traum.
unt komt der vɪntər viːdər, zɪŋ |ɪç nox jeːnən traom.

Ich sing ihn in der Weite, auf Eises Läng und Breite,
ɪç zɪŋ |iːn |ɪn der vaetə, aof |aezəs lɛŋ |unt braetə,

da blüht der Winter schön! Auch diese Blüte schwindet,
daː blyːt der vɪntər ʃøːn! aox diːzə blyːtə ʃvɪndət,

und neue Freude findet sich auf bebauten Höhn.
unt nɔøə frɔødə fɪndət zɪç |aof bəbaotən høːn.

Denn wie ich bei der Linde das junge Völkchen finde,
dɛn viː |ɪç bae der lɪndə das juŋə fœlkçən fɪndə,

so gleich erreg ich sie.
zoː glaeç |ɛrreːk |ɪç ziː.

Der stumpfe Bursche bläht sich,
der ʃtumpfə burʃə blɛːt zɪç,

das steife Mädchen dreht sich nach meiner Melodie.
das ʃtaefə mɛːtçən dreːt zɪç nax maenər melodiː.

Ihr gebt den Sohlen Flügel
iːr geːpt den zoːlən flyːgəl

und treibt durch Tal und Hügel den Leibling weit von Haus.
|unt traept durç taːl |unt hyːgəl den liːplɪŋ vaet fon haos.

Ihr lieben, holden Musen,
iːr liːbən, holdən muːzən,

wann ruh ich ihr am Busen auch endlich wieder aus?
van ruː |ɪç |iːr |am buːzən |aoç |ɛntlɪç viːdər |aos?

Schubert   Der Tod und das Mädchen
              der toːt |unt das mɛːtçən

Vorüber, ach! vorüber geh, wilder Knochenmann!
foryːbər, ax! foryːbər geː, vɪldər knoxənman!

155

Ich bin noch jung, geh, Lieber!
ɪç bɪn nɔx juŋ, ge:, li̱:bər!

und rühre mich nicht an.
ʊnt ry:rə mɪç nɪçt |an.

Gieb deine Hand, du schön und zart Gebild!
gi:p da̱enə hant, du: ʃø:n |ʊnt tsart gəbi̱lt!

bin Freund und komme nicht zu strafen.
bɪn frɔ̱ønt ʊnt kɔmmə nɪçt tsu: ʃtra̱:fən.

Sei gutes Muts! ich bin nicht wild,
za̱e gu̱:təs mu:ts! ɪç bɪn nɪçt vɪlt,

sollst sanft in meinen Armen schlafen!
zɔlst zanft |ɪn ma̱enən |armən ʃla̱:fən!

Schubert   Der Wanderer
             der va̱ndərər

Ich komme vom Gebirge her,
ɪç kɔ̱mmə fɔm gəbi̱rgə he:r,

es dampft das Tal, es braust das Meer.
ɛs dampft das ta:l, ɛs bra̱ost das me:r.

Ich wandle still, bin wenig froh,
ɪç va̱ndlə ʃtɪl, bɪn ve:nɪç fro:,

und immer fragt der Seufzer: wo? immer wo?
ʊnt |ɪmmər fra:kt der zɔøftsər, vo:? |ɪmmər vo:?

Die Sonne dünkt mich hier so kalt,
di zɔ̱nnə dyŋkt mɪç hi:r zo: kalt,

die Blüte welk, das Leben alt,
di bly̱:tə vɛlk, das le̱:bən |alt,

und was sie reden, leerer Schall,
ʊnt vas zi: re̱:dən, le:rər ʃal,

ich bin ein Fremdling überall.
ɪç bɪn |a̱en frɛmtlɪŋ |y̱:bər|al.

Wo bist du, wo bist du
vo: bɪst du:, vo: bɪst du:

mein geliebtes Land?
ma̱en gəli̱:ptəs lant?

gesucht, geahnt, und nie gekannt!
gəzu̯xt, gə|a:nt, ʊnt ni: gəkant!

Das Land, das Land so hoffnungsgrün,
das lant, das lant zo: hɔfnʊŋsgry:n,

das Land, wo meine Rosen blühn,
das lant, vo: ma̯enə ro:zən bly:n,

wo meine Freunde wandeln gehn,
vo: ma̯enə frɔ̯øndə vandəln ge:n,

wo meine Toten auferstehn das Land,
vo: ma̯enə to:tən |a̯of|ɛrʃte:n das lant,

das meine Sprache spricht,
das ma̯enə ʃpra:xə ʃprɪçt,

o Land, wo bist du?
o: lant, vo: bɪst du:?

Ich wandle still, bin wenig froh,
ɪç vandlə ʃtil, bɪn ve:nɪç fro:,

und immer fragt der Seufzer: wo? immer wo?
ʊnt |ɪmmər fra:kt der zɔ̯øftsər, vo:? ɪmmər vo:?

Im Geisterhauch tönt's mir zurück:
ɪm ga̯estərha̯ox tø:nts mi:r tsurʏk,

"Dort, wo du nicht bist, dort ist das Glück!"
"dɔrt, vo: du: nɪçt bɪst, dɔrt |ɪst das glʏk!"

Schubert   Der Wegweiser
              der ve:kva̯ezər

Was vermeid ich denn die Wege,
vas fɛrma̯et |ɪç dɛn di ve:gə,

wo die andern Wandrer gehn,
vo: di |andərn vandrər ge:n,

suche mir versteckte Stege
zu̯xə mi:r fɛrʃtɛktə ʃte:gə

durch verschneite Felsenhöhn?
dʊrç fɛrʃna̯etə fɛlzənhø:n?

Habe ja doch nichts begangen,
ha:bə ja: dɔx nɪçts bəgaŋən,

dass ich Menschen sollte scheun,
das |ɪç mɛnʃən zɔltə ʃøøn,

welch ein törichtes Verlangen
vɛlç |aen tøːrɪçtəs fɛrlaŋən

treibt mich in die Wüstenein?
traept mɪç |ɪn di vyːstənaen?

Weiser stehen auf den Wegen,
vaezər ʃteːən |aof den veːgən,

weisen auf die Städte zu,
vaezən |aof di ʃtɛtə tsuː,

und ich wandre sonder Massen,
ʊnt |ɪç vandrə zɔndər masən,

ohne Ruh, und suche Ruh.
oːnə ruː, ʊnt zuçə ruː.

Einen Weiser seh ich stehen
aenən vaezər zeː |ɪç ʃteːən

unverrückt vor meinem Blick;
|ʊnfɛrrʏkt for maenəm blɪk;

eine Strasse muss ich gehen,
aenə ʃtrasə mʊs |ɪç geːən,

die noch keiner ging zurück.
di nɔx kaenər gɪŋ tsurʏk.

Schubert   Die Allmacht
              di |almaxt

Gross ist Jehova, der Herr!
groːs |ɪst jeːhoːva, der hɛr!

denn Himmel und Erde verkünden seine Macht.
dɛn hɪmməl |ʊnt |eːrdə fɛrkyndən zaenə maxt.

Du hörst sie im brausenden Sturm,
duː høːrst ziː |ɪm braozəndən ʃtʊrm,

in des Waldstroms laut aufrauschendem Ruf;
ɪn dɛs valtʃtroːms laot |aofraoʃəndəm ruːf;

gross ist Jehova, der Herr, gross ist seine Macht.
groːs |ɪst jeːhoːva, der hɛr, groːs |ɪst zaenə maxt.

158

Du hörst sie in des grünenden Waldes Gesäusel,
du: høːrst ziː |ɪn dɛs gryːnəndən va̲ldəs gəzo̲ɔøzəl,

siehst sie in wogender Saaten Gold,
ziːst ziː |ɪn vo̲ːgəndər za̲ːtən gɔlt,

in lieblicher Blumen glühendem Schmelz,
ɪn li̲ːplɪçər blu̲ːmən glyːəndəm ʃmɛlts,

im Glanz des sternebesäeten Himmels.
ɪm glants dɛs ʃtɛ̲rnəbəzɛːətən hɪ̲mməls.

Furchtbar tönt sie im Donnergeroll
fu̲rçtbaːr tøːnt ziː |ɪm dɔ̲nnərgərɔl

und flammt in des Blitzes
|ʊnt flamt |ɪn dɛs blɪ̲tsəs

schnell hinzuckendem Flug,
ʃnɛl hɪ̲ntsʊkəndəm fluːk,

doch kündet das pochende Herz
dɔx ky̲ndət das pɔ̲xəndə hɛrts

dir fühlbarer noch Jehovas Macht,
diːr fy̲ːlbarər nɔx jeːho̲ːvas maxt,

des ewigen Gottes,
dɛs |e̲ːvɪgən gɔ̲təs,

blickst du flehend empor
blɪ̲kst duː fle̲ːənt |ɛmpo̲ːr

und hoffst auf Huld und Erbarmen.
|ʊnt hɔfst |a̲ɔf hʊlt |ʊnt |ɛrba̲rmən.

Gross ist Jehova, der Herr!
groːs |ɪst jeːho̲ːva, der hɛr!

Schubert   Die Forelle
             di fɔrɛ̲llə

In einem Bächlein helle, da schoss in froher Eil
ɪn |a̲ɛnəm bɛ̲çlaɛn hɛ̲llə, daː ʃɔs |ɪn fro̲ːər |a̲ɛl

die launische Forelle vorüber wie ein Pfeil.
di la̲ɔnɪʃə fɔrɛ̲llə fɔry̲ːbər viː |a̲ɛn pfa̲ɛl.

Ich stand an dem Gestade und sah in süsser Ruh
ɪç stant |an dem gəʃta̲ːdə |ʊnt zaː |ɪn zyːsər ruː

159

des muntern Fischleins Bade im klaren Bächlein zu.
dɛs mʊntərn fɪʃlaens baːdə |ɪm klaːrən bɛçlaen tsuː.

Ein Fischer mit der Rute wohl an dem Ufer stand,
aen fɪʃər mɪt der ruːtə voːl |an dem |uːfər ʃtant,

und sah's mit kaltem Blute, wie sich das Fischlein wand.
ʊnt zaːs mɪt kaltəm bluːtə, viː zɪç das fɪʃlaen vant.

So lang' dem Wasser Helle, so dacht ich, nicht gebricht,
zoː laŋ dem vasər hɛllə, zoː daxt |ɪç, nɪçt gəbrɪçt,

so fängt er die Forelle mit seiner Angel nicht.
zoː fɛŋt |er di fɔrɛllə mɪt zaenər |aŋəl nɪçt.

Doch endlich ward dem Diebe die Zeit zu lang.
dɔx |ɛntlɪç vart dem diːbə di tsaet tsuː laŋ.

Er macht das Bächlein tückisch trübe,
ɛr maxt das bɛçlaen tʏkɪʃ tryːbə,

und eh ich es gedacht,
ʊnt |eː |ɪç |ɛs gədaxt,

so zuckte seine Rute,
zoː tsʊktə zaenə ruːtə,

das Fischlein, das Fischlein zappelt dran,
das fɪʃlaen, das fɪʃlaen tsapəlt dran,

und ich mit regem Blute sah die Betrogne an.
ʊnt |ɪç mɪt reːgəm bluːtə zaː di bətroːgnə |an.

Schubert   Die junge Nonne
            di juŋə nɔnnə

Wie braust durch die Wipfel der heulende Sturm!
viː braost dʊrç di vɪpfəl der hɔøləndə ʃtʊrm!

Es klirren die Balken, es zittert das Haus!
ɛs klɪrrən di balkən, ɛs tsɪtərt das haos!

Es rollet der Donner, es leuchtet der Blitz,
ɛs rɔllət der dɔnnər, ɛs lɔøçtət der blɪts,

und finster die Nacht, wie das Grab!
ʊnt fɪnstər di naxt, viː das graːp!

Immerhin, immerhin,
ɪmmərhɪn, ɪmmərhɪn,

160

so tobt' es auch jüngst noch in mir!
zo: to:pt |ɛs |a͜ox jʏŋst nɔx |ɪn mi:r!

Es brauste das Leben, wie jetzo der Sturm,
ɛs bra͜ostə das le:bən, vi jɛtso der ʃtʊrm,

es bebten die Glieder, wie jetzo das Haus,
ɛs be:ptən di gli:dər, vi jɛtso das ha͜os,

es flammte die Liebe, wie jetzo der Blitz,
ɛs flamtə di li:bə, vi: jɛtso der blɪts,

und finster die Brust, wie das Grab.
ʊnt fɪnstər di brʊst, vi: das gra:p.

Nun tobe, du wilder, gewaltger Sturm,
nu:n to:bə, du: vɪldər, gəvaltgər ʃtʊrm,

im Herzen ist Friede, im Herzen ist Ruh,
ɪm hɛrtsən |ɪst fri:də, ɪm hɛrtsən |ɪst ru:,

des Bräutigams harret die liebende Braut,
dɛs brɔ͜øtɪgams harrət di li:bəndə bra͜ot,

gereinigt in prüfender Glut der ewigen,
gəra͜enɪkt |ɪn pry:fəndər glu:t der |e:vɪgən,

ewigen Liebe getraut.
e:vɪgən li:bə gətra͜ot.

Ich harre, mein Heiland! mit sehnendem Blick!
ɪç harrə, ma͜en ha͜elant! mɪt ze:nəndəm blɪk!

komm, himmlischer Bräutigam, hole die Braut,
kɔm, hɪmlɪʃər brɔ͜øtɪgam, ho:lə di bra͜ot,

erlöse die Seele von irdischer Haft!
ɛrlø:zə di ze:lə fɔn |ɪrdɪʃər haft!

Horch, friedlich ertönet das Glöcklein vom Turm!
hɔrç, fri:tlɪç |ɛrtø:nət das glœkla͜en fɔm tʊrm!

Es lockt mich das süsse Getön
ɛs lɔkt mɪç das zy:sə gətø:n

allmächtig zu ewigen Höhn! Alleluja!
|almɛçtɪk tsu: |e:vɪgən hø:n! alləlu:ja!

Schubert   Die Liebe hat gelogen
             di li̱ːbə hat gəlo̱ːgən

Die Liebe hat gelogen,
di li̱ːbə hat gəlo̱ːgən,

die Sorge lastet schwer,
di zo̱rgə lastət ʃveːr,

betrogen, ach! betrogen
bətro̱ːgən, ax! bətro̱ːgən

hat alles mich umher!
hat |alləs mɪç |umhe̱ːr!

Es fliessen heisse Tropfen
ɛs fliːsən haesə tro̱pfən

die Wange stets herab,
di vaṇə ʃteːts hɛra̱p,

lass ab, mein Herz, zu klopfen,
las |ap, ma̱en hɛrts, tsuː klo̱pfən,

du armes Herz, lass ab!
duː |a̱rməs hɛrts, las |ap!

Schubert   Die Post
           di post

Von der Strasse her ein Posthorn klingt.
fon der ʃtra̱ːsə heːr |aen po̱sthorn klɪŋkt.

Was hat es, dass es so hoch aufspringt, mein Herz?
vas hat |ɛs, das |ɛs zoː hoːx |a̱ofʃprɪŋt, ma̱en hɛrts?

Die Post bringt keinen Brief für dich.
di post brɪŋt ka̱enən briːf fyːr dɪç.

Was drängst du denn so wunderlich, mein Herz?
vas drɛṇst duː dɛn zoː vʊndərlɪç, ma̱en hɛrts?

Nun ja, die Post kommt aus der Stadt,
nuːn jaː, di post komt |aos der ʃtat,

wo ich ein liebes Liebchen hatt, mein Herz!
voː |ɪç |aen li̱ːbəs li̱ːpçən hat, ma̱en hɛrts!

Willst wohl einmal hinübersehn
vɪlst voːl |aenmaːl hɪny̱ːbərzeːn

und fragen, wie es dort mag gehn, mein Herz?
|ʊnt fra̱ːgən, viː |ɛs dort maːk geːn, ma̱en hɛrts?

Schubert   Du bist die Ruh
             du: bɪst di ru:

Du bist die Ruh, der Friede mild,
du: bɪst di ru:, der fri:də mɪlt,

die Sehnsucht du, und was sie stillt.
di ze:nzʊxt du:, ʊnt vas zi: ʃtɪlt.

Ich weihe dir voll Lust und Schmerz
ɪç vae̯ə di:r fɔl lʊst |ʊnt ʃmɛrts

zur Wohnung hier mein Aug und Herz.
tsur vo:nʊŋ hi:r mae̯n |ao̯k |ʊnt hɛrts.

Kehr ein bei mir, und schliesse du
ke:r|ae̯n bae̯ mi:r, ʊnt ʃli:sə du:

still hinter dir die Pforten zu.
ʃtɪl hɪntər di:r di pfɔrtən tsu:.

Treib andern Schmerz aus dieser Brust!
trae̯p |andərn ʃmɛrts |ao̯s di:zər brʊst!

voll sei dies Herz von deiner Lust.
fɔl zae̯ di:s hɛrts fɔn dae̯nər lʊst.

Dies Augenzelt, von deinem Glanz
di:s |ao̯gəntsɛlt, fɔn dae̯nəm glants

allein erhellt, o füll es ganz!
|allae̯n |ɛrhɛlt, o: fʏl |ɛs gants!

Schubert   Eifersucht und Stolz
             ae̯fərzʊçt |ʊnt ʃtɔlts

Wohin so schnell, so kraus und wild, mein lieber Bach?
vohɪn zo: ʃnɛl, zo: krao̯s |ʊnt vɪlt, mae̯n li:bər bax?

eilst du voll Zorn dem frechen Bruder Jäger nach?
ae̯lst du: fɔl tsɔrn dem frɛçən bru:dər jɛ:gər nax?

Kehr um, und schilt erst deine Müllerin
ke:r |ʊm, ʊnt ʃɪlt |e:rst dae̯nə mʏllərɪn

für ihren leichten, losen, kleinen Flattersinn, kehr um!
fy:r |i:rən lae̯çtən, lo:zən, klae̯nən flatərzɪn, ke:r|ʊm!

Sahst du sie gestern Abend nicht am Tore stehn,
za:st du: zi: gɛstərn |a:bənt nɪçt |am to:rə ʃte:n,

mit langem Halse nach der grossen Strasse sehn?
mɪt laŋəm halzə nax der gro:sən ʃtrasə ze:n?

163

Wenn von dem Fang der Jäger lustig zieht nach Haus,
vɛn fɔn dem faŋ der jeːgər lustɪç tsiːt nax haos,

da steckt kein sittsam Kind den Kopf zum Fenster 'naus.
daː ʃtɛkt kaen zɪtzam kɪnt den kopf tsum fɛnstər naos.

Geh, Bächlein, hin und sag ihr das;
geː, bɛçlaen, hɪn |unt zaːk |iːr das;

doch sag ihr nicht, hörst du, kein Wort,
dɔx zaːk |iːr nɪçt, høːrst duː, kaen vɔrt,

von meinem traurigen Gesicht; sag ihr:
fɔn maenəm traorɪgən gəzɪçt; zaːk |iːr,

Er schnitzt bei mir sich eine Pfeif aus Rohr,
eːr ʃnɪtst bae miːr zɪç |aenə pfaef |aos roːr,

und bläst den Kindern schöne Tänz
unt blɛːst den kɪndərn ʃøːnə tɛnts

und Lieder vor, sag ihr's!
|unt liːdər for, zaːk |iːrs!

Schubert   Fischerweise
              fɪʃərvaezə

Den Fischer fechten Sorgen und Gram und Leid nicht an,
den fɪʃər fɛçtən zɔrgən |unt graːm |unt laet nɪçt |an,

er löst am frühen Morgen mit leichtem Sinn den Kahn.
eːr løːst |am fryːən mɔrgən mɪt laeçtəm zɪn den kaːn.

Da lagert rings noch Friede auf Wald und Flur und Bach,
daː laːgərt rɪŋs nox friːdə |aof valt |unt fluːr |unt bax,

er ruft mit seinem Liede die goldne Sonne wach.
eːr ruːft mɪt zaenəm liːdə di gɔldnə zɔnnə vax.

Er singt zu seinem Werke aus voller frischer Brust,
eːr zɪŋt tsuː zaenəm vɛrkə |aos fɔllər frɪʃər brust,

die Arbeit gibt ihm Stärke, die Stärke Lebenslust.
di |arbaet giːpt |iːm ʃtɛrkə, di ʃtɛrkə leːbənslust.

Bald wird ein bunt Gewimmel in allen Tiefen laut,
balt vɪrt |aen bunt gəvɪmməl |ın |allən tiːfən laot,

und plätschert durch den Himmel, der sich im Wasser baut.
unt plɛtʃərt durç den hɪmməl, der zɪç |ım vasər baot.

Doch wer ein Netz will stellen, braucht Augen klar und gut,
dɔx veːr |aen nɛts vɪl ʃtɛllən, braoxt |aogən klaːr |ʊnt guːt,

muss heiter gleich den Wellen und frei sein wie die Flut;
mʊs haetər glaeç den vɛllən |ʊnt frae zaen viː di fluːt;

dort angelt auf der Brücke die Hirtin, schlauer Wicht!
dɔrt |aŋəlt |aof der brʏkə di hɪrtɪn, ʃlaoər vɪçt!

gib auf nur deine Tücke, den Fisch betrügst du nicht!
giːp |aof nuːr daenə tʏkə, den fɪʃ betrʏːkst duː nɪçt!

Schubert   Frühlingsglaube
            fryːlɪŋsglaobə

Die linden Lüfte sind erwacht,
di lɪndən lʏftə zɪnt |ɛrvaxt,

sie säuseln und wehen Tag und Nacht,
ziː zɔøzəln |ʊnt veːən taːk |ʊnt naxt,

sie schaffen an allen Enden.
ziː ʃafən |an |allən |ɛndən.

O frischer Duft, o neuer Klang!
oː frɪʃər dʊft, oː nɔøer klaŋ!

Nun, armes Herze, sei nicht bang!
nuːn, arməs hɛrtsə, zaɪ nɪçt baŋ!

nun muss sich alles wenden.
nuːn mʊs zɪç |alləs vɛndən.

Die Welt wird schöner mit jedem Tag,
di vɛlt vɪrt ʃønər mɪt jeːdəm taːk,

man weiss nicht, was noch werden mag,
man vaes nɪçt, vas nɔx veːrdən maːk,

das Blühen will nicht enden, es will nicht enden;
das blyːən vɪl nɪçt |ɛndən, ɛs vɪl nɪçt |ɛndən,

es blüht das fernste, tiefste Thal:
ɛs blyːt das fɛrnstə, tiːfstə taːl:

Nun, armes Herz, vergiss der Qual!
nuːn, arməs hɛrts, fɛrgɪs der kvaːl!

Nun muss sich alles wenden.
nuːn mʊs zɪç |alləs vɛndən.

165

Schubert   Frühlingstraum
            fry:lɪŋstraom

Ich träumte von bunten Blumen,
ɪç trɔømtə fɔn bʊntən blu:mən,

so wie sie wohl blühen im Mai,
zo: vi: zi: vo:l bly:ən |ɪm maen,

ich träumte von grünen Wiesen,
ɪç trɔømtə fɔn gry:nən vi:zən,

von lustigem Vogelgeschrei.
fɔn lʊstɪgəm fo:gəlgəʃrae.

Und als die Hähne krähten,
ʊnt |als di hɛ:nə krɛ:tən,

da ward mein Auge wach;
da: vart maen |aogə vax;

da war es kalt und finster,
da: va:r |ɛs kalt |ʊnt fɪnstər,

es schrieen die Raben vom Dach.
ɛs ʃri:ən di ra:bən fɔm dax.

Doch an den Fensterscheiben,
dɔx |an den fɛnstərʃaebən,

wer malte die Blätter da?
ve:r maltə di blɛtər da:?

Ihr lacht wohl über den Träumer,
i:r laxt vo:l |y:bər den trɔømər,

der Blumen im Winter sah?
der blu:mən |ɪm vɪntər za:?

Ich träumte von Lieb um Liebe,
ɪç trɔømtə fɔn li:p |ʊm li:bə,

von einer schönen Maid,
fɔn |aenər ʃø:nən maet,

von Herzen und von Küssen,
fɔn hɛrtsən |ʊnt fɔn kysən,

von Wonne und Seligkeit.
fɔn vɔnnə |ʊnt ze:lɪçkaet.

Und als die Hähne krähten,
ʊnt |als di hɛ:nə krɛ:tən,

da ward mein Herze wach;
da: vart maen hɛrtsə vax;

166

nun sitz ich hier alleine
nuːn zɪts |ɪç hiːr |allaenə

und denke dem Traume nach.
|unt dɛŋkə dem traomə nax.

Die Augen schliess ich wieder,
di |aogən ʃliːs |ɪç viːdər,

noch schlägt das Herz so warm.
nɔx ʃlɛːkt das hɛrts zoː varm.

Wann grünt ihr Blätter am Fenster?
van gryːnt |iːr blɛtər |am fɛnstər?

wann halt ich mein Liebchen im Arm?
van halt |ɪç maen liːpçən |ɪm |arm?

Schubert   Ganymed
               ganimeːt

Wie im Morgenglanze du rings mich anglühst,
viː |ɪm mɔrgənglantse duː rɪŋs mɪç |anglyːst,

Frühling, Geliebter!
fryːlɪŋ, gəliːptər!

Mit tausendfacher Liebeswonne sich an mein Herze drängt
mɪt taozəntfaxər liːbəsvɔnnə zɪç |an maen hɛrtsə drɛŋt

deiner ewigen Wärme heilig Gefühl,
daenər |eːvɪgən vɛrmə haelɪç gəfyːl,

unendliche Schöne!
un|ɛntlɪçə ʃøːnə!

Dass ich dich fassen möcht in diesen Arm!
das |ɪç dɪç fasən mœçt |ɪn diːzən |arm!

Ach, an deinem Busen lieg ich und schmachte,
ax, an daenəm buːzən liːk |ɪç |unt ʃmaxtə,

und deine Blumen,
unt daenə bluːmən,

dein Gras drängen sich an mein Herz.
daen graːs drɛŋən zɪç |an maen hɛrts.

Du kühlst den brennenden Durst meines Busens,
duː kyːlst den brɛnnəndən durst maenəs buːzəns,

167

lieblicher Morgenwind,
li:plɪçər mɔrgənvɪnt,

ruft drein die Nachtigall
ru:ft draen di naxtigal

liebend nach mir aus dem Nebeltal.
li:bənt nax mi:r |aos dem ne:bəlta:l.

Ich komm! ich komme! ach! wohin?
ɪç kɔm! ɪç kɔmmə! ax! vohɪn?

Hinauf strebt's, hinauf!
hɪnaof ʃtre:pts, hɪnaof!

Es schweben die Wolken abwärts,
ɛs ʃve:bən di vɔlkən |apvɛrts,

die Wolken neigen sich der sehnenden Liebe.
di vɔlkən naegən zɪç der ze:nəndən li:bə.

Mir! in eurem Schosse aufwärts! umfangend umfangen!
mi:r! ɪn |ɔørəm ʃo:sə |aofvɛrts! umfaŋənt |umfaŋən!

aufwärts an deinen Busen, all'liebender Vater!
aofvɛrts |an daenən bu:zən, alli:bəndər fa:tər!

Schubert   Gretchen am Spinnrade
            grɛ:tçən |am ʃpɪnra:də

Meine Ruh ist hin, mein Herz ist schwer;
maenə ru: |ɪst hɪn, maen hɛrts |ɪst ʃve:r,

ich finde sie nimmer und nimmermehr.
ɪç fɪndə zi: nɪmmər |unt nɪmmərme:r.

Wo ich ihn nicht hab, ist mir das Grab,
vo: |ɪç |i:n nɪçt ha:p, ɪst mi:r das gra:p,

die ganze Welt ist mir vergällt.
di gantsə vɛlt |ɪst mi:r fɛrgɛlt.

Mein armer Kopf ist mir verrückt,
maen |armər kɔpf |ɪst mi:r fɛrrykt,

mein armer Sinn ist mir zerstückt.
maen |armər zɪn |ɪst mi:r tsɛrʃtykt.

Meine Ruh ist hin, mein Herz ist schwer;
maenə ru: |ɪst hɪn, maen hɛrts |ɪst ʃve:r,

ich finde sie nimmer und nimmermehr.
ıç fındə zi: nımmər |ʊnt nımmərme:r.

Nach ihm nur schau ich zum Fenster hinaus,
nax |i:m nu:r ʃao |ıç tsum fɛnstər hınaos,

nach ihm nur geh ich aus dem Haus.
nax |i:m nu:r ge: |ıç |aos dem haos.

Sein hoher Gang, sein' edle Gestalt,
zaen ho:ər gaŋ, zaen |e:dlə gəʃtalt,

seines Mundes Lächeln, seiner Augen Gewalt,
zaenəs mʊndəs lɛçəln, zaenər |aogən gəvalt,

und seiner Rede Zauberfluss,
ʊnt zaenər re:də tsaobərflʊs,

sein Händedruck, und ach! sein Kuss!
zaen hɛndədrʊk, ʊnt |ax! zaen kʊs!

Meine Ruh ist hin, mein Herz ist schwer;
maenə ru: |ıst hın, maen hɛrts |ıst ʃve:r;

ich finde sie nimmer und nimmermehr.
ıç fındə zi: nımmər |ʊnt nımmərme:r.

Mein Busen drängt sich nach ihm hin.
maen bu:zən drɛŋt zıç na:x |i:m hın.

Ach! dürft ich fassen und halten ihn!
ax! dyrft |ıç fasən |ʊnt haltən |i:n!

und küssen ihn, so wie ich wollt,
ʊnt kysən |i:n, zo: vi: |ıç vɔlt,

an seinen Küssen vergehen sollt,
an zaenən kysən fɛrge:ən zɔlt,

o könnt ich ihn küssen, so wie ich wollt,
o: kœnt |ıç |i:n kysən, zo: vi: |ıç vɔlt,

an seinen Küssen vergehen sollt!
an zaenən kysən fɛrge:ən zɔlt!

Schubert   Heiden-Röslein
             haedən rø:zlaen

Sah ein Knab ein Röslein stehn, Röslein auf der Heiden,
za: |aen kna:p |aen rø:zlaen ʃte:n, rø:zlaen |aof der haedən,

169

war so jung und morgenschön, lief er schnell,
vaːr zoː juŋ |ʊnt mɔrgənʃøːn, liːf eːr ʃnəl,

es nah zu sehn, sah's mit vielen Freuden.
ɛs naː tsuː zeːn, zaːs mɪt fiːlən frɔødən.

Röslein, Röslein, Röslein rot, Röslein auf der Heiden.
røːzlaen, røːzlaen, røːzlaen roːt, røːzlaen |aof der haɪdən.

Knabe sprach: ich breche dich, Röslein auf der Heiden!
knaːbə ʃpraːx, ɪç brɛçə dɪç, røːzlaen |aof der haedən!

Röslein sprach: ich steche dich,
røːzlaen ʃpraːx, ɪç stɛçə dɪç,

dass du ewig denkst an mich,
das duː |eːvɪç dɛŋkst |an mɪç,

und ich will's nicht leiden.
ʊnt |ɪç vɪls nɪçt laedən.

Und der wilde Knabe brach 's Röslein auf der Heiden;
ʊnt der vɪldə knaːbə braːxs røːzlaen |aof der haedən,

Röslein wehrte sich und stach,
røːzlaen veːrtə zɪç |ʊnt ʃtaːx,

half ihr doch kein Weh und Ach,
half |iːr dɔx kaen veː |ʊnt |ax,

musst es eben leiden.
mʊst |ɛs |eːbən laedən.

Schubert   Ihr Bild
              iːr bɪlt

Ich stand in dunkeln Träumen und starrt' ihr Bildnis an,
ɪç ʃtant |ɪn dʊŋkəln trɔømən |ʊnt ʃtart |iːr bɪltnɪs |an,

und das geliebte Antlitz heimlich zu leben begann.
ʊnt das gəliːptə |antlɪts haemlɪç tsu leːbən bəgan.

Um ihre Lippen zog sich ein Lächeln wunderbar,
ʊm |iːrə lɪpən tsoːk zɪç aen lɛçəln vʊndərbaːr,

und wie von Wehmuthsthränen erglänzte ihr Augenpaar.
ʊnt viː fɔn veːmʊtstrɛːnən |ɛrglɛntstə |iːr |aogənpaːr.

Auch meine Thränen flossen mir von den Wangen herab-
aox maenə trɛːnən flɔsən miːr fɔn den vaŋən hɛrap-

und ach!   ich kann es nicht glauben,
ʊnt |ax!   ɪç kan |ɛs nɪçt glaoben,

dass ich dich verloren hab!
das |ɪç dɪç fɛrlo:rən ha:p!

Schubert   Jägers Abendlied
              jɛ:gərs |abəntli:t

Im Felde schleich ich still und wild,
ɪm fɛldə ʃlaeç |ɪç ʃtɪl |ʊnt vɪlt,

gespannt mein Feuerrohr,
gəʃpant maen foøerro:r,

da schwebt so licht dein liebes Bild,
da: ʃve:pt zo: lɪçt daen li:bəs bɪlt,

dein süsses Bild mir vor.
daen zy:səs bɪlt mi:r for.

Du wandelst jetzt wohl still und mild
du: vandəlst jɛtst vo:l ʃtɪl |ʊnt mɪlt

durch Feld und liebes Thal,
dʊrç fɛlt |ʊnt li:bəs ta:l,

und, ach, mein schnell verrauschend Bild
ʊnt, ax, maen ʃnɛl fɛrraoʃənt bɪlt

stellt sich dir's nicht einmal?
ʃtɛlt zɪç   di:rs nɪçt |aenma:l?

Mir ist es, denk ich nur an dich,
mi:r |ɪst |ɛs, dɛŋk |ɪç nu:r |an dɪç,

als in den Mond zu sehn,
als |ɪn den mo:nt tsu: ze:n,

ein stiller Friede kommt auf mich,
aen ʃtɪlər fri:də kɔmt |aof mɪç,

weiss nicht, wie mir geschehn.
vaes nɪçt, vi: mi:r gəʃe:n.

171

Schubert   Lachen und Weinen
             laxən |ʊnt vaenən

Lachen und Weinen zu jeglicher Stunde
laxən |ʊnt vaenən tsu: je:klɪçər ʃtʊndə

ruht bei der Lieb auf so mancherlei Grunde.
ru:t bae der li:p |aof zo: mançərlae grʊndə.

Morgens lacht' ich vor Lust,
mɔrgəns laxt |ɪç fɔr lʊst,

und warum ich nun weine bei des Abendes Scheine,
ʊnt varʊm |ɪç nu:n vaenə bae des |a:bəndəs ʃaenə,

ist mir selb' nicht bewusst, ist mir selb' nicht bewusst.
ɪst mi:r zɛlp nɪçt bəvʊst, ɪst mi:r zɛlp nɪçt bəvʊst.

Weinen und Lachen zu jeglicher Stunde,
vaenən |ʊnt laxən tsu: je:klɪçər ʃtʊndə,

ruht bei der Lieb auf so mancherlei Grunde.
ru:t bae der li:p |aof zo: mançərlae grʊndə.

Abends weint' ich vor Schmerz;
a:bənts vaent |ɪç fɔr ʃmɛrts;

und warum du erwachen kannst am Morgen mit Lachen,
ʊnt varʊm du: |ɛrvaxən kanst |am mɔrgən mɪt laxən,

muss ich dich fragen, o Herz, muss ich dich fragen, o Herz.
mʊs |ɪç dɪç fra:gən, o: hɛrts, mʊs |ɪç |dɪç fra:gən, o: hɛrts.

Schubert   Liebesbotschaft
             li:bəsbo:tʃaft

Rauschendes Bächlein, so silbern und hell,
raoʃəndəs bɛçlaen, zo: zɪlbərn |ʊnt hɛl,

eilst zur Geliebten so munter und schnell?
aelst tsur gəli:ptən zo: mʊntər |ʊnt ʃnɛl?

ach, trautes Bächlein, mein Bote sei du;
ax, traotəs bɛçlaen, maen bo:tə zae du:,

bringe die Grüsse des Fernen ihr zu.
brɪŋə di gry:sə dɛs fɛrnən |i:r tsu:.

All ihre Blumen im Garten gepflegt,
al |i:rə blu:mən ɪm gartən gəpfle:kt,

172

die sie so lieblich am Busen trägt,
di zi: zo: li:plɪç |am bu:zən trɛ:kt,

und ihre Rosen in purpurner Glut,
ʊnt |i:rə ro:zən |ɪn pʊrpʊrnər glu:t,

Bächlein erquicke mit kühlender Flut.
bɛçlaen |ɛrkvɪkə mɪt ky:ləndər flu:t.

Wenn sie am Ufer, in Träume versenkt,
vɛn zi: |am |u:fər, ɪn trɔømə fɛrzɛŋkt,

meiner gedenkend, das Köpfchen hängt,
maenər gədɛŋkənt, das kœpfçən hɛŋt,

tröste die Süsse mit freundlichem Blick,
trø:stə di zy:sə mɪt frɔøntlɪçəm blɪk,

denn der Geliebte kehrt bald zurück.
dɛn der gəli:ptə ke:rt balt tsuryk.

Neigt sich die Sonne mit röthlichem Schein,
naekt zɪç di zɔnnə mɪt rø:tlɪçəm ʃaen,

wiege das Liebchen in Schlummer ein.
vi:gə das li:pçən |ɪn ʃlʊmmər |aen.

Rausche sie murmelnd in süsse Ruh,
raoʃə zi: mʊrməlnt |ɪn zy:sə ru:,

flüstre ihr Träume der Liebe zu.
flystrə |i:r trɔømə der li:bə tsu:.

Schubert   Lied der Mignon
              li:t der miɲõ

Nur wer die Sehnsucht kennt, weiss, was ich leide!
nu:r ve:r di ze:nzʊxt kɛnt, vaes, vas |ɪç laedə!

Allein und abgetrennt von aller Freude,
allaen |ʊnt |apgətrɛnt fɔn |allər frɔødə,

seh ich ans Firmament nach jener Seite.
ze: |ɪç |ans fɪrmamɛnt nax je:nər zaetə.

Ach! der mich liebt und kennt, ist in der Weite.
ax! der mɪç li:pt |ʊnt kɛnt, ɪst |ɪn der vaetə.

Es schwindelt mir, es brennt mein Eingeweide.
ɛs ʃvɪndəlt mi:r, ɛs brɛnt maen |aengəvaedə.

Schubert   Litanei
             litanae

Ruhn in Frieden alle Seelen,
ruːn |ɪn friːdən |alə zeːlən,

die vollbracht ein banges Quälen,
di fɔlbraxt |aen baŋəs kvɛːlən,

die vollendet süssen Traum,
di fɔl|ɛndət zyːsən traom,

lebenssatt, geboren kaum,
leːbənsat, gəboːrən kaom,

aus der Welt hinüber schieden:
aos der vɛlt hɪnyːbər ʃiːdən,

alle Seelen ruhn in Frieden!
alə zeːlən ruːn |ɪn friːdən!

Liebevoller Mädchen Seelen,
liːbəfɔlər mɛːtçən zeːlən,

deren Thränen nicht zu zählen,
deːrən trɛːnən nɪçt tsuː tsɛːlən,

die ein falscher Freund verliess,
di |aen falʃər frɔønt fɛrliːs,

und die blinde Welt verstiess:
ʊnt di blɪndə vɛlt fɛrʃtiːs,

alle, die von hinnen schieden,
alə, di fɔn hɪnnən ʃiːdən,

alle Seelen ruhn in Frieden!
alə zeːlən ruːn |ɪn friːdən!

Und die nie der Sonne lachten,
ʊnt di niː der zɔnnə laxtən,

unterm Mond auf Dornen wachten,
ʊntərm moːnt |aof dɔrnən vaxtən,

Gott im reinen Himmelslicht
gɔt ɪm raenən hɪmməlslɪçt

einst zu sehn von Angesicht:
aenst tsuː zeːn fɔn |angəsɪçt,

alle, die von hinnen schieden,
alə, di fɔn hɪnnən ʃiːdən,

alle Seelen ruhn in Frieden!
alə zeːlən ruːn |ɪn friːdən!

Schubert   Nacht und Träume
                naxt |ʊnt trɔømə

Heilge Nacht, du sinkest nieder;
haelgə naxt, du: zɪŋkəst ni:dər;

nieder wallen auch die Träume,
ni:dər vallən |aox di trɔømə,

wie dein Mondlicht durch die Räume,
vi: daen mo:ntlɪçt durç di rɔømə,

durch der Menschen stille, stille Brust.
durç der menʃən ʃtɪllə, ʃtɪllə brʊst.

Die belauschen sie mit Lust;
di bəlaoʃən zi: mɪt lʊst;

rufen, wenn der Tag erwacht:
ru:fən, ven der ta:k |ɛrvaxt,

Kehre wieder, heilge Nacht!
ke:rə vi:dər, haelgə naxt!

holde Träume, kehret wieder!
holdə trɔømə, ke:rət vi:dər!

Schubert   Rastlose Liebe
                rastlo:zə li:bə

Dem Schnee, dem Regen, dem Wind entgegen,
dem ʃne:, dem re:gən, dem vɪnt |ɛntge:gən,

im Dampf der Klüfte, durch Nebeldüfte immer zu!
ɪm dampf der klyftə, durç ne:bəldyftə |ɪmmər tsu:!

ohne Rast und Ruh!
o:nə rast |ʊnt ru:!

Lieber durch Leiden wollt ich mich schlagen,
li:bər durç laedən volt |ɪç mɪç ʃla:gən,

als so viel Freuden des Lebens ertragen.
als zo: fi:l frɔødən des le:bəns |ɛrtra:gən.

Alle das Neigen von Herzen zu Herzen,
alləs das naegən fon hɛrtsən tsu: hɛrtsən,

ach, wie so eigen schaffet es Schmerzen!
ax, vi: zo: |aegən ʃafət |ɛs ʃmɛrtsən!

175

Wie, soll ich fliehn? Wälderwärts ziehn?
viː, zɔl |ɪç fliːn? vɛldərvɛrts tsiːn?

Alles vergebens!
aləs fɛrgeːbəns!

Krone des Lebens, Glück ohne Ruh,
kroːnə dɛs leːbəns, glʏk |oːnə ruː,

Liebe bist du, o Liebe bist du!
liːbə bɪst duː, oː liːbə bɪst duː!

Schubert   Sei mir gegrüsst
            zae miːr gəgryːst

O du Entrissne mir und meinem Kusse,
oː duː |ɛntrɪsnə miːr |ʊnt maenəm kʊsə,

sei mir gegrüsst, sei mir geküsst!
zae miːr gəgryːst, zae miːr gəkʏst!

Erreichbar nur meinem Sehnsuchtsgrusse,
ɛrraeçbaːr nuːr maenəm zeːnzʊxtsgruːsə,

sei mir gegrüsst, sei mir geküsst!
zae miːr gəgryːst, zae miːr gəkʏst!

Du von der Hand der Liebe diesem Herzen Gegebne,
duː fɔn der hant der liːbə diːzəm hɛrtsən gəgeːbnə,

du von dieser Brust Genommne mir!
duː fɔn diːzər brʊst gənɔmnə miːr!

mit diesem Tränengusse
mɪt diːzəm trɛːnəngʊsə

sei mir gegrüsst, sei mir geküsst!
zae miːr gəgryːst, zae miːr gəkʏst!

Zum Trotz der Ferne, die sich, feindlich trennend,
tsum trots der fɛrnə, di zɪç, faentlɪç trɛnənt,

hat zwischen mich und dich gestellt;
hat tsvɪʃən mɪç |ʊnt dɪç gəʃtɛlt;

dem Neid der Schicksalsmächte zum Verdrusse
dem naet der ʃɪkzalzmɛçtə tsum fɛrdrʊsə

sei mir gegrüsst, sei mir geküsst!
zae miːr gəgryːst, zae miːr gəkʏst!

Wie du mir je im schönsten Lenz der Liebe
viː duː miːr jeː |ɪm ʃøːnstən lɛnts der liːbə

mit Gruss und Kuss entgegenkamst,
mɪt gruːs |ʊnt kʊs |ɛntgeːgənkaːmst,

mit meiner Seele glühendstem Ergusse
mɪt maenər zeːlə glyːəntstəm |ɛrgʊsə

sei mir gegrüsst, sei mir geküsst!
zae miːr gəgryːst, zae miːr gəkʏst!

Ein Hauch der Liebe tilget Räum' und Zeiten,
aen haox der liːbə tɪlgət rɔøm |ʊnt tsaetən,

ich bin bei dir, du bist bei mir,
ɪç bɪn bae diːr, duː bɪst bae miːr,

ich halte dich in dieses Arms Umschlusse,
ɪç haltə dɪç |ɪn diːzəs |arms |ʊmʃlʊsə,

sei mir gegrüsst, sei mir geküsst!
zae miːr gəgryːst, zae miːr gəkʏst!

Schubert   Ständchen
              ʃtɛntçən

Leise flehen meine Lieder durch die Nacht zu dir;
laezə fleːən maenə liːdər dʊrç di naxt tsuː diːr;

in den stillen Hain hernieder, Liebchen, komm zu mir!
ɪn den ʃtɪllən haen hɛrniːdər, liːpçən, kɔm tsuː miːr!

Flüsternd schlanke Wipfel rauschen in des Mondes Licht,
flʏstərnt ʃlaŋkə vɪpfəl raoʃən |ɪn dɛs moːndəs lɪçt,

des Verräthers feindlich Lauschen fürchte, Holde, nicht.
dɛs fɛrrɛːtərs faentlɪç laoʃən fʏrçtə, hɔldə, nɪçt.

Hörst die Nachtigallen schlagen? ach! sie flehen dich,
høːrst di naxtɪgallən ʃlaːgən? ax! ziː fleːən dɪç,

mit der Töne süssen Klagen flehen sie für mich.
mɪt der tøːnə zyːsən klaːgən fleːən ziː fyːr mɪç.

Sie verstehn des Busens Sehnen, kennen Liebesschmerz,
ziː fɛrʃteːn dɛs buːzəns zeːnən, kɛnnən liːbəsʃmɛrts,

rühren mit den Silbertönen jedes weiche Herz.
ryːrən mɪt den zɪlbərtøːnən jeːdəs vaeçə hɛrts.

177

Lass auch dir die Brust bewegen, Liebchen, höre mich!
las |aox diːr di brust bəveːgən, liːpçən, høːrə mɪç!

bebend harr ich dir entgegen! komm, beglücke mich!
beːbənt har |ɪç diːr |ɛntgeːgən! kɔm, bəglʏkə mɪç!

Schubert   Ungeduld
             ʊngədʊlt

Ich schnitt' es gern in alle Rinden ein,
ɪç ʃnɪt |ɛs gɛrn |ɪn |allə rɪndən |aen,

ich grüb es gern in jeden Kieselstein,
ɪç gryːp |ɛs gɛrn |ɪn jeːdən kiːzəlʃtaen,

ich möcht es sä'n auf jedes frische Beet
ɪç mœçt |ɛs zeːn |aof jeːdəs frɪʃə beːt

mit Kressensamen, der es schnell verrät,
mɪt krɛsənzaːmən, der |ɛs ʃnɛl fɛrreːt,

auf jeden weissen Zettel möcht ich's schreiben:
aof jeːdən vaesən tsɛtəl mœçt |ɪçs ʃraebən,

Dein ist mein Herz, dein ist mein Herz
daen |ɪst maen hɛrts, daen |ɪst maen hɛrts

und soll es ewig, ewig bleiben!
ʊnt zɔl |ɛs |eːvɪç, eːvɪç blaebən!

Ich möcht mir ziehen einen jungen Staar,
ɪç mœçt miːr tsiːən |aenən jʊŋən ʃtaːr,

bis dass er spräch die Worte rein und klar,
bɪs das |eːr ʃprɛç di vɔrtə raen |ʊnt klaːr,

bis er sie spräch mit meines Mundes Klang,
bɪs |eːr ziː ʃprɛç mɪt maenəs mʊndəs klaŋ,

mit meines Herzens vollem, heissen Drang;
mɪt maenəs hɛrtsəns fɔlləm, haesən draŋ,

dann säng er hell durch ihre Fensterscheiben:
dan zɛŋ |eːr hɛl dʊrç |iːrə fɛnstərʃaebən,

Dein ist mein Herz...
daen |ɪst maen hɛrts...

Den Morgenwinden möcht ich's hauchen ein,
den mɔrgənvɪndən mœçt |ɪçs haoxən |aen,

ich möcht es säuseln durch den regen Hain;
ɪç mœçt |ɛs zɔøzəln durç den reːgən haen;

o, leuchtet' es aus jedem Blumenstern!
oː, lɔøçtət |ɛs |aos jeːdəm bluːmənʃtɛrn!

trüg es der Duft zu ihr von nah und fern!
tryːk |ɛs der duft tsuː |iːr fon naː |unt fɛrn!

ihr Wogen, könnt ihr nichts als Räder treiben?
iːr voːgən, kœnt |iːr nɪçts |als rɛːdər traebən?

Ich meint, es müsst in meinen Augen stehn,
ɪç maent, ɛs myst |ɪn maenən |aogən ʃteːn,

auf meinen Wangen müsst man's brennen sehn,
aof maenən vaŋən myst mans brɛnnən zeːn,

zu lesen wär's auf meinem stummen Mund,
tsuː leːzən vɛːrs |aof maenəm ʃtummən munt,

ein jeder Atemzug gäb's laut ihr kund;
aen jeːdər |aːtəmtsuːk gɛːps laot |iːr kunt;

und sie merkt nichts von all dem bangen Treiben.
unt ziː mɛrkt nɪçts fon |al dem baŋən traebən.

Schubert   Wanderers Nachtlied
               vandərərs naxtliːt

Über allen Gipfeln ist Ruh,
yːbər |allən gɪpfəln |ɪst ruː,

in allen Wipfeln spürest du
ɪn |allən vɪpfəln ʃpyːrəst duː

kaum einen Hauch;
kaom |aenən haox,

die Vöglein schweigen,
di føːglaen ʃvaegən,

schweigen im Walde.
ʃvaegən |ɪm valdə.

Warte nur, warte nur,
vartə nuːr, vartə nuːr,

balde ruhest du auch.
baldə ruːəst duː |aox.

179

Schubert   Wiegenlied
            vi:gənli:t

Schlafe, schlafe, holder, süsser Knabe,
ʃla:fə, ʃla:fə, hɔldər, zy:sər kna:bə,

leise wiegt dich deiner Mutter Hand;
laezə vi:kt dɪç daenər mʊtər hant;

sanfte Ruhe, milde Labe
zanftə ru:ə, mɪldə la:bə

bringt dir schwebend dieses Wiegenband.
brɪŋt di:r ʃve:bənt di:zəs vi:gənbant.

Schlafe, schlafe in dem süssen Grabe,
ʃla:fə, ʃla:fə |ɪn dem zy:sən gra:bə,

noch beschützt dich deiner Mutter Arm;
nɔx bəʃʏtst dɪç daenər mʊtər |arm;

alle Wünsche, alle Habe
allə vʏnʃə, allə ha:bə

fasst sie liebend, alle liebewarm.
fast zi: li:bənt, allə li:bəvarm.

Schlafe, schlafe in der Flaumen Schosse,
ʃla:fə, ʃla:fə |ɪn der flaomən ʃo:sə,

noch umtönt dich lauter Liebeston,
nɔx |umtø:nt dɪç laotər li:bəsto:n,

eine Lilie, eine Rose,
aenə li:ljə, aenə ro:zə,

nach dem Schlafe werd sie dir zum Lohn.
nax dem ʃla:fə ve:rt zi: di:r tsum lo:n.

Schubert   Wohin?
            vohɪn?

Ich hört ein Bächlein rauschen wohl aus dem Felsenquell,
ɪç hø:rt |aen bɛçlaen raoʃən vo:l |aos dem fɛlzənkvɛl,

hinab zum Tale rauschen so frisch und wunderhell.
hɪnap tsum ta:lə raoʃən zo: friʃ |unt vundərhɛl.

Ich weiss nicht, wie mir wurde,
ɪç vaes nɪçt, vi: mi:r vʊrdə,

nicht, wer den Rat mir gab,
nɪçt, ve:r den ra:t mi:r ga:p,

180

ich musste auch hinunter mit meinem Wanderstab.
ɪç mʊstə |aox hɪnʊntər mɪt maenəm vandərʃta:p.

Hinunter und immer weiter, und immer dem Bache nach,
hɪnʊntər |ʊnt |ɪmmər vaetər, ʊnt |ɪmmər dem baxə nax,

und immer frischer rauschte und immer heller der Bach.
ʊnt |ɪmmər frɪʃər raoʃtə |ʊnt |ɪmmər hɛllər der bax.

Ist das denn meine Strasse?   O Bächlein, sprich, wohin?
ɪst das dɛn maenə ʃtrasə? o: bɛçlaen, ʃprɪç, vohɪn?

du hast mit deinem Rauschen mir ganz berauscht den Sinn.
du: hast mɪt daenəm raoʃən mi:r gants bəraoʃt den zɪn.

Was sag ich denn vom Rauschen?
vas za:k |ɪç dɛn fɔm raoʃən?

das kann kein Rauschen sein:
das kan kaen raoʃən zaen,

Es singen wohl die Nixen tief unten ihren Reihn.
ɛs zɪŋən vo:l di nɪksən ti:f |ʊntən |i:rən raen.

Lass singen, Gesell, lass rauschen,
las zɪŋən, gəzɛl, las raoʃən,

und wandre fröhlich nach!
ʊnt vandrə frø:lɪç nax!

Es gehn ja Mühlenräder in jedem klaren Bach.
ɛs ge:n ja: my:lənrɛ:dər |ɪn je:dəm kla:rən bax.

Schumann   Dein Angesicht
              daen |angəzɪçt

Dein Angesicht, so lieb und schön,
daen |angəzɪçt, zo: li:p |ʊnt ʃø:n,

das hab' ich jüngst im Traum geseh'n,
das ha:p ɪç jʏŋst |ɪm traom gəze:n,

es ist so mild und engelgleich,
ɛs ɪst zo: mɪlt |ʊnt |ɛŋəlglaeç,

und doch so bleich, so schmerzenreich.
ʊnt dɔx zo: blaeç, zo: ʃmɛrtsənraeç.

181

Und nur die Lippen, die sind roth;
unt nuːr di lɪpən, di zɪnt roːt;

bald aber küsst sie bleich der Tod.
balt ǀaːbər kʏst ziː blɛeç der toːt.

Erlöschen wird das Himmelslicht,
ɛrlœʃən vɪrt das hɪmməslɪçt,

das aus den frommen Augen bricht.
das ǀaos den frɔmmən ǀaogən brɪçt.

Schumann   Der Nussbaum
             der nʊsbaom

Es grünet ein Nussbaum vor dem Haus,
ɛs gryːnət ǀaen nʊsbaom foɾ dem haos,

duftig, luftig breitet er blätt'rig die Äste aus.
dʊftɪç, lʊftɪç braetət ǀeːr blɛtrɪç di ǀɛstə ǀaos.

Viel liebliche Blüthen stehen d'ran;
fiːl liːplɪçə blyːtən ʃteːən dran;

linde Winde kommen, sie herzlich zu umfah'n.
lɪndə vɪndə kɔmmən, ziː hɛrtslɪç tsuː ǀʊmfaːn.

Es flüstern je zwei zu zwei gepaart,
ɛs flʏstərn jeː tsvae tsuː tsvae gəpaːrt,

neigend, beugend zierlich zum Kusse
naegənt, boøgənt tsiːrlɪç tsum kʊsə

die Häuptchen zart.
di hoøptçən tsart.

Sie flüstern von einem Mägdlein,
ziː flʏstərn fɔn ǀaenəm mɛːktlaen,

das dächte die Nächte und Tage lang,
das dɛçtə di nɛçtə ǀʊnt taːgə laŋ,

wusste, ach! selber nicht, was.
vʊstə, ax! zɛlbər nɪçt, vas.

Sie flüstern, wer mag versteh'n so gar leise Weis'?
ziː flʏstərn, veːr maːk fɛrʃteːn zoː gaːr laezə vaes?

flüstern vom Bräut'gam und nächstem Jahr.
flʏstərn fɔm broøtgaːm ǀʊnt nɛçstəm jaːr.

Das Mägdlein horchet, es rauscht im Baum,
das mɛːktlaen hǫrçət, ɛs raoʃt |ɪm baom,

sehnend, wähnend sinkt es
zeːnənt, vɛːnənt zɪŋkt |ɛs

lächelnd in Schlaf und Traum.
lɛçəlnt |ɪn ʃlaːf |ʊnt traom.

Schumann   Frauenliebe und –Leben
               fraoənliːbə |ʊnt leːbən

               1. Seit ich ihn gesehen
                  zaet |ɪç |iːn gəzeːən

Seit ich ihn gesehen,
zaet |ɪç |iːn gəzeːən,

glaub' ich blind zu sein;
glaop |ɪç blɪnt tsuː zaen;

wo ich hin nur blicke,
voː |ɪç hɪn nuːr blɪkə,

seh' ich ihn allein;
zeː |ɪç |iːn |allaen;

wie im wachen Traume
viː |ɪm vaxən traomə

schwebt sein Bild mir vor,
ʃveːpt zaen bɪlt miːr for,

taucht aus tiefstem Dunkel
taoxt |aos tiːfstəm dʊŋkəl

heller, heller nur empor.
hɛllər, hɛllər nuːr |ɛmpoːr.

Sonst ist licht– und farblos
zɔnst |ɪst lɪçt |ʊnt farbloːs

alles um mich her,
|alləs |ʊm mɪç heːr,

nach der Schwestern Spiele
nax der ʃvɛstərn ʃpiːlə

nicht begehr' ich mehr,
nɪçt bəgeːr |ɪç meːr,

183

möchte lieber weinen,
mœçtə liːbər vaenən,

still im Kämmerlein;
ʃtɪl |ɪm kɛmmərlaen;

seit ich ihn gesehen,
zaet |ɪç |iːn gəzeːən,

glaub' ich blind zu sein.
glaop |ɪç blɪnt t͜su: zaen.

Schumann   Frauenliebe und –Leben

　　　　　　2.　Er, der Herrlichste von allen
　　　　　　　　eːr, der hɛrlɪçstə fɔn |allən

Er, der Herrlichste von allen,
eːr, der hɛrlɪçstə fɔn |allən,

wie so milde, wie so gut!
viː zoː mɪldə, viː zoː guːt!

Holde Lippen, klares Auge,
hɔlde lɪpən, klaːrəs |aogə,

heller Sinn und fester Muth.
hɛllər zɪn |ʊnt fɛstər muːt.

So wie dort in blauer Tiefe,
zoː viː dɔrt |ɪn blaoər tiːfə,

hell und herrlich, jener Stern,
hɛl |ʊnt hɛrlɪç, jeːnər ʃtɛrn,

also Er an meinem Himmel,
alzo eːr |an maenəm hɪmməl,

hell und herrlich, hehr und fern.
hɛl |ʊnt hɛrlɪç, heːr |ʊnt fɛrn.

Wandle, wandle deine Bahnen,
vandlə, vandlə daenə baːnən,

nur betrachten deinen Schein,
nuːr bətraxtən daenən ʃaen,

nur in Demuth ihn betrachten,
nuːr |ɪn deːmuːt |iːn bətraxtən,

selig nur, und traurig sein!
zeːlɪç nuːr, |ʊnt traorɪç zaen!

184

Höre nicht mein stilles Beten,
høːrə nɪçt maen ʃtɪlləs beːtən,

deinem Glücke nur geweiht;
daenəm glʏkə nuːr gəvaet;

darfst mich, nied're Magd, nicht kennen,
darfst mɪç, niːdrə maːkt, nɪçt kɛnnən,

hoher Stern der Herrlichkeit.
hoːər ʃtɛrn der hɛrlɪçkaet.

Nur die Würdigste von allen
nuːr di vʏrdɪçstə fɔn |allən

darf beglücken deine Wahl,
darf beglʏkən daenə vaːl,

und ich will die Hohe segnen
ʊnt |ɪç vɪl di hoːə zeːgnən

viele tausendmal.
fiːlə taozəntmaːl.

Will mich freuen dann und weinen,
vɪl mɪç frɔøən dan |ʊnt vaenən,

selig, selig bin ich dann,
zeːlɪç, zeːlɪç bɪn |ɪç dan,

sollte mir das Herz auch brechen,
zɔltə miːr das hɛrts |aox brɛçən,

brich, o Herz, was liegt daran?
brɪç, oː hɛrts, vas liːkt daran?

Schumann   Frauenliebe und —Leben

      3. Ich kann's nicht fassen, nicht glauben
      ɪç kans nɪçt fasən, nɪçt glaobən

Ich kann's nicht fassen, nicht glauben,
ɪç kans nɪçt fasən, nɪçt glaobən,

es hat ein Traum mich berückt;
ɛs hat aen traom mɪç bərʏkt;

wie hätt' er doch unter allen
viː hɛt |eːr dɔx |ʊntər |allən

mich Arme erhöht und beglückt?
mɪç |armə |ɛrhøːt |ʊnt bəglʏkt?

185

Mir war's, er habe gesprochen:
miːr vaːrs, eːr haːbə gəʃprɔxən,

"Ich bin auf ewig dein,"
"ɪç bɪn |aof |eːvɪç daen,"

mir war's ich träume noch immer,
miːr vaːrs |ɪç trɔømə nɔx |ɪmmər,

es kann ja nimmer so sein.
ɛs kan jaː nɪmmər zoː zaen.

O lass im Traume mich sterben,
oː lass |ɪm traomə mɪç ʃtɛrbən,

gewieget an seiner Brust,
gəviːgət |an zaenər brʊst,

den seligen Tod mich schlürfen
den zeːlɪgən toːt mɪç ʃlʏrfən

in Thränen unendlicher Lust.
|ɪn trɛːnən |ʊn|ɛntlɪçər lʊst.

Schumann   Frauenliebe und −Leben

           4. Der Ring
              der rɪŋ

Du Ring an meinem Finger,
duː rɪŋ |an maenəm fɪŋər,

mein goldenes Ringelein,
maen gɔldənəs rɪŋəlaen,

ich drücke dich fromm an die Lippen,
ɪç drʏkə dɪç frɔm |an di lɪpən,

an das Herze mein.
an das hɛrtsə maen.

Ich hatt' ihn ausgeträumet,
ɪç hat |iːn |aosgətrɔømət,

der Kindheit friedlich schönen Traum,
der kɪnthaet friːtlɪç ʃøːnən traom,

ich fand allein mich, verloren
ɪç fant |allaen mɪç, fɛrloːrən

186

im öden, unendlichen Raum.
|ɪm |ø:dən, ʊn|ɛntlɪçən ra̠om.

Du Ring an meinem Finger,
du: rɪŋ |an ma̠enəm fɪ̠ŋər,

da hast du mich erst belehrt,
da: hast‿du: mɪç |e:rst bəle̠:rt,

hast meinem Blick erschlossen
hast ma̠enəm blɪk |ɛrʃlo̠sən

des Lebens unendlichen, tiefen Wert.
dɛs le̠:bəns |ʊn|ɛntlɪçən, ti̠:fən ve:rt.

Ich will ihm dienen, ihm leben,
ɪç vɪl |i:m di̠:nən, i:m le̠:bən,

ihm angehören ganz,
i:m |a̠ngəhø:rən gants,

hin selber mich geben und finden
hɪn ze̠lbər mɪç ge:bən |ʊnt fɪ̠ndən

verklärt mich in seinem Glanz.
fɛrkle̠:rt mɪç |ɪn za̠enəm glants.

Schumann Frauenliebe und –Leben

   5. Helft mir, ihr Schwestern
    hɛlft mi:r, i:r ʃve̠stərn

Helft mir, ihr Schwestern, freundlich mich schmücken,
hɛlft mi:r, i:r ʃve̠stərn, fro̠øntlɪç mɪç ʃmy̠kən,

dient der Glücklichen heute, mir!
di:nt‿der gly̠klɪçən ho̠øtə, mi:r!

Windet geschäftig mir um die Stirne
vɪ̠ndət gəʃɛftɪç mi:r |ʊm di ʃtɪrnə

noch der blühenden Myrthe Zier.
nɔx der bly̠:əndən my̠rtə tsi:r.

Als ich befriedigt, freudigen Herzens,
als |ɪç bəfri̠:dɪçt, fro̠ødɪgən hɛrtsəns,

sonst dem Geliebten im Arme lag,
zɔnst‿dem gəli̠:ptən |ɪm |a̠rmə la:k,

187

immer noch rief er, Sehnsucht im Herzen,
ɪmmər nɔx riːf |eːr, zeːnzʊxt |ɪm hɛrtsən,

ungeduldig den heutigen Tag.
ʊngəduldɪç den hɔøtɪgən taːk.

Helft mir, ihr Schwestern, helft mir verscheuchen
hɛlft miːr, iːr ʃvɛstərn, hɛlft miːr fɛrʃɔøçən

eine thörichte Bangigkeit;
aenə tøːrɪçtə baŋɪçkaet;

dass ich mit klarem Aug' ihn empfange,
das |ɪç mɪt klaːrəm |aok |iːn |ɛmpfaŋə,

ihn, die Quelle der Freudigkeit.
iːn, di kvɛllə der frɔødɪçkaet.

Bist, mein Geliebter, du mir erschienen,
bɪst, maen gəliːptər, duː miːr |ɛrʃiːnən,

giebst du mir, Sonne, deinen Schein?
giːpst duː miːr, zɔnnə, daenən ʃaen?

Lass mich in Andacht, lass mich in Demuth,
las mɪç |ɪn |andaxt, las mɪç |ɪn deːmuːt,

lass mich verneigen, dem Herren mein.
las mɪç fɛrnaegən, dem hɛrrən maen.

Streuet ihm, Schwestern, streuet ihm Blumen,
ʃtrɔøet iːm, ʃvɛstərn, ʃtrɔøet |iːm bluːmən,

bringet ihm knospende Rosen dar.
brɪŋət |iːm knɔspəndə roːzən daːr.

Aber euch, Schwestern, grüss' ich mit Wehmuth,
aːbər |ɔøç, ʃvɛstərn, gryːs |ɪç mɪt veːmuːt,

freudig scheidend aus eurer Schaar.
frɔødɪç ʃaedənt |aos |ɔørər ʃaːr.

Schumann   Frauenliebe und –Leben

    6. Süsser Freund
       zyːsər frɔønt

Süsser Freund, du blickest mich verwundert an,
zyːsər frɔønt, duː blɪkəst mɪç fɛrvʊndərt |an,

kannst es nicht begreifen, wie ich weinen kann;
kanst |ɛs nɪçt bəgraefən, viː |ɪç vaenən kan;

188

lass der feuchten Perlen ungewohnte Zier
las der fͻͻçtən pɛrlən |ʊngəvoːntə tsiːr

freudig hell erzittern in dem Auge mir.
frͻødɪç hɛl |ɛrtsɪtərn |ɪn dem |aͻgə miːr.

Wie so bang mein Busen, wie so wonnevoll!
viː zoː baŋ maͻn buːzən, viː zo vͻnnəfͻl!

wüsst' ich nur mit Worten, wie ich's sagen soll;
vyːst |ɪç nuːr mɪt vͻrtən, viː ɪçs zaːgən zͻl;

komm und birg dein Antlitz hier an meiner Brust,
kͻm |ʊnt bɪrk daͻn |antlɪts hiːr |an maͻnər brʊst,

will in's Ohr dir flüstern alle meine Lust.
vɪl |ɪns |oːr diːr flͻstərn |allə maͻnə lʊst.

Weisst du nun die Thränen, die ich weinen kann,
vaͻst du: nuːn di trɛːnən, di |ɪç vaͻnən kan,

sollst du nicht sie sehen, du geliebter, geliebter Mann!
zͻlst du: nɪçt zi: zɛːən, du: gəliːptər, gəliːptər man!

Bleib an meinem Herzen, fühl'e dessen Schlag,
blaͻp |an maͻnəm hͻrtsən, fyːlə dͻsən ʃlaːk,

dass ich fest und fester nur dich drücken mag,
das |ɪç fͻst |ʊnt fͻstər nuːr dɪç drͻkən maːk,

fest und fester!
fͻst |ʊnt fͻstər!

Hier an meinem Bette hat die Wiege Raum,
hiːr |an maͻnəm bͻtə hat di: viːgə raͻm,

wo sie still verberge meinen holden Traum;
voː zi: ʃtɪl fͻrbͻrgə maͻnən hͻldən traͻm;

kommen wird der Morgen, wo der Traum erwacht,
kͻmmən vɪrt der mͻrgən, voː der traͻm |ɛrvaͻxt,

und daraus dein Bildnis mir entgegen lacht.
ʊnt daraͻs daͻn bͻltnɪs miːr |ɛntgeːgən laxt.

Schumann   Frauenliebe und –Leben

    7. An meinem Herzen
        an maͻnəm hͻrtsən

An meinem Herzen, an meiner Brust,
an maͻnəm hͻrtsən, an maͻnər brʊst,

189

du meine Wonne, du meine Lust!
duː maenə vɔnnə, duː maenə lʊst!

Das Glück ist die Liebe, die Lieb' ist das Glück,
das glʏk |ɪst di liːbə, di liːp |ɪst das glʏk,

ich hab's gesagt und nehm's nicht zurück.
ɪç haps gəzaːkt ʊnt neːms nɪçt tsurʏk.

Hab' überschwenglich mich geschätzt,
haːp |yːbərʃvɛŋlɪç mɪç gəʃɛtst,

bin überglücklich aber jetzt.
bɪn |yːbərglʏklɪç |aːbər jɛtst.

Nur die da säugt, nur die da liebt
nuːr di daː zɔøkt, nuːr di daː liːpt

das Kind, dem sie die Nahrung gibt;
das kɪnt, dem ziː di naːrʊŋ giːpt;

nur eine Mutter weiss allein,
nuːr |aenə mʊtər vaes |allaen,

was lieben heisst und glücklich sein.
vas liːbən haest |ʊnt glʏklɪç zaen.

O wie bedaur' ich doch den Mann,
oː viː bədaor |ɪç dɔx den man,

der Mutterglück nicht fühlen kann!
der mʊtərglʏk nɪçt fyːlən kan!

Du lieber, lieber Engel du,
duː liːbər, liːbər |ɛŋəl duː,

du schauest mich an und lächelst dazu!
duː ʃaoəst mɪç |an |ʊnt lɛçəlst datsuː!

An meinem Herzen, an meiner Brust,
an maenəm hɛrtsən, an maenər brʊst,

du meine Wonne, du meine Lust!
duː maenə vɔnnə, duː maenə lʊst!

Schumann   Frauenliebe und –Leben

8. Nun hast du mir den ersten Schmerz gethan,
   nuːn hast duː miːr den |eːrstən ʃmɛrts gətaːn,

Nun hast du mir den ersten Schmerz gethan,
nuːn hast duː miːr den |eːrstən ʃmɛrts gətaːn,

der aber traf.
der |a̲ːbər traːf.

Du schläfst, du harter, unbarmherz' ger Mann,
duː ʃlɛːfst, duː ha̲rtər, u̲nbarmhɛrtsgər man,

den Todesschlaf.
den to̲ːdəsʃlaːf.

Es blicket die Verlass'ne vor sich hin,
ɛs blɪ̲kət di fɛrla̲snə foːr zɪç hɪn,

die Welt ist leer, ist leer.
di vɛlt |ɪst leːr, ɪst leːr.

Geliebet hab' ich und gelebt,
geli̲ːbət hap |ɪç |ʊnt gəle̲ːpt,

ich bin nicht lebend mehr.
ɪç bɪn nɪçt le̲ːbənt meːr.

Ich zieh' mich in mein Inn'res still zurück,
ɪç tsiː mɪç |ɪn ma̲en |ɪnrəs ʃtɪl tsurʏ̲k,

der Schleier fällt,
der ʃla̲eər fɛlt,

da hab' ich dich und mein verlornes Glück,
daː hap |ɪç dɪç |ʊnt ma̲en fɛrlo̲ːrnəs glʏk,

du meine Welt!
duː ma̲enə vɛlt!

Schumann   Dichterliebe

     1. Im wunderschönen Monat Mai
        ɪm vʊ̲ndərʃøːnən mo̲ːnat ma̲e

Im wunderschönen Monat Mai,
ɪm vʊ̲ndərʃøːnən mo̲ːnat ma̲e,

als alle Knospen sprangen,
als |a̲llə kno̲spən ʃpra̲ŋən,

da ist in meinem Herzen
daː |ɪst |ɪn ma̲enəm hɛrtsən

die Liebe aufgegangen.
di li̲ːbə |a̲ofgəgaŋən.

191

Im wunderschönen Monat Mai,
ɪm vʊndərʃøːnən moːnat maɛ,

als alle Vögel sangen,
als |allə føːgəl zaŋən,

da hab' ich ihr gestanden
daː haːp |ɪç |iːr gəʃtandən

mein Sehnen und Verlangen.
maɛn zeːnən |ʊnt fɛrlaŋən.

Schumann   Dichterliebe
              2. Aus meinen Thränen spriessen
                 aos maɛnən trɛːnən ʃpriːsən

Aus meinen Thränen spriessen
aos maɛnən trɛːnən ʃpriːsən

viel blühende Blumen hervor,
fiːl blyːəndə bluːmən hɛrfoːr,

und meine Seufzer werden
ʊnt maɛnə zɔøftsər veːrdən

ein Nachtigallenchor.
|aɛn naxtigallənkoːr.

Und wenn du mich lieb hast, Kindchen,
ʊnt vɛn duː mɪç liːp hast, kɪntçən,

schenk' ich dir die Blumen all',
ʃɛŋk |ɪç diːr di bluːmən al,

und vor deinem Fenster soll klingen
ʊnt for daɛnəm fɛnstər zol klɪŋən

das Lied der Nachtigall.
das liːt der naxtigal.

Schumann   Dichterliebe

              3. Die Rose, die Lilie
                 di roːzə, di liːljə

Die Rose, die Lilie, die Taube, die Sonne,
di roːzə, di liːljə, di taobə, di zonnə,

die liebt ich einst alle in Liebeswonne.
di liːpt |ɪç |aenst |allə |ın liːbəsvɔnnə.

Ich lieb' sie nicht mehr, ich liebe alleine
ɪç liːp zi: nɪçt meːr, ɪç liːbə |allaenə

die Kleine, die Feine, die Reine, die Eine;
di klaenə, di faenə, di raenə, di |aenə;

sie selber, aller Liebe Wonne,
zi: zɛlbər, allər liːbə vɔnnə,

ist Rose und Lilie und Taube und Sonne,
ɪst roːzə |ʊnt liːljə |ʊnt taobə |ʊnt zɔnnə,

ich liebe alleine die Kleine,
ɪç liːbə |allaenə di klaenə,

die Feine, die Reine, die Eine!
di faenə, di raenə, di |aenə!

Schumann   Dichterliebe

4. Wenn ich in deine Augen seh'
vɛn |ɪç |ın daenə |aogən zeː

Wenn ich in deine Augen seh',
vɛn |ɪç |ın daenə |aogən zeː,

so schwindet all' mein Leid und Weh;
zoː ʃvɪndət |al maen laet |ʊnt veː,

doch wenn ich küsse deinen Mund,
dɔx vɛn |ɪç kysə daenən mʊnt,

so werd ich ganz und gar gesund.
zoː vɛrt |ɪç gants |ʊnt gaːr gəzʊnt.

Wenn ich mich lehn' an deine Brust,
vɛn |ɪç mɪç leːn |an daenə brʊst,

kommt's über mich wie Himmelslust;
kɔmts |yːbər mɪç viː hɪmməlslʊst;

doch wenn du sprichst: ich liebe dich!
dɔx vɛn du: ʃprɪçst,   ɪç liːbə dɪç!

so muss ich weinen bitterlich.
zoː mʊs |ɪç vaenən bɪtərlɪç.

5. Ich will meine Seele tauchen
ɪç vɪl maenə zeːlə taoçən

Ich will meine Seele tauchen
ɪç vɪl maenə zeːlə taoçən

in den Kelch der Lilie hinein;
|ɪn den kɛlç der liːljə hɪnaen;

die Lilie soll klingend hauchen
di liːljə zɔl klɪŋənt haoçən

ein Lied von der Liebsten mein.
|aen liːt fɔn der liːpstən maen.

Das Lied soll schauern und beben,
das liːt zɔl ʃaoərn |ʊnt beːbən,

wie der Kuss von ihrem Mund,
viː der kʊs fɔn |iːrəm mʊnt,

den sie mir einst gegeben
den ziː miːr |aenst gəgeːbən

in wunderbar süsser Stund'!
|ɪn vʊndərbaːr zyːsər ʃtʊnt!

6. Im Rhein
ɪm raen

Im Rhein, im heiligen Strome,
ɪm raen, ɪm haelɪgən ʃtroːmə,

da spiegelt sich in den Well'n,
daː ʃpiːgəlt zɪç |ɪn den vɛln,

mit seinem grossen Dome,
mɪt zaenəm groːsən doːmə,

das grosse, heilige Cöln.
das groːsə, haelɪgə kœln.

Im Dom, da steht ein Bildniss,
ɪm doːm, daː ʃteːt |aen bɪltnɪs,

auf goldenem Leder gemalt;
aof gɔldənəm leːdər gəmalt;

194

in meines Lebens Wildniss
ın mae̯nəs le̲ːbəns vɪltnɪs

hat's freundlich hinein gestrahlt.
hats frɔø̯ntlɪç hɪnae̯n gəʃtraːlt.

Es schweben Blumen und Eng'lein
ɛs ʃveːbən bluːmən |ʊnt |ɛ̲ŋlae̯n

um unsre liebe Frau;
|ʊm |ʊ̲nzrə li̲ːbə frao̯;

die Augen, die Lippen,
di |ao̯gən, di lɪ̲pən,

die Lippen, die Wänglein,
di lɪ̲pən, di vɛ̲ŋlae̯n,

die gleichen der Liebsten genau.
di glae̯çən der li̲ːpstən gənao̯.

Schumann   Dichterliebe
         7. Ich grolle nicht
            ɪç grɔ̲llə nɪçt

Ich grolle nicht, und wenn das Herz auch bricht,
ɪç grɔ̲llə nɪçt, ʊnt vɛn das hɛrts |ao̯x brɪçt,

ewig verlor'nes Lieb, ich grolle nicht.
eːvɪç fɛrlo̲rnəs liːp, ɪç grɔ̲llə nɪçt.

Wie du auch strahlst in Diamantenpracht,
viː duː |ao̯x ʃtraːlst |ɪn diam̲antənpraxt,

es fällt kein Strahl in deines Herzens Nacht,
ɛs fɛlt kae̯n ʃtraːl |ɪn dae̯nəs hɛ̲rtsəns naxt,

das weiss ich längst.
das vae̯s |ɪç lɛŋst.

Ich grolle nicht und wenn das Herz auch bricht.
ɪç grɔ̲llə nɪçt |ʊnt vɛn das hɛrts |ao̯x brɪçt.

Ich sah dich ja im Traume,
ɪç zaː dɪç jaː |ɪm trao̯mə,

und sah die Nacht in deines Herzens Raume,
ʊnt zaː di naxt |ɪn dae̯nəs hɛ̲rtsəns rao̯mə,

und sah die Schlang', die dir am Herzen frisst,
ʊnt zaː di ʃlaŋ,   di diːr |am hɛrtsən frɪst,

ich sah, mein Lieb, wie sehr du elend bist.
ɪç zaː, maɛn liːp, viː zeːr du |eːlənt bɪst.

Ich grolle nicht, ich grolle nicht.
ɪç grɔllə nɪçt, ɪç grɔllə nɪçt.

Schumann   Dichterliebe

      8. Und wüssten's die Blumen
        ʊnt vʏstəns di bluːmən

Und wüssten's die Blumen, die kleinen,
ʊnt vʏstəns di bluːmən, di klaɛnən,

wie tief verwundet mein Herz,
viː tiːf fɛrvʊndət maɛn hɛrts,

sie würden mit mir weinen,
ziː vʏrdən mɪt miːr vaɛnən,

zu heilen meinen Schmerz.
tsuː haɛlən maɛnən ʃmɛrts.

Und wüssten's die Nachtigallen,
ʊnt vʏstəns di naxtigallən,

wie ich so traurig und krank,
viː |ɪç zoː traorɪç |ʊnt kraŋk,

sie liessen fröhlich erschallen
ziː liːsən frøːlɪç |ɛrʃallən

erquickenden Gesang.
ɛrkvɪkəndən gəzaŋ.

Und wüssten sie mein Wehe,
ʊnt vʏstən ziː maɛn veːə,

die goldenen Sternelein,
di gɔldənən ʃtɛrnəlaɛn,

sie kämen aus ihrer Höhe,
ziː kɛːmən |aos |iːrər høːə,

und sprächen Trost mir ein.
ʊnt ʃprɛçən troːst miːr |aen.

Sie alle können's nicht wissen,
zi: |allə kœnnəns nɪçt vɪsən,

nur Eine kennt meinen Schmerz;
nu:r |aenə kɛnt maenən ʃmɛrts;

sie hat ja selbst zerrissen,
zi: hat ja: zɛlpst tsɛrrɪsən,

zerrissen mir das Herz.
tsɛrrɪsən mi:r das hɛrts.

Schumann   Dichterliebe

    9. Das ist ein Flöten und Geigen
      das |ɪst |aen flø:tən |unt gaegən

Das ist ein Flöten und Geigen,
das |ɪst |aen flø:tən |unt gaegən,

Trompeten schmettern darein;
trompe:tən ʃmɛtərn daraen;

da tanzt wohl den Hochzeitreigen
da: tantst vo:l den hoxtsaetraegən

die Herzallerliebste mein.
di hɛrts|allərli:pstə maen.

Das ist ein Klingen und Dröhnen,
das |ɪst |aen klɪŋən |unt drø:nən,

ein Pauken und ein Schalmei'n;
|aen paokən |unt |aen ʃa:lmaen;

dazwischen schluchzen und stöhnen
datsvɪʃən ʃluxtsən |unt ʃtø:nən

die lieblichen Engelein.
di li:plɪçən |ɛŋəlaen.

Schumann   Dichterliebe

    10. Hör' ich das Liedchen klingen
      hø:r |ɪç das li:tçən klɪŋən

Hör' ich das Liedchen klingen,
hø:r |ɪç das li:tçən klɪŋən,

das einst die Liebste sang,
das |a͜enst di li:pstə zaŋ,

so will mir die Brust zerspringen
zo: vɪl mi:r di brust͜ tsɛrʃprɪŋən

von wildem Schmerzensdrang.
fɔn vɪldəm ʃmɛrtsənsdraŋ.

Es treibt mich ein dunkles Sehnen
ɛs tra͜ept mɪç |a͜en duŋkləs ze͜:nən

hinauf zur Waldeshöh',
hɪna͜of tsu:r valdəshø:,

dort löst sich auf in Thränen
dɔrt lø:st zɪç |a͜of |ɪn trɛ͜:nən

mein übergrosses Weh'.
ma͜en |y:bərgro:səs ve:.

Schumann   Dichterliebe

11. Ein Jüngling liebt ein Mädchen
    a͜en jʏŋlɪŋ li:pt a͜en mɛ͜:tçən

Ein Jüngling liebt ein Mädchen,
a͜en jʏŋlɪŋ li:pt |a͜en mɛ͜:tçən,

die hat einen Andern erwählt;
di hat |a͜enən |andərn |ɛrvɛ͜:lt;

der And're liebt eine Andre
der |andrə li:pt |a͜enə |andrə

und hat sich mit dieser vermählt.
unt hat zɪç mɪt di͜:zər fɛrmɛ͜:lt.

Das Mädchen nimmt aus Aerger
das mɛ͜:tçən nɪmt |a͜os |ɛrgər

den ersten besten Mann,
den |e͜:rstən bɛstən man,

der ihr in den Weg gelaufen;
der |i:r |ɪn den ve:k gəla͜ofən;

der Jüngling ist übel d'ran.
der jʏŋlɪŋ |ɪst |y:bəl dran.

Es ist eine alte Geschichte,
ɛs |ɪst |aenə |altə gəʃɪçtə,

doch bleibt sie immer neu;
dɔx blaept ziː |ɪmmər nɔø;

und wem sie just passiret,
ʊnt veːm ziː jʊst pasiːrət,

dem bricht das Herz entzwei.
dem brɪçt das hɛrts |ɛntsvae.

Schumann   Dichterliebe

    12. Am leuchtenden Sommermorgen
       am lɔøçtəndən zɔmmərmɔrgən

Am leuchtenden Sommermorgen
am lɔøçtəndən zɔmmərmɔrgən

geh ich im Garten herum.
geː |ɪç |ɪm gartən hɛrʊm.

Es flüstern und sprechen die Blumen,
ɛs flystərn |ʊnt ʃprɛçən di bluːmən,

ich aber wandle stumm.
ɪç |aːbər vandlə ʃtʊm.

Es flüstern und sprechen die Blumen,
ɛs flystərn |ʊnt ʃprɛçən di bluːmən,

und schau'n mitleidig mich an:
ʊnt ʃaon mɪtlaedɪç mɪç |an,

Sei unsrer Schwester nicht böse,
zae |ʊnzrər ʃvɛstər nɪçt bøːzə,

du trauriger, blasser Mann.
duː traorɪgər blasər man.

Schumann   Dichterliebe

    13. Ich hab' im Traum geweinet
       ɪç haːp |ɪm traom gəvaenət

Ich hab' im Traum geweinet,
ɪç haːp |ɪm traom gəvaenət,

mir träumte, du lägest im Grab.
miːr trøːmtə, duː lɛːgəst |ɪm graːp.

Ich wachte auf, und die Thräne
ɪç vaxtə |aof, ʊnt di trɛːnə

floss noch von der Wange herab.
flɔs nɔx fɔn der vaŋə hɛrap.

Ich hab' im Traum geweinet,
ɪç haːp |ɪm traom gəvaenət,

mir träumt', du verliessest mich.
miːr trøːmt, duː fɛrliːsəst mɪç.

Ich wachte auf, und ich weinte
ɪç vaxtə |aof, ʊnt |ɪç vaentə

noch lange bitterlich.
nɔx laŋə bɪtərlɪç.

Ich hab' im Traum geweinet,
ɪç haːp |ɪm traom gəvaenət,

mir träumte, du wärst mir noch gut.
miːr trøːmtə, duː vɛːrst miːr nɔx guːt.

Ich wachte auf, und noch immer
ɪç vaxtə |aof, ʊnt nɔx |ɪmmər

strömt meine Thränenflut.
ʃtrøːmt maenə trɛːnənfluːt.

Schumann   Dichterliebe

14. Allnächtlich im Traume
    alnɛçtlɪç |ɪm traomə

Allnächtlich im Traume seh' ich dich,
alnɛçtlɪç |ɪm traomə zeː |ɪç dɪç,

und sehe dich freundlich grüssen,
ʊnt zeːə dɪç frøntlɪç gryːsən,

und laut aufweinend stürz' ich mich
ʊnt laot |aofvaenənt ʃtyrts |ɪç mɪç

zu deinen süssen Füssen.
tsuː daenən zyːsən fyːsən.

Du siehest mich an wehmüthiglich
du: zi̯:əst mɪç |an ve̯:mytɪklɪç

und schüttelst das blonde Köpfchen;
ʊnt ʃy̆təlst das blo̯ndə kœpfçən;

aus deinen Augen schleichen sich
a̯os da̯enən |a̯ogən ʃlɛi̯çən zɪç

die Perlenthränentröpfchen.
di pɛrləntrɛ:nəntrœpfçən.

Du sagst mir heimlich ein leises Wort,
du: za:kst mi:r ha̯emlɪç |a̯en la̯ezəs vort,

und giebst mir den Strauss von Cypressen.
ʊnt gi:pst mi:r den ʃtra̯os fon tsy:prɛsən.

Ich wache auf, und der Strauss ist fort,
ɪç vaxə |a̯of, ʊnt der ʃtra̯os |ɪst fort,

und's Wort hab' ich vergessen.
ʊnts vort ha:p |ɪç fɛrgɛsən.

Schumann   Dichterliebe

15. Aus alten Märchen winkt es
    a̯os |altən mɛrçən vɪŋkt |ɛs

Aus alten Märchen winkt es
a̯os |altən mɛrçən vɪŋkt |ɛs

hervor mit weisser Hand,
hɛrfo̯:r mɪt va̯esər hant,

da singt es und da klingt es
da: zɪŋt |ɛs |ʊnt da: klɪŋt |ɛs

von einem Zauberland;
fon |a̯enəm tsa̯obərlant;

wo bunte Blumen blühen
vo: bŭntə blu:mən bly:ən

im gold'nen Abendlicht,
|ɪm go̯ldnən |a:bəntlɪçt,

und lieblich duftend glühen,
ʊnt li̯:plɪç dŭftənt gly:ən,

201

mit bräutlichem Gesicht;
mɪt brɒːtlɪçən gəzɪçt;

und grüne Bäume singen
ʊnt gryːnə bɒːmə zɪŋən

uralte Melodei'n,
|uːr|altə melodaən,

die Lüfte heimlich klingen,
di lʏftə haemlɪç klɪŋən,

und Vögel schmettern drein;
ʊnt føːgəl ʃmɛtərn draen;

und Nebelbilder steigen
ʊnt neːbəlbɪldər ʃtaegən

wohl aus der Erd' hervor,
voːl |aos der eːrt hɛrfoːr,

und tanzen luft'gen Reigen
ʊnt tantsən lʊftgən raegən

im wunderlichen Chor;
|ɪm vʊndərlɪçən koːr;

und blaue Funken brennen
ʊnt blaoə fʊŋkən brɛnnən

an jedem Blatt und Reis,
|an jeːdəm blat |ʊnt raes,

und rothe Lichter rennen
ʊnt roːtə lɪçtər rɛnnən

im irren, wirren Kreis;
ɪm |ɪrrən, vɪrrən kraes;

und laute Quellen brechen
ʊnt laotə kvɛllən brɛçən

aus wildem Marmorstein,
|aos vɪldəm marmorʃtaen,

und seltsam in den Bächen
ʊnt zɛltzam |ɪn den bɛçən

strahlt fort der Wiederschein.
ʃtraːlt fort der viːdərʃaen.

Ach! könnt' ich dorthin kommen,
ax! kœnt |ɪç dɔrthɪn kɔmmən,

und dort mein Herz erfreu'n,
|ʊnt dɔrt maen hɛrts |ɛrfrɒən,

und aller Qual entnommen,
ʊnt |allər kvaːl |ɛntnɔmmən,

und frei und selig sein!
ʊnt fraɛ |ʊnt zeːlɪç zaɛn!

Ach, jenes Land der Wonne,
ax! jeːnəs lant der vɔnnə,

das seh' ich oft im Traum,
das zeː |ɪç |ɔft |ɪm traɔm,

doch kommt die Morgensonne,
dɔx kɔmt di mɔrgənzɔnnə,

zerfliesst's wie eitel Schaum.
tsɛrfliːsts viː |aɛtəl ʃaɔm.

Schumann   Dichterliebe

16. Die alten, bösen Lieder
    di |altən, bøːzən liːdər

Die alten, bösen Lieder,
di |altən, bøːzən liːdər,

die Träume bös' und arg,
di trøømə bøːz |ʊnt |ark,

die lasst uns jetzt begraben,
di last |ʊns jɛtst bəgraːbən,

holt einen grossen Sarg.
hoːlt |aenən groːsən zark.

Hinein leg' ich gar Manches,
hɪnaen leːk |ɪç gaːr mançəs,

doch sag' ich noch nicht was;
dɔx zaːk |ɪç nɔx nɪçt vas;

der Sarg muss sein noch grösser
der zark mʊs zaen nɔx grøːsər

wie's Heidelberger Fass.
viːs haedəlbɛrgər fas.

Und holt eine Todtenbahre,
ʊnt hoːlt |aenə toːtənbaːrə,

203

von Brettern fest und dick;
fon brɛtərn fɛst |ʊnt dɪk;

auch muss sie sein noch länger,
aox mʊs zi: zaen nɔx lɛŋər,

als wie zu Mainz die Brück'.
als vi: tsu: maɪnts di brʏk.

Und holt mir auch zwölf Riesen,
ʊnt ho:lt mi:r |aox tsvœlf ri:zən,

die müssen noch stärker sein,
di mʏsən nɔx ʃtɛrkər zaen,

als wie der starke Christoph,
als vi: der ʃtarkə krɪstɔf,

im Dom zu Cöln am Rhein.
ɪm do:m tsu: kœln |am raen.

Die sollen den Sarg forttragen,
di zɔllən den zark fɔrttra:gən,

und senken in's Meer hinab;
ʊnt zɛŋkən |ɪns me:r hɪnap;

denn solchem grossen Sarge
dɛn zɔlçəm gro:sən zargə

gebührt ein grosses Grab.
gəby:rt |aen gro:səs gra:p.

Wisst ihr, warum der Sarg wohl
vɪst |i:r, varʊm der zark vo:l

so gross und schwer mag sein?
zo: gro:s |ʊnt ʃve:r ma:k zaen?

Ich senkt' auch meine Liebe
ɪç zɛŋkt |aox maenə li:bə

und meinen Schmerz hinein.
|ʊnt maenən ʃmɛrts hɪnaen.

Schumann   Die beiden Grenadiere
                    di baedən grenadi:rə

Nach Frankreich zogen zwei Grenadier',
nax fraŋkraeç tso:gən tsvae grenadi:r,

die waren in Russland gefangen.
di va:rən |ɪn rʊslant gəfaŋən.

Und als sie kamen in's deutsche Quartier,
ʊnt |als zi: ka:mən |ɪns dɔøtʃə kvarti:r,

sie liessen die Köpfe hangen.
zi: li:sən di kœpfə haŋən.

Da hörten sie Beide die traurige Mähr',
da: hœrtən zi: baedə di traorɪgə mɛ:r,

dass Frankreich verloren gegangen,
das fraŋkraeç fɛrlo:rən gəgaŋən,

besiegt und geschlagen das tapfere Heer,
bəzi:kt |ʊnt gəʃla:gən das tapfərə he:r,

und der Kaiser gefangen.
ʊnt der kaezər gəfaŋən.

Da weinten zusammen die Grenadier'
da: vaentən tsuzamən di grenadi:r

wohl ob der kläglichen Kunde.
vo:l |ɔp der klɛ:klɪçən kʊndə.

Der Eine sprach: "Wie weh' wird mir,
der |aenə ʃprax, "vi: ve: vɪrt mi:r,

wie brennt meine alte Wunde!"
vi: brɛnt maenə |altə vʊndə!"

Der Andre sprach: "Das Lied ist aus,
der |andrə ʃprax, "das li:t |ɪst |aos,

auch ich möcht' mit dir sterben,
aox |ɪç mœçt mɪt di:r ʃtɛrbən,

doch hab' ich Weib und Kind zu Haus,
dɔx ha:p |ɪç vaep |ʊnt kɪnt tsu: haos,

die ohne mich verderben."
di |o:nə mɪç fɛrdɛrbən."

"Was schert mich Weib, was schert mich Kind,
"vas ʃe:rt mɪç vaep, vas ʃe:rt mɪç kɪnt,

ich trage weit besser Verlangen;
ɪç tra:gə vaet bɛsər fɛrlaŋən;

lass sie betteln gehn, wenn sie hungrig sind—
las zi: bɛtəln ge:n, vɛn zi: hʊŋrɪç zɪnt—

mein Kaiser, mein Kaiser gefangen!
maen kaezər, maen kaezər gəfaŋən!

Gewähr' mir, Bruder, eine Bitt':
gəveːr miːr, bruːdər, aenə bɪt,

Wenn ich jetzt sterben werde,
vɛn |ɪç jɛtst ʃtɛrbən veːrdə,

so nimm meine Leiche nach Frankreich mit,
zoː nɪm maenə laeçə nax fraŋkraeç mɪt,

begrab' mich in Frankreichs Erde.
bəgraːp mɪç |ɪn fraŋkraeçs |eːrdə.

Das Ehrenkreuz am rothem Band
das |eːrənkrɔøts |am roːtəm bant

sollst du auf's Herz mir legen;
zɔlst duː |aofs hɛrts miːr leːgən;

die Flinte gieb mir in die Hand,
di flɪntə giːp miːr |ɪn di hant,

und gürt' mir um den Degen.
ʊnt gyːrt miːr |ʊm den deːgən.

So will ich liegen und horchen still,
zoː vɪl |ɪç liːgən |ʊnt hɔrçən ʃtɪl,

wie ein Schildwach', im Grabe,
viː |aen ʃɪltvax, ɪm graːbə,

bis einst ich höre Kanonengebrüll
bɪs |aenst |ɪç høːrə kanoːnəngəbryl

und wiehernder Rosse Getrabe.
|ʊnt viːərndər rɔsə gətraːbə.

Dann reitet mein Kaiser wohl über mein Grab,
dan raetət maen kaezər voːl |yːbər maen graːp,

viel Schwerter klirren und blitzen,
fiːl ʃvɛrtər klɪrrən |ʊnt blɪtsən,

dann steig' ich gewaffnet hervor aus dem Grab-
dan ʃtaek |ɪç gəvafnət hɛrfoːr |aos dem graːp-

den Kaiser, den Kaiser zu schützen!"
den kaezər, den kaezər tsuː ʃytsən!"

Schumann   Die Lotosblume
               di lo̠:tosblu:mə

Die Lotosblume ängstigt
di lo̠:tosblu:mə |ɛŋstɪkt

sich vor der Sonne Pracht,
zɪç fɔr der zo̠nnə praxt,

und mit gesenktem Haupte
ʊnt mɪt gəze̠ŋktəm ha̠optə

erwartet sie träumend die Nacht.
ɛrva̠rtət zi: tro̠ømənt di naxt.

Der Mond, der ist ihr Buhle,
der mo:nt, der |ɪst |i:r bu̠:lə,

er weckt sie mit seinem Licht,
e:r vɛkt zi: mɪt za̠enəm lɪçt,

und ihm entschleiert sie freundlich
ʊnt |i:m |ɛntʃla̠eərt zi: fro̠øntlɪç

ihr frommes Blumengesicht.
i:r fro̠mməs blu̠:məngəzɪçt.

Sie blüht und glüht und leuchtet,
zi: bly:t |ʊnt gly:t |ʊnt lo̠øçtət,

und starret stumm in die Höh';
ʊnt ʃta̠rrət ʃtʊm |ɪn di hø:,

sie duftet und weinet und zittert
zi: du̠ftət |ʊnt va̠enət |ʊnt tsɪ̠rtərt

vor Liebe und Liebesweh.
fɔr li̠:bə |ʊnt li̠:bəsve:.

Schumann   Du bist wie eine Blume
              du: bɪst vi: |a̠enə blu̠:mə

Du bist wie eine Blume,
du: bɪst vi: |a̠enə blu̠:mə,

so hold und schön und rein;
zo: hɔlt |ʊnt ʃø:n |ʊnt ra̠en;

ich schau' dich an, und Wehmuth
ɪç ʃa̠o   dɪç |an, ʊnt ve:mʊt

schleicht mir in's Herz hinein.
ʃlae̯çt miːr |ɪns hɛrts hɪnae̯n.

Mir ist, als ob ich die Hände
miːr |ɪst, als |ɔp |ɪç di hɛndə

auf's Haupt dir legen sollt',
|ao̯fs hao̯pt diːr leːgən zɔlt,

betend, dass Gott dich erhalte
beːtənt, das gɔt‿dɪç |ɛrhaltə

so rein und schön und hold.
zoː rae̯n |ʊnt ʃøːn |ʊnt hɔlt.

Schumann   Mondnacht
                moːntnaxt

Es war, als hätt' der Himmel
ɛs vaːr, als hɛt der hɪmməl

die Erde still geküsst,
di eːrdə ʃtɪl gəkyst,

dass sie im Blüthenschimmer
das ziː |ɪm blyːtənʃɪmmər

von ihm nur träumen müsst'.
fɔn |iːm nuːr trɔ̯ɔmən myst.

Die Luft ging durch die Felder,
di lʊft gɪŋ dʊrç di fɛldər,

die Ähren wogten sacht,
di |ɛːrən voːktən zaxt,

es rauschten leis' die Wälder,
ɛs rao̯ʃtən lae̯s di vɛldər,

so sternklar war die Nacht.
zoː ʃtɛrnklaːr vaːr di naxt.

Und meine Seele spannte
ʊnt mae̯nə zeːlə ʃpantə

weit ihre Flügel aus,
vae̯t |iːrə flyːgəl |ao̯s,

flog durch die stillen Lande,
floːk dʊrç di ʃtɪllən landə,

als flöge sie nach Haus.
als fløːgə ziː nax haos.

Schumann   Stille Thränen
              ʃtɪllə trɛːnən

Du bist vom Schlaf erstanden
duː bɪst fɔm ʃlaːf |ɛrʃtandən

und wandelst durch die Au,
|ʊnt vandəlst dʊrç di |ao,

da liegt ob allen Landen
daː liːkt |ɔp |allən landən

der Himmel wunderblau.
der hɪmməl vʊndərblao.

So lang du ohne Sorgen
zoː laŋ duː |oːnə zɔrgən

geschlummert schmerzenlos,
gəʃlʊmmərt ʃmɛrtsənloːs,

der Himmel bis zum Morgen
der hɪmməl bɪs tsum mɔrgən

viel Thränen niedergoss.
fiːl trɛːnən niːdərgɔs.

In stillen Nächten weinet
ɪn ʃtɪllən nɛçtən vaenət

oft mancher aus den Schmerz,
|ɔft mançər |aos den ʃmɛrts,

und morgens dann ihr meinet,
ʊnt mɔrgəns dan |iːr maenət,

stets fröhlich sei sein Herz.
ʃteːts frøːlɪç zae zaen hɛrts.

209

Schumann   Volksliedchen
            fɔlksliːtçən

Wenn ich früh in den Garten geh'
vɛn |ɪç fryː |ɪn den gartən geː

in meinem grünen Hut,
|ɪn maenəm gryːnən huːt,

ist mein erster Gedanke,
ɪst maen |eːrstər gədaŋkə,

was nun mein Liebster tut?
vas nuːn maen liːpstər tuːt?

Am Himmel steht kein Stern,
am hɪmməl ʃteːt kaen ʃtɛrn,

den ich dem Freund nicht gönnte.
den |ɪç dem frɔønt nɪçt gœntə.

Mein Herz gäb' ich ihm gern,
maen hɛrts gɛːp |ɪç |iːm gɛrn,

wenn ich's herausthun könnte.
vɛn |ɪçs hɛraostuːn kœntə.

Schumann   Wanderlied
            vandərliːt

Wohlauf! noch getrunken den funkelnden Wein!
voːl|aof! nɔx gətruŋkən den fuŋkəlndən vaen!

Ade nun, ihr Lieben!   geschieden muss sein.
adeː nuːn, iːr liːbən! gəʃiːdən mʊs‿zaen.

Ade nun, ihr Berge, du väterlich Haus!
adeː nuːn, iːr bɛrgə, duː fɛːtərlɪç haos!

Es treibt in die Ferne mich mächtig hinaus.
ɛs traept |ɪn di fɛrnə mɪç mɛçtɪk hɪnaos.

Die Sonne, sie bleibet am Himmel nicht steh'n,
di zɔnnə, ziː blaebət |am hɪmməl nɪçt ʃteːn,

es treibt sie, durch Länder und Meere zu geh'n.
ɛs traept ziː, dʊrç lɛndər |ʊnt meːrə tsuː geːn.

Die Woge nicht haftet am einsamen Strand,
di voːgə nɪçt haftət |am |aenzaːmən ʃtrant,

210

die Stürme, sie brausen mit Macht durch das Land.
di ʃtʏrmə, ziː braozən mɪt maxt durç das lant.

Mit eilenden Wolken der Vogel dort zieht
mit |aeləndən vɔlkən der foːgəl dort tsiːt

und singt in der Ferne ein heimathlich Lied.
|unt zɪŋt |ɪn der fɛrnə |aen haematlɪç liːt.

So treibt es den Burschen durch Wälder und Feld,
zoː traept |ɛs den burʃən durç vɛldər |unt fɛlt,

zu gleichen der Mutter, der wandernden Welt.
tsuː glaeçən der mutər, der vandərndən vɛlt.

Da grüssen ihn Vögel bekannt über'm Meer,
daː gryːsən |iːn føːgəl bəkant |yːbərm meːr,

sie flogen von Fluren der Heimath hieher;
siː floːgən fon fluːrən der haemat hiːhɛr;

da duften die Blumen vertraulich um ihn,
daː duftən di bluːmən fɛrtraolɪç |um |iːn,

sie trieben vom Lande die Lüfte dahin.
ziː triːbən fom landə di lʏftə dahɪn.

Die Vögel, die kennen sein väterlich Haus,
di føːgəl, di kɛnnən zaen fɛːtərlɪç haos,

die Blumen, die pflanzt er der Liebe zum Strauss,
di bluːmən, di pflantst |eːr der liːbə tsum ʃtraos,

und Liebe, die folgt ihm, sie geht ihm zur Hand:
unt liːbə, di folkt |iːm, ziː geːt |iːm tsur hant,

so wird ihm zur Heimath das ferneste Land.
zoː vɪrt |iːm tsur haemat das fɛrnəstə lant.

Wohlauf! noch getrunken den funkelnden Wein!
voːl|aof! nox gətruŋkən den fuŋkəlndən vaen!

Ade nun, ihr Lieben!   geschieden muss sein.
adeː nuːn, iːr liːbən! gəʃiːdən mus zaen.

Ade nun, ihr Berge, du väterlich Haus!
adeː nuːn, iːr bɛrgə, duː fɛːtərlɪç haos!

Es treibt in die Ferne mich mächtig hinaus!
ɛs traept |ɪn di fɛrnə mɪç mɛçtɪk hɪnaos!

Schumann   Widmung
             vɪdmʊŋ

Du meine Seele, du mein Herz,
duː maenə zeːlə, duː maen hɛrts,

du meine Wonn', o du mein Schmerz,
duː maenə vɔn, oː duː maen ʃmɛrts,

du meine Welt, in der ich lebe,
duː maenə vɛlt, ɪn der |ɪç leːbə,

mein Himmel du, darein ich schwebe,
maen hɪmməl duː, daraen |ɪç ʃveːbə,

o du mein Grab, in das hinab
oː duː maen graːp, ɪn das hɪnap

ich ewig meinen Kummer gab!
|ɪç |eːvɪç maenən kʊmmər gaːp!

Du bist die Ruh', du bist der Frieden,
duː bɪst di ruː, duː bɪst der friːdən,

du bist vom Himmel mir beschieden.
duː bɪst fɔm hɪmməl miːr bəʃiːdən.

Dass du mich liebst, macht mich mir werth,
das duː mɪç liːpst, maxt mɪç miːr veːrt,

dein Blick hat mich vor mir verklärt,
daen blɪk hat mɪç fɔr miːr fɛrklɛːrt,

du hebst mich liebend über mich,
duː heːpst mɪç liːbənt |yːbər mɪç,

mein guter Geist, mein bess'res Ich!
maen guːtər gaest, maen bɛsrəs |ɪç!

Strauss   Allerseelen
           alərzeːlən

Stell' auf den Tisch die duftenden Reseden,
ʃtɛl |aof den tɪʃ di dʊftəndən rəzeːdən,

die letzten roten Astern trag' herbei,
di lɛtstən roːtən |astərn traːk hɛrbae,

und lass uns wieder von der Liebe reden,
ʊnt las |uns viːdər fɔn der liːbə reːdən,

212

wie einst im Mai.
viː |aenst |ɪm mae.

Gieb mir die Hand, dass ich sie heimlich drücke,
giːp miːr di hant, das |ɪç ziː haemlɪç drʏkə,

und wenn man's sieht, mir ist es einerlei,
ʊnt vɛn mans ziːt, miːr |ɪst |ɛs |aenərlae,

gieb mir nur einen deiner süssen Blicke,
giːp miːr nuːr |aenən daenər zyːsən blɪkə,

wie einst im Mai.
viː |aenst |ɪm mae.

Es blüht und duftet heut' auf jedem Grabe,
ɛs blyːt |ʊnt duftət hoøt |aof jeːdəm graːbə,

ein Tag im Jahr ist ja den Toten frei,
aen taːk |ɪm jaːr |ɪst jaː den toːtən frae,

komm an mein Herz, dass ich dich wieder habe
kɔm |an maen hɛrts, das |ɪç dɪç viːdər haːbə

wie einst im Mai.
viː |aenst |ɪm mae.

Strauss   Breit über mein Haupt dein schwarzes Haar
braet |yːbər maen haopt daen ʃvartsəs haːr

Breit über mein Haupt dein schwarzes Haar,
braet |yːbər maen haopt daen ʃvartsəs haːr,

neig' zu mir dein Angesicht,
naek tsuː miːr daen |angəzɪçt,

da strömt in die Seele so hell
daː ʃtrømt |ɪn di zeːlə zoː hɛl

und klar mir deiner Augen Licht.
|ʊnt klaːr miːr daenər |aogən lɪçt.

Ich will nicht droben der Sonne Pracht,
ɪç vɪl nɪçt droːbən der zɔnnə praxt,

noch der Sterne leuchtenden Kranz,
nɔx der ʃtɛrnə loøçtəndən krants,

ich will nur deiner Locken Nacht
ɪç vɪl nuːr daenər lɔkən naxt

und deiner Blicke Glanz.
|ʊnt d̯aenər blɪkə glants.

Strauss   Cäcilie
             tsɛtsi̱ːljə

Wenn du es wüsstest, was träumen heisst
vɛn duː |ɛs vʏstəst, vas tr̥ɔømən h̯aest

von brennenden Küssen, von Wandern
fɔn br̥ɛnnəndən kʏsən, fɔn v̯andərn

und Ruhen mit der Geliebten,
|ʊnt r̯u̱ːən mɪt d̯er gəli̱ːptən,

Aug' in Auge und kosend und plaudernd,
a̯ok |ɪn |aogə |ʊnt ko̱ːzənt |ʊnt pl̯aodərnt,

wenn du es wüsstest, du neigtest dein Herz!
vɛn duː |ɛs vʏstəst, duː n̯aektəst d̯aen hɛrts!

Wenn du es wüsstest, was bangen heisst
vɛn duː |ɛs vʏstəst, vas baŋən h̯aest

in einsamen Nächten, umschauert vom Sturm,
|ɪn |aenzamən nɛ̱çtən, umʃa̱oərt fɔm ʃturm,

da niemand tröstet milden Mundes die kampfmüde Seele,
daː ni̱ːmant tr̯øːstət mɪldən mʊndəs di kampfmyːdə ze̱ːlə,

wenn du es wüsstest, du kämest zu mir.
vɛn duː |ɛs vʏstest, duː kɛ̱ːməst tsuː miːr.

Wenn du es wüsstest, was leben heisst,
vɛn duː |ɛs vʏstəst, was le̱ːbən h̯aest,

umhaucht von der Gottheit weltschaffendem Atem,
umha̯oxt fɔn der go̱thaet vɛltʃafəndəm |a̱ːtəm,

zu schweben empor, lichtgetragen, zu seligen Höh'n,
tsuː ʃve̱ːbən |ɛmpo̱ːr, lɪ̱çtgətraːgən, tsuː ze̱ːlɪgən høːn,

wenn du es wüsstest, du lebtest mit mir.
vɛn duː |ɛs vʏstəst, duː le̱ːptəst mit miːr.

214

Strauss   Die Nacht
           di naxt

Aus dem Walde tritt die Nacht,
aͦos dem valdə trɪt di naxt,

aus den Bäumen schleicht sie leise,
aͦos den boͦømən ʃlaͤeçt ziː laͤezə,

schaut sich um in weitem Kreise, nun gib acht.
ʃaͦot zɪç |um |ɪn vaͤetəm kraͤezə, nuːn giːp |axt.

Alle Lichter dieser Welt,
alə lɪçtər diːzər vɛlt,

alle Blumen, alle Farben löscht sie aus
alə bluːmən, alə farbən lœʃt ziː |aͦos

und stiehlt die Garben weg vom Feld.
|ʊnt ʃtiːlt di garbən vɛk fɔm fɛlt.

Alles nimmt sie, was nur hold,
aləs nɪmt ziː, vas nuːr hɔlt,

nimmt das Silber weg des Stroms,
nɪmt das zɪlbər vɛk dɛs ʃtroːms,

nimmt vom Kupferdach des Doms weg das·Gold.
nɪmt fɔm kʊpfərdax dɛs doːms vɛk das gɔlt.

Ausgeplündert steht der Strauch, rücke näher,
aͦosgəplʏndərt ʃteːt der ʃtraͦox, rʏkə nɛːər,

Seel' an Seele; o die Nacht, mir bangt,
zeːl |an zeːlə, oː di naxt, miːr baŋt,

sie stehle dich mir auch.
ziː ʃteːlə dɪç miːr |aͦoç.

Strauss   Heimkehr
          haͤemkeːr

Leiser schwanken die Äste, der Kahn fliegt uferwärts,
laͤezər ʃvaŋkən di |ɛstə, der kaːn fliːkt |uːfərvɛrts,

heim kehrt die Taube zum Neste,
haͤem keːrt di taͦobə tsum nɛstə,

zu dir kehrt heim mein Herz.
tsuː diːr keːrt haͤem maͤen hɛrts.

215

Genug am schimmernden Tage,
gənuːk |am ʃɪmmərndən taːgə,

wenn rings das Leben lärmt,
vɛn rɪŋs das leːbən lɛrmt,

mit irrem Flügelschlage ist es in's Weite geschwärmt.
mɪt |ɪrrəm flyːgəlʃlaːgə |ɪst |ɛs |ɪns vaetə gəʃvɛrmt.

Doch nun die Sonne geschieden
dɔx nuːn di zɔnnə gəʃiːdən

und Stille sich senkt auf den Hain,
ʊnt ʃtɪllə zɪç zɛŋkt |aof den haen,

fühlt es: bei dir ist der Frieden,
fyːlt |ɛs, bae diːr |ɪst der friːdən,

die Ruh' bei dir allein.
di ruː bae diːr |allaen.

Strauss   Heimliche Aufforderung
               haemlɪçə |aoffordəruŋ

Auf, hebe die funkelnde Schale empor zum Mund,
aof, heːbə di fʊŋkəlndə ʃaːlə |empoːr tsum mʊnt,

und trinke beim Freudenmahle dein Herz gesund.
ʊnt trɪŋkə baem frøødənmaːlə daen hɛrts gəzʊnt.

Und wenn du sie hebst, so winke mir heimlich zu,
ʊnt vɛn duː ziː heːpst, zoː vɪŋkə miːr haemlɪç tsuː,

dann lächle ich und dann trinke ich still wie du...
dan lɛçlə |ɪç |ʊnt dan trɪŋkə |ɪç ʃtɪl viː duː

und still gleich mir betrachte um uns
|ʊnt ʃtɪl glaeç miːr bətraxtə |um |ʊns

das Heer der trunknen Schwätzer-
das heːr der trʊŋknən ʃvɛtsər-

verachte sie nicht zu sehr.
fɛr|axtə ziː nɪçt tsuː zeːr.

Nein, hebe die blinkende Schale, gefüllt mit Wein,
naen, heːbə di blɪŋkəndə ʃaːlə, gəfʏlt mɪt vaen,

und lass beim lärmenden Mahle sie glücklich sein.
ʊnt las baem lɛrməndən maːlə ziː glʏklɪç zaen.

Doch hast du das Mahl genossen, den Durst gestillt,
dɔx hast duː das maːl gənoosən, den dʊrst gəʃtɪlt,

dann verlasse der lauten Genossen festfreudiges Bild
dan fərlasə der laotən gənoosən fɛstfrøødɪgəs bɪlt

und wandle hinaus in den Garten zum Rosenstrauch,
ʊnt vandlə hɪnaos |ɪn den gartən tsum rooːzənʃtraox,

dort will ich dich dann erwarten nach altem Brauch,
dɔrt vɪl |ɪç dɪç dan |ɛrvartən nax |altəm braox,

und will an die Brust dir sinken, eh' du's gehofft,
ʊnt vɪl |an di brʊst diːr zɪŋkən, eː duːs gəhɔft,

und deine Küsse trinken, wie ehmals oft
ʊnt daenə kʏsə trɪŋkən, viː |eːmals |ɔft

und flechten in deine Haare der Rose Pracht
|ʊnt flɛçtən |ɪn daenə haːrə der rooːzə praxt

o komm, du wunderbare ersehnte Nacht!
oː kɔm, duː vʊndərbarə |ɛrzeːntə naxt!

Strauss   Kornblumen
           kɔrnbluːmən

Kornblumen nenn' ich die Gestalten,
kɔrnbluːmən nɛn |ɪç di gəʃtaltən,

die milden mit den blauen Augen,
di mɪldən mɪt den blaoən |aogən,

die, anspruchslos, in stillem Walten
di, |anʃpruxslooːs, ɪn ʃtɪlləm valtən

den Thau des Friedens, den sie saugen
den tao dɛs friːdəns, den ziː zaogən

aus ihren eignen, klaren Seelen,
|aos |iːrən |aegnən, klaːrən zeːlən,

mittheilen allem, dem sie nah'n,
mɪttaelən |alləm, dem ziː naːn,

bewusstlos der Gefühlsjuwelen,
bəvʊstlooːs der gəfyːlsjuveːlən,

die sie von Himmelshand empfah'n.
di ziː fɔn hɪmməlshant |ɛmpfaːn.

217

Dir wird so wohl in ihrer Nähe,
diːr vɪrt zoː voːl |ɪn |iːrər nɛːə,

als gingst du durch ein Saatgefilde,
als gɪŋst duː dʊrç |aen zaːtgəfɪldə,

durch das der Hauch des Abends wehe,
dʊrç das der haox dɛs |aːbənts veːə,

voll frommen Friedens und voll Milde.
fɔl frɔmən friːdəns |ʊnt fɔl mɪldə.

S trauss   Morgen!
                mɔrgən

Und morgen wird die Sonne wieder scheinen
ʊnt mɔrgən vɪrt di zɔnnə viːdər ʃaenən

und auf dem Wege, den ich gehen werde,
ʊnt |aof dem veːgə, den |ɪç geːən veːrdə,

wird uns, die Glücklichen, sie wieder einen
vɪrt |ʊns, di glʏklɪçən, ziː viːdər |aenən

inmitten dieser sonnenatmenden Erde...
|ɪnmɪtən diːzər zɔnnən|aːtməndən |eːrdə...

und zu dem Strand, dem weiten, wogenblauen,
ʊnt tsuː dem ʃtrant, dem vaetən, voːgənblaoən,

werden wir still und langsam niedersteigen,
veːrdən viːr ʃtɪl |ʊnt laŋzam niːdərʃtaegən,

stumm werden wir uns in die Augen schauen,
ʃtʊm veːrdən viːr |ʊns |ɪn di |aogən ʃaoən,

und auf uns sinkt des Glückes stummes Schweigen.
ʊnt |aof |ʊns zɪŋt des glʏkəs ʃtʊmməs ʃvaegən.

S trauss   Nachtgang
                naxtgaŋ

Wir gingen durch die stille, milde Nacht,
viːr gɪŋən dʊrç di ʃtɪllə, mɪldə naxt,

218

dein Arm in meinem, dein Auge in meinem.
daen |arm |ɪn maenəm, daen |aogə |ɪn maenəm.

Der Mond goss silbernes Licht über dein Angesicht,
der moːnt gɔs zɪlbərnəs lɪçt |yːbər daen |angəzɪçt,

wie auf Goldgrund ruhte dein schönes Haupt.
viː |aof gɔltgrʊnt ruːtə daen ʃøːnəs haopt.

Und du erschienst mir wie eine Heilige,
ʊnt duː |ɛrʃiːnst miːr viː |aenə haelɪgə,

mild, mild und gross und seelenübervoll,
mɪlt, mɪlt |ʊnt groːs |ʊnt zeːlən|yːbərfɔl,

heilig und rein, wie die liebe Sonne.
haelɪç |ʊnt raen, viː di liːbə zɔnnə.

Und in die Augen schwoll mir
ʊnt |ɪn di |aogən ʃvɔl miːr

ein warmer Drang wie Tränenahnung.
aen varmər draŋ viː trɛːnən|aːnʊŋ.

Fester fasst' ich dich und küsste,
fɛstər fast |ɪç dɪç |ʊnt kʏstə,

küsste dich ganz leise. Meine Seele weinte.
kʏstə dɪç gants laezə. maenə zeːlə vaentə.

S trauss   S tändchen
              ʃtɛntçən

Mach' auf, mach' auf, doch leise, mein Kind,
max |aof, max |aof, dɔx laezə, maen kɪnt,

um Keinen vom Schlummer zu wecken;
ʊm kaenən fɔm ʃlʊmmər tsuː vɛkən;

kaum murmelt der Bach, kaum zittert im Wind
kaom mʊrməlt der bax, kaom tsɪtərt |ɪm vɪnt

ein Blatt an den Büschen und Hecken.
|aen blat |an den byʃən |ʊnt hɛkən.

Drum leise, mein Mädchen, dass nichts sich regt,
drʊm laezə, maen mɛːtçən, das nɪçts zɪç reːkt,

nur leise die Hand auf die Klinke gelegt.
nuːr laezə di hant |aof di klɪŋkə gəleːkt.

Mit Tritten wie Tritte der Elfen so sacht,
mɪt ˈtrɪtən viː ˈtrɪtə der |ˈɛlfən zoː zaxt,

um über die Blumen zu hüpfen,
um |ˈyːbər di ˈbluːmən tsu ˈhʏpfən,

flieg' leicht hinaus in die Mondscheinnacht
fliːk laɛçt hɪnaos |ɪn di ˈmoːntʃaennaxt

zu mir in den Garten zu schlüpfen.
tsuː miːr |ɪn den ˈgartən tsuː ʃlʏpfən.

Rings schlummern die Blüthen am rieselnden Bach
rɪŋs ˈʃlʊmmərn di ˈblyːtən |am ˈriːzəlndən bax

und duften im Schlaf, nur die Liebe ist wach!
|ʊnt ˈdʊftən |ɪm ʃlaːf, nuːr di ˈliːbə |ɪst vax!

Sitz' nieder, hier dämmert's geheimnissvoll
zɪts ˈniːdər, hiːr ˈdɛmmərts gehaemnɪsfɔl

unter den Lindenbäumen, die Nachtigall
|ˈʊntər den ˈlɪndənboømən, di ˈnaxtigal

uns zu Haüpten soll von uns'ren Küssen träumen,
|ʊns tsuː ˈhoøptən zɔl fɔn |ˈʊnzrən ˈkʏsən ˈtroømən,

und die Rose, wenn sie am Morgen erwacht,
ʊnt di ˈroːzə, vɛn ziː |am ˈmɔrgən |ɛrvaxt,

hoch glühn von den Wonneschauern der Nacht.
hoːx glyːn fɔn den ˈvɔnnəʃaoərn der naxt.

Strauss   Traum durch die Dämmerung
           traom dʊrç di ˈdɛmməruŋ

Weite Wiesen im Dämmergrau;
ˈvaetə ˈviːzən |ɪm ˈdɛmmərgrao;

die Sonne verglomm, die Sterne ziehn,
di ˈzɔnnə fɛrˈglɔm, di ˈʃtɛrnə tsiːn,

nun geh' ich hin zu der schönsten Frau,
nuːn geː |ɪç hɪn tsuː der ˈʃøːnstən frao,

weit über Wiesen im Dämmergrau,
vaet |ˈyːbər ˈviːzən |ɪm ˈdɛmmərgrao,

tief in den Busch von Jasmin.
tiːf |ɪn den buʃ fɔn jasˈmiːn.

Durch Dämmergrau in der Liebe Land;
dʊrç dɛmmərgraʊ |ɪn der li̯:bə lant;

ich gehe nicht schnell, ich eile nicht;
ɪç ge̯:ə nɪçt ʃnɛl, ɪç |aelə nɪçt;

mich zieht ein weiches sammtenes Band
mɪç tsi:t |aen vae̯çəs zamtənəs bant

durch Dämmergrau in der Liebe Land,
dʊrç dɛmmərgraʊ |ɪn der li̯:bə lant,

in ein blaues, mildes Licht.
|ɪn |aen blaoəs, mɪldəs lɪçt.

Strauss   Wiegenlied
             vi̯:gənli:t

Träume, träume, du, mein süsses Leben,
trɔømə, trɔømə, du:, maen zy̯:səs le̯:bən,

von dem Himmel, der die Blumen bringt.
fɔn dem hɪmməl, der di blu̯:mən brɪŋt.

Blüten schimmern da, die beben
bly̯:tən ʃɪmmərn da:, di be̯:bən

von dem Lied, das deine Mutter singt.
fɔn dem li:t, das dae̯nə mu̯tər zɪŋt.

Träume, träume, Knospe meiner Sorgen,
trɔømə, trɔømə, knɔspə mae̯nər zɔrgən,

von dem Tage, da die Blume spross;
fɔn dem ta̯:gə, da: di blu̯:mə ʃprɔs,

von dem hellen Blütenmorgen,
fɔn dem hɛllən bly̯:tənmɔrgən,

da dein Seelchen sich der Welt erschloss.
da: daen ze̯:lçən zɪç der vɛlt |ɛrʃlɔs.

Träume, träume, Blüte meiner Liebe,
trɔømə, trɔømə, bly̯:tə mae̯nər li̯:bə,

von der stillen, von der heil'gen Nacht,
fɔn der ʃtɪllən, fɔn der hae̯lgən naxt,

da die Blume seiner Liebe
da: di blu̯:mə zae̯nər li̯:bə

diese Welt zum Himmel mir gemacht.
di̱ːzə vɛlt tsum hɪmməl miːr gəma̱xt.

Strauss   Wie sollten wir geheim sie halten
            viː zo̱ltən viːr gəha̱em ziː ha̱ltən

Wie sollten wir geheim sie halten,
viː zo̱ltən viːr gəha̱em ziː ha̱ltən,

die Seligkeit, die uns erfüllt?
di ze̱ːlɪçkaet, di |uns |ɛrfy̱lt?

Nein, bis in seine tiefsten Falten
na̱en, bɪs |ɪn za̱enə ti̱ːfstən fa̱ltən

sei allen unser Herz enthüllt!
za̱e |allən |u̱nzər hɛrts |ɛnthy̱lt!

Wenn zwei in Liebe sich gefunden
vɛn   tsva̱e |ɪn li̱ːbə zɪç gəfu̱ndən

geht Jubel hin durch die Natur,
ge̱ːt ju̱ːbəl hɪn dʊrç di natu̱ːr,

in längern wonnevollen Stunden
ɪn lɛŋərn vo̱nnəfɔllən ʃtu̱ndən

legt sich der Tag auf Wald und Flur.
le̱ːkt zɪç der taːk |a̱of valt |ʊnt fluːr.

Selbst aus der Eiche morschem Stamm,
zɛlpst |a̱os der |a̱eçə mo̱rʃəm ʃtam,

die ein Jahrtausend überlebt,
di |a̱en ja̱ːrtaozənt |y̱ːbərle̱ːpt,

steigt neu des Wipfels grüne Flamme
ʃta̱ekt no̱ø dɛs vɪpfəls gry̱ːnə flammə

und rauscht von Jugendlust durchbebt.
|ʊnt ra̱oʃt fɔn ju̱ːgəntlʊst dʊ̱rçbe̱ːpt.

Zu höherm Glanz und Dufte brechen die Knospen auf
tsuː hø̱ːərm glants |ʊnt du̱ftə bre̱çən di kno̱spən |a̱of

beim Glück der Zwei und süsser rauscht es in den Bächen
ba̱em glʏk der tsva̱e |ʊnt zy̱ːsər ra̱oʃt |ɛs |ɪn den bɛ̱çən

und reicher blüht und reicher glänzt der Mai.
|ʊnt ra̱eçər bly̱ːt |ʊnt ra̱eçər glɛntst der ma̱e.

Strauss   Zueignung
              tsu̯aegnʊŋ

Ja, du weisst es, theure Seele,
ja:, du: va̱est |ɛs, to̱ørə ze:lə,

dass ich fern von dir mich quäle,
das |ıç fɛrn fɔn di:r mıç kvɛ̱:lə,

Liebe macht die Herzen krank, habe Dank.
li̱:bə maxt‿di hɛrtsən kraŋk, ha̱:be daŋk.

Einst hielt ich, der Freiheit Zecher,
a̱enst hi:lt |ıç, der fra̱ehaet‿tsɛ̱çər,

hoch den Amethisten Becher
ho:x den |amət̲ıstən bɛ̱çər

und du segnetest den Trank, habe Dank.
|ʊnt du: ze̱:gnətəst‿den traŋk, ha̱:bə daŋk.

Und beschworst darin die Bösen,
ʊnt bəʃvo̱:rst‿dar̲ın di bø:zən,

bis ich, was ich nie gewesen,
bıs |ıç, vas |ıç ni: gəve̱:zən,

heilig, heilig an's Herz dir sank, habe Dank.
ha̱elıç, ha̱elıç |ans hɛrts di:r zaŋk, ha̱:bə daŋk.

Wagner   Allmächt'ge Jungfrau, from "Tannhäuser"
           almɛ̱çtgə   juŋfra̱o   t̲anho̱øzər

Allmächt'ge Jungfrau, hör' mein Flehen!
almɛ̱çtgə juŋfra̱o, hø:r ma̱en fle̱:ən!

Zu dir, Gepries'ne, rufe ich!
tsu: di:r, gəpri̱:snə, ru̱:fə |ıç!

Lass mich im Staub vor dir vergehen,
las mıç |ım ʃta̱op fɔr di:r fɛrge̱:ən,

o! nimm von dieser Erde mich!
o:! nım fɔn di̱:zər |e̱:rdə mıç!

Mach' dass ich rein und engelgleich
max das |ıç ra̱en |ʊnt |ɛŋəlgla̱eç

eingehe in dein selig Reich!
|a̱enge:ə |ın da̱en ze̱:lıç ra̱eç!

Wenn je, in thör'gem Wahn befangen,
vɛn je:, ın tø̱:rgəm va:n bəfa̱ŋən,

mein Herz sich abgewandt von dir,
maen hɛrts zɪç |apgəvant fon diːr,

wenn je ein sündiges Verlangen,
vɛn jeː |aen zyndɪgəs fɛrlaŋən,

ein weltlich Sehnen keimt' in mir:
aen vɛltlɪç zeːnən kaemt |ɪn miːr,

so rang ich unter tausend Schmerzen,
soː raŋ |ɪç |untər taozənt ʃmɛrtsən,

dass ich es töd' in meinem Herzen.
das |ɪç |ɛs tøːt |ɪn maenəm hɛrtsən.

Doch, konnt' ich jeden Fehl nicht büssen,
dox, kont |ɪç jeːdən feːl nɪçt byːsən,

so nimm dich gnädig meiner an!
zoː nɪm dɪç gnɛːdɪç maenər |an!

Dass ich mit demuthvollem Grüssen
das |ɪç mɪt deːmutfolləm gryːsən

als würd'ge Magd dir nahen kann:
als vyrdgə maːkt diːr naːən kan,

um deiner gnadenreichste Huld
um daenər gnaːdənraeçstə hult

nur anzuflehn für seine Schuld!
nuːr |antsufleːn fyːr zaenə ʃult!

Wagner   Dich, theure Halle, from "Tannhäuser"
              dɪç, tøørə hallə   tanhøøzər

Dich, theure Halle, grüss' ich wieder,
dɪç, tøørə hallə, gryːs |ɪç viːdər,

froh grüss' ich dich, geliebter Raum!
froː gryːs |ɪç dɪç, gəliːptər raom!

In dir erwachen seine Lieder und wecken mich aus düst'rem Traum.
ɪn diːr |ɛrvaxən zaenə liːdər |unt vɛkən mɪç |aos dyːstrəm traom.

Da er aus dir geschieden, wie öd' erschienst du mir!
daː eːr |aos diːr gəʃiːdən, viː øːt |ɛrʃiːnst duː miːr!

Aus mir entfloh der Frieden, die Freude zog aus dir!
aos miːr |ɛntfloː der friːdən, di frøødə tsoːk |aos diːr!

Wie jetzt mein Busen hoch sich hebet,
vi: jɛtst mae̯n bu̯:zən ho:x zɪç he̯:bət,

so scheinst du jetzt mir stolz und hehr;
zo: ʃae̯nst du: jɛtst mi:r ʃtɔlts |unt he:r;

der mich und dich so neu belebet,
der mɪç |unt dɪç zo: nọø bəle̯:bət,

nicht weilt er ferne mehr!
nɪçt vae̯lt |e:r fɛrnə me:r!

Sei mir gegrüsst, sei mir gegrüsst!
zae̯ mi:r gəgry:st, zae̯ mi:r gəgry:st!

Du, theure Halle, sei mir gegrüsst!
du: tọørə hallə, zae̯ mi:r gəgry:st!

Wagner   Du bist der Lenz, from "Die Walküre"
              du: bɪst der lɛnts   di valky:rə

Du bist der Lenz, nach dem ich verlangte
du: bɪst der lɛnts, nax dem |ɪç fərlaŋtə

in frostigen Winters Frist.
|ɪn frɔstɪgən vɪntərs frɪst.

Dich grüsste mein Herz mit heiligem Grau'n,
dɪç gry:stə mae̯n hɛrts mɪt hae̯lɪgəm grao̯n,

als dein Blick zuerst mir erblühte.
als dae̯n blɪk tsu|e̯:rst mi:r |ɛrbly:tə.

Fremdes nur sah ich von je,
frɛmdəs nu:r za: |ɪç fɔn je:,

freundlos war mir das Nahe;
frọøntlo:s va:r mi:r das na̱:ə;

als hätt' ich nie es gekannt, war, was immer mir kam.
als hɛt |ɪç ni: |ɛs gəkant, va:r, vas |ɪmmər mi:r ka:m.

Doch dich kannt' ich deutlich und klar:
dɔx dɪç kant |ɪç dọøtlɪç |unt kla:r,

als mein Auge dich sah, war'st du mein Eigen:
als mae̯n |ao̯gə dɪç za:, varst du: mae̯n |ae̯gən,

was im Busen ich barg, was ich bin,
vas |ɪm bu̱:zən |ɪç bark, vas |ɪç bɪn,

hell wie der Tag taucht' es mir auf,
hɛl viː der taːk ta͜oxt |ɛs miːr |a͜of,

wie tönender Schall schlug's an mein Ohr,
viː tøːnəndər ʃal ʃluːks |an ma͜en |oːr,

als in frostig öder Fremde
als |ɪn frɔstɪç |øːdər frɛmdə

zuerst ich den Freund ersah.
tsu|e͜ːrst |ɪç den frɔ͜ønt |ɛrzaː.

Wagner   Einsam in trüben Tagen, from "Lohengrin"
              a͜enzam |ɪn tryːbən taːgən   loːəngrɪn

Einsam in trüben Tagen hab' ich zu Gott gefleht,
a͜enzam |ɪn tryːbən taːgən haːp |ɪç tsuː gɔt gəfle͜ːt,

des Herzens tiefstes Klagen ergoss ich im Gebet,
dɛs hɛrtsəns ti͜ːfstəs klaːgən |ɛrgɔs |ɪç |ɪm gəbe͜ːt,

da drang aus meinem Stöhnen ein Laut so klagevoll,
daː draŋ |a͜os ma͜enəm ʃtøːnən |a͜en la͜ot zoː klaːgəfɔl,

der zu gewalt'gem Tönen weit in die Lüfte schwoll:
der tsuː gəva͜ltgəm tøːnən va͜et |ɪn di lʏftə ʃvɔl,

ich hört' ihn fern hin hallen, bis kaum mein Ohr er traf;
ɪç hø͜ːrt |i͜ːn fɛrn hɪn hallən, bɪs ka͜om ma͜en |oːr |e͜ːr tra͜ːf;

mein Aug' ist zugefallen, ich sank in süssen Schlaf.
ma͜en a͜ok |ɪst tsu͜gəfallən, ɪç zaŋk |ɪn zy͜ːsən ʃlaːf.

In lichter Waffen Scheine ein Ritter nahte da,
ɪn lɪ͜çtər va͜fən ʃa͜enə |a͜en rɪ͜tər na͜ːtə daː,

so tugendlicher Reine ich keinen noch ersah.
zoː tu͜ːgəntlɪçər ra͜enə |ɪç ka͜enən nɔx |e͜ːrzaː.

Ein golden Horn zur Hüften, gelehnet auf sein Schwert,
a͜en gɔldən hɔrn tsur hy͜ftən, gəle͜ːnət a͜of za͜en ʃve͜ːrt,

so trat er aus den Lüften zu mir, der Recke werth,
zoː tra͜ːt |e͜ːr |a͜os den lʏftən tsuː mi͜ːr, der rɛ͜kə ve͜ːrt,

mit züchtigem Gebahren gab Tröstung er mir ein:
mɪt tsy͜çtɪgəm gəba͜ːrən gaːp trœstʊŋ |e͜ːr mi͜ːr a͜en,

des Ritters will, ich wahren, er soll mein Streiter sein!
dɛs rɪ͜tərs vɪl |ɪç va͜ːrən, e͜ːr zɔl ma͜en ʃtra͜etər za͜en!

226

Hört, was dem Gottgesandten ich biete für Gewähr:
høːrt, vas dem gɔtgəzantən |ɪç biːtə fyːr gəvɛːr,

in meines Vaters Landen die Krone trage er,
ɪn maenəs faːtərs landən di kroːnə traːgə |eːr,

mich glücklich soll ich preisen, nimmt er mein Gut dahin,
mɪç glʏklɪç zɔl |ɪç praezən, nɪmt |eːr maen guːt dahɪn,

will er Gemahl mich heissen, geb' ich ihm, was ich bin!
vɪl |eːr gəmaːl mɪç haesən, geːp |ɪç iːm, vas |ɪç bɪn!

Wagner   Morgenlich leuchtend, from "Die Meistersinger"
              mɔrgənlɪç lɔøçtənt   di maestərzɪŋər

Morgenlich leuchtend im rosigen Schein,
mɔrgənlɪç lɔøçtənt |ɪm roːzɪgən ʃaen,

von Blüth' und Duft geschwellt die Luft,
fɔn blyːt |ʊnt duft gəʃvɛlt di luft,

voll aller Wonnen nie ersonnen,
fɔl |allər vɔnnən niː |ɛrzɔnnən,

ein Garten lud mich ein,
aen gartən luːt mɪç |aen,

dort unter einem Wunderbaum, von Früchten reich behangen,
dɔrt |ʊntər |aenəm vʊndərbaom, fɔn frʏçtən raeç bəhaŋən,

zu schau'n im sel'gen Liebestraum,
tsuː ʃaon |ɪm zeːlgən liːbəstraom,

was höchstem Lustverlangen Erfüllung kühn verhiess,
vas høːçstər lʊstfərlaŋən ɛrfʏlluŋ kyːn fərhiːs,

das schönste Weib, Eva, im Paradies!
das ʃøːnstə vaep, eːva, ɪm paradiːs!

Abendlich dämmernd umschloss mich die Nacht;
aːbəntlɪç dɛmmərnt |ʊmʃlɔs mɪç di naxt;

auf steilem Pfad war ich genaht
aof ʃtaeləm pfaːt vaːr |ɪç gənaːt

zu einer Quelle reiner Welle,
tsuː |aenər kvɛllə raenər vɛllə,

die lockend mir gelacht: dort unter einem Lorbeerbaum,
di lɔkənt miːr gəlaxt, dɔrt |ʊntər |aenəm lɔrbeːrbaom,

von Sternen hell durchschienen,
fɔn ʃtɛrnən hɛl dʊrçʃiːnən,

ich schaut' im wachen Dichtertraum,
ɪç ʃaot |ɪm vaxən dɪçtərtraom,

von heilig holden Mienen,
fɔn haelɪç hɔldən miːnən,

mich netzend mit dem edlen Nass,
mɪç nɛtsənt mɪt dem |eːdlən nas,

das hehrste Weib: die Muse des Parnass!
das heːrstə vaep, di muːzə dɛs parnas!

Huldreichster Tag, dem ich aus Dichter's Traum erwacht!
hʊltraeçstər taːk, dem |ɪç |aos dɪçtərs traom ɛrvaxt!

Dass ich erträumt, das Paradies,
das |ɪç |ɛrtrɵmt, das paradiːs,

in himmlisch neu verklärter Pracht
ɪn hɪmlɪʃ nɵ fɛrklɛrtər praxt

hell vor mir lag, dahin lachend
hɛl fɔr miːr laːk, dahɪn laxənt

nun der Quell den Pfad mir wies;
nuːn der kvɛl den pfaːt miːr viːs;

die, dort geboren, mein Herz erkoren,
di, dɔrt gəboːrən, maen hɛrts |ɛrkoːrən,

der Erde lieblichstes Bild,
der |eːrdə liːplɪçstəs bɪlt,

als Muse mir geweit, so heilig
als muːzə miːr gəvaet, zoː haelɪç

ernst als mild, ward kühn von mir gefreit;
ɛrnst |als mɪlt, vart kyːn fɔn miːr gəfraet;

am lichten Tag der Sonnen,
am lɪçtən taːk der zɔnnən,

durch Sanges Sieg gewonnen:
dʊrç zaŋəs ziːk gəvɔnnən,

Parnass und Paradies!
parnas |ʊnt paradiːs!

Wagner   O du mein holder Abendstern, from ''Tannhäuser''
               o: du: maen hͻldər |a:bəntʃtɛrn   tanhͻøzər

Wie Todesahnung Dämm'rung deckt die Lande;
vi: to̝:dəs|a:nυŋ dɛmrυŋ dɛkt di landə;

umhüllt das Thal mit schwärzlichem Gewande,
υmhy̝lt das ta:l mɪt ʃvɛrtslɪçəm gəvandə,

der Seele, die nach jenen Hön'n verlangt,
der ze̝:lə, di nax je̝:nən høːn fɛrlant,

vor ihrem Flug durch Nacht und Grausen bangt.
fͻr |i:rəm flu:k dυrç naxt |υnt graozən bant.

Da scheinest du, o! lieblichster der Sterne,
da: ʃaenəst du:, o:! li:blɪçstər der ʃtɛrnə,

dein sanftes Licht entsendest du der Ferne,
daen zanftəs lɪçt |ɛntzɛndəst du: der fɛrnə,

die nächt'ge Dämm'rung theilt dein lieber Strahl,
di nɛçtgə dɛmrυŋ taelt daen li:bər ʃtra:l,

und freundlich zeigst du den Weg aus dem Thal.
υnt frͻøntlɪç tsaekst du: den ve:k |aos dem ta:l.

O du mein holder Abendstern,
o: du: maen hͻldər |a:bəntʃtɛrn,

wohl grüsst' ich immer dich so gern;
vo:l gry:st |ɪç |ɪmmər dɪç zo: gɛrn;

vom Herzen, das sie nie verrieth,
fͻm hɛrtsən, das zi: ni: fɛrri̝:t,

grüsse sie, wenn sie vorbei dir zieht,
gry:sə zi:, vɛn zi: fͻrbae di:r tsi:t,

wenn sie entschwebt dem Thal der Erden,
vɛn zi: |ɛntʃve̝:pt dem ta:l der |e:rdən,

ein sel'ger Engel dort zu werden.
aen ze̝:lgər |ɛŋəl dͻrt tsu: ve:rdən.

Wagner   Träume
            trͻømə

Sag, welch wunderbare Träume
za:k, vɛlç vυndərba:rə trͻømə

halten meinen Sinn umfangen,
haltən maenən zɪn |υmfaŋən,

229

dass sie nicht wie leere Schäume
das zi: nɪçt vi: le:rə ʃɔømə

sind in ödes Nichts vergangen?
zɪnt ɪn |ø:dəs nɪçts fɛrgaŋən?

Träume, die in jeder Stunde,
trɔømə, di |ɪn je:dər ʃtʊndə,

jedem Tage schöner blün'n,
je:dəm ta:gə ʃø:nər bly:n,

und mit ihrer Himmelskunde
ʊnt mɪt |i:rər hɪmməlskʊndə

selig durch's Gemüte ziehn?
ze:lɪç dʊrçs gəmy:tə tsi:n?

Träume, die wie hehre Strahlen
trɔømə, di vi: he:rə ʃtra:lən

in die Seele sich versenken,
|ɪn di ze:lə zɪç fɛrzɛŋkən,

dort ein ewig Bild zu malen:
dɔrt |aen |e:vɪç bɪlt tsu: ma:lən,

Allvergessen, Eingedenken!
alfɛrgɛsən, aengədɛŋkən!

Träume, wie wenn Frühlingssonne
trɔømə, vi: vɛn fry:lɪŋszɔnnə

aus dem Schnee die Blüten küsst,
|aos dem ʃne: di bly:tən kʏst,

dass zu nie geahnter Wonne
das tsu: ni: gə|a:ntər vɔnnə

sie der neue Tag begrüsst,
zi: der nɔøə ta:k bəgry:st,

dass sie wachsen, dass sie blühen,
das zi: vaksən, das zi: bly:ən,

träumend spenden ihren Duft,
trɔømənt ʃpɛndən |i:rən dʊft,

sanft an deiner Brust verglühen,
zanft |an daenər brʊst fɛrgly:ən,

und dann sinken in die Gruft.
ʊnt dan zɪŋkən |ɪn di grʊft.

Wagner   Winterstürme wichen dem Wonnemond, from "Die Walküre"
             vɪntərʃtyrmə vɪçən dem vɔnnəmoːnt   di valkyːrə

Winterstürme wichen dem Wonnemond,
vɪntərʃtyrmə vɪçən dem vɔnnəmoːnt,

in mildem Lichte leuchtet der Lenz;
ɪn mɪldəm lɪçtə lɔøçtət der lɛnts;

auf linden Lüften, leicht und lieblich,
aof lɪndən lyftən, laeçt |unt liːplɪç,

Wunder webend er sich wiegt;
vundər veːbənt |eːr zɪç viːkt;

durch Wald und Auen weht sein Athem,
durç valt |unt |aoən veːt zaen |aːtəm,

weit geöffnet lacht sein Aug';
vaet gə|øfnət laxt zaen aok;

aus sel'ger Vöglein Sange süss er tönt,
aos zeːlgər føːglaen zaŋə zyːs |eːr tøːnt,

holde Düfte haucht er aus;
hɔldə dyftə haoxt |eːr |aos;

seinem warmen Blut entblühen wonnige Blumen,
zaenəm varmən bluːt |ɛntblyːən vɔnnɪgə bluːmən,

Keim und Spross entspringt seiner Kraft.
kaem |unt ʃprɔs |ɛntʃprɪŋt zaenər kraft.

Mit zarter Waffen Zier bezwingt er die Welt,
mɪt tsartər vafən tsiːr bətsvɪŋkt |eːr di vɛlt,

Winter und Sturm wichen der starken Wehr:
vɪntər |unt ʃturm vɪçən der ʃtarkən veːr,

wohl musste den tapfern Streichen
voːl mustə den tapfərn ʃtraeçən

die strenge Thüre auch weichen,
di ʃtrɛŋə tyːrə |aox vaeçən,

die trotzig und starr uns trennte von ihm.
di trɔtsɪç |unt ʃtar |uns trɛntə fon |iːm.

Zu seiner Schwester schwang er sich her;
tsuː zaenər ʃvɛstər ʃvaŋ |eːr zɪç heːr;

die Liebe lockte den Lenz:
di liːbə lɔktə den lɛnts,

in uns'rem Busen barg sie sich tief;
ɪn |unzrəm buːzən bark ziː zɪç tiːf;

231

nun lacht sie selig dem Licht.
nuːn laxt ziː zeːlɪç dem lɪçt.

Die bräutliche Schwester befreite der Bruder;
di brɔøtlɪçə ʃvɛstər bəfraetə der bruːdər;

zertrümmert liegt, was je sie getrennt;
tsɛrtrʏmmərt liːkt, vas jeː ziː gətrɛnt;

jauchzend grüsst sich das junge Paar:
jaoxtsənt gryːst zɪç das juŋə paːr,

vereint sind Liebe und Lenz!
fɛr|aent zɪnt liːbə |ʊnt lɛnts!

Weber   Leise, leise, fromme Weise, from "Der Freischütz"
         laezə, laezə, frɔmmə vaezə   der fraeʃʏts

Wie nahte mir der Schlummer bevor ich ihn gesehn?
viː naːtə miːr der ʃlʊmmər bəfɔr |ɪç |iːn gəzeːn?

Ja, Liebe pflegt mit Kummer stets Hand in Hand zu gehn.
jaː, liːbə pfleːkt mɪt kʊmmər ʃteːts hant |ɪn hant tsuː geːn.

Ob Mond auf seinem Pfad wohl lacht? Wie schön die Nacht!
ɔp moːnt |aof zaenəm pfaːt voːl laxt? viː ʃøːn di naxt!

Leise, fromme Weise, schwing' dich auf zum Sternenkreise!
laezə, frɔmmə vaezə, ʃvɪŋ dɪç |aof tsum ʃtɛrnənkraezə!

Lied erschalle, feiernd walle mein Gebet zur Himmelshalle!
liːt |ɛrʃallə, faeərnt vallə maen gəbeːt tsur hɪmməlshallə!

O wie hell die gold'nen Sterne,
oː viː hɛl di gɔldnən ʃtɛrnə,

mit wie reinem Glanz sie glühn!
mɪt viː raenəm glants ziː glyːn!

Nur dort in der Berge Ferne scheint ein Wetter aufzuziehn,
nuːr dort |ɪn der bɛrgə fɛrnə ʃaent |aen vɛtər |aoftsutsiːn,

dort am Wald auch schwebt ein Heer
dort |am valt |aox ʃveːpt |aen heːr

dunkler Wolken dumpf und schwer.
dʊŋklər vɔlkən dʊmpf |ʊnt ʃveːr.

Zu dir wende ich die Hände,
tsuː diːr vɛndə |ɪç di hɛndə,

232

Herr, ohn' Anfang und ohn' Ende.
hɛr, oːn |anfaŋ |ʊnt |oːn |ɛndə.

Vor Gefahren uns zu wahren, sende deine Engelschaaren!
foːr gəfaːrən |ʊns tsu vaːrən, zɛndə daenə |ɛŋəlʃaːrən!

Alles pflegt schon längst der Ruh!
aləs pfleːkt ʃoːn lɛŋst der ruː!

Trauter Freund, wo weilest du?
traotər frɔønt, voː vaeləst duː?

Ob mein Ohr auch eifrig lauscht,
ɔp maen |oːr |aox |aefrɪç laoʃt,

nur der Tannen Wipfel rauscht,
nuːr der tannən vɪpfəl raoʃt,

nur das Birkenlaub im Hain
nuːr das bɪrkənlaop |im haen

flüstert durch die hehre Stille,
flʏstərt dʊrç di heːrə ʃtɪllə,

nur die Nachtigall und Grille
nuːr di naxtigal |ʊnt grɪllə

scheint der Nachtluft sich zu freu'n.
ʃaent der naxtlʊft zɪç tsuː frøøn.

Doch wie! täuscht mich nicht mein Ohr?
dɔx viː! tøøʃt mɪç nɪçt maen |oːr?

Dort klingt's wie Schritte!
dɔrt klɪŋts viː ʃrɪtə!

Dort aus der Tannen Mitte kommt was hervor! Er ist's!
dɔrt |aos der tannən mɪtə kɔmt vas hɛrfoːr! eːr |ɪsts!

die Flagge der Liebe mag weh'n!
di flagə der liːbə maːk veːn!

Dein Mädchen wacht noch in der Nacht!
daen mɛːtçən vaxt nɔx |ɪn der naxt!

Er scheint mich noch nicht zu sehn.
ɛːr ʃaent mɪç nɔx nɪçt tsuː zeːn.

Gott! täuscht das Licht des Mond's mich nicht,
gɔt! tøøʃt das lɪçt des moːnts mɪç nɪçt,

so schmückt ein Blumenstrauss den Hut!
zoː ʃmʏkt |aen bluːmənʃtraos den huːt!

Gewiss, er hat den besten Schuss gethan;
gəvɪs, eːr hat den bɛstən ʃʊs getaːn;

das kündet Glück für morgen an!
das kʏndət glʏk fyːr mɔrgən |an!

O süsse Hoffnung!   Neu belebter Muth!
oː syːsə hɔfnʊŋ!   nɔø bəleːptər muːt!

All' meine Pulse schlagen,
al maenə pʊlsə ʃlaːgən,

und das Herz wallt ungestüm
ʊnt das hɛrts valt |ʊŋgəʃtyːm

süss entzückt entgegen ihm!
zyːs |ɛnttsʏkt |ɛntgeːgən |iːm!

Konnt' ich das zu hoffen wagen?
kɔnt |ɪç das tsuː hɔfən vaːgən?

Ja! es wandte sich das Glück
jaː ɛs vandtə zɪç das glʏk

zu dem theuren Freund zurück,
tsuː dem tɔørən frɔønt tsurʏk,

will sich morgen treu bewähren!
vɪl zɪç mɔrgən trɔø bəvɛːrən!

Ist's nicht Täuschung, ist's nicht Wahn?
ɪsts nɪçt tɔøʃʊŋ,   ɪsts nɪçt vaːn?

Himmel, nimm des Dankes Zähren
hɪmməl, nɪm dɛs daŋkəs tsɛːrən

für dies Pfand der Hoffnung an!
fyːr diːs pfant der hɔfnʊŋ |an!

Wolf, H.   Alle gingen, Herz, zur Ruh
allə gɪŋən, hɛrts, tsur ruː

Alle gingen, Herz, zur Ruh,
allə gɪŋən, hɛrts, tsur ruː,

Alle schlafen, nur nicht du.
allə ʃlaːfən, nuːr nɪçt duː.

Denn der hoffnungslose Kummer
dɛn der hɔfnʊŋsloːzə kʊmmər

scheucht von deinem Bett den Schlummer,
ʃɔøçt fɔn daenəm bɛt den ʃlʊmmər,

und dein Sinnen schweift in stummer
ʊnt daen zɪnnən ʃvaeft |ɪn ʃtʊmmər

Sorge seiner Liebe zu.
zɔrgə zaenər liːbə tsuː.

Wolf, H.   Anakreons Grab
               anaːkreɔns graːp

Wo die Rose hier blüht,
voː di roːzə hiːr blyːt,

wo Reben und Lorbeer sich schlingen,
voː reːbən |ʊnt lɔrbeːr zɪç ʃlɪŋən,

wo das Turtelchen lockt,
voː das tʏrtəlçən lɔkt,

wo sich das Grillchen ergötzt,
voː zɪç das grɪlçən |ɛrgœtst,

welch ein Grab ist hier,
vɛlç |aen graːp |ɪst hiːr,

das alle Götter mit Leben
das |allə gœtər mɪt leːbən

schön bepflanzt und geziert?
ʃøːn bəpflantst |ʊnt gətsiːrt?

Es ist Anakreons Ruh.
ɛs |ɪst |anaːkreɔns ruː.

Frühling, Sommer und Herbst
fryːlɪŋ, zɔmmər |ʊnt hɛrpst

genoss der glückliche Dichter;
gənɔs der glʏklɪçə dɪçtər;

vor dem Winter hat ihn endlich
fɔr dem vɪntər hat |iːn |ɛntlɪç

der Hügel geschützt.
der hyːgəl gəʃʏtst.

Wolf, H.   Auch kleine Dinge
              aͦox klae̯nə dɪŋə

Auch kleine Dinge können uns entzücken,
aͦox klae̯nə dɪŋə kœnnən |ʊns |ɛntt͜sy̆kən,

auch kleine Dinge können theuer sein.
aͦox klae̯nə dɪŋə kœnnən tɔ̈ø̈r zae̯n.

Bedenkt, wie gern wir uns mit Perlen schmücken,
bədɛŋkt, vi: gɛrn vi:r |ʊns mɪt p̬ɛrlən ʃmy̆kən,

sie werden schwer bezahlt und sind nur klein.
zi: vɛrdən ʃve:r bətsa̲:lt |ʊnt zɪnt nu:r klae̯n.

Bedenkt, wie klein ist die Olivenfrucht,
bədɛŋkt, vi: klae̯n |ɪst d̬i |oli̯:vənfrʊxt,

und wird um ihre Güte doch gesucht.
ʊnt vɪrt |ʊm |i:rə gy̆:tə dɔx gəzu̲:xt.

Denkt an die Rose nur, wie klein sie ist,
dɛŋkt |an di ro̲:zə nu:r, vi: klae̯n zi: |ɪst,

und duftet doch so lieblich, wie ihr wisst.
ʊnt d̬u̲ftət dɔx zo: li̲:plɪç, vi: |i:r vɪst.

Wolf, H.   Auf dem grünen Balkon
              aͦof dem gry̆:nən balkõ

Auf dem grünen Balkon mein Mädchen
aͦof dem gry̆:nən balkõ mae̯n mɛ̲:tçən

schaut nach mir durchs Gitterlein.
ʃaͦot nax mi:r dʊrçs gɪtərlae̯n.

Mit den Augen blinzelt sie freundlich,
mɪt d̬en |aͦogən blɪ̲ntsəlt zi: frɔø̈ntlɪç,

mit dem Finger sagt sie mir: Nein!
mɪt d̬em fɪŋər za:kt zi: mi:r, nae̯n!

Glück, das nimmer ohne Wanken
glʏk, das nɪ̲mmər |o:nə vaŋkən

junger Liebe folgt hienieden,
ju̲ŋər li:bə fɔlkt hi:ni̲:dən,

hat mir eine Lust beschieden,
hat mi:r |ae̯nə lʊst bəʃi̲:dən,

und auch da noch muss ich schwanken.
ʊnt |aͦox da: nɔx mʊs |ɪç ʃvaŋkən.

236

Schmeicheln hör ich oder Zanken,
ʃmaeçəln høːr |ɪç |oːdər tsaŋkən,

komm ich an ihr Fensterlädchen.
kɔm |ɪç |an |iːr fɛnstərlɛːtçən.

Immer nach dem Brauch der Mädchen
ɪmmər nax dem braox der mɛːtçən

träuft ins Glück ein bisschen Pein:
trɔøft |ɪns glʏk |aen bɪsçən paen,

Mit den Augen blinzelt sie freundlich,
mɪt den |aogən blɪntsəlt ziː frɔøntlɪç,

mit dem Finger sagt sie mir: Nein!
mɪt dem fɪŋər zaːkt ziː miːr, naen!

Wie sich nur in ihr vertragen
viː zɪç nuːr |ɪn |iːr fɛrtraːgən

ihre Kälte, meine Gluth?
|iːrə kɛltə, maenə gluːt?

Weil in ihr mein Himmel ruht,
vael |ɪn |iːr maen hɪmməl ruːt,

seh ich Trüb und Hell sich jagen.
zeː |ɪç tryːp |ʊnt hɛl zɪç jaːgən.

In den Wind gehn meine Klagen,
ɪn den vɪnt geːn maenə klaːgən,

dass noch nie die süsse Kleine
das nɔx niː di zyːsə klaenə

ihre Arme schlang um meine;
|iːrə |armə ʃlaŋ |ʊm maenə;

doch sie hält mich hin so fein,
dɔx ziː hɛlt mɪç hɪn zoː faen,

mit den Augen blinzelt sie freundlich,
mɪt den |aogən blɪntsəlt ziː frɔøntlɪç,

mit dem Finger sagt sie mir: Nein!
mɪt dem fɪŋər zaːkt ziː miːr, naen!

Wolf, H.   Auf ein altes Bild
             aof |aen |altəs bɪlt

In grüner Landschaft Sommerflor,
ɪn gryːnər landʃaft zɔmmərflor,

bei kühlem Wasser, Schilf und Rohr,
ba͜e ky:ləm va͜sər, ʃɪlf |ʊnt ro:r,

schau, wie das Knäblein sündelos
ʃa͜o, vi: das kne͜:pla͜en zyndəlo:s

frei spielet auf der Jungfrau Schoss!
fra͜e ʃpi:lət |a͜of der jʊŋfra͜o ʃo:s!

Und dort im Walde wonnesam,
ʊnt‿dɔrt |ɪm valdə vɔnnəza:m,

ach, grünet schon des Kreuzes Stamm!
ax, gry͜:nət ʃo:n des krɔøtsəs ʃtam!

Wolf, H.   Das verlassene Mägdlein
               das fɛrla͜sənə mɛ:ktla͜en

Früh, wann die Hähne krähn,
fry:, van di hɛ͜:nə krɛ:n,

eh die Sternlein schwinden,
e: di ʃtɛ͜rnla͜en ʃvɪndən,

muss ich am Herde stehn,
mʊs |ɪç |am he:rdə ʃte:n,

muss Feuer zünden.
mʊs fɔ͜øər tsyndən.

Schön ist der Flammen Schein,
ʃø:n |ɪst‿der fla͜mmən ʃa͜en,

es springen die Funken;
ɛs ʃprɪŋən di fʊŋkən;

ich schaue so darein,
ɪç ʃa͜oə zo: dara͜en,

in Leid versunken.
ɪn la͜et fɛrzʊŋkən.

Plötzlich, da kommt es mir,
plœtslɪç, da: kɔmt |ɛs mi:r,

treuloser Knabe,
trɔølo:zər kna͜:bə,

dass ich die Nacht von dir
das |ɪç di naxt fɔn di:r

geträumet habe.
gətrɔ̜ømət ha̜ːbə.

Träne auf Träne dann
trɛ̜ːnə |a̜of trɛ̜ːnə dan

stürzet hernieder;
ʃtyᷓtsət hɛrniːdər;

so kommt der Tag heran
zoː kɔmt der ta̜ːk hɛra̜n—

o ging er wieder!
oː gɪŋ |eːr vi̜ːdər!

Wolf, H.   Er ist's
            ɛr |ɪsts

Frühling lässt sein blaues Band
fryːlɪŋ lɛst za̜en bla̜oəs bant

wieder flattern durch die Lüfte;
vi̜ːdər fla̜tərn dʊrç di lyᷓftə;

süsse, wohlbekannte Düfte
zyːsə, vo̜ːlbəkantə dyᷓftə

streifen ahnungsvoll das Land.
ʃtra̜efən |a̜ːnʊŋsfɔl das lant.

Veilchen träumen schon,
fa̜elçən trɔ̜ømən ʃoːn,

wollen balde kommen.
vɔlən ba̜ldə kɔmmən.

Horch, von fern ein leiser Harfenton!
hɔrç, fɔn fɛrn |a̜en la̜ezər ha̜rfəntoːn!

Frühling, ja du bist's!
fryᷓːlɪŋ, ja̜ː duː bɪsts!

Dich hab ich vernommen,
dɪç ha̜ːp |ɪç fɛrnɔ̜mmən,

ja du bist's!
ja̜ː duː bɪsts!

Wolf, H.   Fussreise
              fuːsraɛzə

Am frisch geschnittnen Wanderstab, wenn ich in der Frühe
am frɪʃ gəʃnɪtnən   vandərʃtaːp, vɛn |ɪç |ɪn der fryːə

so durch Wälder ziehe, Hügel auf und ab:
zoː durç vɛldər tsiːə, hyːgəl |aof |unt |ap,

dann, wie's Vöglein im Laube
dan, viːs føːglaen |ɪm laobə

singet und sich rührt,
zɪŋət |unt zɪç ryːrt,

oder wie die goldne Traube
oːdər viː di gɔldnə traobə

Wonnegeister spürt in der ersten Morgensonne:
vɔnnəgaestər ʃpyːrt |ɪn der |eːrstən mɔrgənzɔnnə,

so fühlt auch mein alter, lieber Adam Herbst-
zoː fyːlt |aox maen |altər, liːbər |aːdəm hɛrpst-

und Frühlingsfieber, gottbeherzte,
unt fryːlɪŋsfiːbər, gɔtbəhɛrtstə,

nie verscherzte Erstlings – Paradieseswonne.
niː fɛrʃɛrtstə |ɛrstlɪŋs – paradiːzəsvɔnnə.

Also bist du nicht so schlimm, o alter Adam,
alzo bɪst duː nɪçt zoː ʃlɪm, oː |altər |aːdam,

wie die strengen Lehrer sagen;
viː di ʃtrɛŋən leːrər zaːgən;

liebst und lobst du immer doch,
liːpst |unt loːpst duː |ɪmmər dɔx,

singst und preisest immer noch,
zɪŋst |unt praezəzt |ɪmmər nɔx,

wie an ewig neuen Schöpfungstagen,
viː |an |eːvɪç nɔøən ʃœpfuŋstaːgən,

deinen lieben Schöpfer und Erhalter.
daenən liːbən ʃœpfər |unt |ɛrhaltər.

Möcht es dieser geben, und mein ganzes Leben
mœçt |ɛs diːzər geːbən, unt maen gantsəs leːbən

wär im leichten Wanderschweisse
vɛːr |ɪm laeçtən vandərʃvaesə

eine solche Morgenreise!
|aenə zɔlçə mɔrgənraezə!

240

Wolf, H.   Gebet
            gəbe̠ːt

Herr! schicke was du willt,
hɛr! ʃɪkə   vas duː vɪlt,

ein Liebes oder Leides;
a̠en li̠ːbəs |o̠ːdər la̠edəs,

ich bin vergnügt, dass beides
ɪç bɪn fɛrgny̠ːkt, das ba̠edəs

aus deinen Händen quillt.
|a̠os da̠enən hɛndən kvɪlt.

Wollest mit Freuden
vo̠lləst mɪt frøːdən

und wollest mit Leiden
|ʊnt vo̠lləst mɪt la̠edən

mich nicht überschütten!
mɪç nɪçt |yːbərʃy̠tən!

Doch in der Mitten
dɔx |ɪn der mi̠tən

liegt holdes Bescheiden.
liːkt hɔ̠ldəs bəʃa̠edən.

Wolf, H.   Gesang Weylas
            gəza̠ŋ va̠elas

Du bist Orplid, mein Land!
duː bɪst |ɔrpli̠ːt ma̠en lant!

das ferne leuchtet;
das fɛrnə lo̠øçtət;

vom Meere dampfet dein besonnter Strand
fɔm me̠ːrə dampfət da̠en bəzɔ̠ntər ʃtrant

den Nebel, so der Götter Wange feuchtet.
den ne̠ːbəl, zoː der gœtər va̠ŋə fo̠øçtət.

Uralte Wasser steigen
u̠ːr|altə vasər ʃta̠egən

verjüngt um deine Hüften, Kind!
fɛrjy̠ŋt |ʊm da̠enə hy̠ftən, kɪnt!

Vor deiner Gottheit beugen
fɔr da̠enər gɔ̠thaet bo̠øgən

241

sich Könige, die deine Wärter sind.
zɪç køːnɪgə, di daenə vɛrtər zɪnt.

Wolf, H.   Gesegnet sei
              gəzeːgnət zae

Gesegnet sei, durch den die Welt entstund;
gəzeːgnət zae, dʊrç den di vɛlt |entʃtʊnt;

wie trefflich schuf er sie nach allen Seiten!
viː trɛflɪç   ʃuːf |eːr ziː nax |allən zaetən!

Er schuf das Meer mit endlos tiefem Grund,
eːr ʃuːf das meːr |mɪt |entloːs tiːfəm grʊnt,

er schuf die Schiffe, die hinübergleiten,
eːr ʃuːf di ʃɪfə,   di hɪnyːbərglaetən,

er schuf das Paradies, mit ew'gem Licht,
eːr ʃuːf das paradiːs, mɪt |eːvgəm lɪçt,

er schuf die Schönheit und dein Angesicht.
eːr ʃuːf di ʃøːnhaet |ʊnt daen |angəzɪçt.

Wolf, H.   Ich hab in Penna
              ɪç haːp |ɪn pɛnna

Ich hab in Penna einen Liebsten wohnen,
ɪç haːp |ɪn pɛnna |aenən liːpstən voːnən,

in der Maremmenebne einen andern,
ɪn der marɛmmən|eːbnə |aenən |andərn,

einen im schönen Hafen von Ancona,
aenən |ɪm ʃøːnən haːfən fɔn aŋkona,

zum vierten muss ich nach Viterbo wandern;
tsum fiːrtən mʊs |ɪç nax vitɛrbo vandərn;

ein andrer wohnt in Casentino dort,
aen |andrər voːnt |ɪn kazɛntiːno dɔrt,

der nächste lebt mit mir am selben Ort,
der nɛçstə leːpt mɪt miːr |am zɛlbən |ɔrt,

und wieder einen hab ich in Magione,
ʊnt vi̱ːdər |a̱enən haːp |ɪç |ɪn madʒone,

vier in La Fratta, zehn in Castiglione.
fiːr |ɪn la fra̱tta, tseːn |ɪn kastiʎone.

Wolf, H.   In dem Schatten meiner Locken
             ɪn dem ʃatən   ma̱enər lɔkən

In dem Schatten meiner Locken
ɪn dem ʃa̱tən   ma̱enər lɔkən

schlief mir mein Geliebter ein.
ʃliːf miːr ma̱er   gəli̱ːptər |a̱en.

Weck ich ihn nun auf? Ach nein!
vɛk |ɪç |iːn nuːn |a̱of? ax na̱en!

Sorglich strählt ich meine krausen
zɔ̱rklɪç ʃtrɛːlt |ɪç ma̱enə kra̱ozən

Locken täglich in der Frühe,
lɔkən tɛ̱ːklɪç |ɪn der fryːə,

doch umsonst ist meine Mühe,
dɔx |ʊmzɔ̱nst |ɪst ma̱enə myːə,

weil die Winde sie zersausen.
va̱el di vɪndə ziː tsɛrza̱ozən.

Lockenschatten, Windessausen
lɔkənʃatən,   vɪndəsza̱ozən

schläferten den Liebsten ein.
ʃlɛ̱fərtən   den li̱ːpstən |a̱en.

Weck ich ihn nun auf? Ach nein!
vɛk |ɪç |iːn nuːn |a̱of? ax na̱en!

Hören muss ich, wie ihn gräme,
hø̱ːrən mʊs |ɪç, viː |iːn grɛ̱ːmə,

dass er schmachtet schon so lange,
das |eːr ʃma̱xtət ʃoːn zoː la̱ŋə,

dass ihm Leben geb und nehme
das |iːm leːbən geːp |ʊnt nɛ̱ːmə

diese meine braune Wange.
di̱ːzə ma̱enə bra̱onə va̱ŋə.

Und er nennt mich seine Schlange,
ʊnt |eːr nɛnt mɪç zaɛnə ʃlaŋə,

und doch schlief er bei mir ein.
ʊnt͜ dɔx ʃliːf |eːr bae miːr |aen.

Weck ich ihn nun auf? Ach nein!
vɛk |ɪç |iːn nuːn |aof? ax naen!

Wolf, H.   In der Frühe
              ɪn der fryːə

Kein Schlaf noch kühlt das Auge mir,
kaen ʃlaːf nɔx kyːlt das |aogə miːr,

dort gehet schon der Tag herfür
dɔrt geːət ʃoːn der taːk hɛrfyːr

an meinem Kammerfenster.
|an maenəm kammərfɛnstər.

Es wühlet mein verstörter Sinn
ɛs vyːlət maen fɛrʃtœrtər zɪn

noch zwischen Zweifeln her und hin
nɔx tsvɪʃən tsvaefəln heːr |ʊnt hɪn

und schaffet Nachtgespenster.
|ʊnt ʃafət naxtgəʃpɛnstər.

Ängst'ge, quäle dich nicht länger,
ɛŋstgə, kveːlə dɪç nɪçt lɛŋər,

meine Seele!
maenə zeːlə!

Freu dich! Schon sind da und dorten
frɔø dɪç! ʃoːn zɪnt daː ʊnt dɔrtən

Morgenglocken wach geworden.
mɔrgənglɔkən vax gəvɔrdən.

Wolf, H.   Mausfallen-Sprüchlein
              maosfallən-ʃpryçlaen

Kleine Gäste, kleines Haus,
klaenə gɛstə, klaenəs haos,

liebe Mäusin, oder Maus,
liːbə mo̞ʏzɪn, o̞ːdər ma̞os,

stelle dich nur kecklich ein
ʃtɛllə dɪç nuːr ke̞klɪç |a̞en

heute Nacht bei Mondenschein!
ho̞ʏtə naxt ba̞e mo̞ːndənʃa̞en!

Mach aber die Tür fein hinter dir zu,
max |a̞bər di tyːr fa̞en hɪntər diːr tsuː,

hörst du? hörst du?
høːrst duː? høːrst duː?

Dabei hüte dein Schwänzchen!
dɑba̞e hy̞ːtə da̞en ʃvɛntsçən!

hörst du? hörst du? Dein Schwänzchen?
høːrst duː? høːrst duː? da̞en ʃvɛntsçən?

Nach Tische singen wir,
nax tɪ̞ʃə zɪ̞ŋən viːr,

nach Tische springen wir
nax tɪʃə ʃprɪ̞ŋən viːr

und machen ein Tänzchen, ein Tänzchen!
|ʊnt ma̞xən |a̞en te̞ntsçən, a̞en te̞ntsçən!

Witt, witt! Witt, witt!
vɪt, vɪt! vɪt, vɪt!

Meine alte Katze tanzt wahrscheinlich mit,
ma̞enə |a̞ltə ka̞tsə tantst vaːrʃa̞enlɪç mɪt,

hörst du? hörst du?
høːrst duː? høːrst duː?

Wolf, H.   Nimmersatte Liebe
              nɪmmərzatə li̞ːbə

So ist die Lieb! So ist die Lieb!
zoː |ɪst di liːp! zoː |ɪst di liːp!

Mit Küssen nicht zu stillen:
mɪt ky̞sən nɪçt tsuː ʃtɪllən,

wer ist der Tor und will ein Sieb
veːr |ɪst der toːr |ʊnt vɪl a̞en ziːp

245

mit eitel Wasser füllen?
mɪt |aetəl vasər fyllən?

Und schöpfst du an die tausend Jahr,
ʊnt ʃœpfst du: |an di taozənt ja:r,

und küssest ewig, ewig gar,
ʊnt kysəst |e:vɪç, e:vɪç ga:r,

du tust ihr nie zu Willen.
du: tu:st |i:r ni: tsu: vɪllən.

Die Lieb, die Lieb hat alle Stund
di li:p, di li:p hat |allə ʃtʊnt

neu wunderlich Gelüsten;
nɔø vʊndərlɪç gəlystən;

wir bissen uns die Lippen wund,
vi:r bɪsən |ʊns di lɪpən vʊnt,

da wir uns heute küssten.
da: vi:r |ʊns hɔøtə kystən.

Das Mädchen hielt in guter Ruh,
das me:tçən hi:lt |ɪn gu:tər ru:,

wie's Lämmlein unterm Messer;
vi:s lɛmlaen |ʊntərm mɛsər,

ihr Auge bat: nur immer zu,
i:r |aogə bat, nu:r |ɪmmər tsu:,

je weher, desto besser!
je: ve:ər, dɛsto bɛsər!

So ist die Lieb, und war auch so,
zo: |ɪst di li:p, ʊnt va:r |aox zo:,

wie lang es Liebe gibt,
vi: laŋ |ɛs li:bə gi:pt,

und anders war Herr Salomo,
ʊnt |andərs va:r hɛr za:lomo,

der Weise, nicht verliebt.
der vaezə, nɪçt fɛrli:pt.

Wolf, H.   Nun wandre, Maria
             nuːn vạndrə, mariːa

Nun wandre, Maria, nun wandre nur fort.
nuːn vạndrə, mariːa, nuːn vạndrə nuːr fɔrt.

Schon krähen die Hähne, und nah ist der Ort.
ʃoːn krẹːən di hẹːnə, ʊnt naː |ɪst der |ɔrt.

Nun wandre, Geliebte, du Kleinod mein,
nuːn vạndrə, gəliːptə, duː klạenoːt mạen,

und balde wir werden in Bethlehem sein.
ʊnt baḷdə viːr vẹːrdən |ɪn beːthlehəm zạen.

Dann ruhest du fein und schlummerst dort.
dan rụːəst duː fạen |ʊnt ʃlụmmərst dort.

Schon krähen die Hähne, und nah ist der Ort.
ʃoːn krẹːən di hẹːnə, ʊnt naː |ɪst der |ɔrt.

Wohl seh ich, Herrin, die Kraft dir schwinden;
voːl zeː |ɪç, hẹrrɪn, di kraft diːr ʃvɪndən;

kann deine Schmerzen, ach, kaum verwinden.
kan dạenə ʃmẹrtsən, ax, kạom fɛrvɪndən.

Getrost! wohl finden wir Herberg dort;
gətrọːst! voːl fɪndən viːr hẹrbɛrk dort;

schon krähn die Hähne und nah ist der Ort.
ʃoːn krɛːn di hẹːnə |ʊnt naː |ɪst der |ɔrt.

Wär erst bestanden dein Stündlein, Marie,
vɛːr |eːrst bəʃtạndən dạen ʃtỵntlạen, marịː,

die gute Botschaft gut lohnt ich sie.
di gụtə bọːtʃaft guːt loːnt |ɪç ziː.

Das Eselein hie gäb ich drum fort!
das |ẹːzəlạen hiː gɛːp |ɪç drụm fɔrt!

Schon krähen die Hähne,
ʃoːn krẹːən di hẹːnə,

komm, nah ist der Ort.
kɔm, naː |ɪst der ɔrt.

Wolf, H.   Schlafendes Jesuskind
             ʃlạːfəndəs jẹːzʊskɪnt

Sohn der Jungfrau, Himmelskind!
zoːn der jụŋfraọ, hɪ̣mməlskɪnt!

247

am Boden auf dem Holz der Schmerzen
am boːdən |a͜of dem hɔlts der ʃmɛrtsən

eingeschlafen,
|a͜engəʃlaːfən,

das der fromme Meister
das der frɔmə ma͜estər

sinnvoll spielend deinen leichten
zɪnfɔl ʃpiːlənt‿da͜enən la͜eçtən

Träumen unterlegte;
trɔ͜ømən |ʊntərleːktə;

Blume du, noch in der Knospe
bluːmə duː, nɔx |ɪn der knɔspe

dämmernd eingehüllt
dɛmmərnt |a͜engəhylt

die Herrlichkeit des Vaters!
di hɛrlɪçka͜et‿des faːtərs!

O wer sehen könnte,
oː veːr zeːən kœntə,

welche Bilder hinter dieser Stirne,
vɛlçə bɪldər hɪntər diːzər ʃtɪrnə,

diesen schwarzen Wimpern,
diːzən ʃvartsən vɪmpərn,

sich in sanftem Wechsel malen!
zɪç |ɪn zanftəm vɛksəl maːlən!

Sohn der Jungfrau, Himmelskind!
zoːn der juŋfra͜o, hɪmməlskɪnt!

Wolf, H.   Über Nacht
             yːbər naxt

Über Nacht, über Nacht
yːbər naxt, yːbər naxt

kommt still das Leid,
kɔmt ʃtɪl das la͜et,

und bist du erwacht,
ʊnt bɪst‿duː |ɛrvaxt,

o traurige Zeit,
oː tra͜orɪgə tsa͜et,

248

du grüssest den dämmernden Morgen
du: gry:səst den dɛmmərndən mɔrgən

mit Weinen und mit Sorgen.
mɪt va͟enən |ʊnt mɪt zɔrgən.

Über Nacht, über Nacht
y:bər naxt, y:bər naxt

kommt still das Glück,
kɔmt ʃtɪl das glʏk,

und bist du erwacht, o selig Geschick,
ʊnt bɪst du: |ɛrva͟xt, o: ze͟:lɪç gəʃɪk,

der düstre Traum ist zerronnen,
der dy:strə tra͟om |ɪst tsɛrrɔnnən,

und Freude ist gewonnen.
|ʊnt frɔ͟ødə |ɪst gəvɔnnən.

Über Nacht, über Nacht
y:bər naxt, y:bər naxt

kommt Freud und Leid,
kɔmt frɔ͟øt |ʊnt la͟et,

und eh du's gedacht,
ʊnt |e: du:s gəda͟xt,

verlassen dich beid
fɛrla͟sən dɪç ba͟et

und gehen dem Herrn zu sagen,
ʊnt ge͟:ən dem hɛrn tsu: za͟:gən,

wie du sie getragen.
vi: du: zi: gətra͟:gən.

Wolf, H.   Verborgenheit
                fɛrbɔ͟rgənha͟et

Lass, o Welt, o lass mich sein!
las, o: vɛlt, o: las mɪç za͟en!

locket nicht mit Liebesgaben,
lɔ͟køt nɪçt mɪt li͟:bəsga:bən,

lasst dies Herz alleine haben
last di:s hɛrts |alla͟enə ha͟:bən

249

seine Wonne, seine Pein!
zaenə vɔnnə, zaenə paen!

Was ich traure, weiss ich nicht,
vas |ɪç traorə, vaes |ɪç nɪçt,

es ist unbekanntes Wehe;
ɛs |ɪst |unbəkantəs veːə,

immerdar durch Tränen sehe
ɪmmərdaːr dʊrç trɛːnən zeːə

ich der Sonne liebes Licht.
|ɪç der zɔnnə liːbəs lɪçt.

Oft bin ich mir kaum bewusst
ɔft bɪn |ɪç miːr kaom bəvʊst

und die helle Freude zücket
ʊnt di hɛllə frøødə tsʏkət

durch die Schwere, so mich drücket,
dʊrç di ʃveːrə, zoː mɪç drʏkət,

wonniglich in meiner Brust.
voːnɪklɪç |ɪn maenər brʊst.

Wolf, H.   Zur Ruh, zur Ruh!
             tsuːr ruː, tsuːr ruː!

Zur Ruh, zur Ruh ihr müden Glieder!
tsuːr ruː, tsuːr ruː |iːr myːdən gliːdər!

schliesst fest euch zu, ihr Augenlider!
ʃliːst fɛst |ɔøç tsuː, iːr |aogənliːdər!

ich bin allein, fort ist die Erde;
ɪç bɪn |allaen, fɔrt |ɪst di |eːrdə;

Nacht muss es sein, dass Licht mir werde,
naxt mʊs |ɛs zaen, das lɪçt miːr veːrdə,

o führt mich ganz, ihr innern Mächte!
oː fyːrt mɪç gants, iːr |ɪnnərn mɛçtə!

hin zu dem Glanz der tiefsten Nächte.
hɪn tsuː dem glants der tiːfstən nɛçtə.

Fort aus dem Raum der Erdenschmerzen,
fɔrt |aos dem raom der |eːrdənʃmɛrtsən,

durch Nacht und Traum zum Mutterherzen!
durç naxt |ʊnt traͦm tsum mutͧərhɛrtsən!

FRENCH PHONETICS FOR THE SINGER

Pierre Delattre and Berton Coffin

Open Syllabication

The most characteristic feature of French is that all syllables tend to open, that is, tend to end in a vowel: Avec une amie is pronounced [a-vɛ-ky-na-mi]. English speakers, on the contrary, tend to close all syllables with a consonant: Eat at eight is pronounced by an American [it-æt-eit]. To help avoid such closing of syllables, we have transcribed all syllables as open; we have even separated the final phonetic consonant from the preceding vowel: il observe [i-lɔ-bsɛ-rv].

Stress and Rhythm

The place of stress is always the same in French — the last syllable of a long word or a group of words: Mes amis, mes meilleurs amis. What makes those last syllables stand out is not an increase of force (intensity, loudness) but an increase of length (duration). In fact, all syllables have equal force and all but the last have equal duration. This sort of stress and rhythm pattern should agree very naturally with singing. No special marking is necessary.

The "mute e"

The ə as in demi [dəmi] is an unstable vowel which falls or remains according to very involved rules in speech. In singing, however, two statements will suffice.

a.   Within a word, before a consonant, it is always sung as a syllable: re-ve-nez.
b.   Final after a consonant (toute), or after a vowel (la vie), it can fall [tut la vi] or remain and be sung [tu tə la vi ə], at the fancy of the poet or composer (poetic license). Even if the same words occurred two lines apart, the ə could remain once and be dropped the next. There fore, follow the phonetic transcription.

Liaison

Symbols used in the following explanation:
a.   Compulsory liaison = ⌣
b.   Optional liaison = ⟋
c.   Forbidden liaison = /
(cf. Principes de Phonétique du Français, chart of Liaison, p. 39.)

Another unstable sound peculiar to French is the consonant of liaison, as in mes amis /auront/attendu. Final consonants that are mute in the isolated word can at times be pronounced with the vowel that begins the next word — at times but not always. It is most useful to know which liaisons are quite forbidden:

a.   between two words not closely connected: ils vont/ils viennent...
b.   after a singular noun: un soldat/anglais, une maison/immense.

c. after et: et/ils chantent
d. before the numbers un, huit, onze: cent/un.
e. before an aspirate h: les/haches.

Other liaisons are either compulsory (i.e. article, or adjective before a noun, personal pronoun before or after a verb), or optional. The latter are done more or less frequently depending on (a) the grammatical relation between the two words (in the above example, auront/attendu is more frequent than amis/auront) and (b) the degree of formality (in formal style, both could be made, but especially auront/attendu).

In the phonetic transcriptions for singing, we omitted all the forbidden liaison, and a small portion of the optional ones — just those which we judged would sound much too stuffy.

Nasality

In French, vowel nasality is "distinctive": whether you say [pɛ] paix or [pɛ̃] pain makes a difference in meaning. Every vowel must therefore be completely nasal: mon [mɔ̃], or completely free from nasality: ami [a mi], année [a ne]. If the vowel is nasal, do not pronounce at all the nasal consonant that follows: mondain [mɔ̃ dɛ̃]. The n's are absolutely silent.

Value of the phonetic symbols used in the transcription of French

Phonetic Symbols	Sounds as derived from English sounds	As found in French words
VOWELS		
ɑ	father, arm	âme . . . ɑm
a	father, with tongue more fronted, about central	Madame . . . madam
e	say, but without diphthongization	nez . . . ne
ɛ	sell	plaire . . . plɛr
i	see, but more close	qui . . . ki
o	no, but without dipthongization	nos . . . no
ɔ	law, taught, open midway between ɑ and o	porte . . . port
u	soon, but more close	jour . . . ʒur
ø	no, for lip rounding, but with tongue tip fronted to touch the lower teeth	deux . . . dø

253

œ	<u>law</u>, <u>floor</u>, for lip rounding, but with tongue tip fronted nearly enough to touch the lower teeth	<u>fleur</u>...flœr
y	<u>do</u>, for lip rounding, but with tongue tip fronted to touch firmly the lower teeth and mass of tongue raised forward.	<u>du</u>...dy
ã	somewhat like <u>pond</u> when the n is not pronounced	<u>dans</u>...dã
ɛ̃	somewhat like <u>bent</u> when the n is not pronounced	<u>pain</u>...pɛ̃
ɔ̃	somewhat like <u>haunt</u> when the n is not pronounced	<u>non</u>...nɔ̃
œ̃	somewhat like <u>hunt</u> when the n is not pronounced	<u>un</u>...œ̃
ə	<u>the</u>, but with more lip rounding. Same as œ of French <u>fleur</u>, but somewhat weaker, shorter. In speech it can often disappear, but very seldom in singing.	<u>petit</u>...pəti

CONSONANTS

b	<u>bay</u>	<u>bonne</u>...bɔn
d	<u>day</u>, with tongue more fronted, touching upper teeth	<u>dans</u>...dã
f	<u>fate</u>	<u>fille</u>...fij
g	<u>gate</u>	<u>garçon</u>...garsɔ̃
k	<u>key</u>, without aspiration	<u>comme</u>...kɔm
l	<u>leave</u>, more fronted, tongue touching upper teeth, always clear, even after a vowel	<u>livre</u>...livr
m	<u>mine</u>	<u>maison</u>...mɛzɔ̃
n	<u>nine</u>	<u>nouveau</u>...nuvo
ɲ	<u>pinion</u>, with tongue more fronted, touching upper teeth	<u>gagner</u>...gaɲe
p	<u>pay</u>, without aspiration	<u>petit</u>...pəti
r	tongue tip flap (more lightly rolled than in Italian) is preferred <u>in singing</u> to pharyngeal friction of spoken French.	<u>rue</u>...ry

CONSONANTS continued

s	<u>s</u>ore, more fronted than in English	<u>sœur</u> . . . sœr
ʃ	<u>sh</u>ore, more fronted than in English, lips rounded	<u>ch</u>ez . . . ʃe
t	<u>til</u>e, without aspiration and with tongue more fronted touching upper teeth	<u>tabl</u>e . . . tabl
v	<u>v</u>ile	<u>v</u>ous . . . vu
ʒ	<u>rouge</u>, <u>garage</u>, <u>regime</u>, with tongue more fronted	<u>je</u> . . . ʒə
j	<u>y</u>es, be<u>y</u>ond	<u>réveillé</u> . . . reveje
w	<u>we</u>, a<u>way</u>	<u>oui</u> . . . wi
ɥ	<u>we</u>, but with tongue tip fronted to touch lower teeth	<u>huit</u> . . . ɥit

BIBLIOGRAPHY

Barbeau, Alfred & Èmile Rodhe.   Dictionnaire Phonétique de la Langue Française. 1930.

Coustenoble, Hélène.   A Pronunciation Dictionary of the French Language, Based Upon Gasc's Concise Dictionary. 1929.

Delattre, Pierre.   An Introduction to French Speech Habits. 1947.

Delattre, Pierre.   Les Difficultés Phonétiques du Français. 1948.

Delattre, Pierre.   Advanced Training in French Pronunciation. 1949.

Delattre, Pierre.   Principes de Phonétique Française, à l'usage des Etudiants Anglo-Américains. 1951.

Delattre, Pierre.   "Les Modes Phonétiques du Français". The French Review, 27: 59 – 63. Oct. 1953.

Fouché, Pierre.   Traité de Prononciation Française. 1956.

Mansion's   French and English Dictionary. (in America, D.C. Heath and Company, Boston).

Bachelet   Chère Nuit
baʃle   ʃɛr nɥi

Voici l'heure bientôt.
vwa si lœ rə bjɛ̃ to.

Derrière la colline
dɛ rjɛ rə la kɔ li nə,

Je vois le soleil qui décline
ʒə vwa lə sɔ lɛ jki de kli nə,

Et cache ses rayons jaloux.
e ka ʃə se rɛ jɔ̃ ʒa lu.

J'entends chanter l'âme des choses
ʒɑ̃ tɑ̃ ʃɑ̃ te la mə de ʃo zə,

Et les narcisses et les roses
e le na rsi sə ze le ro zə

M'apportent des parfums plus doux!
ma pɔ rtə de pa rfœ̃ ply du!

Chère nuit aux clartés sereines,
ʃɛ rə nɥi o kla rte sə rɛ nə,

Toi qui ramènes Le tendre amant,
twa ki ra mɛ nə lə tɑ̃ dra mɑ̃,

Ah! descends et voile la terre
ɑ dɛ sɑ̃ ze vwa lə la tɛ rə,

De ton mystère, Calme et charmant.
də tɔ̃ mi stɛ rə, ka lme ʃa rmɑ̃.

Mon bonheur renaît sous ton aile,
mɔ̃ bɔ nœ rrə nɛ su tɔ̃ nɛ lə,

O nuit plus belle Que les beaux jours:
o nɥi ply bɛ lə kə le bo ʒu r:

Ah! lève-toi! Pour faire encore
ɑ lɛ və twa! pu rfɛ rɑ̃ kɔ rə

Briller l'aurore De mes amours!
bri je lɔ rɔ rə, də me za mu r!

Berlioz   L'absence
bɛrljoz   l absɑ̃s

Reviens, reviens, ma bien aimée!
rə vjɛ̃ rə vjɛ̃, ma bjɛ̃ ne me ə!

256

Comme une fleur loin du soleil,
kɔ my nə flœ r, lwɛ̃ dy so lɛ j,

La fleur de ma vie est fermée
la flœ rdə ma vi ɛ, fɛ rme ə,

Loin de ton sourire vermeil.
lwɛ̃ də tɔ̃ su ri rə vɛ rmɛ j.

Entre nos coeurs quelle distance!
ã trə no kœ rkɛ lə di stã sə!

Tant d'espace entre nos baisers!
tã dɛ spa sã trə no bɛ ze!

O sort amer! ô dure absence!
o sɔ ra mɛ r! o dy ra psã sə!

O grand désirs inapaisés!
o grã de zi ri na pɛ ze!

D'ici là—bas que de campagnes,
di si la bɑ kə də kã pa ɲə,

Que de villes et de hameaux,
kə də vi lə e də a mo,

Que de vallons et de montagnes,
kə də va lɔ̃ e də mɔ̃ ta ɲə,

A lasser le pied des chevaux!
a lɑ se lə pje de ʃə vo!

Bizet   Habanera, from "Carmen"
bizɛ   abanera   karmɛn

L'amour est un oiseau rebelle
la mu rɛ tɛ̃ nwa zo rə bɛ lə

Que nul ne peut apprivoiser,
kə ny lnə pø ta pri vwa ze,

Et c'est bien en vain qu'on l'appelle,
e sɛ bjɛ̃ nã vɛ̃ kɔ̃ la pɛ lə,

S'il lui convient de refuser.
si llɥi kɔ̃ vjɛ̃ də rə fy ze

Rien n'y fait, menace ou prière,
rjɛ̃ ni fɛ, mə na su pri jɛ rə,

L'un parle bien, l'autre se tait;
lœ̃ pa rlə bjɛ̃ lo trə sə tɛ;

Et c'est l'autre que je préfère
e sɛ lo trə kə ʒə pre fɛ rə,

Il n'a rien dit; mais il me plait.
i lna rjɛ̃ di mɛ zi lmə plɛ.

L'amour est enfant de Bohême,
la mu rɛ tɑ̃ fɑ̃ də bo ɛ m,

Il n'a jamais, jamais connu de loi,
i lna ʒa mɛ ʒa mɛ ko ny də lwa,

Si tu ne m'aimes pas, je t'aime;
si ty nə mɛ mə pa, ʒə tɛ mə;

Si je t'aime, prends garde à toi!
si ʒə tɛ mə prɑ̃ ga rda twa!

Mais si je t'aime, si je t'aime, prends garde à toi!
mɛ si ʒə tɛ mə, si ʒə tɛ mə prɑ̃ ga rda twa!

L'oiseau que tu croyais surprendre
lwa zo kə ty krwa jɛ sy rprɑ̃ drə

Battit de l'aile et s'envola;
ba ti də lɛ le sɑ̃ vɔ la;

L'amour est loin, tu peux l'attendre;
la mu rɛ lwɛ̃, ty pø la tɑ̃ drə;

Tu ne l'attends plus, il est la!
ty nə la tɑ̃ ply i lɛ la!

Tout autour de toi vite, vite,
tu to tu rdə twa vi tə vi tə,

Il vient, s'en va, puis il revient;
i lvjɛ̃, sɑ̃ va pчi zi lrə vjɛ̃

Tu crois le tenir, il t'évite;
ty krwa lə tə ni r, i lte vi tə;

Tu crois l'éviter, il te tient!
ty krwa le vi te, i ltə tjɛ̃!

258

Bizet   Je dis que rien ne m'épouvante, from "Carmen"
bizɛ   ʒə di kə rjɛ̃ nə mepuvɑ̃t   karmɛn

C'est des contrebandiers le refuge ordinaire.
sɛ de kɔ̃ trə bɑ̃ dje lə rə fy ʒɔ rdi nɛ rə.

Il est ici, je le verrai
i lɛ ti si ʒə lə vɛ re,

Et le devoir que m'imposa sa mère
e lə də vwa rkə mɛ̃ po za sa mɛ rə,

Sans trembler je l'accomplirai.
sɑ̃ trɑ̃ ble ʒə la kɔ̃ pli re.

Je dis, que rien ne m'épouvante
ʒə di kə rjɛ̃ nə me pu vɑ̃ tə,

Je dis, hélas! que je réponds de moi;
ʒə di e lɑs, kə ʒə re pɔ̃ də mwa;

Mais j'ai beau faire la vaillante,
mɛ ʒe bo fɛ rə la va jɑ̃ tə,

Au fond du coeur je meurs d'effroi!
o fɔ̃ dy kœ r, ʒə mœ rdɛ frwa!

Seule en ce lieu sauvage,
sœ lɑ̃ sə ljø so va ʒə,

Toute seule j'ai peur, mais j'ai tort d'avoir peur;
tu tə sœ lə ʒe pœ r, mɛ ʒe tɔ rda vwa rpœ r;

Vous me donnerez du courage,
vu mə dɔ nə re dy ku ra ʒə,

Vous me protégerez, Seigneur!
vu mə pro te ʒə re sɛ ɲœ r!

Je vais voir de près cette femme
ʒə vɛ vwa rdə prɛ sɛ tə fa mə,

Dont les artifices maudits
dɔ̃ le za rti fi sə mo di,

Ont fini par faire un in- fâme
ɔ̃ fi ni pa rfɛ rœ̃ nɛ̃ fɑ mə,

De celui que j'aimais jadis!
də sə lɥi kə ʒe mɛ ʒa di!

Elle est dangereuse elle est belle!
ɛ lɛ dɑ̃ ʒə rø zə, ɛ lɛ bɛ lə!

Mais je ne veux pas avoir peur! Non – – –
mɛ ʒə nə vø pa za vwa rpœ r!   nɔ̃ – – –

259

Je parlerai haut devant elle
ʒə pa rlə re o də vã tɛ lə,

Ah! vous me protégerez! donnez moi du courage!
a!   vu mə prɔ te ʒə re! dɔ ne mwa dy ku ra ʒə!

Bizet   La fleur que tu m'avais jetée, from "Carmen"
bizɛ   la flœr kə ty m avɛ ʒəte   karmɛn

La fleur que tu m'avais jetée,
la flœ rkə ty ma vɛ ʒə te ə,

Dans ma prison m'était restée,
dã ma pri zõ me tɛ rɛ ste ə,

Flétrie et sèche, cette fleur
fle tri e sɛ ʃə sɛ tə flœ r,

Gardait toujours sa douce odeur;
ga rdɛ tu ʒu rsa du so dœ r;

Et pendant des heures entières,
e pã dã de zœ rə zã tjɛ rə,

Sur mes yeux, fermant mes paupières,
sy rme zjø fɛ rmã me po pjɛ rə,

De cette odeur je m'enivrais
də sɛ to dœ rʒə mã ni vrɛ,

Et dans la nuit je te voyais!
e dã la nɥi ʒə tə vwa jɛ!

Je me prenais à te maudire,
ʒə mə prə nɛ a tə mo di rə,

A te détester, à me dire:
a tə de tɛ ste a mə di rə:

Pourquoi faut il que le destin
pu rkwa fo ti lkə lə dɛ stɛ̃,

L'ait mise là sur mon chemin!
lɛ mi zə la, sy rmõ ʃə mɛ̃!

Puis je m'accusais de blasphème,
pɥi, ʒə ma ky zɛ də bla sfɛ mə,

Et je ne sentais en moi même,
e ʒə nə sã tɛ zã mwa mɛ mə,

260

Je ne sentais qu'un seul désir,
ʒə nə sɑ̃ tɛ kɶ̃ sœ lde zi r,

un seul désir, un seul espoir:
ɶ̃ sœ lde zi r, ɶ̃ sœ lɛ spwa r:

Te revoir, ô Carmen, oui, te revoir!
tə rə vwa ro ka rmɛ n, wi tə rə vwa r!

Car tu n'avais eu qu'a paraître,
ka rty na vɛ zy ka pa rɛ trə,

Qu'à jeter un regard sur moi,
ka ʒə te ɶ̃ rə ga rsy rmwa,

Pour t'emparer de tout mon être,
pu rtɑ̃ pa re də tu mɔ̃ nɛ trə,

O ma Carmen!   Et j'étais une chose à toi!
o ma ka rmɛ n! e ʒe tɛ zy nə ʃo za twa!

Carmen, je t'aime!
ka rmɛ n, ʒə tɛ mə!

Bizet   Ouvre ton coeur
bizɛ   uvrə tɔ̃ kœr

La marguerite a fermé sa corolle,
la ma rgə ri t, a fɛ rme sa kɔ rɔ lə,

L'ombre a fermé les yeux du jour.
lɔ̃ bra fɛ rme le zjø dy ʒu r.

Belle, me tiendras tu parole?
bɛ lə, mə tjɛ̃ dra ty pa rɔ lə?

Ouvre ton coeur à mon amour.
u vrə tɔ̃ kœ ra mɔ̃ na mu r.

O jeune ange, à ma flamme,
o ʒœ nɑ̃ ʒa ma fla mə,

Qu'un rêve charme ton sommeil,
kɶ̃ rɛ və ʃa rmə tɔ̃ sɔ mɛ j,

Je veux reprendre mon âme,
ʒə vø rə prɑ̃ drə mɔ̃ nɑ mə,

Ouvre ton coeur, ô jeune ange, à ma flamme,
u vrə tɔ̃ kœ ro ʒœ nɑ̃ ʒa ma fla mə

Comme une fleur s'ouvre au soleil!
kɔ my nə flœ r, su vro sɔ lɛ j

Bizet   Seguidilla, from "Carmen"
bizɛ   segidija   karmɛn

Près des remparts de Séville,
prɛs de rɑ̃ pa rdə se vi lə,

Chez mon ami Lillas Pastia
ʃe mɔ̃ na mi li la pa stja

J'irai danser la Séguedille
ʒi re dɑ̃ se la se gə di j

Et boire du Manzanilla.
e bwa rə dy mɑ̃ za ni ja.

J'irai chez mon ami Lillas Pastia
ʒi re ʃe mɔ̃ na mi li la pa stja.

Oui, mais toute seule on s'ennuie,
wi, mɛ tu tə sœ lɔ̃ sɑ̃ nɥi ə,

Et les vrais plaisirs sont à deux;
e le vrɛ plɛ zi rsɔ̃ ta dø;

Donc, pour me tenir compagnie,
dɔ̃ k, pu rmə tə ni rkɔ̃ pa ɲi ə,

J'emmènerai mon amoureux!
ʒɑ̃ mɛ nə re mɔ̃ na mu rø!

Mon amoureux il est au diable,
mɔ̃ na mu rø, i lɛ to dja blə,

Je l'ai mis à la porte hier!
ʒə le mi a la pɔ rtə jɛ r!

Mon pauvre coeur très consolable,
mɔ̃ po vrə kœ rtrɛ kɔ̃ sɔ la blə,

Mon coeur est libre comme l'air!
mɔ̃ kœ rɛ li brə kɔ mə lɛ r!

J'ai des galants à la douzaine,
ʒe de ga lɑ̃ a la du zɛ nə,

Mais ils ne sont pas à mon gré.
mɛ i lnə sɔ̃ pa za mɔ̃ gre.

262

Voici la fin de la semaine:
vwa si la fɛ̃ də la sə mɛ nə:

Qui veut m'aimer? je l'aimerai!
ki vø mɛ me? ʒə lɛ mə re!

Qui veut mon âme? Elle est à prendre!
ki vø mɔ̃ na mɛ lɛ ta prɑ̃ drə!

Vous arrivez au bon moment!
vu za ri ve o bɔ̃ mɔ mɑ̃!

Je n'ai guère le temps d'attendre,
ʒə ne gɛ rə lə tɑ̃ da tɑ̃ drə,

Car avec mon nouvel amant, . . .
ka ra vɛ kmɔ̃ nu vɛ la mɑ̃, . . .

Bizet   Votre toast, je peux vous le rendre, from "Carmen"
bizɛ   votrə tost ʒə pø vu lə rɑ̃dr   karmɛn

Votre toast, je peux vous le rendre,
vɔ trə to st, ʒə pø vu lə rɑ̃ drə,

Señors, señors, car avec les soldats
se ɲo rse ɲo r, ka ra vɛ kle sɔ lda,

Oui, les Toréros, peuvent s'entendre;
wi le tɔ re ro, pœ və sɑ̃ tɑ̃ drə;

Pour plaisirs, pour plaisirs, ils ont les combats!
pu rplɛ zi rpu rplɛ si r, i lzɔ̃ le kɔ̃ ba!

Le cirque est plein, c'est jour de fête!
lə si rkɛ plɛ̃ sɛ ʒu rdə fɛ tə!

Le cirque est plein du haut en bas;
lə si rkɛ plɛ̃ dy o tɑ̃ ba;

Les spectateurs, perdant la tête,
le spɛ kta tœ r, pɛ rdɑ̃ la tɛ tə,

Les spectateurs s'interpellent à grand fracas!
le spɛ kta tœ r, sɛ̃ tɛ rpɛ lə ta grɑ̃ fra ka!

Apostrophes, cris et tapage
a pɔ strɔ fə kri ze ta pa ʒə,

Poussés jusques à la fureur!
pu se ʒy skə za la fy rœ r!

Car c'est la fête du courage!
ka rsɛ la fɛ tə dy ku ra ʒə!

C'est la fête des gens de coeur!
sɛ la fɛ tə de ʒã də kœ r!

Allons! en garde! ah!
a lõ! ã ga rdə! a!

Toréador, en garde!
tɔ re a dɔ r ã ga rdə!

Et songe bien, oui, songe en combattant,
e sõ ʒə bjɛ̃ wi sõ ʒã kõ ba tã,

Qu'un oeil noir te regarde, Et que l'amour t'attend,
kœ̃ nœ jnwa rtə rə ga rd, e kə la mu rta tã,

Toréador, l'amour t'attend!
tɔ re a dɔ r, la mu rta tã!

Tout d'un coup, on fait silence...
tu dœ̃ ku, õ fɛ si lã sə...

Ah! que se passe−t−il?
a kə sə pa sə ti l?

Plus de cris, c'est l'instant!
ply də kri sɛ lɛ̃ stã!

Le taureau s'élance En bondissant hors du Toril!
lə tɔ ro se lã sã bõ di sã ɔ rdy tɔ ri l!

Il s'élance, il entre, il frappe!
i lse lã sə, i lã tri lfra pə!

un cheval roule, Entraînant un Picador,
œ̃ ʃə va lru lə, ã trɛ nã tœ̃ pi ka dɔ r,

" Ah! bravo! Toro! " hurle la foule!
a bra vo tɔ ro! y rlə la fu lə!

Le taureau va, il vient, et frappe encor!
lə tɔ ro va, i lvjɛ̃, e fra pã kɔ r!

En secouant ses banderilles,
ã sə ku ã se bã də ri jə,

Plein de fureur, il court! Le cirque est plein de sang!
plɛ̃ də fy rœ r, i lku r! lə si rkɛ plɛ̃ də sã!

On se sauve, on franchit les grilles!
õ sə so v, õ frã ʃi le gri jə!

C'est ton tour maintenant!   Allons! en garde! ah!
sɛ tɔ̃ tu rmɛ̃ tə nɑ̃! a lɔ̃! ɑ̃ ga rdə! a!

Charpentier Depuis le jour, from "Louise"
ʃarpɑ̃tje   dəpɥi lə ʒur   luiz

Depuis le jour où je me suis donnée,
də pɥi lə ʒu r, u ʒə mə sɥi do ne ə,

Toute fleurie semble ma destinée.
tu tə flœ ri ə sɑ̃ blə ma dɛ sti ne ə.

Je crois rêver sous un ciel de féerie,
ʒə krwa rɛ ve, su zœ̃ sjɛ ldə fe ri ə,

l'âme encore grisée de ton premier baiser!
la mɑ̃ ko rə gri ze ə, də tɔ̃ prə mje bɛ ze!

Quelle belle vie! Mon rêve n'était pas un rêve!
kɛ lə bɛ lə vi ə! mɔ̃ rɛ və ne tɛ pa zœ̃ rɛ və!

Ah! je suis heureuse!
a! ʒə sɥi zø rø zə!

L'amour étend sur moi ses ailes!
la mu re tɑ̃ sy rmwa se zɛ lə!

Au jardin de mon coeur chante une joie nouvelle!
o ʒa rdɛ̃ də mɔ̃ kœ r, ʃɑ̃ ty nə ʒwa nu vɛ lə!

Tout vibre, tout se réjouit de mon triomphe!
tu vi brə tu sə re ʒu i də mɔ̃ tri jɔ̃ fə!

Autour de moi tout est sourire, lumière et joie!
o tu rdə mwa tu tɛ su ri rə, ly mjɛ re ʒwa ə!

et je tremble délicieusement
e ʒə trɑ̃ blə, de li si ø zə mɑ̃

au souvenir charmant du premier jour d'amour!
o su və ni rʃa rmɑ̃, dy prə mje ʒu rda mu r!

Je suis heureuse! trop heureuse.
ʒə sɥi zø rø zə! trɔ pø rø zə.

265

Chausson   Les Papillons
ʃosɔ̃   lə papijɔ̃

Les papillons couleur de neige
le pa pi jɔ̃ ku lœ rdə nɛ ʒə,

Volent par essaims sur la mer;
vɔ lə pa rɛ sɛ̃ sy rla mɛ r;

Beaux papillons blancs,
bo pa pi jɔ̃ blɑ̃,

quand pourrai-je Prendre le bleu chemin de l'air!
kɑ̃ pu rɛ ʒə prɑ̃ drə lə blø ʃə mɛ̃ də lɛ r!

Savez-vous, ô belle des belles,
sa ve vu, o bɛ lə de bɛ lə,

Ma bayadère aux yeux de jais,
ma ba ja dɛ ro zjø də ʒɛ,

S'ils me voulaient prêter leurs ailes,
si lmə vu lɛ prɛ te lœ rzɛ lə,

Dites, savez vous où j'irais?
di tə sa ve vu u ʒi rɛ?

Sans prendre un seul baiser aux roses,
sɑ̃ prɑ̃ drœ̃ sœ lbɛ ze o ro zə,

A travers vallons et forêts
a tra vɛ rva lɔ̃ ze fɔ rɛ,

J'irais à vos lèvres mi closes,
ʒi rɛ za vo lɛ vrə mi klo zə,

Fleur de mon âme, et j'y mourrais.
flœ rdə mɔ̃ nɑ mə, e ʒi mu rrɛ.

Chausson   Le Temps des lilas
ʃosɔ̃   lə tɑ̃ de lila

Le temps des lilas et le temps des roses
lə tɑ̃ de li la e lə tɑ̃ de ro zə

Ne reviendra plus à ce printemps-ci;
nə rə vjɛ̃ dra ply a sə prɛ̃ tɑ̃ si;

Le temps des lilas et le temps des roses
lə tɑ̃ de li la e lə tɑ̃ de ro zə

Est passé le temps des oeillets aussi.
ɛ pa se, lə tɑ̃ de zœ jɛ o si.

Le vent a changé, les cieux sont moroses,
lə vɑ̃ a ʃɑ̃ ʒe, le sjø sɔ̃ mɔ ro zə,

Et nous n'irons plus courir, et cueillir
e nu ni rɔ̃ ply ku ri r, e kœ ji r

Les lilas en fleur et les belles roses;
le li la zɑ̃ flœ re le bɛ lə ro zə;

Le printemps est triste et ne peut fleurir.
lə prɛ̃ tɑ̃ ɛ tri ste nə pø flœ ri r.

Oh! joyeux et doux printemps de l'année,
o ʒwa jø ze du prɛ̃ tɑ̃ də la ne ə,

Qui vins, l'an passé, nous ensoleiller;
ki vɛ̃ lɑ̃ pa se, nu zɑ̃ sɔ lɛ je;

Notre fleur d'amour est si bien fanée.
nɔ trə flœ rda mu rɛ si bjɛ̃ fa ne ə.

Las! que ton baiser ne peut l'éveiller!
lɑs! kə tɔ̃ bɛ ze nə pø le vɛ je!

Et toi, que fais tu? pas de fleurs écloses,
e twa, kə fɛ ty? pa də flœ rze klo zə,

Point de gai soleil ni d'ombrages frais;
pwɛ̃ də ge sɔ lɛ jni dɔ̃ bra ʒə frɛ;

Le temps des lilas et le temps des roses
lə tɑ̃ de li la e lə tɑ̃ de ro zə,

Avec notre amour est mort à jamais.
a vɛ knɔ tra mu rɛ mɔ ra ʒa mɛ.

Debussy   Recit et Air de Lia from "L'Enfant Prodigue"
dəbysi   resi e ɛr də lia   l ɑ̃fɑ̃ prɔdig

L'année en vain chasse l'année!
la ne ə ɑ̃ vɛ̃ ʃa sə la ne ə!

A chaque saison ramenée,
a ʃa kə sɛ zɔ̃ ra mə ne ə,

Leurs jeux et leurs ébats m'attristent malgré moi;
lœ rʒø e lœ rze ba ma tri stə ma lgre mwa;

Ils rouvrent ma blessure et mon chagrin s'accroît...
i lru vrə ma blɛ sy rə, e mɔ̃ ʃa grɛ̃ sa krwa...

267

Je viens chercher la grève solitaire...
ʒə vjɛ̃ ʃɛ rʃe la grɛ və sɔ li tɛ rə...

Douleur involontaire!   Efforts superflus!
du lœ rɛ̃ vɔ lɔ̃ tɛ rə! ɛ fɔ rsy pɛ rfly!

Lia pleure toujours l'enfant qu'elle n'a plus!
li a, plœ rə tu ʒu r, lɑ̃ fɑ̃ kɛ lə na ply!

Azaël! Azaël!   Pourquoi m'as–tu quittée?
a za ɛ l! a za ɛ l! pu rkwa ma ty ki te ə?

En mon coeur maternel ton image est restée.
ɑ̃ mɔ̃ kœ rma tɛ rnɛ l, tɔ̃ ni ma ʒɛ rɛ ste.

Azaël! Azaël! Pourquoi m'as–tu quittée?
a za ɛ l! a za ɛ l! pu rkwa ma ty ki te ə?

Cependant les soirs étaient doux,
sə pɑ̃ dɑ̃ le swa re tɛ du,

Dans la plaine d'ormes plantée,
dɑ̃ la plɛ nə dɔ rmə plɑ̃ te ə,

Quand, sous la charge récoltée,
kɑ̃ su la ʃa rʒə re kɔ lte ə,

On ramenait les grands boeufs roux.
ɔ̃ ra mə nɛ le grɑ̃ bø ru.

Lorsque la tâche était finie,
lɔ rskə la tɑ ʃe tɛ fi ni,

Enfants, vieillards et serviteurs,
ɑ̃ fɑ̃, vjɛ ja re sɛ rvi tœ r,

Ouvriers des champs ou pasteurs,
u vri je de ʃɑ̃ u pa stœ r,

Louaient, de Dieu la main bénie.
lu ɛ, də djø la mɛ̃ be ni ə,

Ainsi les jours suivaient les jours
ɛ̃ si le ʒu rsɥi vɛ le ʒu r

Et dans la pieuse famille,
e dɑ̃ la pi ø zə fa mi jə,

Le jeune homme et la jeune fille
lə ʒœ nɔ mə, e la ʒœ nə fi j

268

Echangeaient leurs chastes amours.
e ʃɑ̃ ʒɛ lœ rʃa stə za mu r.

D'autres ne sentent pas le poids de la vieillesse;
do trə nə sɑ̃ tə pa lə pwa, də la vjɛ jɛ sə;

Heureux dans leurs enfants,
ø rø dɑ̃ lœ rzɑ̃ fɑ̃,

Ils voient couler les ans
i lvwa ku le le zɑ̃

sans regret comme sans tristesse...
sɑ̃ rə grɛ kɔ mə sɑ̃ tri stɛ sə...

Aux coeurs inconsolés que les temps sont pesants! ...
o kœ rɛ̃ kɔ̃ sɔ le, kə le tɑ̃ sɔ̃ pə zɑ̃! ...

Azaël! Azaël! Pourquoi m'as-tu quittée?
a za ɛ l! a za ɛ l! pu rkwa ma ty ki te ə?

Debussy   Beau soir
dəbysi   bo swar

Lorsque au soleil couchant les rivières sont roses,
lɔ rsko sɔ lɛ jku ʃɑ̃, le ri vjɛ rə sɔ̃ ro zə,

Et qu'un tiède frisson court sur les champs de blé.
e kœ̃ tjɛ də fri sɔ̃ ku rsy rle ʃɑ̃ də ble.

Un conseil d'être heureux semble sortir des choses
œ̃ kɔ̃ sɛ jdɛ trø rø sɑ̃ blə sɔ rti rde ʃo zə

Et monter vers le coeur troublé
e mɔ̃ te vɛ rlə kœ rtru ble

Un conseil de goûter le charme d'être au monde
œ̃ kɔ̃ sɛ jdə gu te lə ʃa rmə dɛ tro mɔ̃ də

Cependant qu'on est jeune et que le soir est beau,
sə pɑ̃ dɑ̃ kɔ̃ nɛ ʒœ ne kə lə swa rɛ bo,

Car nous nous en allons, Comme s'en va cette onde;
ka rnu nu zɑ̃ na lɔ̃, kɔ mə sɑ̃ va sɛ tɔ̃ də;

Elle à la mer, Nous au tombeau.
ɛ la la mɛ r, nu o tɔ̃ bo

Debussy   C'est l'Extase
dəbysi   sɛ l ekstaz

C'est l'extase langoureuse
sɛ lɛ ksta zə lɑ̃ gu rø zə

C'est la fatigue amoureuse
sɛ la fa ti ga mu rø zə

C'est tous les frissons des bois
sɛ tu le fri sɔ̃ de bwa

Parmi l'étreinte des brises
pa rmi le trɛ̃ tə de bri zə

C'est, vers les ramures grises,
sɛ, vɛ rle ra my rə gri zə,

Le choeur des petites voix.
lə kœ rde pə ti tə vwa.

O le frêle et frais murmure
o lə frɛ le frɛ my rmy rə

Cela gazouille et susurre,
sə la ga zu je sy sy rə,

Cela ressemble au cri doux.
sə la rə sɑ̃ blo kri du.

que l'herbe agitée expire.
kə lɛ rba ʒi te ɛ kspi rə.

Tu dirais, sous l'eau qui vire
ty di rɛ, su lo ki vi rə

Le roulis sourd des cailloux.
lə ru li su rde ka ju.

Cette âme qui se lamente
sɛ ta mə ki sə la mɑ̃ tə

En cette plainte dormante
ɑ̃ sɛ tə plɛ̃ tə dɔ rmɑ̃ tə

C'est la nôtre, n'est-ce pas?
sɛ la no trə, nɛ sə pa?

La mienne, dis, et la tienne
la mjɛ nə, di, e la tjɛ nə

Dont s'exhale l'humble antienne
dɔ̃ sɛ gza lə lœ̃ blɑ̃ tjɛ nə

Par ce tiède soir, tout bas.
pa rsə tjɛ də swa r, tu bɑ.

270

Debussy   Chevaux de bois
dəbysi   ʃəvo d bwa

Tournez, tournez, bons chevaux de bois
tu rne, tu rne, bõ ʃə vo də bwa

Tournez, cent tours, tournez mille tours
tu rne sã tu r, tu rne mi lə tu r

Tournez souvent et tournez toujours
tu rne su vã e tu rne tu ʒu r

Tournez tournez au son des hautbois.
tu rne tu rne o sõ de o bwa.

L'enfant tout rouge et la mère blanche
lã fã tu ru ʒə, e la mɛ rə blɑ ʃə

Le gars en noir et la fille en rose
lə gɑ ã nwa re la fi jã ro zə

L'une à la chose et l'autre à la pose,
ly na la ʃo ze lo tra la po zə,

Chacun se paie un sou de dimanche
ʃa kœ̃ sə pɛ œ̃ su də di mã ʃə

Tournez, tournez, chevaux de leur coeur,
tu rne, tu rne, ʃə vo də lœ rkœ r,

Tandis qu'autour de tous vos tournois
tã di ko tu rdə tu vo tu rnwa

Clignote l'oeil du filou sournois
kli ɲo tə lœ jdy fi lu su rnwa

Tournez au son du piston vainqueur!
tu rne o sõ dy pi stõ vɛ̃ kœ r!

C'est étonnant comme ça vous soûle
sɛ te tɔ nã kɔ mə sa vu su lə

D'aller ainsi dans ce cirque bête:
da le ɛ̃ si dã sə si rkə bɛ tə:

Rien dans le ventre et mal dans la tête,
rjɛ̃ dã lə vã tre ma ldã la tɛ tə,

Du mal en masse et du bien en foule
dy ma lã ma se dy bjɛ̃ ã fu lə

Tournez dadas, sans qu'il soit besoin
tu rne da da, sã ki lswa bə zwɛ̃

D'user jamais de nuls éperons
dy ze ʒa mɛ də ny lze pə rõ

271

Pour commander à vos galops ronds.
pu rkɔ mã de, a vo ga lo rɔ̃,

Tournez, tournez, sans espoir de foin
tu rne, tu rne, sã zɛ spwa rdə fwɛ̃

Et dépêchez, chevaux de leur âme
e de pe ʃe, ʃə vo də lœ ra mə

Déjà voici que sonne à la soupe
de ʒa vwa si kə so na la su pə

La nuit qui tombe et chasse la troupe
la nɥi ki tɔ̃ be ʃa sə la tru pə

De gais buveurs que leur soif affame.
də gɛ by vœ rkə lœ rswa fa ʃa mə.

Tournez, tournez! Le ciel en velours
tu rne, tu rne! lə sjɛ lã və lu r

D'astres en or se vêt lentement,
da strə zã nɔ rsə vɛ lã tə mã,

L'Eglise tinte un glas tristement.
le gli zə tɛ̃ tœ̃ gla tri stə mã.

Tournez au son joyeux des tambours, tournez.
tu rne o sɔ̃ ʒwa jø de tã bu r, tu rne.

Debussy   Clair de lune
dəbysi   klɛr də lyn

Votre âme est un paysage choisi
vɔ tra mɛ tœ̃ pe i za ʒə ʃwa zi

Que vont charmants masques et bergamasques
kə vɔ̃ ʃa rmã ma skə ze bɛ rga ma skə

Jouant du luth et dansant et quasi
ʒu ã dy ly te dã sã, e ka zi

tristes sous leurs déguisements fantasques,
tri stə, su lœ rde gi zə mã fã ta skə,

Tout en chantant sur le mode mineur
tu tã ʃã tã sy rlə mo də mi nœ r

L'amour vainqueur et la vie opportune,
la mu rvɛ̃ kœ re la vi o pɔ rty nə,

272

Ils n'ont pas l'air de croire à leur bonheur,
i lnɔ̃ pa lɛ rdə krwa ra lœ rbɔ nœ r,

Et leur chanson se mêle au clair de lune,
e lœ rʃɑ̃ sɔ̃ sə mɛ lo klɛ rdə ly nə,

Au calme clair de lune triste et beau,
o ka lmə klɛ rdə ly nə, tri stə bo,

Qui fait rêver les oiseaux dans les arbres
ki fɛ rɛ ve le zwa zo dɑ̃ le za rbrə

Et sangloter d'extase les jets d'eau
e sɑ̃ glɔ te dɛ kstɑ zə le ʒɛ do

Les grands jets d'eau sveltes parmi les marbres.
le grɑ̃ ʒɛ do svɛ ltə pa rmi le ma rbrə.

Debussy   De Fleurs (Proses Lyriques)
dəbysi   də flœr   proz lirik

Dans l'ennui si désolément vert de la serre de douleur,
dɑ̃ lɑ̃ nɥi, si de zɔ le mɑ̃ vɛ r də la sɛ rə də du lœ r,

les Fleurs enlacent mon coeur de leurs tiges méchantes.
le flœ rzɑ̃ la sə mɔ̃ kœ r, də lœ rti ʒə me ʃɑ̃ tə.

Ah! quand reviendront autour de ma tête les chères mains
ɑ kɑ̃ rə vjɛ̃ drɔ̃ o tu rdə ma tɛ tə, le ʃɛ rə mɛ̃

si tendrement désenlaceuses?
si tɑ̃ drə mɑ̃ de zɑ̃ la sø zə?

Les grand Iris violets violèrent méchamment tes yeux,
le grɑ̃ di ri svjɔ le, vjɔ lɛ rə me ʃa mɑ̃ te zjø,

en semblant les refléter, Eux, qui furent l'eau du songe
ɑ̃ sɑ̃ blɑ̃ le rə fle te, ø ki fy rə lo dy sɔ̃ ʒə

où plongèrent mes rêves
u plɔ̃ ʒɛ rə me rɛ və,

si doucement enclos en leur couleur;
si du sə mɑ̃ tɑ̃ klo ɑ̃ lœ rku lœ r;

Et les lys, blancs jets d'eau de pistils embaumés,
e le li s, blɑ̃ ʒe do də pi sti lɑ̃ bo me,

ont perdu leur grâce blanche
ɔ̃ pɛ rdy lœ rgrɑ sə blɑ̃ ʃə

273

Et ne sont plus que pauvres malades sans soleil!
e nə sɔ̃ ply kə po vrə ma la də sɑ̃ sɔ lɛ j!

Soleil! ami des fleurs mauvaises,
sɔ lɛ j! a mi de flœ rm vɛ zə,

Tueur de rêves! Tueur d'illusions ce pain béni
ty œ rdə rɛ və! ty œ rdi ly zjɔ̃, sə pɛ̃ be ni

des âmes misérables! Venez!
de zɑ mə mi ze ra blə! və ne!

Les mains salvatrices Brisez les vitres de mensonge,
le mɛ̃ sa lva tri sə, bri ze le vi trə də mɑ̃ sɔ̃ ʒə,

Brisez les vitres de maléfice, mon âme meurt de
bri ze le vi trə də ma le fi sə, mɔ̃ nɑ mə mœ rdə

trop de soleil! Mirages!
trɔ də sɔ lɛ j! mi ra ʒə!

Plus ne refleurira la joie de mes yeux
ply nə rə flœ ri ra la ʒwa də me zjø

Et mes mains sont lasses de prier,
e me mɛ̃ sɔ̃ lɑ sə də pri je,

Mes yeux sont las de pleurer!
me zjø sɔ̃ lɑ də plœ re!

Eternellement ce bruit fou des pétales noirs
e tɛ rnɛ lə mɑ̃, sə brɥi fu de pe ta lə nwa r

de l'ennui tombant goutte à goutte sur ma tête
də lɑ̃ nɥi tɔ̃ bɑ̃ gu ta gu tə, sy rma tɛ tə

Dans le vert de la serre de douleur!
dɑ̃ lə vɛ rdə la sɛ rə də du lœ r!

Debussy   De Grève (Proses Lyriques)
dəbysi   də grɛv   proz lirik

Sur la mer les crépuscules tombent,
sy rla mɛ rle kre py sky lə tɔ̃ bə,

Soie blanche effilée.
swa blɑ̃ ʃe fi le ə.

Les vagues comme de petites folles Jasent,
le va gə kɔ mə də pə ti tə fɔ lə ʒa zə,

petites filles sortant de l'école,
pə ti tə fi jə so rtɑ̃ də le kɔ lə,

Parmi les froufrous de leur robe,
pa rmi le fru fru də lœ rrɔ bə,

Soie verte irisée!
swa vɛ rti ri ze ə!

Les nuages, graves voyageurs,
le ny a ʒə, grɑ və vwa ja ʒœ r,

se concertent sur le prochain orage,
sə kɔ̃ sɛ rtə sy rlə prɔ ʃɛ nɔ ra ʒə,

Et c'est un fond vraiment trop grave
e sɛ tœ̃ fɔ̃ vrɛ mɑ̃ trɔ grɑ və

à cette anglaise aquarelle.
a sɛ tɑ̃ glɛ za kwa rɛ lə.

Les vagues, les petites vagues,
le va gə, le pe ti tə va gə,

ne savent plus où se mettre,
nə sa və ply u sə mɛ trə.

car voici la méchante averse,
ka rvwa si la me ʃɑ̃ ta vɛ rsə,

Frou frous de jupes envolées,
fru fru də ʒy pə zɑ̃ vɔ le ə,

Soie verte affolée.
swa vɛ rta fɔ le ə.

Mais la lune, compatissante à tous!
mɛ la ly nə, kɔ̃ pa ti sɑ̃ ta tu s!

Vient apaiser ce gris conflit
vjɛ̃ ta pɛ ze sə gri kɔ̃ fli

Et caresse lentement ses petites amies
e ka rɛ sə lɑ̃ tə mɑ̃ se pə ti tə za mi

qui s'offrent comme lèvres aimantes
ki sɔ frə kɔ mə lɛ vrə zɛ mɑ̃ tə

A ce tiède et blanc baiser.
a sə tjɛ de blɑ̃ bɛ ze.

Puis, Plus rien Plus que les cloches attardées
pɥi, ply rjɛ̃, ply kə le klɔ ʃə za ta rde ə

des flottantes églises!
de flɔ tɑ̃ tə ze gli zə!

Angélus des vagues, Soie blanche apaisée!
ã ʒe ly sde va gə, swa blã ʃa pɛ ze ə!

Debussy   De Rêve (Proses Lyriques)
dəbysi   də rɛv   proz lirik

La nuit a des douceurs de femme
la nyi a de du sœ rdə fa mə

Et les vieux arbes, sous la lune d'or, Songent!
e le vjø za rbrə su la ly nə do r, sõ ʒə!

A Celle qui vient de passer la tête emperlée,
a sɛ lə ki vjɛ̃ də pa se, la tɛ tã pɛ rle ə,

Maintenant navrée, à jamais navrée,
mɛ̃ tə nã na vre ə, a ʒa mɛ na vre ə,

Ils n'ont pas su lui faire signe.
i lnõ pa sy lyi fɛ rə si ɲə.

Toutes! Elles ont passé: les Frêles, les Folles,
tu tə!   ɛ lə zõ pa se, le frɛ lə, le fɔ lə,

Semant leur rire au gazon grêle, aux brises frôleuses
sə mã lœ rri ro ga zõ grɛ lə, o bri zə fro lø zə

la caresse charmeuse des hanches fleurissantes.
la ka rɛ sə ʃa rmø zə, de ã ʃə flœ ri sã tə.

Hélas! de tout ceci, plus rien qu'un blanc frisson.
e la s, də tu sə si, ply rjɛ̃ kœ̃ blã fri sõ.

Les vieux arbres sous la lune d'or pleurent
le vjø za rbrə su la ly nə do r, plœ rə

leurs belles feuilles d'or!
lœ rbɛ lə fœ jə do r!

Nul ne leur dédiera plus la fierté
ny lnə lœ rde di ra ply, la fjɛ rte

des casques d'or
de ka skə do r

Maintenant ternis, à jamais ternis.
mɛ̃ tə nã tɛ rni, a ʒa mɛ tɛ rni.

Les chevaliers sont morts Sur le chemin du Grâal!
le ʃə va lje sõ mo r, sy rlə ʃə mɛ̃ dy grɑ l!

La nuit a des douceurs de femme, Das mains semblent
la nɥi a de du sœ rdə fa mə, de mɛ̃, sɑ̃ blə

frôler les âmes, mains si folles, si frêles,
fro le le zɑ mə, mɛ̃ si fɔ lə, si frɛ lə,

Au temps où les épées chantaient pour Elles!
o tɑ̃ u le ze pe ə, ʃɑ̃ tɛ pu rɛ lə!

D'étranges soupirs s'élèvent sous les arbres.
de trɑ̃ ʒə su pi r, se lɛ və su le zɑ rbrə.

Mon âme c'est du rêve ancien qui t'étreint!
mɔ̃ nɑ mə sɛ dy rɛ vɑ̃ sjɛ̃, ki te trɛ̃!

Debussy   De Soir (Proses Lyriques)
dəbysi   də swar   proz lirik

Diamanche sur les villes, Dimanche dans les coeurs!
di mɑ̃ ʃə sy rle vi lə, di mɑ̃ ʃə dɑ̃ le kœ r!

Diamanche chez les petites filles chantant
di mɑ̃ ʃə ʃe le pə ti tə fi jə ʃɑ̃ tɑ̃

d'une voix informée des rondes obstinées
dy nə vwa ɛ̃ fɔ rme, de rɔ̃ də zɔ psti ne ə

ou de bonnes Tours n'en ont plus que pour quelques jours!
u də bɔ nə tu r, nɑ̃ nɔ̃ ply kə pu rkɛ lkə ʒu r!

Dimanche, les gares sont folles!
di mɑ̃ ʃə, le ga rə sɔ̃ fɔ lə!

Tout le monde appareille pour des banlieues d'aventure
tu lə mɔ̃ da pa rɛ jə, pu rde bɑ̃ ljø da vɑ̃ ty rə

en se disant adieu avec des gestes éperdus!
ɑ̃ sə di zɑ̃ a djø, a vɛ kde ʒɛ stə ze pɛ rdy!

Dimanche les trains vont vite,
di mɑ̃ ʃə, le trɛ̃ vɔ̃ vi tə,

dévorés par d'insatiables tunnels;
de vɔ re pa rdɛ̃ sa sja blə ty nɛ l;

Et les bons signaux des routes échangent d'un oeil unique
e le bɔ̃ si ɲo de ru tə, e ʃɑ̃ ʒə dœ̃ nœ jy ni kə

des impressions toutes mécaniques.
de zɛ̃ prɛ si jɔ̃, tu tə me ka ni kə.

277

Dimanche, dans le bleu de mes rêves
di mã ʃə, dã lə blø də me rɛ və

Où mes pensées tristes de feux d'artifices manqués
u me pã se tri stə, də fø da rti fi sə mã ke

Ne veulent plus quitter le deuil
nə vœ lə ply ki te lə dœ j

de vieux Dimanches trépassés.
de vjø di mã ʃə, tre pa se.

Et la nuit à pas de velours vient endormir
e la nɥi a pɑ də və lu r, vjɛ̃ tã dɔ rmi r

le beau ciel fatigué, et c'est Dimanche
lə bo sjɛ lfa ti ge, e sɛ di mã ʃə,

dans les avenues d'étoiles;
dã le za və ny de twa lə;

la Vierge or sur argent
la vjɛ rʒə ɔ rsy ra rʒã

laisse tomber les fleurs de sommeil!
lɛ sə tõ be, le flœ rdə sɔ mɛ j!

Vite, les petits anges Dépassez les hirondelles
vi tə, le pə ti zã ʒə, de pa se le zi rõ dɛ lə,

afin de vous coucher forts d'absolution!
a fɛ̃ də vu ku ʃe, fɔ rda psɔ ly si jõ!

Prenez pitié des villes, Prenez pitié des coeurs,
prə ne pi tje de vi lə, prə ne pi tje de kœ r,

Vous, la Vierge or sur argent!
vu la vjɛ rʒə, ɔ rsy ra rʒã!

Debussy   En sourdine
dəbysi   ã surdin

Calmes dans le demi-jour
ka lmə dã lə də mi ʒu r

Que les branches hautes font,
kə le brã ʃə o tə fõ,

Pénétrons bien notre amour
pe ne trõ bjɛ̃ nɔ tra mu r

278

De ce silence profond.
də sə si lɑ̃ sə prɔ fɔ̃.

Fondons nos âmes, nos coeurs
fɔ̃ dɔ̃ no zɑ mə, no kœ r

et nos sens extasiés,
e no sɑ̃ sɛ ksta zi e,

Parmi les vagues langueurs
pa rmi le va gə lɑ̃ gœ r

Des pins et des arbousiers.
de pɛ̃ e de za rbu zje.

Ferme tes yeux à demi,
fɛ rmə te zjø a də mi,

Croise tes bras sur ton sein,
krwa zə te bra sy rtɔ̃ sɛ̃,

Et de ton coeur endormi
e də tɔ̃ kœ rɑ̃ dɔ rmi

Chasse à jamais tout dessein.
ʃa sa ʒa mɛ tu dɛ sɛ̃.

Laissons-nous persuader
lɛ sɔ̃ nu pɛ rsy a de

Au souffle berceur et doux
o su flə bɛ rsœ re du

Qui vient à tes pieds rider
ki vjɛ̃ a te pje ri de

Les ondes de gazon roux.
le zɔ̃ də də ga zɔ̃ ru.

Et quand solennel, le soir,
e kɑ̃ sɔ la nɛ llə swa r,

Des chênes noirs tombera,
de ʃɛ nə nwa rtɔ̃ bə ra,

Voix de notre désespoir,
vwa də nɔ trə de zɛ spwa r,

Le rossignol chantera.
lə rɔ si ɲɔ lʃɑ̃ tə ra.

279

Debussy   Fantoches
dəbysi   fɑ̃tɔʃ

Scaramouche et Pulcinella
ska ra mu ʃe py lsi nɛ la

Qu'un mauvais dessein rassembla
kœ̃ mɔ vɛ dɛ sɛ̃ ra sɑ̃ bla

Gesticulent noirs sous la lune. la la la...
ʒɛ sti ky lə nwa rsu la ly nə. la la la...

Cependant l'excellent docteur Bolonais
sə pɑ̃ dɑ̃ lɛ ksɛ lɑ̃ dɔ ktœ rbɔ lɔ nɛ

Cueille avec lenteur des simples
kœ ja vɛ klɑ̃ tœ rde sɛ̃ plə

Parmi l'herbe brune.
pa rmi lɛ rbə bry nə.

Lors sa fille, piquant minois
lɔ rsa fi jə, pi kɑ̃ mi nwa

Sous la charmille, en tapinois,
su la ʃa rmi jə, ɑ̃ ta pi nwa,

Se glisse demi-nue la la la
sə gli sə də mi ny ə la la la

En quête de son beau pirate espagnol,
ɑ̃ kɛ tə də sɔ̃ bo pi ra tɛ spa ɲɔ l,

Dont un amoureux rossignol
dɔ̃ tœ̃ na mu rø rɔ si ɲɔ l

Clame la détresse à tue-tête.
kla mə la de trɛ sa ty tɛ tə.

Debussy   Green
dəbysi   grin

Voici des fruits, des fleurs, des feuilles et des branches,
vwa si de frɥi, de flœ r, de fœ jə ze de brɑ̃ ʃə,

Et puis voici mon coeur, qui ne bat que pour vous;
e pɥi vwa si mɔ̃ kœ r, ki nə ba kə pu rvu;

Ne le déchirez pas avec vos deux mains blanches,
nə lə de ʃi re pa, a vɛ kvo dø mɛ̃ blɑ̃ ʃə,

Et qu'à vos yeux si beaux l'humble présent soit doux.
e ka vo zjø si bo, lœ̃ blə prɛ zɑ̃ swa du.

J'arrive tout couvert encore de rosée
ʒa ri və tu ku vɛ rɑ̃ ko rə də ro ze ə

Que le vent du matin vient glacer à mon front,
kə lə vɑ̃ dy ma tɛ̃ vjɛ̃ gla se à mɔ̃ frɔ̃,

Souffrez que ma fatigue à vos pieds reposée
su fre kə ma fa ti gə, a vo pje rə po ze ə

Rêve des chers instants qui la délasseront.
rɛ və de ʃɛ rzɛ̃ stɑ̃ ki la de lɑ sə rɔ̃.

Sur votre jeune sein, laissez rouler ma tête.
sy rvɔ trə ʒœ nə sɛ̃, lɛ se ru le ma tɛ tə.

Toute sonore encore de vos derniers baisers.
tu tə so nɔ rɑ̃ ko rə, də vo dɛ rnje bɛ ze.

Laissez-la s'apaiser de la bonne tempête,
lɛ se la sa pɛ ze də la bɔ nə tɑ̃ pɛ tə,

Et que je dorme un peu puisque vous reposez.
e kə ʒə dɔ rmœ̃ pø, pɥi skə vu rə po ze.

Debussy   Harmonie du soir
dəbysi   armɔni dy swar

Voici venir les temps où vibrant sur sa tige
vwa si və ni rle tɑ̃ u vi brɑ̃ sy rsa ti ʒə

Chaque fleur s'évapore ainsi qu'un encensoir;
ʃa kə flœ rse va po rɛ̃ si kœ̃ nɑ̃ sɑ̃ swa r;

Les sons et les parfums tournent dans l'air du soir;
le sɔ̃ ze le pa rfœ̃ tu rnə dɑ̃ lɛ rdy swa r;

Valse mélancolique et langoureux vertige,
va lsə me lɑ̃ kɔ li ke lɑ̃ gu rø vɛ rti ʒə,

Chaque fleur s'évapore ainsi qu'un encensoir;
ʃa kə flœ rse va po rɛ̃ si kœ̃ nɑ̃ sɑ̃ swa r;

Le violon frémit comme un coeur qu'on afflige,
lə vi o lɔ̃ fre mi kɔ mœ̃ kœ rkɔ̃ na fli ʒə,

Valse mélancolique et langoureux vertige,
va lsə me lɑ̃ kɔ li ke lɑ̃ gu rø vɛ rti ʒə,

Le ciel est triste et beau comme un grand reposoir
lə sjɛ lɛ tri stə bo kɔ mœ̃ grɑ̃ rə po zwa r

Le violon frémit comme un coeur qu'on afflige;
lə vi ɔ lɔ̃ fre mi kɔ mœ̃ kœ rkɔ̃ na fli ʒə;

Un coeur tendre, qui hait le néant vaste et noir!
œ̃ kœ rtɑ̃ drə, ki ɛ lə ne ɑ̃ va ste nwa r!

Le ciel est triste et beau comme un grand reposoir;
lə sjɛ lɛ tri ste bo kɔ mœ̃ grɑ̃ rə po zwa r;

Le soleil s'est noyé dans son sang qui se fige...
lə sɔ lɛ jsɛ nwa je dɑ̃ sɔ̃ sɑ̃ ki sə fi ʒə...

Un coeur tendre, qui hait le néant vaste et noir,
œ̃ kœ rtɑ̃ drə, ki ɛ lə ne ɑ̃ va ste nwa r,

Du passé lumineux recueille tout vestige
dy pa se ly mi nø rə kœ jə tu vɛ sti ʒə

Le soleil s'est noyé dans son sang qui se fige
lə sɔ lɛ jsɛ nwa je dɑ̃ sɔ̃ sɑ̃ ki sə fi ʒə

Ton souvenir en moi luit comme un ostensoir.
tɔ̃ su və ni rɑ̃ mwa lɥi, kɔ mœ̃ nɔ stɑ̃ swa r.

Debussy   Il pleure dans mon coeur
debysi   il plœr dɑ̃ mɔ̃ kœr

Il pleure dans mon coeur
i lplœ rə dɑ̃ mɔ̃ kœ r

comme il pleut sur la ville.
kɔ mi lplø sy rla vi lə.

Quelle est cette langueur
kɛ lɛ sɛ tə lɑ̃ gœ r

Qui pénètre mon coeur?
ki pe nɛ trə mɔ̃ kœ r?

O bruit doux de la pluie
o brɥi du də la plɥi ə

Par terre et sur les toits!
pa rtɛ re sy rle twa!

Pour un coeur qui s'ennuie
pu rœ̃ kœ rki sɑ̃ nɥi ə

O le bruit de la pluie!
o lə brɥi də la plɥi!

Il pleure sans raison
i lpœ rə sɑ̃ rɛ z�õ

Dans ce coeur qui s'écoeure.
dɑ̃ sə kœ rki se kœ rə.

Quoi! nulle trahison?
kwa! ny lə tra i z�õ?

Ce deuil est sans raison.
sə dœ j ɛ sɑ̃ rɛ zõ.

C'est bien la pire peine
sɛ bjɛ̃ la pi rə pɛ nə

De ne savoir pourquoi,
də nə sa vwa rpu rkwa,

sans amour et sans haine,
sɑ̃ za mu re sɑ̃ ɛ nə,

Mon coeur a tant de peine.
mõ kœ ra tɑ̃ də pɛ nə.

Debussy   L'échelonnement des haies
dəbysi   l eʃlɔnmɑ̃ de ɛ

L'échelonnement des haies
le ʃə lɔ nə mɑ̃ de ɛ

Moutonne à l'infini, mer
mu tɔ na lɛ̃ fi ni, mɛ r

Claire dans le brouillard clair
klɛ rə dɑ̃ lə bru ja rklɛ r

Qui sent bon les jeunes baies.
ki sɑ̃ bõ le ʒœ nə bɛ.

Des arbres et des moulins
de za rbrə ze de mu lɛ̃

Sont légers sur le vert tendre
sõ le ʒe sy rlə vɛ rtɑ̃ drə

Où vient s'ébattre et s'étendre
u vjɛ̃ se ba tre se tɑ̃ drə

L'agilité des poulains.
la ʒi li te de pu lɛ̃.

283

Dans ce vague d'un Dimanche
dã sə va gə dœ̃ di mã ʃə

Voici se jouer aussi
vwa si sə ʒu e o si,

De grandes brebis aussi
də grã də brə bi o si

Douces que leur laine blanche.
du sə kə lœ rlɛ nə blã ʃə.

Tout à l'heure déferlait
tu ta lœ rə de fɛ rlɛ

L'onde roulée en volutes
lõ də, ru le ə ã vɔ ly tə

De cloches comme des flûtes
də klɔ ʃə kɔ mə de fly tə

Dans le ciel comme du lait.
dã lə sjɛ l, kɔ mə dy lɛ.

Debussy   Les cloches
dəbysi   le klɔʃ

Les feuilles s'ouvraient sur le bord des branches,
le fœ jə su vrɛ sy r lə bɔ rde brã ʃə,

Délicatement,
de li ka tə mã,

Les cloches tintaient, légères et franches,
le klɔ ʃə tɛ̃ tɛ le ʒɛ rə ze frã ʃə,

Dans le ciel clément.
dã lə sjɛ lkle mã.

Rythmique et fervent comme une antienne,
ri tmi ke fɛ rvã kɔ my nã ti ɛ nə,

Ce lointain appel
sə lwɛ̃ tɛ na pɛ l

Me remémorait la blancheur chrétienne,
mə rə me mɔ rɛ la blã ʃœ rkre tjɛ nə,

Des fleurs de l'autel.
de flœ rdə lo tɛ l.

284

Ces cloches parlaient d'heureuses années,
se klɔ ʃə pa rlɛ dø rø zə za ne ə,

Et dans le grand bois
e dɑ̃ lə grɑ̃ bwa

Semblaient reverdir les feuilles fanées
sɑ̃ blɛ rə vɛ rdi rle fœ jə fa ne ə,

Des jours d'autrefois.
de ʒu rdo trə fwa.

Debussy   L'ombre des arbres
dəbysi   l ɔ̃brə de zarbr

L'ombre des arbres dans la rivière embrumée
lɔ̃ brə de za rbrə dɑ̃ la ri vjɛ rɑ̃ bry me ə,

Meurt comme de la fumée,
mœ rkɔ mə də la fy me ə,

Tandis qu'en l'air, parmi les ramures réelles
tɑ̃ di kɑ̃ lɛ r, pa rmi le ra my rə re ɛ lə,

Se plaignent les tourterelles
sə plɛ ɲə le tu rtə rɛ lə,

Combien ô voyageur, ce paysage blême
kɔ̃ bjɛ̃, o vwa ja ʒœ r, sə pe i za ʒə blɛ mə,

Te mira blême toi-même
tə mi ra blɛ mə twa mɛ mə,

Et que tristes pleuraient dans les hautes feuillées,
e kə tri stə plœ rɛ dɑ̃ le o tə fœ je ə,

Tes espérances noyées.
te zɛ spe rɑ̃ sə, nwa je ə.

Debussy   Mandoline
dəbysi   mɑ̃dɔlin

Les donneurs de sérénades
le dɔ nœ rdə se re na də,

Et les belles écouteuses
e le bɛ lə ze ku tø zə,

285

Echangent des propos fades
e ∫ã ʒə de prɔ po fa də

Sous les ramures chanteuses.
su le ra my rə ∫ã tø zə.

C'est Tircis et c'est Aminte,
sɛ ti rsi se sɛ ta mɛ̃ tə,

Et c'est l'éternel Clitandre,
e sɛ le tɛ rnɛ lkli tã drə,

Et c'est Damis qui pour mainte
e sɛ da mi ski pu rmɛ̃ tə

Cruelle fait maint vers tendre.
kry ɛ lə fɛ mɛ̃ vɛ rtã drə.

Leurs courtes vestes de soie,
lœ rku rtə vɛ stə də swa,

Leurs longues robes à queues,
lœ rlɔ̃ gə rɔ bə za kø,

Leur élégance, leur joie
lœ re le gã sə, lœ rʒwa

Et leurs molles ombres bleues,
e lœ rmɔ lə zɔ̃ brə blø,

Tourbillonnent dans l'extase
tu rbi jɔ nə dã lɛ ksta zə,

D'une lune rose et grise,
dy nə ly nə ro ze gri zə,

Et la mandoline jase,
e la mã dɔ li nə ʒa zə

parmi les frissons de brise La, la...
pa rmi le fri sɔ̃ də bri zə la, la...

Debussy   Nuit d'étoiles
dəbysi   nɥi d etwal

Nuit d'étoiles sous tes voiles,
nɥi de twa lə, su te vwa lə,

Sous ta brise et tes parfums,
su ta bri ze te pa rfœ̃,

286

Triste lyre qui soupire,
tri stə li rə, ki su pi rə,

Je rêve aux amours défunts.
ʒə rɛ vo za mu rde fœ̃.

La sereine mélancolie
la sə rɛ nə me lɑ̃ kɔ li ə

Vient éclore au fond de mon coeur,
vjɛ̃ te klɔ ro fɔ̃ də mɔ̃ kœ r,

Et j'entends l'âme de ma mie
e ʒɑ̃ tɑ̃, la mə də ma mi ə

Tressaillir dans le bois rêveur.
trɛ sa ji rdɑ̃ lə bwa rɛ vœ r.

Je revois à notre fontaine
ʒə rə vwa za nɔ trə fɔ̃ tɛ nə

Tes regards bleus comme les cieux,
te rə ga rblø kɔ mə le sjø,

Cette rose, c'est ton haleine,
sɛ tə ro zə, sɛ tɔ̃ na lɛ nə,

Et ces étoiles sont tes yeux.
e sɛ ze twa lə sɔ̃ te zjø.

Debussy   Romance
dəbysi   rɔmɑ̃s

L'âme évaporée et souffrante,
la me va pɔ re e su frɑ̃ tə,

L'âme douce, l'âme odorante,
la mə du sə, la mɔ dɔ rɑ̃ tə,

Des lis divins que j'ai cueillis
de li sdi vɛ̃, kə ʒe kœ ji

Dans le jardin de ta pensée,
dɑ̃ lə ʒa rdɛ̃, də ta pɑ̃ se,

Où donc les vents l'ont-ils chassée,
u dɔ̃ kle vɑ̃ lɔ̃ ti lʃa se,

Cette âme adorable des lis?
sɛ ta ma dɔ ra blə de li s?

N'est—il plus un parfum qui reste
nɛ ti lply zṏ pa rfṏ ki rɛ stə

De la suavité céleste,
də la sy a vi te se lɛ stə,

Des jours où tu m'enveloppais
de ʒu ru ty mã və lɔ pɛ,

D'une vapeur surnaturelle,
dy nə va pœ rsy rna ty rɛ lə,

Faite d'espoir, d'amour fidèle,
fɛ tə dɛ spwa r, da mu rfi dɛ lə,

De béatitude et de paix?
də be a ti ty d, e də pɛ?

Debussy   Spleen
dəbysi   splin

Les roses étaient toutes rouges,
le ro zə ze tɛ tu tə ru ʒə,

Et les lierres étaient tout noirs.
e le ljɛ rə ze tɛ tu nwa r.

Chère, pour peu que tu te bouges,
ʃɛ rə, pu rpø kə ty tə bu ʒə,

Renaissent tous mes désespoirs.
rə nɛ sə tu me de zɛ spwa r.

Le ciel était trop bleu, trop tendre,
lə sjɛ le tɛ tro blø tro tã drə,

La mer trop verte et l'air trop doux.
la mɛ rtrɔ vɛ rte lɛ rtrɔ du.

Je crains toujours, ce qu'est d'attendre!
ʒə krɛ̃ tu ʒu r, sə kɛ da tã drə!

Quelque fuite atroce de vous.
kɛ lkə fyi ta trɔ sə də vu.

Du houx à la feuille vernie
dy u a la fœ jə vɛ rni,

Et du luisant buis je suis las
e dy lyi zã byi ʒə syi la,

288

Et de la campagne infinie,
e də la kɑ̃ pa ɲɛ̃ fi ni ə,

Et de tout, fors de vous.   Hélas!
e də tu, fɔ rdə vu. e lɑ!
   (s not pronounced here, archaic
     to rime with <u>las</u>.)

Delibes   Bell Song, from "Lakmé"
dəlib   lakme

Ah, Où va la jeune Indoue, Fille des Parias,
a u va la ʒœ nɛ̃ du ə, fi jə de pa ri ja,

Quand la lune se joue dans les grands mimosas?
kɑ̃ la ly nə sə ʒu ə, dɑ̃ le grɑ̃ mi mo za?

Elle court sur la mousse et ne se souvient pas
ɛ lə ku rsy rla mu sə, e nə sə su vjɛ̃ pa,

Que partout on repousse l'enfant des Parias.
kə pa rtu ɔ̃ rə pu sə, lɑ̃ fɑ̃ de pa ri ja.

Le long des lauriers roses, Rêvant de douces choses,
lə lɔ̃ de lo rje ro zə, rɛ vɑ̃ də du sə ʃo zə,

Ah! Elle passe sans bruit Et riant à la nuit!
a ɛ lə pɑ sə sɑ̃ brɥi, e ri jɑ̃ ta la nɥi!

Là—bas dans la forêt plus sombre, Quel est ce voyageur perdu?
la bɑ dɑ̃ la fɔ rɛ ply sɔ̃ brə, kɛ lɛ sə vwa ja ʒœ rpɛ rdy?

Autour de lui des yeux brillent dans l'ombre,
o tu rdə lɥi de zjø bri jə dɑ̃ lɔ̃ brə,

Il marche encore au hasard, éperdu
i lma rʃɑ̃ ko rə o a za r, e pɛ rdy,

Les fauves rugissent de joie,
le fo və ry ʒi sə də ʒwa ə,

Ils vont se jeter sur leur proie,
i lvɔ̃ sə ʒə te sy rlœ rprwa ə,

La jeune fille accourt et brave leurs fureurs:
la ʒœ nə fi ja ku r, e bra və lœ rfy rœ r,

Elle a dans sa main la baguette,
ɛ la dɑ̃ sa mɛ̃ la ba gɛ tə,

289

Où tinte la clochette, des charmeurs! Ah!
u tɛ̃ tə la klɔ ʃɛ tə, de ʃa rmœ r!   a!

L'étranger la regarde, Elle reste éblouie.
le trɑ̃ ʒe la rə ga rdə, ɛ lə rɛ ste blu i ə.

Il est plus beau que les Rajahs!
i lɛ ply bo kə le ra ʒa!

Il rougira, S'il sait qu'il doit la vie
i lru ʒi ra, si lsɛ ki ldwa la vi ə,

A la fille des Parias.
a la fi jə de pa ri ja.

Mais lui, l'endormant dans un rêve,
mɛ lɥi lɑ̃ dɔ rmɑ̃ dɑ̃ zɛ̃ rɛ və,

Jusque dans le ciel il l'enlève,
ʒy skə dɑ̃ lə sjɛ li llɑ̃ lɛ və,

En lui disant: ta place est là!
ɑ̃ lɥi di zɑ̃, ta pla sɛ la!

C'était Vishnou fils de Brahma!
se tɛ vi ʃnu, fi sdə bra ma!

Depuis ce jour au fond des bois,
də pɥi sə ʒu ro fɔ̃ de bwa,

Le voyageur entend parfois
lə vwa ja ʒœ rɑ̃ tɑ̃ pa rfwa,

Le bruit léger de la baguette,
lə brɥi le ʒe də la ba gɛ tə,

Où tinte la clochette, des charmeurs!
u tɛ̃ tə la klɔ ʃɛ tə, de ʃa rmœ r

Delibes   Bonjour, Suzon!
dəlib   bɔ̃ʒur syzɔ̃

Bonjour, Suzon, ma fleur des bois!
bɔ̃ ʒu rsy zɔ̃ ma flœ rde bwa!

Es-tu toujours la plus jolie?
ɛ ty tu ʒu rla ply ʒo li ə

Je reviens tel que tu me vois,
ʒə rə vjɛ̃ tɛ lkə ty mə vwa,

290

D'un grand voyage en Italie.
dœ̃ grã vwa ja ʒã ni ta li ə.

Du paradis j'ai fait le tour.
dy pa ra di ʒe fɛ lə tu r.

J'ai fait des vers, j'ai fait l'amour,
ʒe fɛ de vɛ rʒe fɛ la mu r,

Mais que t'importe?
mɛ kə tɛ̃ pɔ rtə?

Je passe devant ta maison, Ouvre ta porte!
ʒə pɑ sə də vã ta mɛ zɔ̃, u vrə ta pɔ rtə!

Je t'ai vue au temps des lilas,
ʒə te vy o tã de li lɑ,

Ton coeur joyeux venait d'éclore.
tɔ̃ kœ rʒwa jø və nɛ de klɔ rə,

Et tu disais, je ne veux pas qu'on m'aime encore.
e ty di zɛ, ʒə nə vø pa kɔ̃ mɛ mã ko rə.

Qu'as tu fait depuis mon départ?
ka ty fɛ də pɥi mɔ̃ de pa r?

Qui part trop tôt revient trop tard.
ki pa rtrɔ to rə vjɛ̃ tro ta r.

Mais que m'importe?
mɛ kə mɛ̃ pɔ rtə?

Delibes   Les filles de Cadix
dəlib   le fij də kadiks

Nous venions de voir le taureau,
nu və njɔ̃ də vwa rlə tɔ ro,

Trois garçons, trois fillettes,
trwa ɡa rsɔ̃ trwa fi jɛ tə,

Sur la pelouse il faisait beau,
sy rla pə lu zi lfə zɛ bo,

Et nous dansions un boléro Au son des castagnettes:
e nu dã sjɔ̃ zœ̃ bɔ le ro, o sɔ̃ de ka sta ɲɛ tə,

Dites—moi, voisin, Si j'ai bonne mine,
di tə mwa vwa zɛ̃, si ʒe bɔ nə mi n,

291

Et si ma basquine Va bien ce matin.
e si ma ba ski nə va bjɛ̃ sə ma tɛ̃.

Vous me trouvez la taille fine? ah!
vu mə tru ve la ta jə fi nə? ɑ!

Les filles de Cadix aiment assez cela, ah! la ra la.
le fi jə də ka di ksɛ mə ta se sə la, ɑ la ra la

Et nous dansions un boléro Un soir, c'était dimanche.
e nu dɑ̃ sjɔ̃ zœ̃ bo le ro œ̃ swa rse tɛ di mɑ̃ ʃə.

Vers nous s'en vient un hidalgo,
vɛ rnu sɑ̃ vjɛ̃ tœ̃ i da lgo,

Cousu d'or, la plume au chapeau,
ku zy dɔ rla ply mo ʃa po,

Et le poing sur la hanche: Si tu veux de moi,
e lə pwɛ̃ sy rla ɑ̃ ʃə, si ty vø də mwa,

Brune au doux sourire, Tu n'as qu'à le dire.
bry no du su ri rə, ty na ka lə di rə

Cet or est à toi. Passez votre chemin beau sire,
sɛ tɔ rɛ ta twa. pa se vɔ trə ʃə mɛ̃ bo si rə,

Les filles de Cadix n'entendent pas cela,
le fi jə də ka di ksnɑ̃ tɑ̃ də pa sə la,

la ra la, ah.
la ra la, ɑ.

Duparc   Chanson triste
dypark   ʃɑ̃sɔ̃ trist

Dans ton coeur dort un clair de lune,
dɑ̃ tɔ̃ kœ rdɔ rœ̃ klɛ rdə ly nə,

un doux clair de lune d'été,
œ̃ du klɛ rdə ly nə de te,

Et pour fuir la vie importune,
e pu rfɥi rla vi ɛ̃ pɔ rty nə,

Je me noierai dans ta clarté.
ʒə mə nwa re, dɑ̃ ta kla rte.

J'oublierai les douleurs passées
ʒu bli re le du lœ rpa se ə,

292

Mon amour; quand tu berceras
mõ na mu r; kã ty bɛ rsə ra

Mon triste coeur et mes pensées
mõ tri stə kœ re me pã se ə,

Dans le calme aimant de tes bras!
dã lə ka lmɛ mã də te bra!

Tu prendras ma tête malade
ty prã dra ma tɛ tə ma la də,

Oh! quelquefois sur tes genoux,
o kɛ lkə fwa sy rte ʒə nu,

Et lui diras une ballade,
e lμi di ra y nə ba la də,

Une ballade, qui semblera parler de nous,
y nə ba la də, ki sã blə ra pa rle də nu,

Et dans tes yeux pleins de tristesses,
e dã te zjø plɛ̃ də tri stɛ sə,

Dans tes yeux alors je boirai
dã te zjø a lɔ rʒə bwa re,

Tant de baisers et de tendresses,
tã də bɛ ze e də tã drɛ sə,

Que peut-être je guérirai.
kə pø tɛ trə ʒə ge ri re.

Duparc   Extase
dypark   ɛkstaz

Sur un lys pâle mon coeur dort
sy rœ̃ li spa lə, mõ kœ rdɔ r,

D'un sommeil doux comme la mort,
dœ̃ sɔ mɛ jdu kɔ mə la mɔ r,

Mort exquise, mort parfumée
mɔ rɛ kski zə, mɔ rpa rfy me ə,

Du souffle de la bien-aimée.
dy su flə də la bjɛ̃ ne me ə.

Sur ton sein pâle mon coeur dort
sy rtõ sɛ̃ pa lə, mõ kœ rdɔ r,

D'un sommeil doux comme la mort.
dœ̃ so mɛ jdu kɔ mə la mɔ r.

Duparc   Le Manoir de Rosemonde
dypark   lə manwar də rozmɔ̃d

De sa dent soudaine et vorace,
də sa dɑ̃ su dɛ ne vɔ ra sə,

Comme un chien l'amour m'a mordu.
kɔ mœ̃ ʃjɛ̃ la mu rma mɔ rdy.

En suivant mon sang répandu,
ɑ̃ sɥi vɑ̃ mɔ̃ sɑ̃ re pɑ̃ dy,

Va, tu pourras suivre ma trace.
va, ty pu ra sɥi vrə ma tra sə.

Prends un cheval de bonne race,
prɑ̃ zœ̃ ʃə va ldə bɔ nə ra sə,

Pars, et suis mon chemin ardu,
pa r, e sɥi mɔ̃ ʃə mɛ̃ a rdy,

Fondrière ou sentier perdu,
fɔ̃ dri jɛ ru sɑ̃ tje pɛ rdy,

Si la course ne te harasse!
si la ku rsə nə tə a ra sə!

En passant par où j'ai passé,
ɑ̃ pa sɑ̃ pa ru ʒe pa se,

Tu verras que seul et blessé,
ty vɛ ra, kə sœ l, e blɛ se,

J'ai parcouru ce triste monde,
ʒe pa rku ry sə tri stə mɔ̃ də,

Et qu'ainsi je m'en fus mourir Bien loin,
e kɛ̃ si ʒə mɑ̃ fy mu ri r, bjɛ̃ lwɛ̃,

sans découvrir Le bleu manoir de Rosemonde.
sɑ̃ de ku vri r, lə blø ma nwa rdə ro zə mɔ̃ də.

294

Duparc   L'invitation au voyage
dypark   l ɛ̃vitasjɔ̃ o vwajaʒ

Mon enfant, ma soeur, Songe à la douceur
mɔ̃ nɑ̃ fɑ̃, ma sœ r, sɔ̃ ʒa la du sœ r,

D'aller là-bas vivre ensemble, Aimer à loisir,
da le la bɑ vi vrɑ̃ sɑ̃ blə, ɛ me a lwa zi r,

Aimer et mourir Au pays qui te ressemble!
ɛ me e mu ri r, o pe i ki tə rə sɑ̃ blə!

Les soleils mouillés De ces ciels brouillés
le sɔ lɛ jmu je, də se sjɛ lbru je,

Pour mon esprit ont les charmes Si mystérieux
pu rmɔ̃ nɛ spri ɔ̃ le ʃa rmə, si mi ste ri jø,

De tes traîtres yeux, Brillant à travers leurs larmes.
də te trɛ trə zjø, bri jɑ̃ ta tra vɛ rlœ rla rmə.

Là, tout n'est qu'ordre et beauté, Luxe, calme et volupté!
la, tu nɛ kɔ rdre bo te, ly ksə, ka lmə, e vɔ ly pte!

Vois sur ces canaux Dormir ces vaisseaux
vwa sy rse ka no dɔ rmi rse vɛ so,

Dont l'humeur est vagabonde;
dɔ̃ ly mœ rɛ va ga bɔ̃ də;

C'est pour assouvir Ton moindre désir
sɛ pu ra su vi rtɔ̃ mwɛ̃ drə de zi r,

Qu'ils viennent du bout du monde.
ki lvjɛ nə dy bu dy mɔ̃ də.

Les soleils couchants Revêtent les champs,
le sɔ lɛ jku ʃɑ̃, rə vɛ tə le ʃɑ̃,

Les canaux, la ville entière, D'hyacinthe et d'or;
le ka no, la vi lɑ̃ tjɛ rə, di a sɛ̃ te dɔ r;

Le monde s'endort Dans une chaude lumière!
lə mɔ̃ də sɑ̃ dɔ r, dɑ̃ zy nə ʃo də ly mjɛ rə!

Là, tout n'est qu'ordre et beauté,
la, tu nɛ kɔ rdre bo te,

Luxe, calme et volupté!
ly ksə, ka lmə, e vɔ ly pte!

Duparc   Phidylé
dypark   fidile

L'herbe est molle au sommeil
lɛ rbɛ mɔ lo sɔ mɛ j,

295

sous les frais peupliers,
su le fre pœ pli je,

Aux pentes des sources moussues,
o pã tə de su rsə mu sy ə,

Qui dans les prés en fleurs
ki dã le pre zã flœ r,

germant par mille issues,
ʒɛ rmã pa rmi li sy ə,

Se perdent sous les noirs halliers.
sə pɛ rdə su le nwa ra lje.

Repose, ô Phidylé.
rə po zə, o fi di le.

Midi sur les feuillages Rayonne,
mi di sy rle fœ ja ʒə rɛ jo n,

et t'invite au sommeil.
e tã vi to so mɛ j.

Par le trèfle et le thym, seules,
pa rlə trɛ fle lə tã, sœ lə,

en plein soleil,
ã plã so lɛ j,

Chantent les abeilles volages;
ʃã tə le za bɛ jə vo la ʒə;

Un chaud parfum circule au détour des sentiers,
œ̃ ʃo pa rfã si rky lo de tu rde sã tje,

La rouge fleur des blés s'incline,
la ru ʒə flœ rde ble sã kli nə,

Et les oiseaux, rasant de l'aile la coline,
e le zwa zo ra zã də lɛ lə la kɔ li nə,

Cherchent l'ombre des églantiers.
ʃɛ rʃə lõ brə de ze glã tje.

Repose, ô Phidylé, Repose, ô Phidylé.
rə po zə, o fi di le, rə po zə, o fi di le.

Mais, quand l'Astre incliné sur sa courbe éclatante,
mɛ kã la strã kli ne, sy rsa ku rbe kla tã tə,

Verra ses ardeurs s'apaiser,
vɛ ra se za rdœ rsa pɛ ze,

Que ton plus beau sourire
kə tõ ply bo su ri r

296

et ton meilleur baiser Me récompensent,
e tɔ̃ mɛ jœ rbɛ ze, mə re kɔ̃ pã sə,

me récompensent de l'attente!
mə re kɔ̃ pã sə, də la tã tə!

Duparc   Soupir
dypark   supir

Ne jamais la voir ni l'entendre,
nə ʒa mɛ la vwa rni lã tã drə,

Ne jamais tout haut la nommer,
nə ʒa mɛ tu o la nɔ me,

Mais, fidèle, toujours l'attendre, Toujours l'aimer.
mɛ fi dɛ lə tu ʒu rla tã drə, tu ʒu rlɛ me.

Ouvrir les bras, et, las d'attendre,
u vri rle bra e lɑ da tã drə,

Sur le néant les refermer,
sy rlə ne ã le rə fɛ rme,

Mais encor, toujours les lui tendre, Toujours l'aimer.
mɛ zã kɔ r, tu ʒu rle lyi tã drə, tu ʒu rlɛ me.

Ah! ne pouvoir que les lui tendre,
a nə pu vwa rkə le lyi tã drə,

Et dans les pleurs se consumer,
e dã le plœ rsə kɔ̃ sy me,

Mais ces pleurs toujours lès répandre,
mɛ se plœ r, tu ʒu rle re pã drə,

Toujours l'aimer.
tu ʒu rlɛ me.

Fauré   Après un rêve
fore   aprɛ zœ̃ rɛv

Dans un sommeil que charmait ton image
dã zœ̃ sɔ mɛ jkə ʃa rmɛ tɔ̃ ni ma ʒə,

297

Je rêvais le bonheur, ardent mirage;

ʒə rɛ vɛ lə bɔ nœ r a rdɑ̃ mi ra ʒə;

Tes yeux étaient plus doux, ta voix pure et sonore.

te zjø e tɛ ply du ta vwa py re sɔ nɔ rə.

Tu rayonnais comme un ciel éclairé par l'aurore;

ty rɛ jɔ nɛ kɔ mœ̃ sjɛ le klɛ re pa rlɔ rɔ rə;

Tu m'appelais, et je quittais la terre

ty ma pə lɛ e ʒə ki tɛ la tɛ rə,

Pour m'enfuir avec toi vers la lumière;

pu rmɑ̃ fɥi ra vɛ ktwa vɛ rla ly mjɛ rə;

Les cieux pour nous entr'ouvraient leurs nues,

le sjø pu rnu ɑ̃ tru vrɛ lœ rny ə,

Splendeurs inconnues, lueurs divines entrevues...

splɑ̃ dœ rzɛ̃ kɔ ny ə, ly œ rdi vi nə zɑ̃ trə vy ə...

Hélas! Hélas, triste réveil des songes!

e la se la s, tri stə re vɛ jde sɔ̃ ʒə!

Je t'appelle, ô nuit, rends—moi tes mensonges;

ʒə ta pɛ lo nɥi rɑ̃ mwa te mɑ̃ sɔ̃ ʒə;

Reviens, reviens radieuse,

rə vjɛ̃, rə vjɛ̃ ra di ø zə,

Reviens, ô nuit mystérieuse!

rə vjɛ̃, o nɥi mi ste ri ø zə!

Fauré   Au bord de l'eau

fore   o bɔr də l o

S'asseoir tous deux au bord du flot qui passe,

sa swa rtu dø o bɔ rdy flo ki pa sə,

Le voir passer;

lə vwa rpa se;

Tous deux s'il glisse un nuage en l'espace,

tu dø si lgli sœ̃ ny a ʒɑ̃ lɛ spa sə,

Le voir glisser;

lə vwa rgli se;

A l'horizon s'il fume un toit de chaume,

a lɔ ri zɔ̃ si lfy mœ̃ twa də ʃo mə,

Le voir fumer;
lə vwa rfy me

Aux alentours, si quelque fleur embaume,
o za lɑ̃ tu r, si kɛ lkə flœ rɑ̃ bo mə,

S'en embaumer;
sɑ̃ nɑ̃ bo me;

Entendre au pied du saule où l'eau murmure,
ɑ̃ tɑ̃ dro pje dy so lu lo my rmy rə,

L'eau murmurer,
lo my rmy re,

Ne pas sentir tant que ce rêve dure
nə pa sɑ̃ ti rtɑ̃ kə sə rɛ və dy rə,

Le temps durer,
lə tɑ̃ dy re,

Mais n'apportant de passion profonde
mɛ na pɔ rtɑ̃ də pa si ɔ̃ pro fɔ̃ də,

Qu'à s'adorer,
ka sa dɔ re

Sans nul souci des querelles du monde,
sɑ̃ ny lsu si, de kə rɛ lə dy mɔ̃ də,

Les ignorer,
le zi ɲo re,

Et seuls tous deux devant tout ce qui lasse,
e sœ ltu dø də vɑ̃ tu sə ki lɑ sə,

Sans se lasser;
sɑ̃ sə lɑ se;

Sentir l'amour devant tout ce qui passe,
sɑ̃ ti rla mu rdə vɑ̃ tu sə ki pɑ sə,

Ne point passer!
nə pwɛ̃ pɑ se!

Fauré   Aurore
fore   ɔrɔr

Des jardins de la nuit s'envolent les étoiles.
de ʒa rdɛ̃ də la nɥi sɑ̃ vɔ lə le ze twa lə.

299

Abeilles d'or qu'attire un invisible miel;
a bɛ jə dɔ rka ti rœ̃ nɛ̃ vi zi blə mjɛ l;

Et l'aube, au loin, tendant la candeur de ses toiles,
e lo bo lwɛ̃ tɑ̃ dɑ̃ la kɑ̃ dœ rdə se twa lə,

trame de fils d'argent le manteau bleu du ciel.
tra mə də fi lda rʒɑ̃ lə mɑ̃ to blø dy sjɛ l.

Du jardin de mon coeur qu'un rêve lent enivre,
dy ʒa rdɛ̃ də mõ kœ r kœ̃ rɛ və lɑ̃ ɑ̃ ni vrə,

S'envolent mes désirs sur les pas du matin,
sɑ̃ vɔ lə me de zi r, sy rle pɑ dy ma tɛ̃,

Comme un essaim léger qu'à l'horizon de cuivre,
kɔ mœ̃ nɛ sɛ̃ le ʒe ka lo ri zõ də kɥi vrə,

appelle un chant plaintif, éternel et lointain.
a pɛ lœ̃ ʃɑ̃ plɛ̃ ti f, e tɛ rnɛ le lwɛ̃ tɛ̃.

Ils volent à tes pieds, astres chassés des nues,
i lvɔ lə ta te pje a strə ʃa se de ny ə,

Exilés du ciel d'or où fleurit ta beauté,
ɛ gzi le dy sjɛ ldɔ ru flœ ri ta bo te,

Et, cherchant jusqu'à toi des routes inconnues,
e ʃɛ rʃɑ̃ ʒy ska twa de ru tə zɛ̃ kɔ ny ə,

Mêlent au jour naissant leur mourante clarté.
mɛ lə to ʒu rnɛ sɑ̃ lœ rmu rɑ̃ tə kla rte.

Fauré   Automne
fore   otɔn

Automne au ciel brumeux, aux horizons navrants,
o tɔ no sjɛ lbry mø, o zɔ ri zõ na vrɑ̃,

Aux rapides couchants, aux aurores pâlies,
o ra pi də ku ʃɑ̃, o zɔ rɔ rə pɑ li ə,

Je regarde couler comme l'eau du torrent,
ʒə rə ga rdə ku le kɔ mə lo dy tɔ rɑ̃,

Tes jours faits de mélancolie.
te ʒu rfɛ də me lɑ̃ kɔ li ə.

Sur l'aile des regrets, mes esprits emportés,
sy rlɛ lə de rə grɛ me zɛ spri zɑ̃ pɔ rte,

Comme s'il se pouvait que notre âge renaisse,
kɔ mə si lsə pu vɛ kə nɔ tra ʒə rə nɛ sə,

Parcourent en rêvant les coteaux enchantés,
pa rku rə tã rɛ vã le kɔ to zã ʃã te,

Où, jadis, sourit ma jeunesse!
u ʒa di ssu ri ma ʒœ nɛ sə!

Je sens au clair soleil du souvenir vainqueur,
ʒə sã o klɛ rsɔ lɛ jdy su və ni rvɛ̃ kœ r,

Refleurir en bouquet les roses déliées,
rə flœ ri rã bu kɛ le ro zə de li e ə,

Et monter à mes yeux des larmes, qu'en mon coeur
e mõ te a me zjø de la rmə kã mõ kœ r,

Mes vingt ans avaient oubliées!
me vɛ̃ tã a vɛ tu bli je ə!

Fauré   En prière
fore   ã prijɛr

Si la voix d'un enfant peut monter jusqu'à Vous,
si la vwa dœ̃ nã fã pø mõ te ʒy ska vu,

O mon Père,
o mõ pɛ rə,

Écoutez de Jésus, devant Vous à genoux,
e ku te də ʒe zy də vã vu a ʒə nu,

La prière!
la pri jɛ rə!

Si Vous m'avez choisi pour enseigner vos lois
si vu ma ve ʃwa zi, pu rã sɛ ɲe vo lwa

sur la terre,
sy rla tɛ rə,

Je saurai Vous servir, auguste Roi des rois,
ʒə sɔ re vu sɛ rvi ro gy stə rwa de rwa,

O Lumiére!
o ly mjɛ rə!

Sur mes lèvres, Seigneur,
sy rme lɛ vrə sɛ ɲœ r,

mettez la vérité Salutaire,
mɛ te la ve ri te sa ly tɛ rə,

Pour que celui qui doute,
pu rkə sə lɥi ki du t,

avec humilité, Vous révère!
a vɛ ky mi li te vu re vɛ rə!

Ne m'abandonnez pas,
nə ma bɑ̃ dɔ ne pa,

donnez—moi la douceur Nécessaire,
dɔ ne mwa la du sœ rne sɛ sɛ rə,

Pour apaiser les maux, soulager la douleur,
pu ra pɛ ze le mo su la ʒe la du lœ r,

la misère!
la mi zɛ rə!

Révélez-Vous à moi, Seigneur en qui je crois,
re ve le vu za mwa, sɛ pœ rɑ̃ ki ʒə krwa,

et j'espère
e ʒɛ spɛ rə,

Pour Vous je veux souffrir, et mourir sur la croix,
pu rvu ʒə vø su fri r, e mu ri rsy rla krwa,

Au calvaire!
o ka lvɛ rə!

Fauré   Fleur jetée
fore   flœr ʒəte

Emporte ma folie au gré du vent,
ɑ̃ pɔ rtə ma fɔ li ə o gre dy vɑ̃,

Fleur en chantant cueillie
flœ rɑ̃ ʃɑ̃ tɑ̃ kœ ji ə,

Et jetée en rêvant,
e ʒə te ɑ̃ rɛ vɑ̃,

Emporte ma folie, au gré du vent,
ɑ̃ pɔ rtə ma fɔ li o gre dy vɑ̃,

Comme la fleur fauchée périt l'amour.
kɔ mə la flœ rfo ʃe ə pe ri la mu r.

302

La main qui t'a touchée
la mɛ̃ ki ta tu ʃe ə

Fuit ma main sans retour,
fᵱi ma mɛ̃ sɑ̃ rə tu r,

Que le vent qui te séche, ô pauvre fleur,
kə lə vɑ̃ ki tə sɛ ʃə, o po vrə flœ r,

Tout à l'heure si fraiche,
tu ta lœ rə si frɛ ʃə,

Et demain sans couleur,
e də mɛ̃ sɑ̃ ku lœ r,

Que le vent qui te sèche, ô pauvre fleur,
kə lə vɑ̃ ki tə sɛ ʃə, o po vrə flœ r,

Que le vent qui te sèche,
kə lə vɑ̃ ki tə sɛ ʃə,

Sèche mon coeur.
sɛ ʃə mɔ̃ kœ r.

Fauré   Ici — bas
fɔre   isi bɑ

Ici — bas tous les lilas meurent,
i si bɑ tu le li la mœ rə,

Tout les chants des oiseaux sont courts,
tu le ʃɑ̃ de zwa zo sɔ̃ ku r,

Je rêve aux étés qui demeurent toujours!
ʒə rɛ vo ze te ki də mœ rə tu ʒu r!

Ici — bas les lèvres effleurent
i si bɑ le lɛ vrə zɛ flœ rə,

Sans rien laisser de leur velours,
sɑ̃ rjɛ̃ lɛ se də lœ rvə lu r,

Je rêve aux baisers qui demeurent toujours!
ʒə rɛ vo bɛ ze ki də mœ rə tu ʒu r!

Ici — bas, tous les hommes pleurent
i si bɑ tu le zɔ mə plœ rə,

Leurs amitiés ou leurs amours,
lœ rza mi tje u lœ rza mu r,

Je rêve aux couples qui demeurent,
ʒə rɛ vo ku plə ki də mœ rə,

Qui demeurent toujours!
ki də mœ rə tu ʒu r!

Fauré   Les berceaux
fɔre   le bɛrso

Le long du Quai, les grands vaisseaux,
lə lɔ̃ dy ke le grɑ̃ vɛ so,

Que la houle incline en silence,
kə la u lɛ̃ kli nɑ̃ si lɑ̃ sə,

Ne prennent pas garde aux berceaux,
nə prɛ nə pa ga rdo bɛ rso,

Que la main des femmes balance.
kə la mɛ̃ de fa mə ba lɑ̃ sə.

Mais viendra le jour des adieux,
mɛ vjɛ̃ dra lə ʒu rde za djø,

Car il faut que les femmes pleurent,
ka ri lfo kə le fa mə plœ rə,

Et que les hommes curieux
e kə le zɔ mə ky ri ø,

Tentent les horizons qui leurrent!
tɑ̃ tə le zɔ ri zɔ̃ ki lœ rə!

Et ce jour—là les grands vaisseaux,
e sə ʒu rla le grɑ̃ vɛ so,

Fuyant le port qui diminue,
fɥi jɑ̃ lə pɔ rki di mi ny ə,

Sentent leur masse retenue
sɑ̃ tə lœ rma sə rə tə ny ə,

Par l'âme des lointains berceaux.
pa rlɑ mə de lwɛ̃ tɛ̃ bɛ rso.

Fauré   Les roses d'Ispahan
fɔre   le roz d ispaɑ̃

Les roses d'Ispahan dans leur gaîne de mousse,
le ro zə di spa ɑ̃ dɑ̃ lœ rgɛ nə də mu sə,

Les jasmins de Mossoul, les fleurs de l'oranger,
le ʒa smɛ̃ də mo su l, le flœ rdə lɔ rɑ̃ ʒe,

Ont un parfum moins frais, ont une odeur moins douce,
ɔ̃ tœ̃ pa rfœ̃ mwɛ̃ frɛ ɔ̃ ty no dœ rmwɛ̃ du sə,

O blanche Leïlah! que ton souffle léger.
o blɑ̃ ʃə le i la! kə tɔ̃ su flə le ʒe.

Ta lèvre est de corail et ton rire léger
ta lɛ vrə də kɔ ra je tɔ̃ ri rə le ʒe,

Sonne mieux que l'eau vive et d'une voix plus douce.
sɔ nə mjø kə lo vi ve dy nə vwa ply du sə.

Mieux que le vent joyeux qui berce l'oranger,
mjø kə lə vɑ̃ ʒwa jø ki bɛ rsə lɔ rɑ̃ ʒe,

Mieux que l'oiseau qui chante au bord d'un nid de mousse.
mjø kə lwa zo ki ʃɑ̃ to bɔ rdœ̃ ni də mu sə.

O Leïlah! depuis que de leur vol léger
o le i la də pɥi kə də lœ rvɔ llə ʒe,

Tous les baisers ont fui de ta lèvre si douce
tu le bɛ ze ɔ̃ fɥi də ta lɛ vrə si du sə,

Il n'est plus de parfum dans le pâle oranger,
i lnɛ ply də pa rfœ̃ dɑ̃ lə pɑ lɔ rɑ̃ ʒe,

Ni de céleste arome aux roses dans leur mousse.
ni də se lɛ sta ro mo ro zə dɑ̃ lœ rmu sə.

Oh! que ton jeune amour, ce papillon léger
o kə tɔ̃ ʒœ na mu r, sə pa pi jɔ̃ le ʒe,

Revienne vers mon coeur d'une aile prompte et douce,
rə vjɛ nə vɛ rmɔ̃ kœ rdy nɛ lə prɔ̃ te du sə,

Et qu'il parfume encor la fleur de l'oranger,
e ki lpa rfy mɑ̃ kɔ rla flœ rdə lɔ rɑ̃ ʒe,

Les roses d'Ispahan dans leur gaine de mousse.
le ro zə di spa ɑ̃, dɑ̃ lœ rgɛ nə də mu sə.

Fauré   Lydia
fore   lidja

Lydia sur tes roses joues
li di a sy rte ro zə ʒu ə,

Et sur ton col frais et si blanc,
e sy rtõ kɔ lfrɛ ze si blɑ̃,

Roule étincelant L'or fluide que tu dénoues;
ru le tɛ̃ sə lɑ̃, lɔ rfly i də kə ty de nu ə;

Le jour qui luit est le meilleur,
lə ʒu rki lɥi ɛ lə mɛ jœ r,

Oublions l'éternelle tombe;
u bli jõ le tɛ rnɛ lə tõ bə;

Laisse tes baisers, tes baisers de colombe
lɛ sə te bɛ ze, te bɛ ze də kɔ lõ bə,

Chanter sur ta lèvre en fleur.
ʃɑ̃ te sy rta lɛ vrɑ̃ flœ r.

Un lys caché répand sans cesse
œ̃ li ska ʃe re pɑ̃ sɑ̃ sɛ sə,

Une odeur divine en ton sein;
y no dœ rdi vi nɑ̃ tõ sɛ̃;

Les délices comme un essaim Sortent de toi,
le de li sə kɔ mœ̃ nɛ sɛ̃ sɔ rtə də twa,

jeune déesse
ʒœ nə de ɛ sə,

Je t'aime et meurs, ô mes amours,
ʒə tɛ me mœ ro me za mu r,

Mon âme en baisers m'est ravie!
mõ nɑ mɑ̃ bɛ ze mɛ ra vi ə!

O Lydia rends—moi la vie, Que je puisse mourir toujours!
o li di a rɑ̃ mwa la vi ə, kə ʒə pɥi sə mu ri rtu ʒu r!

Fauré   Mai
fore   me

Puisque Mai tout en fleurs dans les prés nous réclame,
pɥi skə me tu tɑ̃ flœ r, dɑ̃ le pre nu re kla mə,

Viens, ne te lasse pas de mêler à ton âme
vjɛ̃ nə tə lɑ sə pa də mɛ le a tõ nɑ mə,

La campagne, les bois, les ombrages charmants,
la kã pa ɲə le bwa le zõ bra ʒə ʃa rmã,

Les larges clairs de lune au bord des flots dormants;
le la rʒə klɛ rdə ly no bo rde flo do rmã;

Le sentier qui finit où le chemin commence,
lə sã tje ki fi ni u lə ʃə mɛ̃ ko mã sə,

Et l'air, et le printemps et l'horizon immense,
e lɛ re lə prɛ̃ tã e lo ri zõ i mã sə,

L'horizon que ce monde attache humble et joyeux,
lo ri zõ kə sə mõ da ta ʃœ̃ ble ʒwa jø,

Comme une lèvre au bas de la robe des cieux.
ko my nə lɛ vro ba də la ro bə de sjø.

Viens, et que le regard des pudiques étoiles,
vjɛ̃ e kə lə rə ga rde py di kə ze twa lə,

Qui tombe sur la terre à travers tant de voiles
ki tõ bə sy rla tɛ rə a tra vɛ rtã de rwa lə,

Que l'arbre pénétré de parfums et de chants,
kə la rbrə pe ne tre də pa rfœ̃ ze də ʃã,

Que le souffle embrasé de midi dans les champs,
kə lə su flã bra ze də mi di dã le ʃã,

Et l'ombre et le soleil, et l'onde, et la verdure,
e lõ bre lə so lɛ j, e lõ de la vɛ rdy rə,

Et le rayonnement de toute la nature,
e lə rɛ jo nə mã, də tu tə la na ty rə,

Fassent épanouir, comme une double fleur,
fa sə te pa nu i r, ko my nə du blə flœ r,

La beauté sur ton front et l'amour dans ton coeur!
la bo te sy rtõ frõ e la mu rdã tõ kœ r!

Fauré   Nell
fore   nɛl

Ta rose de poupre à ton clair soleil,
ta ro zə də pu rpra tõ klɛ rso lɛ j,

O Juin, étincelle enivrée,
o ʒɥɛ̃ e tɛ̃ sɛ lã ni vre ə,

Penche aussi vers moi ta coupe dorée:
pã ʃo si vɛ rmwa ta ku pə dɔ re ə:

Mon coeur à ta rose est pareil.
mɔ̃ kœ ra ta ro zɛ pa rɛ j.

Sous le mol abri de la feuille ombreuse
su lə mɔ la bri də la fœ jɔ̃ brø zə,

Monte un soupir de volupté;
mɔ̃ tœ̃ su pi rdə vɔ ly pte;

Plus d'un ramier chante au bois écarté,
ply dœ̃ ra mje ʃã to bwa e ka rte,

O mon coeur, sa plainte amoureuse.
o mɔ̃ kœ r, sa plɛ̃ ta mu rø zə.

Que ta perle est douce au ciel enflammé,
kə ta pɛ rlɛ du so sjɛ lã fla me,

Etoile de la nuit pensive!
e twa lə də la nɥi pã si və!

Mais combien plus douce est la clarté vive
mɛ kɔ̃ bjɛ̃ ply du sɛ la kla rte vi və,

Qui rayonne en mon coeur, en mon coeur charmé!
ki rɛ jɔ nã mɔ̃ kœ r, ã mɔ̃ kœ rʃa rme!

La chantante mer, le long du rivage,
la ʃã tã tə mɛ rlə lɔ̃ dy ri va ʒə,

Taira son murmure éternel,
tɛ ra sɔ̃ my rmy re tɛ rnɛ l,

Avant qu'en mon coeur, chère amours, ô Nell,
a vã kã mɔ̃ kœ r, ʃɛ ra mu r, o nɛ l,

Ne fleurisse plus ton image!
nə flœ ri sə ply tɔ̃ ni ma ʒə!

Fauré   Prison (fɔre — prizɔ̃)
Hahn   D'une prison (an — d yn prizɔ̃)

Le ciel est par dessus le toit, si bleu, si calme...
lə sjɛ lɛ pa rdə sy lə twa, si blø si ka lmə...

Un arbre, par dessus le toít, berce sa palme...
œ̃ na rbrə pa rdə sy lə twa, bɛ rsə sa pa lmə...

La cloche dans le ciel qu'on voit, doucement tinte,
la klɔ ʃə dã lə sjɛ lkõ vwa, du sə mã tẽ tə,

Un oiseau sur l'arbre qu'on voit, chante sa plainte...
ẽ nwa zo sy rla rbrə kõ vwa, ʃã tə sa plẽ tə...

Mon Dieu, mon Dieu! La vie est là simple et tranquille!
mõ djø, mõ djø! la vi ɛ la sẽ ple trã ki lə!

Cette paisible rumeur là vient de la ville...
sɛ tə pɛ zi blə ry mœ rla vjẽ də la vi lə...

Qu'as-tu fait, ô toi que voilà, pleurant sans cesse
ka ty fɛ o twa kə vwa la, plœ rã sã sɛ sə,

Dis, qu'as-tu fait, toi que voilà, de ta jeunesse?
di ka ty fɛ, twa kə vwa la, də ta ʒœ nɛ sə?

Fifteenth Century Song   L'Amour de Moi
                          l amur də mwa

L'amour de moi s'y est enclose
la mu rdə mwa si ɛ tã klo zə,

Dedans un joli jardinet,
də dã zẽ ʒo li ʒa rdi nɛ,

Où croît la rose et le muguet,
u krwa la ro ze lə my gɛ,

Et aussi fait la passerose.
e o si fɛ la pa sə ro zə.

Ce jardin est bel et plaisant,
sə ʒa rdẽ ɛ bɛ le plɛ zã,

Il est garni de toutes flours.
i lɛ ga rni də tu tə flu r.

Hélas! il n'est si douce chose
e lɑ si lnɛ si du sə ʃo zə,

Que de ce doux rossignolet
kə də sə du rɔ si ɲo lɛ,

Qui chante au soir, au matinet:
ki ʃã to swa r, o ma ti nɛ:

Quand il est las, il se repose.
kã ti lɛ lɑ, i lsə rə po zə.

309

Je l'ai regardée une pose:
ʒə le rə ga rde y nə po zə:

Elle était blanche comme lait
ɛ le tɛ blɑ̃ ʃə kɔ mə lɛ,

Et douce comme un agnelet,
e du sə kɔ mœ̃ na ɲə lɛ,

Vermeille et fraîche comme rose.
vɛ rmɛ je frɛ ʃə, kɔ mə ro zə.

Fourdrain   Carnaval
furdrɛ̃   karnaval

Carnaval!   Joyeux Carnaval!
ka rna va l!   ʒwa jø ka rna va l!

On s'élance La foule assiège
ɔ̃ se lɑ̃ sə, la fu la sjɛ ʒə,

Des hérauts à pied, à cheval,
de e ro za pje a ʃə va l,

Précédant un riche cortège!   Une fanfare
pre se dɑ̃ tœ̃ ri ʃə kɔ rtɛ ʒə! y nə fɑ̃ fa rə,

des clameurs s'él vent stridentes, sonores!
de kla mœ rsə lɛ və stri dɑ̃ tə, so nɔ rə!

Du haut des chars il pleut des fleurs
dy o de ʃa ri lplø de flœ r,

Et des papiers multicolores Saluez!
e de pa pje my lti kɔ lo rə, sa ly e!

Voici la Reine tenant sa marotte;
vwa si la rɛ nə tə nɑ̃ sa ma rɔ t,

Elle a sa traine de gala,
ɛ la sa trɛ nə də ga la,

Et des cheveux couleur carotte;
e de ʃə vø ku lœ rka rɔ tə;

Elle taquine son bouffon
ɛ lə ta ki nə sɔ̃ bu fɔ̃

Dont les lèvres restent muettes,
dɔ̃ le lɛ vrə rɛ stə my ɛ tə,

310

Elle lui montre comment
ε lə lɥi mɔ̃ trə kɔ mã

"font" Font font les petites marionettes.
fɔ̃, fɔ̃ fɔ̃ le pə ti tə ma rjɔ nε tə.

Il lui répond: Merci, m'amour;
i llɥi re pɔ̃: mε rsi, ma mu r;

De ces leçons-là je me passe
də se lə sɔ̃ la ʒə mə pa sə,

J'écoute l'âme du faubourg
ʒe ku tə la mə dy fo bu r,

Jusqu'à toi monter dans l'espace.
ʒy ska twa mɔ̃ te dã lε spa sə.

Je vois là haut, je vois soudain
ʒə vwa la o, ʒə vwa su dɛ̃,

Le soleil s'exalter lui-même
lə sɔ lε jsε gza lte lɥi mε mə,

Reine, il baise ta main
rε nə, i lbε zə ta mɛ̃,

Et fait flamber ton diadème.
e fε flã be, tɔ̃ di a dε mə.

Fourdrain   Le Papillon
furdrɛ̃   lə papijɔ̃

Gai papillon, papillon d'or
ge pa pi jɔ̃, pa pi jɔ̃ dɔ r

Qui t'envoles rapide et frêle,
ki tã vɔ lə ra pi de frε lə,

Au bout des doigts je garde encor
o bu de dwa ʒə ga rdã kɔ r,

Un peu de cendre de ton aile!
ɶ̃ pø də sã drə də tɔ̃ nε lə!

Tu venais voir la blonde enfant
ty və nε vwa rla blɔ̃ dã fã,

Qui babille dans ma chambrette,
ki ba bi jə dã ma ʃã brɛ tə,

Tu venais, Monsieur le passant
ty və nɛ, mə sjø lə pa sã,

Dire bonjour à ma grisette
di rə bõ ʒu ra ma gri zɛ tə.

Ah! vraiment elle est bien ta soeur,
a! vrɛ mã ɛ lɛ bjɛ̃ ta sœ r,

Comme toi légère et volage,
kɔ mə twa le ʒɛ re vɔ la ʒə,

Elle sait endormir le coeur Et le bercer
ɛ lə sɛ tã dɔ rmi rlə kœ re lə bɛ rse,

en un mirage.
ã nœ̃ mi ra ʒə.

Mais papillon, dès le printemps,
mɛ pa pi jõ, dɛ lə prɛ̃ tã,

Elle s'enfuira la méchante,
ɛ lə sã fu̯i ra la me ʃã tə,

Laissant de tous ses grands serments
lɛ sã də tu se grã sɛ rmã,

Un peu de poussiére qui chante.
œ̃ pø də pu sjɛ rə, ki ʃã tə.

Franck   La procession
frãk   la prɔsɛsjõ

Dieu s'avance à travers les champs
djø sa vã sa tra vɛ rle ʃã

Par les landes, les prés, les verts taillis de hêtres.
pa rle lã də, le pre, le vɛ rta ji də ɛ trə.

Il vient, suivi du peuple, et porté par les prêtres:
i lvjɛ̃, su̯i vi dy pœ plə, e pɔ rte pa rle prɛ trə:

Aux cantiques de l'homme, oiseaux, mêlez vos chants!
o kã ti kə də lɔ mə, wa zo, mɛ le vo ʃã!

On s'arrête. La foule autour d'un chêne antique
õ sa rɛ tə. la fu lo tu rdœ̃ ʃɛ nã ti kə,

S'incline, en adorant, sous l'ostensoir mystique:
sɛ̃ kli nã na dɔ rã, su lɔ stã swa rmi sti kə:

Soleil! darde sur lui tes longs rayons couchants!
sɔ lɛ jda rdə sy rlɥi, te lõ rɛ jõ ku ʃã!

Aux cantiques de l'homme, oiseaux, mêlez vos chants!
o kã ti kə də lɔ mə, wa zo mɛ le vo ʃã!

Vous, fleurs, avec l'encens exhalez votre arôme!
vu, flœ r, a vɛ klã sã ɛ gza le vɔ tra ro mə!

O fête! tout reluit, tout prie et tout embaume!
o fɛ tə! tu rə lɥi, tu pri e tu tã bo mə!

Dieu s'avance à travers les champs.
djø sa vã sa tra vɛ rle ʃã.

Franck Le mariage des roses
frãk   lə mariaʒ de roz

Mignonne, sais-tu comment S'épousent les roses?
mi ɲo nə sɛ ty kɔ mã se pu zə le ro zə?

Ah! cet hymen est charmant, cet hymen est charmant!
a sɛ ti mɛ nɛ ʃa rmã, sɛ ti mɛ nɛ ʃa rmã!

Quelles tendres choses Elles disent en ouvrant
kɛ lə tã drə ʃo zə ɛ lə di zə tã nu vrã

Leurs paupières closes!
lœ rpo pjɛ rə klo zə!

Mignonne, sais-tu comment S'épousent les roses?
mi ɲo nə sɛ ty kɔ mã se pu zə le ro zə?

Elles disent: aimons nous! Si courte est la vie!
ɛ lə di zə, ɛ mõ nu! si ku rtɛ la vi ə!

Ayons les baisers plus doux, L'âme plus ravie!
ɛ jõ le bɛ ze ply du, la mə ply ra vi ə!

Pendant que l'homme à genoux Doute, espère ou prie!
pã dã kə lɔ ma ʒə nu du tɛ spɛ ru pri ə!

O mes soeurs, embrassons-nous! Si courte est la vie!
o me sœ r ã bra sõ nu! si ku rtɛ la vi ə!

Crois—moi, mignonne, crois—moi, Aimons—nous comme elles,
krwa mwa mi ɲo nə krwa mwa ɛ mõ nu kɔ mɛ lə,

Vois, le printemps vient à toi, Le printemps vient à toi.
vwa lə prɛ̃ tɑ̃ vjɛ̃ ta twa, lə prɛ̃ tɑ̃ vjɛ̃ ta twa.

Et des hirondelles, Aimer est l'unique loi
e de zi rõ dɛ lə ɛ me ɛ ly ni kə lwa

A leurs nids fidèles.
a lœ rni fi dɛ lə.

O ma reine, suis ton roi, Aimons—nous comme elles.
o ma rɛ nə sɥi tõ rwa, ɛ mõ nu kɔ mɛ lə,

Excepté d'avoir aimé, Qu'est—il donc sur terre?
ɛ ksɛ pte da vwa rɛ me, kɛ ti ldõ ksy rtɛ rə?

Votre horizon est fermé Ombre, nuit, mystère!
vɔ trɔ ri zõ ɛ fɛ rme õ brə nɥi mi stɛ rə!

Un seul phare est allumé L'amour nous l'éclaire,
œ̃ sœ lfa rɛ ta ly me, la mu rnu le klɛ rə,

Excepté d'avoir aimé Qu'est—il donc sur terre?
e ksɛ pte da vwa rɛ me, kɛ ti ldõ ksy rtɛ rə?

Franck   Lied
frɑ̃k   lid

Pour moi sa main cueillait des roses A ce buisson,
pu rmwa sa mɛ̃ kœ jɛ de ro zə a sə bɥi sõ,

Comme elle encore à peine écloses, Chère moisson.
kɔ mɛ lɑ̃ kɔ ra pɛ ne klo zə ʃɛ rə mwa sõ.

La gerbe, hélas! en est fanée Comme elle aussi;
la ʒɛ rbe la sɑ̃ nɛ fa ne ə kɔ mɛ lo si;

La moissonneuse moissonnée Repose ici.
la mwa sɔ nø zə mwa sɔ ne ə rə po zi si.

Mais sur la tombe qui vous couvre, O mes amours!
mɛ sy rla tõ bə ki vu ku vrə, o me za mu r!

Une églantine, qui s'entr'ouvre, Sourit toujours.
y ne glɑ̃ ti nə ki sɑ̃ tru vrə, su ri tu ʒu r.

Et sous le buisson qui surplombe, Quand je reviens,
e su lə bɥi sõ ki sy rplõ bə, kɑ̃ ʒə rə vjɛ̃,

Une voix me dit sous la tombe: "Je me souviens."
y nə vwa mə di su la tõ bə: ʒə mə su vjɛ̃.

Gluck   Divinités du Styx (Alceste)
glyk   divinite dy stiks alsɛst

Divinités du Styx, ministres de la mort,
di vi ni te dy sti ks, mi ni strə də la mɔ r,

je n'invoquerai point, votre pitié cruelle,
ʒə nɛ̃ vɔ kə re pwɛ̃, vɔ trə pi tje kry ɛ lə,

J'enlève un tendre époux à son funeste sort,
ʒã lɛ vɛ̃ tã dre pu, a sõ fy nɛ stə sɔ r,

mais je vous abandonne une épouse fidèle.
mɛ ʒə vu za bã dɔ ny ne pu zə fi dɛ lə.

Divinités du Styx, ministres de la mort,
di vi ni te dy sti ks, mi ni strə də la mɔ r,

mourir pour ce qu'on aime est un trop doux effort,
mu ri rpu rsə kõ nɛ mə, ɛ tɛ̃ tro du zə fɔ r,

une vertu si naturelle, mon coeur est animé
y nə vɛ rty si na ty rɛ lə, mõ kœ rɛ ta ni me,

du plus noble transport!
dy ply nɔ blə trã spɔ r!

Je sens une force nouvelle,
ʒə sã zy nə fɔ rsə nu vɛ lə,

Je vais où mon amour m'appelle,
ʒə vɛ zu mõ na mu rma pɛ lə,

mon coeur est animé du plus noble transport.
mõ kœ rɛ ta ni me, dy ply nɔ blə trã spɔ r.

Gounod   Ah! Je veux vivre, from "Roméo et Juliette"
guno   a ʒə vø vivr   rɔmeo e ʒyljɛt

Ah! Je veux vivre Dans le rêve qui m'enivre
a ʒə vø vi vrə dã lə rɛ və ki mã ni vrə

Longtemps encor!   Douce flamme, Je te garde
lɔ̃ tɑ̃ zɑ̃ kɔ r, du sə fla mə ʒə tə ga rdə

dans mon âme Comme un trésor!
dɑ̃ mɔ̃ na mə kɔ mœ̃ tre zɔ r!

Cette ivresse De jeunesse Ne dure, hélas! qu'un jour.
sɛ ti vrɛ sə də ʒœ nɛ sə, nə dy re la skœ̃ ʒu r.

Puis vient l'heure Où l'on pleure,
pɥi vjɛ̃ lœ rə u lɔ̃ plœ rə,

Le coeur cède à l'amour,
lə kœ rsɛ da la mu r,

Et le bonheur fuit sans retour.
e lə bɔ nœ rfɥi sɑ̃ rə tu r.

Loin de l'hiver morose
lwɛ̃ də li vɛ rmɔ ro zə,

laisse-moi, laisse-moi sommeiller,
lɛ sə mwa, lɛ sə mwa sɔ mɛ je,

Et respirer la rose,
e rɛ spi re la ro zə,

respirer la rose avant de l'effeuiller.
rɛ spi re la ro za vɑ̃ də lɛ fœ je.

Reste dans mon âme
rɛ stə dɑ̃ mɔ̃ na mə,

Comme un doux trésor Longtemps encor!
kɔ mœ̃ du tre zɔ r, lɔ̃ tɑ̃ zɑ̃ kɔ r!

Gounod   Ah! lève-toi, soleil!, from Roméo et Juliette"
guno   a lɛv twa sɔlɛj   rɔmeo e ʒyljɛt

L'amour! oui, son ardeur a troublé tout mon être!
la mu r! wi, sɔ̃ na rdœ ra tru ble tu mɔ̃ nɛ trə!

Mais quelle soudaine clarté resplendit
mɛ kɛ lə su dɛ nə kla rte rɛ splɑ̃ di

à cette fenêtre?
a sɛ tə fə nɛ trə?

C'est là que dans la nuit rayonne sa beauté!
sɛ la kə dɑ̃ la nɥi rɛ jɔ nə sa bo te!

Ah! lève-toi, soleil! fais pâlir les étoiles
ɑ! lɛ və twa, sɔ lɛ j! fɛ pɑ li rlɛ ze twa lə,

Qui, dans l'azur sans voiles,
ki, dɑ̃ la ʒy rsɑ̃ vwa lə,

Brillent au firmament.
bri jə to fi rma mɑ̃.

Ah! lève-toi, parais! Astre pur et charmant!
ɑ! lɛ və twa, pa rɛ! a strɛ̀ py re ʃa rmɑ̃!

Elle rêve! elle dénoue
ɛ lə rɛ və! ɛ lə de nu ə,

Une boucle de cheveux Qui vient caresser sa joue
y nə bu klə də ʃə vø, ki vjɛ̃ ka re se sa ʒu ə,

Amour! porte-lui mes voeux! Elle parle!
a mu r! pɔ rtə lɥi me vø! ɛ lə pa rlə!

Qu'elle est belle!
kɛ lɛ bɛ lə!

Ah! je n'ai rien entendu!
ɑ! ʒə ne rjɛ̃ nɑ̃ tɑ̃ dy!

Mais ses yeux parlent pour elle,
mɛ se zjø pa rlə pu rɛ lə,

Et mon coeur a répondu! Viens, parais!
e mɔ̃ kœ ra re pɔ̃ dy! vjɛ̃, pa rɛ!

Gounod   Avant de quitter ces lieux, from "Faust"
guno   avɑ̃ də kite se ljø   Fr. fɔst Ger. faost

Avant de quitter ces lieux,
a vɑ̃ də ki te se ljø,

Sol natal des mes aïeux
sɔ lna ta ldə me za jø,

A toi, Seigneur et roi des cieux,
a twa sɛ ɲœ re rwa de sjø,

Ma soeur je confie!
ma sœ rʒə kɔ̃ fi ə!

Daigne de tout danger
dɛ ɲə də tu dɑ̃ ʒe,

317

Toujours, toujours la protéger,
tu ʒu rtu ʒu rla prɔ te ʒe,

Cette soeur si chérie;
sɛ tə sœ rsi ʃe ri ə;

Daigne la protéger de tout danger.
dɛ ɲə la prɔ te ʒe də tu dɑ̃ ʒe.

Délivré d'une triste pensée,
de li vre dy nə tri stə pɑ̃ se ə,

J'irai chercher la gloire au sein des ennemis,
ʒi re ʃɛ rʃe la glwa ro sɛ̃ de zə nə mi,

Le premier, le plus brave au fort de la mêlée
lə prə mje lə ply bra vo fɔ rdə la mɛ le ə

J'irai combattre pour mon pays.
ʒi re kɔ̃ ba trə pu rmɔ̃ pe i.

Et si vers lui Dieu me rappelle,
e si vɛ rlɥi djø mə ra pɛ lə,

Je veillerai sur toi fidèle, O Marguerite!
ʒə vɛ je re sy rtwa fi dɛ lə, o ma rgə ri tə,

...O Roi des cieux, jette les yeux,
o rwa de sjø ʒɛ tə le zjø,

protège Marguerite, Roi des cieux!
prɔ tɛ ʒə ma rgə ri tə, rwa de sjø!

Gounod   Faites—lui mes aveux, from "Faust"
guno   fɛtə lɥi me zavø   Fr. fɔst Ger. f<u>a</u>ost

Faites—lui mes aveux, Portez mes voeux!
fɛ tə lɥi me za vø pɔ rte me vø!

Fleurs écloses près d'elle, Dites—lui qu'elle est belle,
flœ rze klo zə prɛ dɛ lə, di tə lɥi kɛ lɛ bɛ lə,

Que mon coeur nuit et jour Languit d'amour!
kə mɔ̃ kœ rnɥi te ʒu r, lɑ̃ gi da mu r!

Révélez à son âme Le secret de ma flamme,
re ve le za sɔ̃ na mə, lə sə kre də ma fla mə,

Qu'il s'exhale avec vous Parfums plus doux!
ki lsɛ gza la vɛ kvu pa rfœ̃ ply du!

318

Fanée! hélas! ce sorcier, que Dieu damne,
fa ne ə! e la ssə sɔ rsje kə djø da nə,

M'a porté malheur!
ma pɔ rte ma lœ r!

Je ne puis, sans qu'elle se fane,
ʒə nə pɥi sɑ̃ kɛ lə sə fa nə,

Toucher une fleur! Si je trempais mes doigts
tu ʃe ry nə flœ r! si ʒə trɑ̃ pɛ me dwa

dans l'eau bénite!
dɑ̃ lo be ni tə!

C'est là que chaque soir vient prier Marguerite!
sɛ la kə ʃa kə swa r, vjɛ̃ pri je ma rgə ri tə!

Voyons maintenant! voyons vite! Elles se fanent?
vwa jɔ̃ mɛ̃ tə nɑ̃! vwa jɔ̃ vi tə! ɛ lə sə fa nə?

non! Satan, je ris de toi!
nɔ̃! sa tɑ̃, ʒə ri də twa!

C'est en vous que j'ai foi; Parlez pour moi!
sɛ tɑ̃ vu kə ʒe fwa pa rle pu rmwa!

Qu'elle puisse connaître L'émoi qu'elle a fait naître,
kɛ lə pɥi sə kɔ nɛ trə, le mwa kɛ la fɛ nɛ trə,

Et dont mon coeur troublé N'a point parlé!
e dɔ̃ mɔ̃ kœ rtru ble na pwɛ̃ pa rle!

Si l'amour l'effarouche, Que la fleur sur sa bouche
si la mu rle fa ru ʃə, kə la flœ rsy rsa bu ʃə,

Sache au moins déposer Un doux baiser!
sa ʃo mwɛ̃ de po ze œ̃ du bɛ ze!

Gounod   Il était un roi de Thulé, from "Faust"
guno   il etɛ tœ̃ rwa də tyle   Fr. fɔst Ger. faost

Je voudrais bien savoir quel était ce jeune homme;
ʒə vu drɛ bjɛ̃ sa vwa rkɛ le tɛ sə ʒœ nɔ mə;

Si c'est un grand seigneur, et comment il se nomme?
si sɛ tœ̃ grɑ̃ sɛ ɲœ r, e kɔ mɑ̃ i lsə nɔ mə?

Il était un Roi de Thulé, Qui, jusqu'à la tombe fidèle,
i le tɛ tœ̃ rwa də ty le ki, ʒy ska la tɔ̃ bə fi dɛ lə,

319

Eut, en souvenir de sa belle,
y tã su və ni rdə sa bɛ lə,

Une coupe en or ciselé.
y nə ku pã nɔ rsi zə le.

Il avait bonne grâce, à ce qu'il m'a semblé.
i la vɛ bɔ nə grɑ sə, a sə ki lma sã ble.

Nul trésor n'avait tant de charmes,
ny ltre zɔ rna vɛ tã də ʃa rmə,

Dans les grand jours il s'en servait,
dã le grã ʒu ri lsã sɛ rvɛ,

Et chaque fois qu'il y buvait,
e ʃa kə fwɑ ki li by vɛ,

Ses yeux se remplissaient de larmes!
se zjø sə rã pli sɛ də la rmə!

Quand il sentit venir la mort,
kã ti lsã ti və ni rla mɔ r,

Etendu sur sa froide couche,
e tã dy sy rsa frwa də ku ʃə,

Pour la porter jusqu'à sa bouche,
pu rla pɔ rte ʒy ska sa bu ʃə,

Sa main fit un suprême effort!
sa mɛ̃ fi tœ̃ sy prɛ mɛ fɔ r!

Je ne savais que dire, Et j'ai rougi d'abord.
ʒə nə sa vɛ kə di rə, e ʒe ru ʒi da bɔ r.

Et puis, en l'honneur de sa dame,
e pɥi, ã lɔ nœ rdə sa da mə,

Il but une dernière fois.
i lby ty nə dɛ rnjɛ rə fwa.

La coupe trembla dans ses doigts,
la ku pə trã bla dã se dwa,

Et doucement il rendit l'âme!
e du sə mã i lrã di la mə!

Gounod   Je ris de me voir si belle, from "Faust"
guno   ʒə ri də mə vwar si bɛl Fr. fɔst Ger. fa̲ost

Je ris de me voir Si belle en ce miroir, Ah!
ʒə ri də mə vwa rsi bɛ lã sə mi rwa r, ɑ!

Est—ce toi, Marguerite, Est—ce toi?
ɛ sə twa, ma rgə ri tə, ɛ sə twa?

Réponds—moi, réponds vite!
re põ mwa, re põ vi tə!

Non! ce n'est plus toi! non,
nõ! sə nɛ ply twa! nõ,

Ce n'est plus ton visage; C'est la fille d'un roi,
sə nɛ ply tõ vi za ʒə; sɛ la fi jə dœ̃ rwa,

Qu'on salue au passage!
kõ sa ly ɔ pa sa ʒə!

Ah s'il était ici! S'il me voyait ainsi!
ɑ si le tɛ ti si! si lmə vwa jɛ tɛ̃ si!

Comme une demoiselle Il me trouverait belle,
kɔ my nə də mwa zɛ lə, i lmə tru və rɛ bɛ lə,

Achevons la métamorphose.
a ʃə võ la me ta mɔ rfo zə.

Il me tarde encor d'essayer Le bracelet et le collier!
il mə ta rdɑ̃ kɔ rdɛ sɛ je lə bra sə le e lə kɔ lje!

Dieu! c'est comme une main, qui sur mon bras se pose!
djø! sɛ kɔ my nə mɛ̃, ki sy rmõ brɑ sə po zə!

Gounod   Le veau d'or est toujours debout, from "Faust"
guno   lə vo dɔr ɛ tuʒur dəbu, Fr. fɔst Ger. f<u>a</u>ost

Le veau d'or est toujours debout!
lə vo dɔ rɛ tu ʒu r də bu!

On encense Sa puissance,
õ nɑ̃ sɑ̃ sə sa pɥi sɑ̃ sə,

D'un bout du monde à l'autre bout!
dœ̃ bu dy mõ da lo trə bu!

Pour fêter l'infâme idole,
pu rfɛ te lɛ̃ fa mi dɔ lə,

Rois et peuples confondus,
rwa ze pœ plə kõ fõ dy,

Au bruit sombre des écus,
o brɥi sõ brə de ze ky,

321

Dansent une ronde folle,
dɑ̃ sə ty nə rɔ̃ də fɔ lə,

Autour de son piédestal!
o tu rdə sɔ̃ pje də sta l!

Et Satan conduit le bal, conduit le bal!
e sa tɑ̃ kɔ̃ dɥi lə ba l, kɔ̃ dɥi lə ba l!

Le veau d'or est vainqueur des dieux!
lə vo dɔ rɛ vɛ̃ kœ rde djø!

Dans sa gloire Dérisoire,
dɑ̃ sa glwa rə de ri zwa rə,

Le monstre abject insulte aux cieux!
lə mɔ̃ stra bʒɛ ktɛ̃ sy lto sjø!

Il contemple, ô rage étrange!
i lkɔ̃ tɑ̃ plo ra ʒe trɑ̃ ʒə!

A ses pieds le genre humain,
a se pje lə ʒɑ̃ ry mɛ̃,

Se ruant, le fer en main,
sə ry ɑ̃ lə fɛ rɑ̃ mɛ̃,

Dans le sang et dans la fange,
dɑ̃ lə sɑ̃ e dɑ̃ la fɑ̃ ʒə,

Où brille l'ardent métal!
u bri jə la rdɑ̃ me ta l!

Et Satan conduit le bal, conduit le bal!
e sa tɑ̃ kɔ̃ dɥi lə ba l, kɔ̃ dɥi lə ba l!

Gounod   Salut! demeure chaste et pure, from "Faust"
guno   saly dəmœr ʃast e pyr   Fr. fɔst Ger. f<u>a</u>ost

Quel trouble inconnu me pénètre?
kɛl tru blɛ̃ kɔ ny mə pe nɛ trə?

Je sens l'amour s'emparer de mon être!
ʒə sɑ̃ la mu rsɑ̃ pa re də mɔ̃ nɛ trə!

O Marguerite, à tes pieds me voici!
o ma rgə ri tə, a te pje mə vwa si!

Salut! demeure chaste et pure,
sa ly də mœ rə ʃa ste py rə,

où se devine La présence d'une âme innocente et divine!
u sə də vi nə la pre zã sə, dy nɑ mi nɔ sã te di vi nə!

Que de richesse en cette pauvreté!
kə də ri ʃɛ sã sɛ tə po vrə te!

En ce réduit, que de félicité!
ã sə re dɥi kə də fe li si te!

O nature, c'est là que tu la fis si belle!
o na ty rə, sɛ la kə ty la fi si bɛ lə!

C'est là que cette enfant a dormi sous ton aîle,
sɛ la kə sɛ tã fã a dɔ rmi su tõ nɛ l,

A grandi sous tes yeux.
a grã di su te zjø.

Là que de ton haleine enveloppant son âme,
la kə də tõ na lɛ nə, ã və lɔ pã sõ na mə,

Tu fis avec amour épanouir la femme
ty fi a vɛ ka mu r, e pa nu i rla fa

En cet ange des cieux! C'est là! oui! c'est là!
mã sɛ tã ʒə de sjø! sɛ la! wi! sɛ la!

Gounod   Sérénade
guno   serenad

Quand tu chantes bercée Le soir entre mes bras,
kã ty ʃã tə bɛ rse ə lə swa rã trə me bra,

Entends-tu ma pensée, Qui te répond tout bas?
ã tã ty ma pã se ə ki tə re põ tu ba?

Ton doux chant me rappelle Les plus beaux de mes jours.
tõ du ʃã mə ra pɛ lə le ply bo də me ʒu r.

Ah! Chantez, chantez, ma belle, Chantez, chantez toujours,
a ʃã te ʃã te ma bɛ lə,   ʃã te ʃã te tu ʒu r,

Chantez, chantez, ma belle, Chantez toujours!
ʃã te, ʃã te, ma bɛ lə, ʃã te tu ʒu r!

Quand tu ris, sur ta bouche L'amour s'épanouit;
kã ty ri sy rta bu ʃə la mu rse pa nu i;

Et soudain le farouche Soupçon s'évanouit.
e su dɛ̃ lə fa ru ʃə su psõ se va nu i.

Ah! le rire fidèle Prouve un coeur sans détours.
a lə ri rə fi 'dɛ lə pru vœ̃ kœ rsɑ̃ de tu r.

Ah! Riez, riez, ma belle, Riez, riez toujours,
a ri je, ri je, ma bɛ lə, ri je, ri je tu ʒu r,

Quand tu dors, calme et pure Dans l'ombre sous mes yeux,
kɑ̃ ty do rka lme py rə dɑ̃ lõ brə su me zjø,

Ton haleine murmure Des mots harmonieux.
tõ na lɛ nə my rmy rə de mo za rmɔ ni ø.

Ton beau corps se révèle sans voile et sans atours.
tõ bo kɔ rsə re vɛ lə sɑ̃ vwa le sɑ̃ za tu r.

Ah! Dormez, dormez, ma belle, Dormez, dormez toujours,
a dɔ rme, dɔ rme, ma bɛ lə, dɔ rme, dɔ rme tu ʒu r,

Dormez, dormez, ma belle, Dormez toujours!
dɔ rme, dɔ rme, ma bɛ lə, dɔ rme tu ʒu r!

Gounod   Si le bonheur à sourire t'invite, from "Faust"
guno   si lə bɔnœr a surir tɛ̃vit Fr. fɔst Ger. fa͜ost

Si le bonheur à sourire t'invite,
si lə bɔ nœ ra su ri rə tɛ̃ vi tə,

Joyeux alors je sens un doux émoi;
ʒwa jø a lɔ rʒə sɑ̃ zõ du ze mwa;

Si la douleur t'accable, Marguerite,
si la du lœ rta ka blə, mar gə ri tə,

O Marguerite, je pleure alors,
o ma rgə ri tə, ʒə plœ ra lɔ r,

je pleure comme toi!
ʒə plœ rə kɔ mə twa!

Comme deux fleurs sur une même tige,
kɔ mə dø flœ rsy ry nə mɛ mə ti ʒə,

Notre destin suivant le même cours,
nɔ trə dɛ stɛ̃ sɥi vɑ̃ lə mɛ mə ku r,

De tes chagrins en frère je m'afflige,
də te ʃa grɛ̃ ɑ̃ frɛ rə ʒə ma fli ʒə,

O Marguerite, Comme une soeur je t'aimerai toujours!
o ma rgə ri tə, kɔ my nə sœ rʒə tɛ mə re tu ʒu r!

324

Gounod   Vous qui faites l'endormie, "Faust"
guno   vu ki fɛ tə lɑ̃dɔrmi   Fr. fɔst   Ger. f̲a̲ost

Vous qui faites l'endormie, N'entendez-vous pas,
vu ki fɛ tə lɑ̃ dɔ rmi ə, nɑ̃ tɑ̃ de vu pɑ,

O Catherine, ma mie, N'entendez-vous pas
o ka tə ri nə ma mi ə, nɑ̃ tɑ̃ de vu pɑ

Ma voix et mes pas?
ma vwa e me pɑ?

Ainsi ton galant t'appelle,
ɛ̃ si tɔ̃ ga lɑ̃ ta pɛ lə,

Et ton coeur l'en croit. Ah!
e tɔ̃ kœ rlɑ̃ krwa. ɑ!

N'ouvre ta porte, ma belle,
nu vrə ta pɔ rtə ma bɛ lə,

Que la bague au doigt!
kə la ba go dwa!

Catherine que j'adore, Pourquoi refuser
ka tə ri nə ke ʒa dɔ rə, pu rkwa rə fy ze,

A l'amant qui vous implore,
a la mɑ̃ ki vu zɛ̃ plɔ rə,

Pourquoi refuser Un si doux baiser?
pu rkwa rə fy ze, œ̃ si du bɛ ze?

Ainsi ton galant supplie, Et ton coeur l'en croit.
ɛ̃ si tɔ̃ ga lɑ̃ sy pli ə, e tɔ̃ kœ rlɑ̃ krwa.

Ah! Ne donne un baiser, ma mie,
ɑ! nə dɔ nœ̃ bɛ ze, ma mi ə,

Que la bague au doigt! Ah!
kə la ba go dwa! ɑ!

Hahn   L'heure exquise
an   l œr ɛkskiz

La lune blanche Luit dans les bois;
la ly nə blɑ̃ ʃə lɥi dɑ̃ le bwa;

De chaque branche Part une voix Sous la ramée
də ʃa kə brɑ̃ ʃə pa ry nə vwa su la ra me ə,

O bienaimée.
o bjɛ̃ nɛ me ə.

325

L'étang reflète, Profond miroir
le tɑ̃ rə flɛ tə, prɔ fɔ̃ mi rwa r,

La silhouette Du saule noir
la si lu ɛ tə dy so lə nwa r

Où le vent pleure Rêvons! c'est l'heure! . . .
u lə vɑ̃ plœ rə, rɛ vɔ̃! sɛ lœ rə! . . .

Un vaste et tendre Apaisement, Semble descendre
œ̃ va stə tɑ̃ dra pɛ zə mɑ̃ sɑ̃ blə də sɑ̃ drə

Du firmament Que l'astre irise . . .
dy fi rma mɑ̃ kə la stri ri zə . . .

C'est l'heure exquise.
sɛ lœ rə kski zə.

Hahn   Si mes vers avaient des ailes!
an   si me vɛr avɛ de zɛl

Mes vers fuiraient, doux et frêles,
me vɛ rfɥi rɛ du ze frɛ lə,

Vers votre jardin si beau
vɛ rvɔ trə ʒa rdɛ̃ si bo,

Si mes vers avaient des ailes Comme l'oiseau!
si me vɛ ra vɛ de zɛ lə, kɔ mə lwa zo!

Ils voleraient, étincelles,
i lvɔ lə rɛ e tɛ̃ sɛ lə,

Vers votre foyer qui rit
vɛ rvɔ trə fwa je ki ri,

Si mes vers avaient des ailes Comme l'esprit.
si me vɛ ra vɛ de zɛ lə, kɔ mə lɛ spri.

Près de vous, purs et fidèles,
prɛ də vu py re fi dɛ lə,

Ils accourraient, nuit et jour
i lza ku rrɛ, nɥi te ʒu r,

Si mes vers avaient des ailes
si me vɛ ra vɛ de zɛ lə,

Comme l'amour!
kɔ mə la mu r!

Halévy   Si la rigueur, from "La Juive"
alevi   si la rigœr   la ʒɥiv

Si la rigueur ou la vengeance
si la ri gœ ru la vã ʒã sə,

Leur font haïr ta sainte loi,
lœ rfɔ̃ a i rta sɛ̃ tə lwa,

Que le pardon, que la clémence, mon Dieu,
kə lə pa rdɔ̃, kə la kle mã sə, mɔ̃ djø,

Les ramène en ce jour vers toi,
le ra mɛ nã sə ʒu rvɛ rtwa,

Rapelons-nous son précepte sacré,
ra pə lɔ̃ nu sɔ̃ pre sɛ ptə sa kre,

Ouvrons nos bras à l'enfant égaré,
u vrɔ̃ no bra a lã fã e ga re,

Nous rappelant son précepte sacré,
nu ra pə lã sɔ̃ pre sɛ ptə sa kre,

oh, mon Dieu, les ramène vers toi,
o, mɔ̃ djø, le ra mɛ nə vɛ rtwa,

en ce jour vers toi.
ã sə ʒu rvɛ rtwa.

Hüe   A des oiseaux
y   a de zwazo

Bonjour, bonjour les fauvettes,
bɔ̃ ʒu rbɔ̃ ʒu rle fo vɛ tə,

Bonjour les joyeux pinsons,
bɔ̃ ʒu rle ʒwa jø pɛ̃ sɔ̃,

Eveillez les pâquerettes
e vɛ je le pa kə rɛ tə

Et les fleurs des verts buissons!
e le flœ rde vɛ rbɥi sɔ̃!

Toujours votre âme est en fête,
tu ʒu rvo tra mɛ tã fɛ tə,

Gais oiseaux qu'on aime à voir,
ge zwa zo kɔ̃ nɛ ma vwa r,

Pour l'amant et le poète,
pu rla mã e lə pɔ ɛ tə,

Vous chantez matin et soir!
vu ʃã te ma tɛ̃ e swa r!

Mais dans la plaine, il me semble
mɛ dã la plɛ ni lmə sã blə

Qu'on a tendu des réseaux;
kɔ̃ na tã dy de re zo;

Voltigez toujours ensemble:
vɔ lti ʒe tu ʒu rzã sã blə:

En garde, petits oiseaux!
ã ga rdə, pə ti zwa zo!

Penchez—vous sans toucher terre,
pã ʃe vu sã tu ʃe tɛ rə,

Voyez—vous au coin du bois,
vwa je vu o kwɛ̃ dy bwa,

Vous guettant avec mystère,
vu gɛ tã ta vɛ kmi stɛ rə,

Ces enfants à l'oeil sournois?
se zã fã a lœ jsu rnwa?

Ah, bien vite à tire d'aile,
a bjɛ̃ vi ta ti rə dɛ lə,

Fuyez, fuyez leurs appâts;
fɥi je, fɥi je lœ rza pɑ;

Venez avec l'hirondelle,
və ne a vɛ kli rɔ̃ dɛ lə,

Qui, dans son vol, suit mes pas.
ki dã sɔ̃ vɔ lsɥi me pɑ.

Dans mon jardin nulle crainte;
dã mɔ̃ ʒa rdɛ̃ ny lə krɛ̃ tə;

Vous pourrez, d'un bec léger,
vu pu re dœ̃ bɛ kle ʒe,

Piller, piller sans contrainte,
pi je pi je sã kɔ̃ trɛ̃ tə,

Tous les fruits mûrs du verger.
tu le frɥi my rdy vɛ rʒe.

Bonsoir, bonsoir les fauvettes,
bɔ̃ swa rbɔ̃ swa rle fo vɛ tə,

Bonsoir les joyeux pinsons,
bõ swa rle ʒwa jø pɛ̃ sõ,

Endormez les pâquerettes
ã dɔ rme le pa kə rɛ tə,

Et les fleurs des verts buissons!
e le flœ rde vɛ rbɥi sõ!

Hüe	J'ai pleuré en rêve
y	ʒe plœre ã rɛv

J'ai pleuré en rêve: J'ai rêvé que tu étais morte;
ʒe plœ re ã rɛ və: ʒe rɛ ve kə ty e tɛ mɔ rtə;

Je m'éveillai et les larmes coulèrent de mes joues.
ʒə me vɛ je, e le la rmə ku lɛ rə də me ʒu ə.

J'ai pleuré en rêve: J'ai rêvé que tu me quittais;
ʒe plœ re ã rɛ və: ʒe rɛ ve kə ty mə ki tɛ;

Je m'éveillai et je pleurai amèrement longtemps après.
ʒə me vɛ je, e ʒə plœ re a mɛ rə mã lõ tã za prɛ.

J'ai pleuré en rêve: J'ai rêvé que tu m'aimais encore;
ʒe plœ re ã rɛ və: ʒe rɛ ve kə ty mɛ mɛ zã kɔ rə;

et le torrent de mes larmes coule toujours, toujours.
e lə tɔ rã də me la rmə ku lə tu ʒu r, tu ʒu r.

Koechlin	Si tu le veux
keklɛ̃	si ty lə vø

Si tu le veux, ô mon amour,
si ty lə vø o mõ na mu r

Ce soir dès que la fin du jour Sera venue,
sə swa rdɛ kə la fɛ̃ dy ʒu rsə ra və ny ə,

Quand les étoiles surgiront,
kã le ze twa lə sy rʒi rõ

Et mettront des clous d'or au fond
e mɛ trɔ̃ de klu dɔ ro fɔ̃

Bleu de la nue,
blø də la ny ə,

Nous partirons seuls tous les deux
nu pa rti rɔ̃ sœ ltu le dø,

Dans la nuit brune en amoureux,
dã la nɥi bry nã na mu rø,

Sans qu'on nous voie; Et tendrement je te dirai
sã kɔ̃ nu vwa ə; e tã drə mã ʒə tə di re,

Un chant d'amour où je mettrai Toute ma joie.
œ̃ ʃã da mu ru ʒə mɛ tre, tu tə ma ʒwa ə.

Mais quand tu rentreras chez toi,
mɛ kã ty rã trə ra ʃe twa,

Si l'on te demande pourquoi,
si lɔ̃ tə də mã də pu rkwa,

Mignonne fée, Tes cheveux sont plus fous qu'avant,
mi ɲɔ nə fe ə, te ʃə vø sɔ̃ ply fu ka vã

Tu répondras que seul le vent T'a décoiffée,
ty re pɔ̃ dra kə sœ llə vã, ta de kwa fe ə,

Si tu le veux, ô mon amour.
si ty lə vø, o mɔ̃ na mu r.

Lully   Bois épais
lyli   bwa zepɛ

Bois épais, redouble ton ombre;
bwa ze pɛ, rə du blə tɔ̃ nɔ̃ brə;

Tu ne saurais être assez sombre,
ty nə sɔ rɛ zɛ tra se sɔ̃ brə,

Tu ne peux trop cacher
ty nə pø tro ka ʃe,

Mon malheureux amour.
mɔ̃ ma lø rø za mu r.

Je sens un désespoir
ʒə sɑ̃ zœ̃ de ze spwa r,

Dont l'horreur est extrême,
dɔ̃ lɔ rœ rɛ tɛ kstrɛ mə,

Je ne dois plus voir ce que j'aime,
ʒə nə dwa ply vwa rsə kə ʒɛ mə,

Je ne veux plus souffrir le jour.
ʒə nə vø ply su fri rlə ʒu r.

Martini   Plaisir d'Amour
martini   plɛzir d amur

Plaisir d'amour ne dure qu'un moment
plɛ zi rda mu r, nə dy rə kœ̃ mɔ mɑ̃,

Chagrin d'amour dure toute la vie
ʃa grɛ̃ da mu r dy rə tu tə la vi ə,

J'ai tout quitté pour l'ingrate Silvie
ʒe tu ki te pu rlɛ̃ gra tə si lvi ə

Elle me quitte et prend un autre amant.
ɛ lə mə ki te prɑ̃ tœ̃ no tra mɑ̃.

Plaisir d'amour ne dure qu'un moment
plɛ zi rda mu r, nə dy rə kœ̃ mɔ mɑ̃

Chagrin d'amour dure toute la vie.
ʃa grɛ̃ da mu rdy rə tu tə la vi ə.

Tant que cette eau coulera doucement
tɑ̃ kə sɛ to ku lə ra du sə mɑ̃,

Vers ce ruisseau qui borde la prairie,
vɛ rsə rɥi so ki bɔ rdə la prɛ ri ə,

Je t'aimerai me répétait Silvie.
ʒə tɛ mə re, mə re pe tɛ si lvi ə.

L'eau coule encor, elle a changé pourtant.
lo ku lɑ̃ kɔ r, e la ʃɑ̃ ʒe pu rtɑ̃.

Massenet   Ah! fuyez, douce image, from "Manon"
masne   a fɥije dus imaʒ   manõ

Je suis seul! Seul enfin! c'est le moment suprême!
ʒə sɥi sœ l! sœ lã fɛ̃! sɛ lə mɔ mã sy prɛ mə!

Il n'est plus rien que j'aime
i lnɛ ply rjɛ̃ kə ʒɛ mə

Que le repos sacré que m'apporte la foi!
kə lə rə po sa kre kə ma pɔ rtə la fwa!

Oui, j'ai voulu mettre Dieu même
wi, ʒe vu ly mɛ trə djø mɛ mə,

Entre le monde et moi!
ã trə lə mõ d, e mwa!

Ah! fuyez, douce image, à mon âme trop chère;
a fɥi je du si ma ʒ, a mõ na mə trɔ ʃɛ rə;

Respectez un repos cruellement gagné,
rɛ spɛ kte zœ̃ rə po kry ɛ lə mã ga ɲe,

Et songez, si j'ai bu dans une coupe amère,
e sõ ʒe, si ʒe by dã zy nə ku pa mɛ rə,

Que mon coeur l'emplirait de ce qu'il a saigné!
kə mõ kœ rlã pli rɛ, də sə ki la sɛ ɲe!

Ah, fuyez! loin de moi!
a, fɥi je! lwɛ̃ də mwa!

Que m'importe la vie et ce semblant de gloire?
kə mɛ̃ pɔ rtə la vi ə e sə sã blã də glwa rə?

Je ne veux que chasser du fond de ma mémoire
ʒə nə vø kə ʃa se dy fõ də ma me mwa rə,

Un nom maudit! ce nom qui m'obsède et pourquoi?
œ̃ nõ mo di! sə nõ, ki mɔ psɛ də, e pu rkwa?

Mon Dieu! De votre flamme
mõ djø! də vɔ trə fla mə,

Purifiez mon âme, Et dissipez à sa lueur
py ri fi e mõ na mə, e di si pe a sa ly œ r,

L'ombre qui passe encor dans le fond de mon coeur!
lõ brə ki pa sã kɔ rdã lə fõ də mõ kœ r!

Massenet   Il est doux, il est bon, from "Hérodiade"
masne   il ɛ du il ɛ bõ   erɔdjad

Celui dont la parole efface toutes peines,
sə lɥi dõ la pa rɔ le fa sə tu tə pɛ nə,

332

Le Prophète est ici! c'est vers lui que je vais!
lə pro fɛ tɛ ti si! sɛ vɛ rlɥi kə ʒə vɛ!

Il est doux, il est bon, sa parole est sereine:
i lɛ du, i lɛ bõ, sa pa ro lɛ sə rɛ nə,

Il parle, tout se tait. Plus léger sur la plaine
i lpa rlə, tu sə tɛ, ply le ʒe sy rla plɛ nə,

L'air attentif, passe sans bruit. Il parle!
lɛ ra tã ti fpɑ sə sã brɥi. i lpa rlə!

Ah! quand reviendra-t-il? quand pourrai-je l'entendre?
ɑ kã rə vjɛ̃ dra ti l? kã pu rɛ ʒə lã tã drə?

Je souffrais j'étais seule et mon coeur s'est calmé
ʒə su frɛ, ʒe tɛ sœ le mõ kœ rsɛ ka lme,

En écoutant sa voix mélodieuse et tendre,
ã ne ku tã sa vwa me lɔ di ø ze tã drə,

Mon coeur s'est calmé!
mõ kœ rsɛ ka lme!

Prophète bien aimé, puis-je vivre sans toi!
pro fɛ tə bjɛ̃ nɛ me pɥi ʒə vi vrə sã twa!

C'est là! dans ce désert où la foule étonnée
sɛ la! dã sə de zɛ ru la fu le tɔ ne,

Avait suivi ses pas, Qu'il m'accueillit un jour,
a vɛ sɥi vi se pɑ, ki lma kœ ji tɛ̃ ʒu r,

enfant abandonnée! Et qu'il m'ouvrit ses bras!
ã fã a bã dɔ ne ə! e ki lmu vri se bra!

Massenet   Le Rêve, from "Manon"
masne   lə rɛv   manõ

Instant charmant Où la crainte fait trève,
ɛ̃ stã ʃa rmã u la krɛ̃ tə fɛ trɛ və,

Où nous sommes deux seulement! Tiens, Manon,
u nu sɔ mə dø sœ lə mã, tjɛ̃, ma nõ,

en marchant Je viens de faire un rêve!
ã ma rʃã, ʒə vjɛ̃ də fɛ rœ̃ rɛ və!

En fermant les yeux je vois
ã fɛ rmã le zjø ʒə vwa

Là—bas une humble retraite
la bɑ, y nœ̃ blə rə trɛ tə,

Une maisonnette Toute blanche au fond des bois!
y nə mɛ zɔ nɛ tə tu tə blɑ̃ ʃo fɔ̃ de bwa!

Sous ces tranquilles ombrages
su se trɑ̃ ki lə zɔ̃ bra ʒə,

Les clairs et joyeux ruisseaux
le klɛ rze ʒwa jø rʮi so,

Où se mirent les feuillages Chantent avec les oiseaux!
u sə mi rə le fœ ja ʒə, ʃɑ̃ tə ta vɛ kle zwa zo!

C'est le paradis! Oh! non!
sɛ lə pa ra di! o nɔ̃

Tout est là triste et morose,
tu tɛ la tri stə mɔ ro zə,

Car il y manque une chose Il y faut encor Manon!
ka ri li mɑ̃ ky nə ʃo z, i li fo tɑ̃ kɔ r, ma nɔ̃!

Viens! Là sera notre vie,
vjɛ̃! la sə ra nɔ trə vi ə,

Si tu le veux, ô Manon!
si ty lə vø, o ma nɔ̃!

Massenet   Obéissons, quand leur voix appelle, from "Manon"
masnɛ   ɔbeisɔ̃ kɑ̃ lœr vwa apɛlə   manɔ̃

Obéissons, quand leur voix appelle,
ɔ be i sɔ̃ kɑ̃ lœ rvwa a pɛ lə,

Aux tendres amours toujours!
o tɑ̃ drə za mu rtu ʒu r!

Tant que vous êtes belle, usez sans les compter
tɑ̃ kə vu zɛ tə bɛ ly ze sɑ̃ le kɔ̃ te

vos jours! tous vos jours!
vo ʒu r! tu vo ʒu r!

Profitons bien de la jeunesse,
prɔ fi tɔ̃ bjɛ̃ də la ʒœ nɛ sə,

Des jours qu'amène le printemps;
de ʒu rka mɛ nə lə prɛ̃ tɑ̃;

334

Aimons, chantons, rions sans cesse,
ɛ mõ, ʃã tõ ri jõ sã sɛ sə,

Nous n'avons encor que vingt ans! Ah!
nu na võ zã kɔ rkə vɛ̃ tã.! ɑ

Le cœur, hélas! le plus fidèle,
lə kœ re lɑ s! lə ply fi dɛ lə,

Oublie en un jour l'amour,
u bli ã nœ̃ ʒu rlɑ mu r,

Et la jeunesse ouvrant son aile A disparu sans retour.
e la ʒœ nɛ su vrã sõ nɛ la di spa ry sã rə tu r.

Bien court, hélas, est le printemps!
bjɛ̃ ku re lɑ sɛ lə prɛ̃ tã!

Massenet   Ouvre tes yeux bleus
masne   uvrə te zjø blø

Ouvre tes yeux bleus, ma mignonne:
u vrə te zjø blø ma mi ɲo nə:

Voici le jour.
vwa si lə ʒu r.

Déjà la fauvette fredonne
de ʒa la fo vɛ tə frə dɔ nə,

Un chant d'amour.
œ̃ ʃã da mu r.

L'aurore épanouit la rose:
lɔ rɔ re pa nu i la ro zə:

Viens avec moi Cueillir la marguerite éclose.
vjɛ̃ za vɛ kmwa, kœ ji rla ma rgə ri te klo zə.

Réveille-toi!
re vɛ jə twa!

A quoi bon contempler la terre Et sa beauté?
a kwa bõ kõ tã ple la tɛ rə, e sa bo te?

L'amour est un plus doux mystère
la mu rɛ tœ̃ ply du mi stɛ rə,

Qu'un jour d'été;
kœ̃ ʒu rde te;

335

C'est en moi que l'oiseau module
sɛ tã mwa kə lwa zo mɔ dy

Un chant vainqueur,
lœ̃ ʃã vɛ̃ kœ r,

Et le grand soleil qui nous brûle
e lə grã sɔ lɛ jki nu bry lə,

Est dans mon coeur!
ɛ dã mõ kœ r!

Massenet   Pleurez! pleurez, mes yeux! , from ''Le Cid''
masne   plœre plœre me zjø   lə sid

De cet affreux combat je sors l'âme brisée!
də sɛ ta frø kõ ba, ʒə sɔ rlɑ mə bri ze ə!

Mais enfin je suis libre et je pourrai du moins
mɛ zã fɛ̃, ʒə sɥi li brə, e ʒə pu re dy mwɛ̃

Soupirer sans contrainte et souffrir sans témoins.
su pi re sã kõ trɛ̃ t, e su fri rsã te mwɛ̃.

Pleurez, mes yeux! tombez triste rosée
plœ re me zjø, tõ be tri stə rɔ ze ə

Qu'un rayon de soleil ne doit jamais tarir!
kœ̃ rɛ jõ də sɔ lɛ jnə dwa ʒa mɛ ta ri r!

S'il me reste un espoir, c'est de bientôt mourir!
si lmə rɛ stœ̃ nɛ spwa r, sɛ də bjɛ̃ to mu ri r!

Pleurez, mes yeux, pleurez toutes vos larmes!
plœ re me zjø, plœ re tu tə vo la rmə!

Mais qui donc a voulu l'éternité des pleurs?
mɛ ki dõ ka vu ly, le tɛ rni te de plœ r?

O chers ensevelis, trouvez-vous tant de charmes
o ʃɛ rzã sə və li, tru ve vu tã də ʃa rmə

A léguer aux vivants d'implacables douleurs?
a le ge ro vi vã dɛ̃ pla ka blə du lœ r?

Hélas! je me souviens il me disait:
e lɑ sʒə mə su vjɛ̃ i lmə di zɛ,

Avec ton doux sourire
a vɛ ktõ du su ri rə,

336

Tu ne saurais jamais conduire
ty nə sɔ rɛ ʒa mɛ, kõ dɥi rə

Qu'aux chemins glorieux ou qu'aux sentiers bénis!
ko ʃə mɛ̃ glɔ ri ø, u ko sɑ̃ tje be ni!

Ah! mon père! Hélas!
ɑ mõ pɛ rə, e lɑ s!

Massenet   Vision fugitive, from "Hérodiade"
masne   vizjõ fyʒitiv   erɔdjad

Ce breuvage pourrait me donner un tel rêve!
sə brœ va ʒə pu rɛ mə dɔ ne œ̃ tɛ lrɛ və!

Je pourrais la revoir...Contempler sa beauté!
ʒə pu rɛ la rə vwa r, kõ tɑ̃ ple sa bo te!

Divine volupté à mes regards promise!
di vi nə vɔ ly pte a me rə ga rprɔ mi zə!

Espérance trop brève qui viens bercer mon coeur
ɛ spe rɑ̃ sə trɔ brɛ və, ki vjɛ̃ bɛ rse mõ kœ r

et troubler ma raison...
e tru ble ma rɛ zõ...

Ah! ne t'enfuis pas, douce illusion!
a! nə tɑ̃ fɥi pa, du si ly zi õ!

Vision fugitive et toujours poursuivie,
vi zi õ fy ʒi ti ve tu ʒu rpu rsɥi vi ə,

Ange mystérieux qui prends toute ma vie...
ɑ̃ ʒə mi ste ri jø ki prɑ̃ tu tə ma vi ə...

Ah! c'est toi que je veux voir,
a sɛ twa kə ʒə vø vwa r,

O mon amour! ô mon espoir!
o mõ na mu r! o mõ nɛ spwa r!

Te presser dans mes bras!
tə prɛ se dɑ̃ me bra!

Sentir battre ton coeur
sɑ̃ ti rba trə tõ kœ r

D'une amoureuse ardeur!
dy na mu rø za rdœ r!

Puis, mourir enlacés
pɥi mu ri rɑ̃ la se,

dans une même ivresse,
dɑ̃ zy nə mɛ mi vrɛ sə,

Pour ces transports, pour cette flamme,
pu rse trɑ̃ spɔ r, pu rsɛ tə fla mə,

Ah! sans remords et sans plainte
a! sɑ̃ rə mɔ re sɑ̃ plɛ̃ tə,

Je donnerais mon âme pour toi,
ʒə do nə rɛ mɔ̃ na mə pu rtwa,

mon amour! mon espoir!
mɔ̃ na mu r! mɔ̃ nɛ spwa r!

Meyerbeer   Ah! mon fils, from "Le Prophète"
Fr. mejɛrbɛr ɑ mɔ̃ fis   lə prɔfɛt
Ger. maeərbeːr

Ah! mon fils, sois béni!
ɑ mɔ̃ fi s, swa be ni!

Ta pauvre mère te fut plus chère
ta po vrə mɛ rə, tə fy ply ʃɛ rə,

que ta Bertha, que ton amour!
kə ta bɛ rta, kə tɔ̃ na mu r!

Ah! mon fils! tu viens, hélas!
ɑ mɔ̃ fi s! ty vjɛ̃, e lɑ s,

de donner pour ta mère plus que la vie,
də do ne, pu rta mɛ rə, ply kə la vi,

en donnant ton bonheur!
ɑ̃ do nɑ̃ tɔ̃ bɔ nœ r!

Ah! mon fils! que vers le ciel
ɑ mɔ̃ fi s! kə vɛ rlə sjɛ l,

s'élève ma prière,
se lɛ və ma pri jɛ rə,

et sois béni dans le Seigneur! Jean! ah!
e swa be ni dɑ̃ lə sɛ ɲœr! ʒɑ̃! ɑ!

338

Offenbach   Les oiseaux dans la charmille, from "Les Contes d'Hoffmann"
ɔfɛnbak   le zwazo dɑ̃ la ʃarmij   le kɔ̃t d ɔfman

Les oiseaux dans la charmille,
le zwa zo dɑ̃ la ʃa rmi jə,

Dans les cieux l'astre du jour,
dɑ̃ le sjø la strə dy ʒu r,

Tout parle à la jeune fille D'amour! Ah!
tu pa rlɑ la ʒœ nə fi jə da mu r! ɑ!

tout parle d'amour! Ah!
tu pa rlə da mu r! ɑ!

Voilà la chanson gentille,
vwa la la ʃɑ̃ sɔ̃ ʒɑ̃ ti jə,

La chanson d'Olympia!
la ʃɑ̃ sɔ̃ dɔ lɛ̃ pi a!

Tout ce qui chante et résonne
tu sə ki ʃɑ̃ te re zɔ nə,

Et soupire, tour à tour,
e su pi rə tu ra tu r,

Emeut son coeur qui frissonne D'amour!
e mø sɔ̃ kœ rki fri sɔ nə da mu r!

Voilà la chanson mignonne, la chanson d'Olympia!
vwa la la ʃɑ̃ sɔ̃ mi ɲɔ nə, la ʃɑ̃ sɔ̃ dɔ lɛ̃ pi a!

Offenbach   Scintille, diamant, from "Les Contes d'Hoffmann"
ɔfɛnbak   sɛ̃tij djamɑ̃   le kɔ̃t d ɔfman

Scintille, diamant, Miroir où se prend l'alouette,
sɛ̃ ti jə di a mɑ̃, mi rwa ru sə prɑ̃ la lu ɛ tə,

Scintille, diamant, fascine, attire-la;
sɛ̃ ti jə di a mɑ̃, fa si na ti rə la;

L'alouette ou la femme A cet appas vainqueur
la lu ɛ tə, u la fa mə, a sɛ ta pɑ vɛ̃ kœ r,

Vont de l'aile ou du coeur;
vɔ̃ də lɛ lu dy kœ r;

L'une y laisse la vie Et l'autre y perd son âme!
ly ni lɛ sə la vi ə, e lo tri pɛ rsɔ̃ na mə!

339

Beau diamant, attire-la!
bo di a mã, a ti rə la!

Paladilhe   Psyché
paladij   psiʃe

Je suis jaloux, Psyché, de toute la nature!
ʒə sɥi ʒa lu psi ʃe, də tu tə la na ty rə

Les rayons du soleil vous baisent trop souvent,
le rɛ jõ dy so lɛ j, vu bɛ zə tro su vã,

Vos cheveux souffrent trop les caresses du vent.
vo ʃə vø su frə tro le ka rɛ sə dy vã.

Quand il les flatte, j'en murmure!
kã ti lle fla tə, ʒã my rmy rə!

L'air même que vous respirez
lɛ rmɛ mə kə vu rɛ spi re,

Avec trop de plaisir passe sur votre bouche.
a vɛ ktro də plɛ zi rpa sə sy rvo trə bu ʃə.

Votre habit de trop près vous touche!
vo tra bi də tro prɛ vu tu ʃə!

Et sitôt que vous soupirez
e si to kə vu su pi re,

Je ne sais quoi qui m'effarouche
ʒə nə sɛ kwa ki mɛ fa ru ʃə,

Craint, parmi vos soupirs, des soupirs égarés!
krɛ̃, pa rmi vo su pi r, de su pi rze ga re!

Ravel   Chanson à boire (Don Quichotte à Dulcinée)
ravɛl   ʃãsõ a bwar dõ kiʃot a dylsine

Foin du bâtard, illustre Dame,
fwɛ̃ dy ba ta ri ly strə da mə,

340

Qui pour me perdre à vos doux yeux
ki pu rmə pɛ rdra vo du zjø,

Dit que l'amour et le vin vieux
di kə la mu re lə vɛ̃ vjø,

Mettent en deuil mon coeur, mon âme! Ah!
mɛ tə tɑ̃ dœ jmɔ̃ kœ r, mɔ̃ nɑ mə! ɑ!

Je bois A la joie!
ʒə bwa, a la ʒwa!

La joie est le seul but Où je vais droit...
la ʒwa ɛ lə sœ lby u ʒə vɛ drwa...

lorsque j'ai lorsque j'ai bu!
lɔ rskə ʒe, lɔ rskə ʒe by!

Ah! la joie! Là Je bois A la joie!
a la ʒwa! la, ʒə bwa a la ʒwa!

Foin du jaloux, brune maîtresse,
fwɛ̃ dy ʒa lu bry nə mɛ trɛ sə,

Qui geint, qui pleure et fait serment
ki ʒɛ̃ ki plœ re fɛ sɛ rmɑ̃

D'être toujours ce pâle amant,
dɛ trə tu ʒu rsə pɑ la mɑ̃

Qui met de l'eau dans son ivresse!
ki mɛ də lo dɑ̃ sɔ̃ ni vrɛ sə!

Ah! Je bois à la joie!
a! ʒə bwa, a la ʒwa!

La joie est le seul but Où je vais droit
la ʒwa ɛ lə sœ lbu u ʒə vɛ drwa,

lorsque j'ai bu!
lɔ rskə ʒe by!

Ah! la joie! Là, Je bois A la joie!
a la ʒwa! la, ʒə bwa a la ʒwa!

Permission for reprinting of the original
lyrics in phonetics granted by Durand et Cie.,
Paris, and Elkan—Vogel Co., Inc., Philadelphia,
Pennsylvania.

Ravel   Chanson épique (Don Quichotte a Dulcinée)
ravɛl   ʃɑ̃sɔ̃ epik   dɔ̃ kiʃɔt a dylsine

Bon Saint Michel qui me donnez loisir
bɔ̃ sɛ̃ mi ʃɛ lki mə dɔ ne lwa zi r,

De voir ma Dame et de l'entendre,
də vwa rma da me də lɑ̃ tɑ̃ drə,

Bon Saint Michel qui me daignez choisir
bɔ̃ sɛ̃ mi ʃɛ lki mə dɛ ɲe ʃwa zi r,

Pour lui complaire et la défendre,
pu rlɥi kɔ̃ plɛ re la de fɑ̃ drə,

Bon Saint Michel veuillez descendre
bɔ̃ sɛ̃ mi ʃɛ lvœ je dɛ sɑ̃ drə,

Avec Saint Georges sur l'autel
a vɛ ksɛ̃ ʒɔ rʒə sy rlo tɛ l,

De la Madone au bleu mantel.
də la ma dɔ no blø mɑ̃ tɛ l.

D'un rayon du ciel bénissez ma lame
dœ̃ rɛ jɔ̃ dy sjɛ l, be ni se ma la mə,

Et son égale en pureté Et son égale en piété
e sɔ̃ ne ga lɑ̃ py rə te, e sɔ̃ ne ga lɑ̃ pi e te,

Comme en pudeur et chasteté: Ma Dame,
kɔ mɑ̃ py dœ re ʃa stə te: ma da mə,

(O grands Saint Georges et Saint Michel)
o grɑ̃ sɛ̃ ʒɔ rʒə e sɛ̃ mi ʃɛ l,

L'ange qui veille sur ma veille,
lɑ̃ ʒə ki vɛ jə sy rma vɛ jə,

Ma douce Dame si pareille A Vous,
ma du sə da mə si pa rɛ j, a vu

Madone au bleu mantel! Amen.
ma dɔ no blø mɑ̃ tɛ l! a mɛ n.

> Permission for reprinting of the original
> lyrics in phonetics granted by Durand et Cie.,
> Paris, and Elkan—Vogel Co., Inc., Philadelphia,
> Pennsylvania.

Ravel   Chanson romanesque (Don Quichotte a Dulcinée)
ravɛl   ʃɑ̃sɔ̃ rɔmanɛsk   dɔ̃ kiʃɔt a dylsine

Si vous me disiez que la terre
si vu mə di zje kə la tɛ rə,

A tant tourner vous offensa,
a tã tu rne vu zɔ fã sa,

Je lui dépêcherais Pança:
ʒə lɥi de pɛ ʃə rɛ pã sa:

Vous la verriez fixe et se taire.
vu la vɛ rje fi kse sə tɛ rə.

Si vous me disiez que l'ennui
si vu mə di zje kə lã nɥi,

Vous vient du ciel trop fleuri d'astres,
vu vjɛ̃ dy sjɛ ltrɔ flœ ri da strə,

Déchirant les divins cadastres,
de ʃi rã le di vɛ̃ ka da strə,

Je faucherais d'un coup la nuit.
ʒə fo ʃə rɛ dœ̃ ku la nɥi.

Si vous me disiez que l'espace
si vu mə di zje kə lɛ spa sə

Ainsi vidé ne vous plaît point,
ɛ̃ si vi de nə vu plɛ pwɛ̃,

Chevalierdieu, la lance au poing,
ʃə va lje djø, la lã so pwɛ̃,

J'étoilerais le vent qui passe.
ʒe twa lə rɛ lə vã ki pa sə.

Mais si vous disiez que mon sang
mɛ si vu di zje kə mõ sã,

Est plus à moi qu'à vous, ma Dame,
ɛ ply za mwa ka vu, ma da mə,

Je blêmirais dessous le blâme,
ʒə blɛ mi rɛ də su lə bla mə,

Et je mourrais, vous bénissant.
e ʒə mu rrɛ vu be ni sã.

O Dulcinée.
o dy lsi ne ə.

Ravel   Sainte
ravɛl   sɛ̃t

A la fenêtre recélant
a la fə nɛ trə rə se lɑ̃

Le santal vieux qui se dédore
lə sɑ̃ ta lvjø ki sə de dɔ rə,

De la viole étincelant
də la vi ɔ le tɛ̃ sə lɑ̃

Jadis selon flûte ou mandore.
ʒa di ssə lɔ̃ fly tu mɑ̃ dɔ r.

Est la sainte pâle étalant
ɛ la sɛ̃ tə pɑ le ta lɑ̃

Le livre vieux qui se déplie
lə li vrə vjø ki sə de pli ə,

Du Magnificat ruisselant
dy ma ɲi fi ka trɥi sə lɑ̃

Jadis selon vêpre ou complie.
ʒa di ssə lɔ̃ vɛ pru kɔ̃ pli.

A ce vitrage d'ostensoir
a sə vi tra ʒə dɔ stɑ̃ swa r,

Que frôle une harpe par l'Ange
kə fro ly nə a rpə pa rlɑ̃ ʒə

Formée avec son vol du soir.
fɔ rme a vɛ ksɔ̃ vɔ ldy swa r.

Pour la délicate phalange
pu rla de li ka tə fa lɑ̃ ʒə

Du doigt que sans le vieux santal
dy dwa kə sɑ̃ lə vjø sɑ̃ ta l,

Ni le vieux livre elle balance
ni lə vjø li vrɛ lə ba lɑ̃ sə,

Sur le plumage instrumental
sy rlə ply ma ʒɛ̃ stry mɑ̃ ta l,

Musicienne du silence.
my zi si ɛ nə dy si lɑ̃ s.

Permission for reprinting of the original
lyrics in phonetics granted by Durand et Cie.,
Paris, and Elken-Vogel Co., Inc., Philadelphia,
Pennsylvania.

Saint-Saëns Amour, viens aider, from "Samson et Dalila"
sɛ̃ sɑ̃s   amur vjɛ̃ zede   sɑ̃sɔ̃ e dalila

Samson recherchant ma présence,
sɑ̃ sɔ̃ rə ʃɛ rʃɑ̃ ma pre zɑ̃ sə,

Ce soir doit venir en ces lieux.
sə swa rdwa və ni rɑ̃ se ljø.

Voici l'heure de la vengeance
vwa si lœ rə də la vɑ̃ ʒɑ̃ sə

Qui doit satisfaire nos Dieux!
ki dwa sa ti sfɛ rə no djø!

Amour! viens aider ma faiblesse!
a mu rvjɛ̃ zɛ de ma fɛ blɛ sə!

Verse le poison dans son sein!
vɛ rsə lə pwa zɔ̃ dɑ̃ sɔ̃ sɛ̃!

Fais que, vaincu par mon adresse,
fɛ kə vɛ̃ ky pa rmɔ̃ na drɛ sə,

Samson soit enchaîné demain!
sɑ̃ sɔ̃ swa tɑ̃ ʃe ne də mɛ̃!

Il voudrait en vain de son âme
i lvu drɛ tɑ̃ vɛ̃ də sɔ̃ na mə,

Pouvoir me chasser, me bannir!
pu vwa rmə ʃa se, mə ba ni r!

Pourrait-il éteindre la flamme
pu rɛ ti le tɛ̃ drə la fla mə

Qu'alimente le souvenir?
ka li mɑ̃ tə lə su və ni r?

Il est à moi! c'est mon esclave!
i lɛ ta mwa! sɛ mɔ̃ nɛ skla və!

Mes frères craignent son courroux;
me frɛ rə krɛ ɲə sɔ̃ ku ru;

Moi, seule entre tous, je le brave,
mwa, sœ lɑ̃ trə tu s, ʒə lə bra və,

Et le retiens à mes genoux!
e lə rə tjɛ̃ za me ʒə nu!

Amour! viens aider ma faiblesse!
a mu rvjɛ̃ zɛ de ma fɛ blɛ sə!

Contre l'amour sa force est vaine;
kɔ̃ trə la mu rsa fɔ rsɛ vɛ nə;

Et lui, le fort parmi les forts,
e lɥi lə fɔ rpa rmi le fɔ r,

345

Lui, qui d'un peuple rompt la chaîne,
lꭗi ki dœ̃ pœ plə rɔ̃ la ʃɛ nə,

Succombera sous mes efforts!
sy kɔ̃ bə ra su me zɛ fɔ r!

Saint-Saëns Danse Macabre
sɛ̃ sɑ̃s   dɑ̃s makabr

Zig et zig et zig, La mort en cadence
zi ge zi ge zig la mɔ rɑ̃ ka dɑ̃ sə

Frappant une tombe avec son talon,
fra pɑ̃ ty nə tɔ̃ ba vɛ ksɔ̃ ta lɔ̃,

La mort à minuit joue un air de dance,
la mɔ ra mi nꭗi ʒu œ̃ nɛ rdə dɑ̃ sə

Zig et zig et zag, sur son violon.
zi ge zi ge zag sy rsɔ̃ vi ɔ lɔ̃.

Le vent d'hiver souffle, et la nuit est sombre;
lə vɑ̃ di vɛ rsu fle la nꭗi ɛ sɔ̃ brə;

Des gémissements sortent des tilleuls;
de ʒe mi sə mɑ̃ sɔ rtə de ti jœ l;

Les squelettes blancs vont à travers l'ombre,
le skə lɛ tə blɑ̃ vɔ̃ ta tra vɛ rlɔ̃ brə,

Courant et sautant sous leur grands linceuls.
ku rɑ̃ te so tɑ̃ su lœ rgrɑ̃ lɛ̃ sœ l.

Zig et zig et zig, chacun se trémousse.
zi ge zi ge zig ʃa kœ̃ sə tre mu s

On entend claquer les os des danseurs;
ɔ̃ nɑ̃ tɑ̃ kla ke le zo de dɑ̃ sœ r;

Un couple lascif s'asseoit sur la mousse,
œ̃ ku plə la si fsa swa sy rla mu sə

Comme pour goûter d'anciennes douceurs.
kɔ mə pu rgu te dɑ̃ sjɛ nə du sœ r.

Zig et zig et zag, la mort continue
zi ge zi ge zag la mɔ rkɔ̃ ti ny ə

De racler sans fin son aigre instrument.
də ra kle sɑ̃ fɛ̃ sɔ̃ nɛ grɛ̃ stry mɑ̃.

Un voile est tombé! La danseuse est nue,
œ̃ vwa lɛ tɔ̃ be! la dɑ̃ sø zɛ ny ə

346

son danseur la serre amoureusement.
sõ dã sœ rla sɛ ra mu rø zə mã.

La dame est, dit-on, marquise ou baronne,
la da mɛ, di tõ, ma rki zu ba ro nə,

Et le vert galant un pauvre charron; Horreur!
e lə vɛ rga lã œ̃ po vrə ʃa rõ; ɔ rœ r!

et voilà qu'elle s'abandonne
e vwa la kɛ lə sa bã do nə

Comme si le rustre était un baron.
kɔ mə si lə ry strɛ tɛ tœ̃ ba rõ.

Zig et zig et zig, quelle sarabande!
zi ge zi ge zig kɛ lə sa ra bã də

Quels cercles de morts se donnant la main!
kɛ lsɛ rklə də mɔ rsə do nã la mɛ̃!

Zig et zig et zag, on voit dans la bande
zi ge zi ge zag õ vwa dã la bã də

Le roi gambader auprès du vilain.
lə rwa gã ba de o prɛ dy vi lɛ̃.

Mais psit! tout à coup on quitte la ronde,
mɛ psi t! tu ta ku, õ ki tə la rõ də,

On se pousse, on fuit, le coq a chanté.
õ sə pu s, õ fɥi, lə kɔ ka ʃã te.

Oh! la belle nuit pour le pauvre monde,
o la bɛ lə nɥi pu rlə po vrə mõ də,

Et vivent la mort et l'égalité!
e vi və la mɔ r, e le ga li te!

Saint-Saëns Mon coeur s'ouvre à ta voix, from "Samson et Dalila"
sɛ̃ sãs   mõ kœr s uvr a ta vwa   sãsõ e dalila

Mon coeur s'ouvre à ta voix comme s'ouvrent les fleurs
mõ kœ rsu vra ta vwa, kɔ mə su vrə le flœ r,

Aux baisers de l'aurore!
o bɛ ze də lɔ rɔ rə!

Mais, ô mon bien-aimé, pour mieux sécher mes pleurs,
mɛ o mõ bjɛ̃ nɛ me, pu rmjø se ʃe me plœ r,

Que ta voix parle encore!
kə ta vwa pa rlɑ̃ kɔ rə!

Dis-moi, qu'à Dalila tu reviens pour jamais,
di mwa ka da li la, ty rə vjɛ̃ pu rʒa mɛ,

Redis à ma tendresse Les serments d'autrefois,
rə di za ma tɑ̃ drɛ sə, le sɛ rmɑ̃ do trə fwa,

ces serments que j'aimais!
se sɛ rmɑ̃ kə ʒɛ mɛ!

Ah! réponds à ma tendresse,
ɑ re põ za ma tɑ̃ drɛ sə,

Verse-moi, verse-moi l'ivresse!
vɛ rsə mwa, vɛ rsə mwa li vrɛ sə!

Réponds à ma tendresse!
re põ za ma tɑ̃ drɛ sə!

Ainsi qu'on voit des blés les épis onduler
ɛ̃ si kõ vwa de ble le ze pi zõ dy le,

Sous la brise légère,
su la bri zə le ʒɛ rə,

Ainsi frémit mon coeur, prêt à se consoler,
ɛ̃ si fre mi mõ kœ r, prɛ ta sə kõ sɔ le,

A ta voix qui m'est chère!
a ta vwa ki mɛ ʃɛ rə!

La flèche est moins rapide à porter le trépas,
la flɛ ʃɛ mwɛ̃ ra pi d, a pɔ rte lə tre pɑ,

Que ne l'est ton amante à voler dans tes bras!
kə nə lɛ tõ na mɑ̃ ta vɔ le dɑ̃ te bra!

Samson! je t'aime!
sɑ̃ sõ! ʒə tɛ mə!

Saint-Saëns Printemps qui commence, from "Samson et Dalila"
sɛ̃ sɑ̃s   prɛ̃tɑ̃ ki kɔmɑ̃s   sɑ̃sõ e dalila

Printemps qui commence, Portant l'espérance
prɛ̃ tɑ̃ ki kɔ mɑ̃ sə, pɔ rtɑ̃ lɛ spe rɑ̃ sə,

Aux coeurs amoureux, Ton souffle qui passe,
o kœ rza mu rø, tõ su flə ki pɑ sə,

De la terre efface Les jours malheureux.
də la tɛ rɛ fa sə, le ʒu rma lø rø.

Tout brûle en notre âme Et ta douce flamme
tu bry lã no tra mə, e ta du sə fla mə

Vient sécher nos pleurs;
vjɛ̃ se ʃe no plœ r;

Tu rends à la terre, Par un doux mystère,
ty rã za la tɛ rə, pa rœ̃ du mi stɛ rə,

Les fruits et les fleurs.
le frɥi ze le flœ r.

En vain je suis belle! Mon coeur plein d'amour,
ã vɛ̃ ʒə sɥi bɛ lə! mɔ̃ kœ rplɛ̃ da mu r,

Pleurant l'infidèle Attend son retour!
plœ rã lɛ̃ fi dɛ lə a tã sɔ̃ rə tu r!

Vivant d'espérance, Mon coeur désolé
vi vã dɛ spe rã sê, mɔ̃ kœ rde zo le,

Garde souvenance Du bonheur passé.
ga rdə su və nã sə, dy bo nœ rpa se.

A la nuit tombante J'irai triste amante
a la nɥi tɔ̃ bã tə, ʒi re tri sta mã tə,

M'asseoir au torrent, L'attendre en pleurant!
ma swa ro to rã, la tã drã plœ rã!

Chassant ma tristesse, S'il revient un jour,
ʃa sã ma tri stɛ sə, si lrə vjɛ̃ tœ̃ ʒu r,

à lui ma tendresse Et la douce ivresse
a lɥi ma tã drɛ sə, e la du si vrɛ sə

Qu'un brûlant amour Garde à son retour.
kœ̃ bry lã ta mu r, ga rda sɔ̃ rə tu r.

Chassant ma tristesse,
ʃa sã ma tri stɛ sə,

S'il revient un jour, à lui ma tendresse!
si lrə vjɛ̃ tœ̃ ʒu r, a lɥi ma tã drɛ sə!

Et la douce ivresse
e la du si vrɛ sə,

Qu'un brûlant amour Garde à son retour!
kœ̃ bry lã ta mu r, ga rda sɔ̃ rə tu r!

Thomas   Connais tu le pays, from "Mignon"
tɔma   kɔnɛ ty lə pei   miɲɔ̃

Connais-tu le pays où fleurit l'oranger,
kɔ nɛ ty lə pe i, u flœ ri lɔ rɑ̃ ʒe,

Le pays des fruits d'or et des roses vermeilles,
lə pe i de frɥi dɔ r, e de ro zə vɛ rmɛ jə,

Où la brise est plus douce, et l'oiseau plus léger,
u la bri zə ply du s, e lwa zo ply le ʒe,

Où dans toute saison butinent les abeilles,
u dɑ̃ tu tə sɛ zɔ̃, by ti nə le za bɛ jə,

Où rayonne et sourit, comme un bienfait de Dieu,
u rɛ jɔ ne su ri kɔ mœ̃ bjɛ̃ fɛ də djø,

Un éternel printemps sous un ciel toujours bleu?
œ̃ ne tɛ rnɛ lprɛ̃ tɑ̃ su zœ̃ sjɛ ltu ʒu rblø?

Hélas! que ne puis-je te suivre
e lɑ skə nə pɥi ʒə tə sɥi vrə,

Vers ce rivage heureux, d'où le sort m'exila!
vɛ rsə ri va ʒø rø du lə sɔ rmɛ gzi la!

C'est là, que je voudrais vivre,
sɛ la kə ʒə vu drɛ vi vrə,

Aimer, aimer et mourir! C'est là! oui, c'est là!
ɛ me, ɛ me re mu ri r! sɛ la! wi sɛ la!

Connais-tu la maison où l'on m'attend là-bas,
kɔ nɛ ty la mɛ zɔ̃, u lɔ̃ ma tɑ̃ la bɑ,

La salle aux lambris d'or, où des hommes de marbre
la sa lo lɑ̃ bri dɔ r, u də zɔ mə də ma rbrə,

M'appellent dans la nuit en me tendant les bras?
ma pɛ lə dɑ̃ la nɥi, ɑ̃ mə tɑ̃ dɑ̃ le bra?

Et la cour où l'on danse à l'ombre d'un grand arbre?
e la ku ru lɔ̃ dɑ̃ s, a lɔ̃ brə dœ̃ grɑ̃ ta rbrə?

Et le lac transparent, où glissent sur les eaux
e lə la ktrɑ̃ spa rɑ̃, u gli sə sy rle zo,

Mille bateaux légers, pareils à des oiseaux!
mi lə ba to le ʒe, pa rɛ ja de zwa zo!

Vers ce pays lointain d'où le sort m'exila!
vɛ rsə pe i lwɛ̃ tɛ̃ du lə sɔ rmɛ gzi la!

Thomas   Elle ne croyait pas, from "Mignon"
tɔma   ɛl nə krwajɛ pa   miɲɔ̃

Elle ne croyait pas, dans sa candeur naïve,
ɛ lə nə krwa jɛ pa, dɑ̃ sa kɑ̃ dœ rna i və,

Que l'amour innocent qui dormait dans son coeur,
kə la mu ri nɔ sɑ̃ ki dɔ rmɛ dɑ̃ sɔ̃ kœ r,

Dût se changer un jour en une ardeur plus vive
dy sə ʃɑ̃ ʒe rœ̃ ʒu rɑ̃ ny na rdœ rply vi və,

Et troubler à jamais son rêve de bonheur.
e tru ble ra ʒa mɛ, sɔ̃ rɛ və də bo nœ r.

Pour rendre à la fleur épuisée
pu rrɑ̃ dra la flœ re pɥi ze ə,

Sa fraîcheur, son éclat vermeil,
sa frɛ ʃœ rsɔ̃ ne kla vɛr mɛ j,

O printemps, donne-lui ta goutte de rosée!
o prɛ̃ tɑ̃, dɔ nə lɥi ta gu tə də rɔ ze ə!

O mon coeur, donne-lui ton rayon de soleil!
o mɔ̃ kœ r, dɔ nə lɥi tɔ̃ rɛ jɔ̃ də sɔ lɛ j!

C'est en vain que j'attends un aveu de sa bouche,
sɛ tɑ̃ vɛ̃ kə ʒa tɑ̃ zœ̃ na vø də sa bu ʃə,

Je veux connaître en vain ses secrètes douleurs,
ʒə vø kɔ nɛ trɑ̃ vɛ̃ se sə krɛ tə du lœ r,

Mon regard l'intimide et ma voix l'effarouche,
mɔ̃ rə ga rlɛ̃ ti mi də, e ma vwa le fa ru ʃə,

Un mot trouble son âme et fait couler ses pleurs!
œ̃ mo tru blə sɔ̃ na m, e fɛ ku le se plœ r!

Thomas   Je suis Titania, from "Mignon"
tɔma   ʒə sɥi titanja   miɲɔ̃

Oui! pour ce soir, je suis reine des fées!
wi pu rsə swa r, ʒə sɥi rɛ nə de fe ə!

Voici mon sceptre d'or et voici mes trophées!
vwa si mɔ̃ sɛ ptrə dɔ r, e vwa si me trɔ fe ə!

Je suis Titania la blonde
ʒə sɥi ti ta ni a la blɔ̃ də,

351

Je suis Titania fille de l'air
ʒə sɥi ti ta ni a fi jə də lɛ r,

En riant je parcours le monde,
ã ri jã ʒə pa rku rlə mõ də,

Plus vive que l'oiseau,
ply vi və kə lwa zo

plus prompte que l'éclair!
ply prõ tə kə le klɛ r!

La troupe folle des lutins suit mon char qui vole et
la tru pə fɔ lə de ly tɛ̃, sɥi mõ ʃa rki vɔ le

dans la nuit Fuit! autour de moi toute ma cour,
dã la nɥi, fɥi, o tu rdə mwa tu tə ma ku r,

court, chantant le plaisir et l'amour.
ku rʃã tã lə plɛ zi re la mu r.

du rayon de Phoebé qui luit!
dy rɛ jõ də fe be ki lɥi!

Parmi les fleurs que l'aurore Fait éclore,
pa rmi le flœ rkə lɔ rɔ rə fɛ te klɔ rə,

Par les bois et par les prés Diaprés
pa rle bwa e pa rle pre di a pre,

Sur les flots converts d'écume, dans la brume,
sy rle flo ku vɛ rde ky mə dã la bry mə,

On me voit d'un pied léger voltiger!
õ mə vwa dœ̃ pje le ʒe vɔ lti ʒe!

D'un pied léger par les bois, par les prés
dœ̃ pje le ʒe pa rle bwa pa rle pre,

Et dans la brume on me voit voltiger, ah!
e dã la bry mõ mə vwa vɔ lti ʒe, a!

Voilà Titania! En riant je parcours le monde,
vwa la, ti ta ni a! ã ri jã ʒə pa rku rlə mõ də,

Plus vive que l'oiseau, plus prompte que l'éclair.
ply vi və kə lwa zo ply prõ tə kə le klɛ r!

Je suis Titania, fille de l'air.
ʒə sɥi ti ta ni a fi jə də lɛ r.

Tchaikowsky   Adieu, forêts, from ''Jeanne d'Arc''
           adjø fɔrɛ   ʒɑn d ark

Oui, Dieu le veut!   Je dois suivre ton ordre,
wi djø lə vø!   ʒə dwa, sɥi vrə t�õ nɔ rdrə,

obéir à ton appel, sainte Vierge!
ɔ be i̥ ra tõ na pɛ l, sɛ̃ tə vjɛ rʒə!

Pourquoi, mon coeur, pourquoi bats tu si fort?
pu rkwa mõ kœ r, pu rkwa ba ty si fɔ r?

Pourquoi frémir? L'effroi remplit mon âme!
pu rkwa fre mi r? lɛ frwa rɑ̃ pli mõ nɑ mə!

Adieu, forêts, adieu, prés fleuris, champs d'or,
a djø fɔ rɛ, a djø pre flœ ri ʃɑ̃ dɔ r,

Et vous, paisibles vallons, adieu!
e vu pɛ zi blə va lõ, a djø!

Jeanne aujourd'hui vous dit à jamais adieu.
ʒa no ʒu rdɥi vu di ta ʒa mɛ a djø.

Oui, pour toujours, toujours, adieu!
wi, pu rtu ʒu r, tu ʒu r, a djø!

Mes prés fleuris et mes forêts ombreuses,
me pre flœ ri e me fɔ rɛ zõ brø zə,

Vous fleurirez pour d'autres que pour moi.
vu flœ ri re pu rdo trə kə pu rmwa.

Adieu, forêts, eau pure de la source: Je vais partir
a djø fɔ rɛ, o py rə də la su rsə, ʒə vɛ pa rti r,

et ne vous verrai plus, Jeanne vous fuit, et pour jamais.
e nə vu vɛ re ply, ʒa nə vu fɥi, e pu rʒa mɛ.

O doux vallon où j'ai connu la joie!
o du va lõ u ʒe kɔ ny la ʒwa ə!

Aujourd'hui je te quitte, doux vallon!
o ʒu rdɥi ʒə tə ki tə, du va lõ!

Et mes agneaux, dans les vertes prairies
e me za ɲo, dɑ̃ le vɛ rtə prɛ ri ə,

demanderont en vain leur guide!
də mɑ̃ də rõ tɑ̃ vɛ̃ lœ rgi də!

Au champ d'honneur je dois guider les braves,
o ʃɑ̃ dɔ nœ r, ʒə dwa gi de le bra və,

cueillir les palmes sanglantes de la victoire!
kœ ji rle pa lmə sɑ̃ glɑ̃ tə də la vi ktwa rə!

353

Je vais où les voix m'appellent, Voix saintes,
ʒə vɛ u le vwa ma pɛ lə, vwa sɛ̃ tə,

Seigneur, vous voyez au fond de mon âme!
sɛ ɲœ r, vu vwa je zo fɔ̃ də mɔ̃ na mə!

Mon coeur se brise, Mon âme souffre, mon coeur saigne!
mɔ̃ kœ rsə bri zə, mɔ̃ na mə su frə, mɔ̃ kœ rsɛ ɲə!

O monts aimés, adieu, forêts ombreuses,
o mɔ̃ zɛ me, a djø fɔ rɛ zɔ̃ brø zə,

Et vous, paisibles vallons, adieu!
e vu pɛ zi blə va lɔ̃ a djø!

Jeanne aujourd'hui vous dit à jamais adieu!
ʒɑ no ʒu rdɥi vu di ta ʒa mɛ a djø!

Oui, pour toujours, adieu.
wi pu rtu ʒu r, a djø

Prés fleuris, arbres verts, Si chers à mon enfance,
pre flœ ri a rbrə vɛ r, si ʃe ra mɔ̃ nɑ̃ fɑ̃ sə,

Vous fleurissez pour d'autres que pour moi.
vu flœ ri se pu rdo trə kə pu rmwa.

Adieu, mes champs, adieu, vallon, source pure,
a djø me ʃɑ̃ a djø, va lɔ̃ su rsə py rə,

Il faut partir et pour toujours!
i lfo pa rti re pu rtu ʒu r!

Ah! recevez mon éternel adieu!
ɑ! rə sə ve mɔ̃ ne tɛ rnɛ la djø!

INDEX OF TITLES AND FIRST LINES